Servants of the Law

Judicial Politics on the California Frontier 1849–89

An Interpretive Exploration of the Field-Terry Controversy

Donald R. Burrill

UNIVERSITY PRESS OF AMERICA,® INC.
Lanham • Boulder • New York • Toronto • Plymouth, UK

4501 Forbes Boulevard
Suite 200
Lanham, Maryland 20706
UPA Acquisitions Department (301) 459-3366

Estover Road
Plymouth PL6 7PY
United Kingdom

Printed in the United States of America
British Library Cataloging in Publication Information Available

Library of Congress Control Number: 2009933543
ISBN: 978-0-7618-4891-2 (paperback : alk. paper)
eISBN: 978-0-7618-4892-9

∞™ The paper used in this publication meets the minimum requirements of American National Standard for Information Sciences—Permanence of Paper for Printed Library Materials, ANSI Z39.48—1992

To Lois Gene

For invaluable service
Carol & Mark Burrill
Elizabeth & Kate Burrill

The chief success in life is the development of character and capacity, and this was the distinctive feature of pioneer times. In the early years after the gold discovery, California brought out all there was in men. It stimulated their strong points and exposed their weak ones. It opened their minds, it tested their courage, it awakened their ambitions, it repaired their judgments, it rewarded their industry and made them feel that life was worth living and had given them a fair share of its good.

John Shertzer Hittell
The Discovery of Gold in California, 1893

It is the first duty of Judges to obey the law. Judges are but the servants of the law.

Stephen J. Field
Associate Justice United States Supreme Court
San Francisco Daily Alta, August 17, 1889

Contents

Foreword vii

Preface ix

1 El Dorado 1

2 A Hasty Footpath to Statehood 28

3 From Roman Law to Common Law: *Juris Civilus* of Use and Custom 52

4 A Judicial Activist 72

5 Justices of the Supreme Court of California 106

6 *Persona non Grata* 130

7 Growing Resentments 143

8 Political Dreams 169

9 *Jus et Fraus Numquam Cohabitant* (Law and Fraud Never Cohabit) 196

10 Injury Unrequited 230

11 Dishonor in Absentia 254

Selected Bibliography 277

Index 287

Foreword

From the state of California's inception in 1850 the judicial architects who fashioned its first statewide notions of law and order brought west with them, along with their dreams and traveling bags, a hodgepodge of political and legal ideologies. During California's first decade of statehood, ambitious men of diverse abilities and perspectives sat on the state's highest court. Many contributed to making California an orderly place, but there were others who were out of place and came and went from the court causing barely a ripple. Then there were those who found the compensation wholly incommensurate to the task and left within a year's cycle.

Among the judicial immigrants who left significant marks, however, were the southerner David S. Terry of Texas and the northerner Stephen J. Field of New York. These men served on California's highest court during its formative, strenuous years from 1855 to 1863. Terry was the court's ninth justice and, depending upon how one counts, the fourth or fifth chief justice, while Field was its eleventh justice and its sixth or seventh chief justice.

The intellectual similarities and differences that these two shared with one another played themselves out over a period of 35 years and brought about a series of events that neither man could have envisioned. Their exchanges began as wary judicial amity within the courtroom, but in short order spilled out into the community as public grudges. Neither judge could tolerate the other's regional provincialism; hence, lifelong resentments inevitably turned into a bitterness that led to tragedy.

In brief, neither judge could abide the political ambitions of the other; hence each was forced to evaluate the other from the contrariety of his own cultural and regional predispositions. Field, the patrician, and Terry, the populist, doggedly measured one another through the smoky glass of their own pedagogic biographies. The relationship conflicted or misconceived as it was, makes for a lively tale of two judicial forefathers creating a historical niche for themselves on the California frontier. In the eyes of their judicial brethren, Terry's years on the bench began in promise and ended in disgrace, while Field's years began in promise and led to the nation's legal pantheon.

Malcolm M. Lucas,
Chief Justice of the California State Supreme Court, 1987–1996

Preface

Before the North Americans came to California, the tranquility of the land's denizens lay in the hands of a widely dispersed, relatively contented agrarian aristocracy. The private constabularies who were fed and sheltered by these Mexican *Californios* were, as a rule, sufficient enough to keep order along the clement coastal plains of the region. The land was called Alta California.

In 1848, however, the Treaty of Guadalupe Hidalgo between Mexico and the United States changed this arrangement—not so much by an overpowering show of force as by the emergence of an aggressive Anglo-Saxon immigration and its voracious hip-to-thigh institutions of law and merchantry. When it came to pursuing the good life, however, the Mexican *rancheros* and the Anglo "free-booters" shared a common point of view—the land, or more aptly, whatever the land might yield, was the wellspring of striving for early invaders of Alta California, be they Mexicans or *Norte Americanos*.

In the generation that followed the treaty, to have expectation of prosperity in the "golden land" meant paying whatever price was necessary to control and own the land. It was a price that embodied elements of financial and commercial competition that held only limited promise for most Mexicans but which was second nature to the invaders from the continent's eastern shore. These eastern/southern immigrants, however, were never fully entrenched and in control until the judicial system in California had become thoroughly "anglicized," and for this to take place Mexico's hoary tradition of Roman law had to disappear.

The Roman, or civil, legal tradition, was rooted in the secular and religious doctrinal notions that originated along the northern shores of the Mediterranean, and was litigated before regional courts through the logical application of the syllogism. By contrast, the promoters of anglicized law—English and Scottish common law—conceived the judicial system as a relationship between the government and its citizens under an intuitive perception of an Anglo-Norman theory of equity.

A month after California's first state constitution was ratified on November 13, 1849, it was announced that the "common sense" of common law would define civil and criminal procedures. It fell to the newly elected legislators, therefore, to develop a system of trial courts, appellate courts and, ultimately, a "court of last resort." This highest court, called "The Supreme Court," was to be the repository of equity as well as the linchpin of all well settled commercial and criminal law.

Initially the court consisted of three judges elected by the citizens at staggered six-year intervals, and excepting the newly appointed judges to the first court, who were elected by legislators, and replacements to the court who were appointed by governors, these mid-century justices were required to win periodic election in order to secure a seat on California's supreme bench.

The subject matter of this book traces the lives of two such elected judges who, through widely disparate circumstances, exercised an indelible influence on the legal and political history of the California court during its embryonic years from 1855 through 1863. These two men shared the bench from 1857 to 1859 and, as circumstances would later determine, were to confront one another off and on in the California's courts for almost 35 years. The circumstances that linked their lives together during this era could serve as a living metaphor of the cultural and legal diversity that so many 19th-century judicial immigrants held toward one another. Their resentments only magnified the bitterness that swirled about California's inception as a state in the midst of the malevolent and unforgiving Civil War.

David Smith Terry, who held his judicial post from 1855 to 1859, was elected as the court's ninth justice, while Stephen Johnson Field, who served from 1857 to 1863, was elected its eleventh justice. During his tenure, each man held the position of chief justice, and each played a seminal role in deciphering and interpreting the oftentimes vague and sometimes idiosyncratic legislation that the new state's independent pistol-packing frontier legislators produced. This occurred at a time when regional territorial law, on its best days, was desultory and, on its worst, was anonymous or non-existent. Miners writing letters home routinely described California, with only slight exaggeration, as "a fearful and lawless place"—and woe to those who would find themselves victims of spontaneous vigilantism.

This description, however, was only partially true; for no matter how disorganized the mining camps, it was inevitable that at times miners would find it necessary to support an assortment of self-governing regulation—for after all, the essence of social order is "the ordination of rules secured by sanctions." In other words, the argument that mining camps were always "lawless" did not fully describe California during these years, because there were some successful attempts to maintain order in the camps. Yet the success of orderly communities would often falter when these camps or townships attempted to expand jurisdiction or were carried from one place to another. But it was also a time when miners and migrants condoned or tolerated, under a pretense of a "law and order," the implantations of rules no matter how conflicted and contradictory the might prove be. Any schematic concept of what a community's law was or should be was just beginning to emerge from the disarray that had been California's cultural heterogeneity, and it was a sad occasion when some people seemingly effortlessly survived penalties for murder, rape or mayhem, while others were lucky to survive rude language or horse stealing.

The western historian Robert Cleland, in his *History of California* (1922) speaking of the territory's idiosyncratic lawlessness, wrote, "[T]here was a tolerance for venality among doxies, dandies and merchants, but absolutely no tolerance for stealing a person's property. Hotels, bordellos and saloons flourished almost spontaneously, but institutions that could predictably stabilize the events of time and place were slow to make an appearance."

From the outset, the frontier community's legal system, that is, its formal codification, and the duties of suitably efficient administrators and enforcement officials—the glue of a judicial system—ended a mile or so beyond a settlement's outskirts. Local judges administered the law, but, even more significantly, they were forced to create it. Moreover, because the territories requiring legal administration were so vast, their jurisdictional congruity frequently fell by the wayside. The lack of efficient and trustworthy judicial intercourse between communities and encampments, and the broad ethnic and cultural diversity that made up these ever-burgeoning populations, made California law exceedingly difficult to administer and standardize.

Overnight, the Mexicans who had been sheltered by the land for generations became its "foreigners," while hordes of transitory "newcomers," who counted their time in the territory by weeks, or even days, began demanding "possessory right" to the land and to the minerals that they were extracting from it. What impoverished these circumstances even more was the transient nature of the fortune seekers who, without a trace of remorse, willingly eviscerated the land in the winnowing.

California's celebrated 19th-century historian Hubert Howe Bancroft wrote in disgust, "[I]t was the rudest times of the rudest epoch in California history."[1] But it was much more than that. It was also a bitter, greedy, and vengeful time. In the oft-repeated slang of the era, most of the early immigrants were "ramblers" and rightly deserved the damning they were given as "squatters." It is reliable to argue that only on infrequent occasions was a native Californian likely to find a "settler" among them. And when it came to describing California's judicial and social stability, even the resolutely ebullient *New York Tribune* journalist and traveler Bayard Taylor was unable to bring himself to file his customarily glossy report once fortune seekers had become thoroughly ensconced in the territory. He wrote:

> The history of law and society in California from the period of the golden discoveries, would furnish many instructive lessons to the philosopher and the statesman. The first consequence of the unprecedented rush of emigration from all parts of the world into a country almost unknown, and but half reclaimed from its original barbarism, was to render all law virtually null, and bring the established authorities to depend entirely on the humor of the population for the observance of their orders. [T]he readiness with which the worthless and depraved class of our [c]ountry came to the Pacific coast [threatened the land with serious consequences]. From the beginning, a state of things little short of anarchy might have been reasonably awaited. Instead of this, a disposition to maintain order and secure the rights of all was shown throughout the mining districts. In the absence of all law or available protection, the people met and adopted rules for their mutual security rules adapted to their situation, where they had neither guards nor prisons, and where the slightest license given to crime or trespass of any kind must inevitably have led to terrible disorders. Small thefts were punished by banishment from the placers, while for those of large amount or for more serious crimes, there was the single alternative of hanging.[2]

It was in this legal climate during these rapacious days that Justice David Terry, the combative southwestern Confederate, and Justice Stephen Field, the manipulating northeastern Brahmin, shared the duties on the state's highest court. More often than not, they were inclined to share common goals, for in a majority of cases that came before them they agreed that frontier law lacked the scope and coherence that was essential for making California a judicially stable place. In a handful of critical state-changing decisions, however, their disagreements could not have been more conflicted. On these occasions, the indelible fissures that lay soul-deep within each man inevitably manifested themselves as intractable convictions that would eventually turn their communal tenure from quiet deference into whispered calumny. The relationship between them eventually became one of cultivated suspicion, rancor, mistrust, and open conflict. The origin for much of this uneasiness was fostered by the social and regional impulses that they both brought with them from the south and the north respectively—moral notions that had been implanted during their formative years.

Field's emotional outlook could be counted on to be confident and full of expectations, even as he showed himself to be inordinately unforgiving, manipulative and, at times, even vengeful, while Terry's sentiments were driven by his unflagging sense of honor, and an unrelenting burden of manliness that was incipient to his southern culture. It caused him to be pessimistic, suspicious, unforgiving, and predictably intemperate. Both judges' dispositions were reflected in the divergent assessment of the nascent legal system in which both men labored.

Time will be given to examining each man's life in greater detail, but for now consider the ordered and contemplative fashion in which Justice Field commented on the necessity of melding California's two legal bloodlines—civil and common law—in contrast to Judge Terry's earthy, brooding need to accommodate the moment. Field wrote:

> [A] legal system had to be created out of chaos. The common law gave no clue to many pressing questions. Little was known and not much was ascertainable about Mexican law, but enormously valuable rights depended on it. The Mexican land grants were so vast that American settlers could not be reconciled to them and considered them a monstrous wrong. Yet the United States was bound by the Treaty of Guadalupe Hidalgo to protect property rights in territory ceded by Mexico.[3]

One can see in this quotation Field's schematic approach to the law that left little doubt in the minds of his colleagues that he was legally gifted in a fashion that few immigrant lawyers were. The contemporary legal scholar Charles McCurdy, in *The Fields and the Law* (1986), puts it this way: "What made [Stephen] Field so formidable was his skill in translating the featureless generalities of the Constitution into a coherent system of principled standards. He had an uncanny ability to diagnose recurrent problem-situations [that] accommodated his value laden premises. [For] Field these solutions were neither contingent nor variable; they were 'true.'"[4]

Terry, on the other hand, perceived territorial law not so much as the systematic merging of historically legal systems, but rather as a set of rules *sui generis* that were appropriate to a given time and place. Society's laws were for Terry practical rules for finding solutions to the community's pressing problems. Consider how unapologetic he was defending his earliest courtroom appearances, bedecked with firearm and shoulder scabbard. He was fully prepared to settle the community's disputes through trials or by histrionic ordeal. Terry wrote the following of a case he was trying in his hometown of Stockton City:

> A great deal [was] made of the fact that I was armed when [I made an] attack [within] the Court House. [Yet] if any of you [had ever] lived in California as early as 1851, you will remember that the carrying of arms was an almost

universal custom. You will also know that [Stockton] had not the most quiet and orderly reputation; and that a Justice's Court in those days, was not a place of any great sanctity. I know if a lawyer was in the habit of doing his duty faithfully he was liable at any time to be attacked for calling things by their proper names. I was not accustomed to permit myself to be governed, in the discharge of my duty to clients, by the character of the other party, or the probability of being attacked by him. I have on more than one occasion, been compelled not only to go armed into a Court House, but to have a man stand behind me, whilst arguing a case, to prevent an attack from the rear.

On this [particular] occasion I was armed because I thought that arms were necessary for my defense, in a community, almost all of whom were armed and because I had frequently, in the course of my practice, been compelled to speak plainly of desperate characters, and I was liable to be called to account by them at any moment, and I always thought that the best way to prevent an attack was to be prepared to repel it. [I]f the character of the place did not shield me from insult I saw no reason why it should shield the aggressor from punishment.[5]

A. E. Wagstaff, Terry's earliest biographer, sums up Terry's legal abilities with much less fulsomeness than can be found when Field's friends speak of his legal skills. Wagstaff writes:

Terry insisted that opinions handed down in the law should be written so that the wayfaring man, though a fool, should be able to read and understand a properly written legal decision for "Judges are writing absolutely binding judicial decisions and extra-judicial decisions, [that the average man might never] consider authoritative.'[6]

The narrative of this book is a selected account of shared and conflicted episodes that were to take place over a period of 30-plus years, when at certain times and certain places each judge's life touched the other's, and when ambient political and social events of a contentious generation of imported Californians played a part in stifling both man's deepest aspirations, eventually ending in devastating consequences. If ever events confirmed the old adage that "reality's narratives can be more fanciful than fiction's fables," the ceaseless enmity between these two men and its consequences surely did. In the turmoil of the times, these two judges were faced with the transition from one judicial system to another, with the incipient changes that included recognition of legal absolutes across national boundaries; determination of personal and religious conduct in the face of unending immigration; regulation of amorphous mineral, water and land-ownership rights; and the authorization of domains for taxing individuals and corporations. In the early days of statehood, the nature of such laws were in innumerable ways quixotic, irrepressible and fortuitous; yet, laced as they were with Latin and Teutonic temperaments and the jurisprudential disquisitions of northern and southern Europeans, they were so much more.

This book, however, does not pretend to be a precise judicial history of early California. Rather, it is the fascinating life that both Terry and Field lived that lies at the heart of the narrative. It is a story about two terrene individuals and the judicial and personal confrontations that were to unfold between them during the latter half of the nineteenth-century. The performance of these men against the backdrop of California's burgeoning judicial legacy makes for a lively, multi-faceted tale. It is a story that was pieced together from an array of records—in particular, written chronicles, booklets and pamphlets, state documents, private letters, memoirs and newspapers. In the telling, an effort was made to present the information accurately, but it must be admitted that some of the unrecorded gaps between events are filled with extrapolations of what most probably happened. Such inferences, however, were always made within the context of what was reported and what it is reasonable to believe had occurred—given the nature of the events and the temper of the era in which these two strenuous and irrepressible men lived their lives.

Chapter 1 sketches Field's and Terry's journey to the Supreme Court of California from their eastern and southern beginnings. Chapters 2 and 3, by contrast, trace the nature of the law they faced when they took their places on the bench. These chapters consider briefly California's historic transition from territory to statehood and from its so-called "lawless" era to its position as a fledgling state caught in the tug and haul of Mexican and Anglo-Saxon jurisprudence. Specifically, Chapter 2 discusses California making its way from a territory to a state and the creation of its first constitution, while Chapter 3 considers some of the reasons that brought about the replacement of Mexico's civil law system with the United States common law system. Thereafter, Chapters 4 through 11 offer a chronographic account of the judges' ongoing private and public engagements. More specifically, while Chapters 4, 5, 6 and 7 concentrate on the events that shaped each man's life, Chapters 8 through 11 investigate the discrete legal conflicts that inevitably were to determine the outcome of the colorful, yet in many ways forlorn, saga of judicial casuistry.

NOTES

1. Hubert Howe Bancroft. *History of California* (San Francisco: The History Company. 1898). VII, 223.

2. Bayard Taylor, *Eldorado, or Adventures in the Path of Empire* (Lincoln, NE: University of Nebraska Press. 1949). 77.

3. Cited in Edward Johnson. *History of the Supreme Court Justices of California, 1850 to 1900* (San Francisco: Bender-Moss. 1963). 69.

4. Cited in Christian G. Fritz, *Federal Justice in California.* 1851–1891 (Lincoln, NE: University of Nebraska Press, 1991). 37–38.

5. Charles L. Case. *Trial of David S. Terry* (R. C. Moore & Co. 1856). 24.

6. Cited in A. E. Wagstaff, *The Life of Ex. Chief Justice of the Supreme Court of California: David S. Terry* (San Francisco).

Chapter One

El Dorado

Judges Stephen J. Field and David S. Terry did not come to the California Territory to practice law. They each came to get "quick and easy" fortunes. They were not the first lawyers to arrive, but they stayed longer than most, and when, early on, they realized that the gold was not there "just for the taking," they wasted little time returning to the skill that they had each brought with them from the east and the south—lawyering. Within the limits of this adventitious time and place, Field's legal training was thorough and confirming, while Terry's was, by any measure, modest. Field used his unmatched intellectual powers to tower over his contemporaries, while Terry succeeded by the sheer force of will and physicality. Yet, in one sense they were very much alike: Each applied the law as jurists in the fashion of the Victorians—as an instrument for advancing social order and moral rectitude. Both wanted to influence the lives of contemporary Californians, and each man was an unabashed moralizer quick to judge his adversaries as enemies of virtue. But perhaps in many respects what was most important was that both had the temperament and skills necessary to find money making easy. The pages that follow are an account of how these two men rose to the highest court in California and how each left an indelible mark on California's frontier law for better and for worse.

In a certain sense, the early lives of Field and Terry could hardly have been more dissimilar. Field's progenitors on both sides of the family were Congregational ministers, or children of ministers, most of who lived and died in New England, while Terry's roots came from a collection of Scotch-Irish emigrants of modest means, but who were eventually to become successful cotton growers in Virginia, Mississippi and Texas. The socially well-born Field began life in Haddam, Connecticut, but, for the most part, was raised in Stockbridge, Massachusetts. He was brought up in the orderly fashion that was common for a cleric's household. Terry, in contrast, was born in Kentucky, raised on the Mississippi and Texas deltas, and grew to manhood in a home that made him fatherless at ten and motherless by thirteen. Field at thirteen was working in a missionary school, studying ancient languages and attending to the children of the wealthy. Terry at thirteen had left school behind and traipsed off to fight the "ragabush" Mexicans in Texas' War for Independence (1835). Yet, twenty-five years later, despite their diverse beginnings, the two men sat together on the California Supreme Court where they began to take the measure of each another.

Stephen Johnson Field, born November 4, 1816, the sixth of nine children, had been named to honor the memory of a Congregational minister revered by the family. Field's mother's given name was "Submit," but she and the family knew better. She may have emulated that Christian virtue, but tenacity and fortitude were also aspects of her nature—and these traits she passed on to her sons. Two older brothers, David Dudley and Cyrus West, were particularly influential in young Stephen's life. The oldest, "Dudley," became a distinguished lawyer and legal scholar whose most noteworthy life contribution was his oversight of the formulation of the New York State Codes of Legal Procedure (he was fond of saying that the sun never set on the codes that had come under his influence). Brother Cyrus, not to be over-shadowed, became a wealthy entrepreneur and a financial force behind the laying of the first and second transatlantic cables in 1856. Other family notables included brother Jonathan who was president of the Massachusetts State Senate, and sister Ellen's son, David Josiah Brewer, who was a justice of the United States Supreme Court from 1889 to 1910. The Field clan, in fact, had been an integral part of New England's puritan landscape since the middle of the 17th century. Grandfather David Dudley Field had served as a captain in the America's War for Independence. His heirs' unswerving devotion to institutional religion had given them the forbearance and self-assured piety to be missionaries in New York's northwestern hill country. Stephen Field's great biographer, Carl Brent Swisher, summed up the family's devout efforts this way: The Field family were people who "prayed earnestly, worked strenuously, and shot with unerring aim."[1] He continued: "In the hard life to which they were forced to accustom themselves, the fundamentals of their existence were their religious faith and creed and the material elements of property that provided food, clothing, and shelter. The struggle developed strength and power of resistance, but it left also the inevitable mark of narrowness that comes with unrelenting concentration on a few things.[2]

The family's youngest, Henry Martyn Field, the son who would follow his father David into the ministry, remembered his childhood days not as the struggle and sacrifice that the biographer describes but as days of Elysium:

> Our whole domestic life received its tone from this unaffected piety of our parents, who taught their children to lie down and rise up in that fear of the Lord which is the beginning of wisdom. The sweetest and tenderest moments of the day were at morning and evening prayers. We read the Bible 'in course' beginning at Genesis and going straight through to Revelation. All sat around the fireplace in a circle. Father began, reading three verses, and we followed, from the oldest to the youngest. Sometimes my sister Mary, who had a sweet voice, sang a hymn. [T]hen the picture in Burn's 'Cotter's Saturday Night' was fulfilled to the letter except in one point the 'kneeling down.' The stern old Puritans had such rigid notions that they would not kneel even to God, as if it were a sign of formality. But rising, our reverend sire took his stand behind a tall chair, as in a pulpit, and then, when all was hushed in silence, the saint, the husband and the father prayed.[3]

In stark contrast, David Smith Terry, a child of the South, born in Kentucky on March 8, 1823, and raised in Baptist Biblicism, would have felt out of place in the Field's structured formalities. Seven years younger than Field, his childhood training had been molded on much craggier soil. His ancestors' lives had been formed on the dank hillsides of Ireland. Members on both sides of the family were known to be people of unflagging resolve and stubbornness. Records indicate that after 1746, Terry's father's family farmed in Virginia, while his mother's family, the Smiths, farmed in the Carolinas. Both Grandfather Terry and Grandfather Smith were military officers in the Revolutionary War (America's War for Independence). Nathaniel Terry was a colonel in the battalion that accepted Cornwallis' surrender at Yorktown, and Colonel David Smith (after whom David Terry was named) joined the colonial forces in 1780 and remained under arms until the war was over. Colonel Smith's son, David Smith II, helped the charismatic Andrew Jackson defeat a seasoned British force at the battle of New Orleans in 1815. Jackson would later describe the young Smith as "the bravest man I have ever met."[4] Smith II's sister, Sarah, married Joseph Terry in Christian County Kentucky in 1816.

Little is known of "Joe" Terry except that he and Sarah were living in Mississippi by 1824, and that they were the parents of four sons—Benjamin Franklin (called Frank), David, Aurelius and Clinton—and that sometime around 1833 or 1834, Sarah separated from her husband because he had "contracted [troublesome] habits" (apparently too much hard liquor).[5] Taking her four boys, Sarah joined her mother, Obedience Smith, on a cotton farm in southeastern Texas. Grandma Smith, along with two of her sisters, owned large sections of the swampy delta land near the Gulf of Mexico—land that today makes up parts of the city of Houston.

For three years, Sarah and her boys labored on this resistive land. It was grinding work, and in the third year, Sarah, became a victim of her labor succumbing to malaria. With the boys now parentless, the oldest, 15-year-old Frank, was left to run the farm and do the best he could with his three younger brothers. Sadly, it is to be reported that when news of Sarah's death reached the boy's father, Joe Terry, he did not send for the motherless children; on the contrary, he lost no time finding a new wife. Sparse accounts show only that he raised a large second family and apparently never again had any contact with his four older boys.

In the chilly winter of 1829, under the consoling hands of the Ladies' Greek Association of New Haven, The Reverend Josiah Brewer and his new bride Emelia Field Brewer set sail for Athens. They were planning to start a school for "young ladies." Joining them was Emelia's little brother Stephen Johnson Field. Stephen and Emelia's father believed that the boy might profit from the study of near eastern languages should he later choose to follow his father's footsteps into the ministry. The three messengers of the gospel on their way to Athens by way of Smyrna discovered in the bustling Turkish seaport a large population of Greeks. Since Athens was under a lethal siege of plague they decided to change plans and set up a school for young women in Smyrna. For the pubescent Stephen it was an adventuresome time. His little family traveled from Smyrna to Athens to Malta and back again, often just fleeing the eruption of cholera that drove 30,000+ people from their homes in Smyrna between 1828 and 1832. The disease brought a frightful cycle of death and sickness, and before running its course, it left its mark on the lives of thousands of families in the eastern Mediterranean.

Both Field's and Terry's lives at 13 were filled with adventures, but in Terry's case these adventures were tinged with feelings of loneliness, for when his mother died and his father had apparently forgotten him, he found himself under the guiding hand of his oldest brother Frank. Yet, taking direction from one who is but two years older than he was, was tenuous indeed. David Terry chose to listen to his brother's advice when it suited him and to ignore it when it did not. The day he abandoned the tedium of school and set off with a boyhood friend to fight for Texas' independence was a day that his brother's advice did not suit him. Twenty years later, he reminisced about these youthful impulses in a letter to his wife:

> [A]t my mother's death, I was left [to] my own guardianship, my only counselor, who had influence with me, being my brother who was but two years older than myself. From that age I counted myself a man, and associated with men, and played a man's part in the struggle which secured the independence of Texas. Acknowledging no control upon my actions, I could not sink from the soldier into the schoolboy; so, what education I have acquired above what a boy of

> twelve gathers at common schools I acquired by reading at home all the books I owned or could borrow during the time I was not engaged on the frontier.[6]

Five years later, while Field was finishing his education at Williams College in Massachusetts, Terry was slogging Texas's parched lands in search of independence from Mexico. Terry claims to have "played a man's part" in the war, but chances are at 13 he was much more a tag-along than a fighter even though years later, the family would insist that he had killed a Mexican officer in the war with a Bowie knife. One thing known for certain, however, is that nine years later in the Mexican War of 1846, Terry was clearly no tag-along. As a member of the Texas Rangers he fought with Captain Sam Ballowe's First Regiment of Texas Volunteers. Fighting with Ballowe enabled him to fight in the war's principal battle at Monterrey. His exploits during this battle go generally unrecorded, but his contemporary biographer A. Russell Buchanan writes, "Virtually the only way for a common soldier to gain notice in accounts of the Mexican War was to be killed or wounded, and since Terry was unscathed he was also unsung"—unsung, of course, except in the voices of Terry's loyal family.[7]

But soldiering was not the only influence in young Terry's life. Between forays of camping and drilling he would make his way home to share the labor of the family farm and read law books in his uncle's law office in Galveston. One can assume that the vivid experiences of military life and the study of law had the effect of nurturing in him the impulse of combativeness and, at times, a much too rudimentary notion of loyalty and honor. Unfortunately, his inability to separate the somatic responses of military life from the reasoned responses of juristic restraint would afflict him throughout life—and the military virtues of courage and honor that he so cherished would not always serve him well. However, there were times when these conflicting intuitions enabled him to realize what many of his military comrades failed to sense, that is: when the struggle is no longer physical, one must find and defend the higher ground of legal and social order. As time passed he was able to cast aside many of the baser impulsive elements of military life, in part through the influence of his wife's counsel and in part, one might judge, through the memory of his mother and her admonitions. A lifetime of recollections and testimony from friend and foe avowed that Terry rarely drank, had never been seen drunk and was never a womanizer or gambler. And moreover, he remained a loyal parishioner in the Southern Baptist Church, which was also a lasting source of circumspection and pride.

Terry's lawyer uncle, T. J. B. Hadley, described Terry as "[N]ot bright, but deep and possessed of a remarkable memory. [N]ot quarrelsome, never offered an insult to anyone, but was prompt to resent one when offered."[8] Later circumstances would prove Colonel Hadley wrong about his nephew's intelligence but not about his temperament. Terry possessed a remarkable degree of analytical intelligence. Apparently his uncle was looking for something that his young nephew did not, at the time, possess—a mesmerizing devotion to the study of law. But intelligence and temperament aside, he had enough commitment to his legal labors to pass the Texas bar in November of 1845. Several months after the battle at Monterrey in 1846, Terry again was in Texas running for district attorney of Galveston. Not surprisingly he lost; at twenty-three, his electioneering performance was at best desultory and passionless—as it would prove to be throughout his life.

This political setback, however, did give him the time to travel east into Mississippi delta country and visit his mother's relatives, including his aunt Ophelia, who was married to Hiram Runnels, a two-term Mississippi Congressman and a politically ambitious man who would later become the governor of both Mississippi and Texas. Terry's eastern visit was a lengthy one—and one which brought the rudderless young man into contact with Uncle Hiram's young ward, Cornelia "Neal" Runnels. From their very first meeting, Cornelia Runnels' poise and placidity beguiled Terry, but sadly she shared no fascination for him. Sensing that her interest lay with a childhood companion, Terry reluctantly ended his visit to Mississippi and returned to his home in Texas in 1848.

He arrived just in time to persuade his brother Frank, who was preparing to join an expedition to the California gold fields, to remain in Texas and look after the farm while he, as the second son, would shoulder the family's pecuniary responsibilities and search for a quick fortune in California. Somehow Frank agreed, and while Terry's westward record is sparse, A. Russell Buchanan pieces together this account: "The expedition was well outfitted and included in the group of twenty or thirty men [some] prominent Texans and four slaves. The party passed through Austin about the middle of April 1849, and by the time it reached El Paso late in June, Terry had become its leader. The expedition continued on [and] Terry was in California on September 3, 1849."[9] Years later, Terry family members would give those willing to listen a much more rousing rendition of his journey west. They told of skirmishes with Indians in which many Indians were killed while Terry and his persistent and durable trekkers suffered the loss of but a single man.

Two solitary years followed but in October of 1851 he received a note from Cornelia Runnels indicating that she still regarded him as a friend. Terry needed no more prompting; and in November he renewed his effort to seek her consent in marriage, and a year later, probably in November of 1852 they were married in Galveston, Texas. Six months later, in February of 1853, they started a home together in California. Cornelia straightaway understood that she had entered the domain of Western frontiersmen when the Stockton paper's account of their marriage read more like a livestock report than a wedding announcement: "David S. Terry, Esq., one of our first, most able and useful citizens, returned by the Golden Gate from a visit to the Atlantic States. He brings with him a wife a valuable acquisition to society in the San Joaquin County."[10] In short order, friends agreed that the refined, politically well-connected Mrs. Terry would eventually round and smooth the coarser edges of the hulking, six-foot-two, 230 pound tempestuous Terry.

At the end of the summer of 1833 Stephen Field, after four years in southern Europe, returned to Massachusetts anxious to enroll at Williams College. Two older brothers had proceeded him at Williams, but neither persevered long enough to earn a baccalaureate degree. Stephen at 17, however, was determined to restore the family's scholarly reputation. Not only did he graduate, but he was also class valedictorian. The classical curriculum at Williams and his earlier training in Adriatic languages suited him well; he immediately became a faculty favorite. Mark Hopkins, president of Williams and one of the country's foremost scholars of moral theology, gave his young charge special attention, and in return, Field was expected to perform—and on this count he did not disappoint. Along the way, Field mastered the works of three of England's leading moral philosophers: Joseph Butler, Francis Whately and William Paley. Writers, as it happened, who were not unfamiliar with the theological determinism of Field's childhood. These three men reinforced the metaphysical convictions that would serve Field well the rest of his life. The world of nature, these teleologists argued, manifested a rational design and therefore proved the existence of a rational designer; and what is more, those who failed to heed the insinuated ratiocinations of this designer were likely to face a life of foolish, even calamitous consequences. In brief, they believed that human beings' and, indeed, *in toto* humankind's "irrationalities" would not go unattended or unpunished. Throughout life, Field embraced these notions of cosmic order and power, and even after he was no longer sentimentally beholden to the concepts, they continued to generate within him much impatience toward those he judged to be suffering from a weakness of moral will.

If Stephen Field was not going to follow his father, the Reverend David Dudley Field, into the ministry, as seemed to be the case, then the family hoped the years he had spent in the Middle East might at least have prepared him for a career teaching ancient languages. (It was said that Field could converse with ease in Greek, Italian and French). But Field's years in Europe only convinced him that the life of a professor of near-Eastern languages did not hold enough promise or enough excitement to be worthy a lifetime of labor. He clearly had the brain for it but not the stomach. Field viewed the teaching of ancient languages in the isolation of a small tutorial school as something akin to monastic life—and he was certain the academy could offer neither the excitement nor the recognition he so fervently wanted.

After matriculating at Williams, however, and with no certain direction settled in his mind, Field was invited by his oldest brother, David Dudley Field, to move to New York City and read law in the family's law firm. In two years, Field's brilliant intellectual performance qualified him for a full-fledged partnership, but sadly, he and his brother's unyielding temperaments made working together day after day a burden he need not carry—both men understood that a partnership keeping them side-by-side was unnecessary. Stephen, who had been traveling in Europe with his father, needed very little persuading, for he had been wholly absorbed by the "gold-for-the-taking" accounts that filled Europe's daily newspapers. By then Stephen Field had contracted a full-blown case of gold fever.

On November 13, 1849, with his father's blessing and a ticket to the Pacific Coast, Field took leave from 10 years in his brother Dudley's law firm and booked passage on the steamship Crescent City bound for Panama. Several weeks later, he found himself at the Isthmus of Panama in the "old Latin American town" of Chagres where again he was stimulated by accounts of a fortune in gold ore that was available to anyone willing to dig for it. From Chagres, Field chartered a pole boat to the town of Cruces, and from there he traveled by mule over the hills into Panama City. There he boarded the shuttle ship California, which carried him north to the San Francisco Bay. Twelve hundred passengers had packed this vessel from stem to stern. Reaching San Francisco on December 28, 1849, he wrote his family expressing gratitude to Providence for letting him endure the 22-day ocean trip without falling ill to malaria. He told his father that he was keenly aware of his good fortune to have escaped the lethal disease. Courageously he had placed himself at risk assisting an exhausted physician who was caring for passengers. It must surely have been an event that stirred memories of the days when he had assisted his brother-in-law attending to the needs of the plague-ridden Athenians. Later when Field was to describe this harrowing trip, he reminded listeners that he had faced the scourge of rampant disease before and had lived to tell about it. Perhaps these early episodes confirmed what he had learned so well at hearthside: Providence determines why some people reap fortunate consequences in life while others do not. But of even greater importance, the trip must have helped confirm for him, once and for all, that the universe is an orderly and rational place, and that by choosing to go west he had made a wise and morally appropriate decision. When Field arrived in San Francisco, he was to learn that people traveling to California overland had their own version of the plague—something called "land scurvy," which left the victim weak and lethargic for months (a malady caused by a deprivation of vegetables).

Field and Terry both came to California as restless young men with unclear lifetime prospects. The chance for overnight wealth, however, while initially alluring, would not turn out to be the driving force in either man's career. Nor did it take either of them long to decide that prospecting was a risky business and that the promise of success had been greatly exaggerated by the gossip-mongering vagabonds and the information-starved journalists who wrote about frontier adventuring. Seizing the moment, both men individually put aside their fading pipe dreams for overnight riches and directed their energies toward building reputations as political lawyers.

In mid-January 1850, after luxuriating in San Francisco's December sun for a fortnight, Field headed upstream by steamer to the sprawling canvas-tent town of Sacramento. It was customary for most passengers to disembark in Sacramento, but Field had other plans; he chose to stay aboard and see what lay farther north.[11] In particular, he was looking for a place where he might employ his legal services while trying his hand at mining and land speculation. He had planned initially to stop in the hamlet of Vernon where he was told prospects for a young lawyer were good, however, upon arriving he discovered that, save for a single house, Vernon was underwater from the incessant rain, so he decided to stay aboard the steamer and look even farther north. What he found was a sandy strip of land at the confluence of the Feather and the Yuba Rivers. (It was the Feather that had given up the first published reports of gold nuggets in California). Field disembarked and scrambled a muddy embankment that placed him squarely before a shabby adobe shack surrounded by a cluster of miners' tents. The adobe, he recounts, was serving as an all-purpose meeting house, courtroom, and assay office. Once inside the musty mud structure he was drawn to a land auction taking place. It proved to be the sort of situation for which he was looking. Moreover the time was right. Field approached the proprietor-auctioneer—a man by the name of Charles Cavillaud—and pushed into his hands a fading copy of *The New York Evening Post* in which Field's name appeared on the paper's travel manifest. Field's name was underlined in ink. The notice read: "Prominent New York City attorney S.J. Field on his way to California." The notice produced the results he had hoped for—it generated enough on-the-spot credit to buy him 65 parcels of land worth $16,250.[12] In reality while bidding on these parcels, he had but 20 dollars in his pocket.

The following morning, Field was approached by Cavillaud with a request to draw up deeds for several leagues of land upon which Cavillaud and a French comrade, Sicard, were planning to develop an entire town. Field wasted no time drawing the boundaries, making sure that the conveyance fell outside any land owned by Captain John A. Sutter. Sutter praised him publicly for his skill and honesty—a gesture that enhanced Field's reputation as a skilled, fair-minded lawyer. The endorsement served him well and gave him a competitive advantage over other "gypsy" lawyers who were in the region.

(Field writes that the size of Sutter's property required title transference of a tract larger than he had ever before placed in conveyance.)[13] Not only did Field play a vital role in establishing permanent borders for the township, he also developed an effective compensation strategy for those suffering property losses as a result of shifting boundaries—a legally necessary tool for dealing with the never-ending flow of intruding squatters.

As a result of his acumen, Field wrote, the land speculators were eager to accept his counsel and asked him to draw up "a deed of township" with "rules of incorporation" and "documents of conveyance" that would secure the transferred title to the residents of the new township. Literally, with Field's help, *sui generis*, a town had sprung up overnight. The next day, Field persuaded his neighbors that now it would be time to establish a town government. Field later wrote, that in the breadth of a single week, the new landowners were ready to elect the town's first *ayuntamiento* (town council) its *first and second alcalde* (mayor and vice mayor) and its sheriff. Moreover, he declared, he was not in the least fainthearted when it came to placing his own name before the assembled as first alcalde. Unfortunately, this time his status as a "New York lawyer" worked against him. Southerner miners in particular were suspicious of what they called his "hidden desires." Nonetheless, his effort on behalf of the new landowners engendered enough support to allow him to squeeze through with a narrow nine-vote victory. It was now time to name their town. They called it "Marysville" after the wife of one of the town's property owners. She had become celebrated for having been one of but a handful of survivors from the ill fated Donner Party expedition of 1846. Astoundingly, in less than five day's time, on January 22, 1850, as Marysville's new first alcalde Field traveled to Sacramento's courthouse, and with few impediments filed the deed of township that put Marysville on the map.

The California mining districts at mid-century were lawless enclaves, so lawless, in fact, that even "camp" transients were agitating for minimal "rules of civil and criminal conduct." Field, of course, was as prepared as anyone to give the residents of Marysville a workable set of rules and regulations. Seemingly overnight he produced an abridged version of his brother Dudley Field's 1847 New York Codes of Legal Procedure. As one never burdened by undue modesty, he summarized his performance as follows:

> [T]o make a long story short, until I was superseded by officers under the United States government, I superintended municipal affairs and administered justice in Marysville with success. Whilst there was a large number of residents there of high character and culture, who would have done honor to any city, there were also unfortunately many desperate persons, gamblers, blackguards, thieves, and

> cut-throats; yet the place was as orderly as a New England village. There were no disturbances at night, no riots and no lynching. It was the model town of the whole country for peacefulness and respect for [the new] laws.[14]

This self-assuredness provoked Carl Swisher, Field's biographer, to write:

> Field's own pronouncements lead to the suspicion that he was a bit intoxicated by his rise in position from obscurity in his brother's law office to czardom in a frontier town. He gloried in applying to others principles of justice derived from his own inner consciousness, principles which had been instilled in him by the years of his early training. He seems never to have doubted his own wisdom in the selection and interpretation of fundamental principles. With deepest satisfaction he looked upon his work and saw that it was good.[15]

Swisher might have added that Field's sense of rectitude, so manifest at thirty-three years of age, had deserted him at 83. His early style as first alcalde of Marysville was portentous of his later judicial perspectives. But immodesty aside, Field had a legitimate reason to be proud, for an alcalde's most formidable task was to bring order to a territory where there had been none, and within a week he had done just that.

Imposing punishments and penalties in a township where the militia was several marching days away (or too busy policing itself) was an exacting task, and not every alcalde proved as successful as Field had in this undertaking. Convicted troublemakers, particularly people who had very little chance of winning an appeal, might easily run off or enlist friends to help them resist arrest. And even when such people were in custody, it was often impossible to control them, because there were no jails, or the jails were too dilapidated to hold them. Frequently, these small mining towns were unwilling to spend the money needed to build jails or even to pay the transfer fees necessary to have their prisoners sent to jails in Sacramento and San Francisco. Miners in these alcalde-run towns generally agreed that if law-breakers were to be dealt with at all, the punishment should be swift. This usually meant banishment or hanging.

Field considered the matter of punishment to be one of his most difficult problems, for it required imposing sanctions on a population that was too much in a hurry to think of civic permanence.[16] Field is to be admired, for even without the help of a militia, he implemented a system in which the punishment usually fit the crime. He aimed to temporize the miners' needs for revenge with a policy of public whipping, banishments, and monetary fines and, on occasions, a combination of all these remedies. To his credit, sensing the unalterable nature of lynching, Field became its consistent foe. Most especially, he fought against hasty lynching and spent significant time trying to convince unruly village mobs that other penalties should replace the finality of the noose. He cited an example of a miner who had refused to reveal the whereabouts of $1,500 dollars allegedly stolen from a woman. An impatient mob, Field writes, wanted to hang the thief on the spot, but, "I resisted this measure and ordered fifty lashes, followed by fifty more the next day."[17] It is difficult to know if Field would have continued the beating if the thief had continued to refuse to reveal his hiding place—it is possible that Field might have beaten him to death. Perhaps Field believed that beating the evidence out of the man was more appropriate than hanging him—reasoning that a protracted beating gave the malefactor time to recognize the error of his ways, and unlike irreversible hanging, was the closest facsimile of "judicial review" that one was likely to find on a frontier. (It might seem that Field's solution played havoc with the subtleties of the United States Constitution's Fifth Amendment, but presumably he rated prohibition against torture as a much too rarefied luxury to be applied on the frontier.)

Constitutional government came to California in May of 1850, and with its appearance, Field's stint as alcalde of Marysville came to an end. But this heady experience only generated in him greater political aspiration for he had discovered that he was a man with an "adventurous spirit," a man, one might say, who yearned for recognition that would never be wholly satisfied within the often-prosaic practice of law or the redundancies of real estate speculation. As time passed, more and more he intruded into politics. He insisted that he always ran for office in order to bring about judicial reform, yet everybody who knew him knew there was more to it than that. It also contained for Field the double aphrodisiacs of power and recognition.

When the first state Legislature convened in January of 1851, Field's appetite for political office was still undiminished. It was his intention to become Yuba County's first representative to the California Legislature, but in order to do this he needed the support of the region's dominant political organization, e.g., the Northern California Democratic Committee. This committee controlled most of the pivotal political sites north of Monterey. Field decided to become better known in order to get a more sympathetic hearing before the committee. He published in the county newspapers a series of endorsements from public leaders—endorsements, he insisted, that had come to him unsolicited. His opponents, particularly the Southern Democrats, ridiculed his claimed unsolicited support, labeling it "wholly false." The endorsements were neither spontaneous nor unsolicited, they insisted. What is more, the large contingent of southern miners in Yuba County did not trust him, and made it clear that he would need to look elsewhere for political endorsement. Nonetheless, putting aside whatever misgivings this might have engendered, Field set out to campaign directly before the claim-miners working in the surrounding hills of Yuba County.

At the Democratic Party's summer convention, Field, well aware of the southern Democrats' resentments, was determined to make himself less obtrusive and to let friends promote his case among various political factions. It was his sense that the farther he stayed away from his southern critics the greater his chances would be to gain the confidence of local rank-and-file Democrats, in particular, northern miners. The district southerners, however, were just as determined not to allow him to remain inconspicuous. Contrarily, they accused him of being a cowardly and clandestine supporter of his famous brother Dudley's uncompromising eastern abolitionist politics. On the stump, however, Field seemed to reinforce these charges when he publicly refused to declare outright whether he was in favor slavery or not. "[E]ach State had the right to resolve the matter as it sees fit,"[18] is the most he would say. On the other hand, northern miners had their own reasons to mistrust him, for on the vital question of "land-grant rights," Field was unwilling to endorse their "finders' keepers" position. Yet, as he had been on the slavery issue, he remained obtuse. Did he support the right of miners to stake a claim and by that act establish ownership, or did he support the Mexican American landowners' claim that the land was theirs by historical title? The miners pressed for an undiluted answer on the matter, but Field remained vague and uncommitted. Later in his career it would prove correct that the miners had reason to mistrust Field's position on the issue of "land entitlements."

On nomination day the convention house was packed with southern miners determined to prevent Field's bid to become the Democratic nominee for the California Assembly, and they succeeded—in the caucuses he was roundly defeated. But Field was not prepared to take no for an answer. With little or no public consultation, he temporarily scrapped his Democratic allegiances and set out to campaign for the assembly seat as an Independent. He believed that his chances of winning were good because miners were too undisciplined to care very much about party alliances. His plan was to dog the steps of the officially nominated Democratic candidate, John T. McCarty, contrasting himself and his ability to that of McCarty's. He kept at McCarty's heels in every village and mining camp, currying favor of the miners with clever speeches that contrasted sharply with his opponent's rhetorical dullness. Especially effective with a homesick miners, Field writes, were his dramatic reminiscences of their eastern hearth, homes and mothers. But he was not averse to appealing to their more carnal impulses as well. He bought his share of saloon votes (460 drinks and 275 cigars).[19] In the fall his efforts paid off. He won the legislative seat with votes to spare, even though he publicly lamented that he failed to carry his hometown of Marysville.

Neutral observers were not surprised, however, for in his rigorous efforts as the alcalde of Marysville, he had engendered his share of enemies.

Field's law practice, however, continued to thrive. His law practice was as successful and lucrative a practice as any of the central valley lawyers. Whenever Field decided to focus his intelligence on making money, he was able to make a great deal of it. His heart might have yearned for public recognition but it was his insight into matters of legal commerce that gave his greatest financial return. His wealth would ebb and flow in proportion to the time that he devoted to it. But political power was always the true elixir. What he did not know at the time, was that political power always would remain out of reach. When Field did covet political goals, however, he was always lured into alliances with rich and powerful people. It was a practice that would make him carelessly beholden to them—that is, it was a practice that made powerless people inordinately resentful of him. He accumulated money in a hurry, and lost it just as quickly, and apparently it was whispered that his itch for gambling only worsened his public image.

When Field entered the California Legislature's lower house in January of 1851, he was confronted by a legal system that was floundering in a messy mixture of civil and common law procedures. But because he arrived with a reputation as a gifted legal analyst and organizer, the legislators in short order channeled his efforts into sorting through the new state's legal conundrums, and all this he did, even as he was codifying the burgeoning legislation that the Assembly produced daily. Moreover, he was not modest about his skills, nor did he need to be, for he was as qualified for the task of organizing legal systems as anyone in the State's fledgling government. Unquestionably, above and beyond most Californians, he had the intellectual gifts necessary to produce a workable, coherent judicial system. The ten years he spent in the New York law offices assisting his brother's efforts to codify New York's legal system had given him every confidence that he was prepared to handle a comparable task in California. By the end of the first legislative session, most colleagues were convinced that he was as competent as he said he was, so much so, that many lawmakers implicitly accepted his formulation of the Codes of Civil and Criminal Procedure for California without much debate. As daunting as this task was, Field for the most part dealt with it single-handedly. He modified over three hundred of the codes introduced by his brother in New York while adding one hundred more of his own, including a provision in the Civil Practice Act respecting water and mining claims that would become the foundation for water and mining law throughout the western states. One hundred fifty years after the original formulations, these codes remain the enduring heart of California's Codes of Procedure, in both civil and criminal law. In his *History of the Supreme Court Justices of California:*

1850–1900, J. Edward Johnson writes that it is "beyond belief that Field could have drafted all these statutes in a single term in the California Assembly."[20] Of course, Field did not consider it so; rather, he assessed his performance in his characteristic fashion:

> I devoted so much attention and earnestness to the work that in a short time the Legislature placed implicit confidence in everything relating to the judiciary which I recommended. The Criminal Practice Act, for instance, remodeled as stated, consisting of over six hundred sections, was never read before the Legislature at all. The rules were suspended and the bill read by its title and passed. When it came before the Governor on the last day of the session, he said he could not sign it without reading it, and it was too late for him to do that. I represented to him that its passage was essential to secure harmonious working of laws already passed. Turning to me he said, "You say it is all right?" I replied, "Yes;" and thereupon he signed it.[21]

The legislative term ended in May of 1851, and an understandably weary Field returned to Marysville, emotionally and financially spent. "I am," he wrote, "eighteen thousand dollars in debt" (with an accrual rate of 10 percent per month!). "I entered the Legislature a wealthy man and left it penniless."[22] It was never publicly clear how he had become penniless. "My ventures [had] proved so many maelstroms into which the investments were not only drawn but swallowed up," he wrote.[23] This was the extent of his entire explanation on the matter. A somewhat less obscure observation was entered in a marginal note that he deleted from the final draft of his *Reminiscences.* In the first draft he wrote, "Various losses and numerous adventures and speculations that I entered into [s]wept away my fortune." "Speculations" fits his perception of land investments, but the "numerous adventures" remain to the offhand observer enigmatic. His critics, however, were quick to declare themselves not in the least mystified. For them these "speculations" were meant to disguise "lost gambling money"—yet no one could expect a crafty vicar's son to acknowledge such circumstances publicly. What is known for sure is that when he entered the Legislature in 1850, he had cash assets of $14,000, and by the end of the term he was $18,000 in debt. What's more, Field chooses in his *Reminiscences* not to discuss why he did not seek reelection to the lower house; perhaps money was the principal roadblock. By mid-summer, however, after Field reduced his liabilities (especially the colossal monthly usury fee), his enthusiasm for political office returned, and he again turned to the California Legislature. This time he was after a higher prize: a seat in the upper house—the Senate.

To the astonishment of most and the annoyance of some, he returned again to the Democrats' summer convention seeking their endorsement. As to be expected, their reception was not cordial. John McCarty, the defeated candidate from the year before, and McCarty's henchmen had not forgotten the humiliation they had suffered at Field's hands. McCarty had referred to him as a "liar and coward and a villain."[24] However, nowhere in Field's discussion of these events does he indicate that he was unwelcome at the convention. Quite the contrary, he suggests that his Herculean efforts producing the state's Codes of Procedure had been a *tour de force* sufficient to wash away any lingering political sins that he might have accumulated. Surely the party would forgive him, he must have reasoned, and would recognize that he was easily the most qualified candidate for the Democrats' Senatorial nomination. Field's strategy for gaining the nomination, however, suggests that he was not as sanguine as he wanted people to believe. He attended the convention, but he did not make an appearance on the floor, nor did he take part in the debates. The less the delegates saw of him, he had decided, the better. If he were to win the nomination *absente reo* (by supposed absence), he believed, he could most likely keep recriminations at a minimum. His plan was to put his political fortunes in the hands of a trusted friend who he sent to the convention floor with ten proxies. But this "friend," as it happened, did not vote for him, but traded the proxies for a sheriff's appointment for a partner. Field later wrote, because of the perfidy of the man he lost the nomination for state senator by two votes. At a distance, Field's account seems to need some adjusting. If, as he says, they held his proxies, in what manner were they able to transfer them to other candidates without his permission? Perhaps a more plausible explanation was that they were colleagues who held their own votes conditionally for him, but that, for reasons that are now unclear, they later changed their minds and voted for others. Field insisted upon describing this event as no less than "treachery." In fact, at one point Field is so angered by the outcome that he writes that he had to be restrained from throwing the culprit out a nearby window. So it happened that once again Field failed to get the Democratic Party's nomination, but this time rather than again provoking the wrath of the Party by running as an independent, he returned to Marysville and continued building a lucrative legal practice.

Some time passed, and in 1855, Field returned to the political arena as a candidate for the United States Senate, but on this occasion, at the urging of his legislative colleague David Broderick. Broderick was soon to become California's fourth U.S. senator, and Field believed that this was reason enough to honor this powerful colleague's request—even though most people (including Field) believed he had little or no chance of being elected a senator. He was quite correct to conclude that the Democratic leadership was still in no mood to forgive the disloyalty he had exhibited during the campaign of 1851. However, as became his manner, he entered the fray publicly while feigning disinterest to any higher political ambition—this was a pattern that he employed whenever he ran for political office. "Others were pressing him to fill a public need" he wrote, "but I myself would never seek the office." In point of fact, as far as one can tell, he worked behind the scenes for every public office he sought. The 1855 run for the U.S. Senate was no exception. Unlike his colleague David Terry, Field never pursued public office frivolously.

One journalist of the era, James O'Meara, offers a different and perhaps more believable interpretation of why Field ran for U.S. Senate. He ran, O'Meara says, to enhance his chances of winning Broderick's backing for a seat on the California Supreme Court in 1857, "[a] position more congenial to his nature and training, and much coveted by him. Likewise it was a place he could fairly hope to obtain; one that he could well honor."[25] Let it be said, however, that if by some quirk Field had unpredictably won the senatorial seat, true to his deeper self, he would have jumped nimbly into the role, and doubtless would have become as gifted a senator as he was later to become a jurist—easily setting aside for the time being whatever political aspirations he might have had. If, as O'Meara suggests, getting elected to California's Supreme Court was indeed his true goal, then he had positioned himself perfectly—not because the Democratic leadership had forgiven him for his behavior in the legislative campaign of 1851 (they never did), but simply because rank-and-file voters, of whatever stripe, rightly regarded him as the most qualified candidate for the high court.

By 1857, the Democratic Party was coming apart at the seams as the pressures from an impending Civil War drew closer. Local loyalties were no longer an overriding issue, and Field won election to the Supreme Court easily, primarily because a majority of the state's corporate leadership and land speculators fancied his well-reported inclination toward judicial conservatism. Field was nominated as an Associate Justice to the court on July 14, 1857, and took his seat on the state's highest bench on October 13, 1857. By his side sat Associate Justice Peter Burnett and Chief Justice David Terry. Just as Field was entering the court as the newest associate justice, Terry was taking his place as its newest chief justice. Field's tenure on the court in no time proved a major disappointment to rank-and-file Democrats, but to his wealthy allies, he was all that they had hoped for. Judicial conservatism aside, however, Field was without doubt the most legally gifted jurist that the California Supreme Court had produced.

David Terry's journey to California's highest court was considerably more problematic than Field's. It began in 1849. It was after several months of wandering the dry riverbeds and watershed creeks on the Sierra Nevada's western slopes that the rangy Texan concluded that only massive investment in equipment and manpower would lead to a successful mining career. Most independent miners didn't stand a chance, and six months of fruitless labor in lower Calaveras County had convinced him that without the support of many investors, the search for gold in California's foothills would prove to be a fool's errand. Thus with no gold-mining fortune awaiting, he swapped his mining equipment for an extra horse and struck out across the San Joaquin Valley, where he eventually settled down in the swampy, mosquito-infested town of Stockton City. It was a town situated on delta lands of the San Joaquin River. The river at Stockton City hub cradled the genesis of an estuary that flowed south and west from the lower Sacramento River and on eventually to the Pacific Ocean. Terry would later write that the terrain reminded him of the Huston delta districts of his beloved Texas. The topography of Stockton City gave it great potential as a shipping center, bordered as it was by an inland waterway flowing almost one hundred miles west to the sea. It did not take long for Terry and friends to recognize the commercial potential of the town, and they soon organized a financial assistance company called the Miners' Distribution Center. This company, located about a mile from the estuary, was soon supplying the valley with legal and transport services that were not available anywhere else in the upper San Joaquin Valley.

The twenty-six year old Terry was changing the direction of his life—his days as a "soldier of fortune" were coming to an end, and although his character as an "irascible cavalier" was not likely to desert him, his mind, not his heart, was slowly replacing his sense of wanderlust, even as his rationality was replacing impulse. Such sagacity led him to settle down, find a wife, raise a family and earn a reliable living as a lawyer. Biographer Buchanan sums it up this way: "Mining disputes and frequent acts of violence offered him a chance for a livelihood [in law] that seemed more attractive than the dry diggings in the Sierra foothills to the east."[26]

Also, there is no dismissing the fact that Terry's imposing size and presence made him a colorful figure on Stockton City's streets. He was easily recognizable—over six-foot-two and two hundred twenty pounds, without a mustache but with a heavily matted beard from cheekbone to jowl. And set above the beard was a pair of glowering gray eyes—people remembered his eyes when they spoke of him. Most Stockton City residents, knowing his reputation as a sullen Irishman, respected him, but showed him little affection—they made it a point to stay out of his way. It was in the courtroom where he made his reputation. Expressly, colleagues understood that when he thought the occasion called for it, he could be hot-tempered, sometimes even physically dangerous. In particular, impugning his honor could quickly set him off into a flurry of violent activity—in a moment he could be on the neck of an antagonist. In a shoulder sling Terry carried a Bowie Knife that he was never reluctant to use, and if one were unlucky enough to face him in a fight, it meant face-to-face combat at close range bringing into play not only the razor-sharp knife but also his massive five-inches-across fists. Moreover, he made it clear that he did not limit his weapons to the knife or to "fisty discussions." He was quite prepared to use any object close at hand, from hatchet to inkstand. And where these fights took place—a state courtroom was as good a place as a back alley—did not matter. Yet surprisingly, those who fought him survived, for he refused to carry a pistol, claiming that he lacked both the skill and will to use it. Some years later he offered a much too indulgent assessment of his tempestuous behavior:

> [What do] my violent and turbulent habits prove? That I will promptly resent a personal affront. One of the first lessons I learned was to avoid giving insults, and to allow none to be given to me. I have acted, and expect to continue to act, on this principle. I believe no man has the right to outrage the feelings of another, or to attempt to blast his good name, without being responsible for his actions. I believe, if a gentleman should wound the feeling of any one, he should at once make suitable reparation, either by an ample apology, or, if he feels that circumstances prevent this that is, if he makes charges which he still thinks true should afford him the satisfaction he desires. I know that a great many men differ with me, and look with a degree of horror on anyone entertaining such sentiments. My own experience has taught me, [however], that when the doctrine of personal responsibility obtains, men are seldom insulted without good cause, and private character is safer from attack; that much quarreling and bad blood, and revengeful feeling is avoided.[27]

In spite of his threatening reputation Terry became a respected member of Stockton's political community. Within a few months, he and his partners at the Miners' Distribution Center represented the city of Stockton in a series of large financial settlements, a fact that earned Terry favorable print in *The San Joaquin Republican.* The paper described Terry as "one of the valley's most prominent citizens, [known for] his integrity of conduct in business, his abilities as a lawyer, and his attention to his duties]."[28]

With these successes, friends were soon pressing him to run for mayor of Stockton. Initially, he was reluctant. Perhaps the failure of his run for district attorney of Galveston three years earlier was still on his mind. Eventually, however, he acquiesced. But once the campaign was underway, it was apparent that Terry was a miserable campaigner. His political stump speeches were laced with fiery rhetoric—"rodomontade," the *Stockton Times,* called it—but left the impression that he was committed more to the cause than to the office. Biographer A. E. Wagstaff accurately called him an uncompromising candidate, hence, an unelectable one—"no trimmer and stuffer [was he]."[29] "[T]here was no dignity outside of an honest exposition of principles," Terry himself once wrote, "[if] a man had not the courage of his convictions he would bear watching." Moreover, since Terry was an implacable southerner, and the 1850 mayoralty race of Stockton became not a popularity contest but a battle of regions—northern versus southern immigrants—"New York v. Texas," wrote *The San Joaquin Republican.* Sadly, by Election Day, the electioneering had degenerated into a series of nasty physical skirmishes and strident accusations about "ballot stuffing and stealing." In point of fact, the outcome was never really in doubt. Three of every five votes went to Terry's opponent, Sam Purdy. But as some voters surmised, the loss proved to be of no great consequence to Terry for upon hearing of his landslide defeat, he remarked, "[It is just as well], had I been elected I would not have known what to have done with the office. I would have made a very poor mayor."[30] Later events would prove that he was better at influencing elections than winning them, and even on those rare occasions when he did win, his efforts generally proved ephemeral.

For more than a generation, the Terry family's politics had been intertwined with the southern wing of the Whig Party, the so-called "Cotton Whigs." But when Grandfather Smith pledged himself to Andrew Jackson's radical Democrats in 1828, segments of the family found themselves caught up in a tangle of competing loyalties; and forty years later, grandson David Smith Terry was still grappling with these divided loyalties. It was a situation that was surely apparent during his political pilgrimage throughout the 1850s in California. This dissimilitude began for Terry when the Democratic Party began to fall apart in mid-decade. At loggerheads were the era's perennial enemies, the southern "Chivs" and the northern abolitionists. While each faction was searching for compromise, each faction was also becoming inflexible on the rock-bottom issue of slaves in the new territories. By mid-century, every attempt at compromise had deteriorated into stalemate and political mischief. Complicating matters, the Whig Party in California had dwindled to a handful of politically well-positioned diehards who could offer no opposition; it was a situation that made the dispute internecine and thus even more vicious. During the tumult, Terry, like so many others, left the Whigs in disgust and joined the Democrats. But unfortunately, now the north-south fissures that were destroying Whigs made even the Democrats less appealing to Terry—to such a degree, in fact, that when the California Democratic Party in 1853 nominated the free-soil governor, John Bigler, for a second term, Terry denounced the Democrats as "betrayers of the principles of the national party" and resigned.

He was gone but not for long. A year later when election resentments had cooled, Terry returned to the Democrats determined to press his long-cherished view for dividing California into two states, one open (slave) and one free. By then, however, interest in a divided state had run its course. The traditional grass roots supporters of the Democratic Party, i.e., farmers, miners-turned-farmers, and small business owners who at one point had looked upon the division of the state sympathetically, were no longer in a divisive mood. They no longer believed that a divided state was in their interest. In particular, they were not of a mind to reduce state markets by half, nor did they want to deal with the two sets of rules and regulations that inevitably would follow from the state's division.

All of this factionalism came to a head at the Democratic State Convention of 1854. On July 18, six hundred disgruntled Democrats squeezed into the sanctuary of Sacramento's First Baptist Church and, after some pre-gavel parliamentary maneuvering, formed themselves into two rival factions, and as it turned out, also into two hair-triggered armed camps. Soon pistols were pulled from belts, and when one shot went off accidentally, the pushing and shoving turned into brawling and cursing, which ended only after the benighted minister of the church pleaded for "dignity in God's house" whereupon an offering of $400 was collected to repair any desecration that may have befallen the sanctuary. Shortly thereafter, since neither side could abide the leadership of the opposing side, the southerners decided to withdraw to the city's music hall down the street where they were able to hold their convention in the peace and tranquility of like-minded people.

Terry joined the southerner faction, of course, but when he realized that he could not get even southerners to listen to his plan for dividing the state, he resigned and was once again on the outside of California's political establishment, searching for more compliant and easily led companions. This time he found what he was looking for as a member of the "American Party"—or the misnomer "Native American Party" or, in the parlance of the day, the "Know-Nothings." The occasion of joining remains unrecorded, or at least undiscovered, but presumably Terry was a member by August of 1855, when he delivered a speech at their inaugural convention. In the speech, he proclaimed that both the Democrats and the Whigs had fallen into the moral morass of compromise, a situation that had forced him to join the Know-Nothings, who, he declared, remained the only truly principled and uncompromising "national party." Quoting a political slogan of the day, he reminded listeners that only the American Party was a party "of the Union Degree" *a rappel*, standing for the preservation of the Union above all other sectional issues. Solidarity to the "Union Degree," he declared, was the true measure of "Americanism" which in Terry's mind meant white Americans ruling white Americans. In this fleeting moment before the country fell into the viciousness of the Civil War, Terry, and others like him, embraced the notion that the American Party was the only party that could provide sufficient resolve to hold the country together. But to the critics who argued that the issue of slavery was much too divisive to preserve the Union, Terry had an answer: "The Border States know how to get along. [It is only the radicals] in Massachusetts and Mississippi that cause all the rancor; they should stay at home, solve their local problems [and allow the moderates] to solve the problems of the fatherland."[31]

The Know-Nothings had first appeared on the political scene somewhere near the end of the 18th century.[32] Originally, their ranks had been filled with northern European Protestants. They began as a secret society of "white nativists" who employed an elaborate set of clandestine hand signals and symbols to identify each other in public places. (An interesting oddity, they supported political candidates as a voting block and kept their preferences hidden right up until the day they were to vote—hence, the name "Know-Nothings".) By mid-19th century they were particularly strong along the northeastern seaboard with large concentrations in New York, New Jersey and Maryland, and by the onset of the fifth decade of the century, they had become politically strong enough to give the country's traditional political powers a reason to be concerned. It is interesting to note that for every three immigrants who came to America's eastern shores during this period one would return home—disillusioned about "new beginnings" in the new world,

Once the Know-Nothings were large enough to come out of the shadows, they attracted strong working class support. In California, their national platform held great appeal—reduced taxes, aggressive punishment of criminals, settling of legally stalled land titles, controlling capitalists and speculators, freeing schools from their sectarian influences, building up the country's shore defenses against "our enemies at sea," regulating railroads and eliminating the presidential patronage system (which was, for the most part, nepotism). Of greatest appeal perhaps, was the party's allegiance to personal morality—it was a form of "no nonsense" conservatism. They crusaded against public drunkenness, fighting, dueling and prostitution.

Insofar as the critics were concerned, however, the Know-Nothings remained a single-issue party. They supported the introduction of "naturalization laws" that would establish "quotas" for immigrants. The names on the earliest rosters of the society were chock-full of Anglo-Saxons eager to put an end to the never-ending waves of jobless Germans, Irish and Eastern European Catholics who were "inundating" the country. Of foremost concern to the Know-Nothings was the influx of Roman Catholics who were settling the northern cities and towns in such numbers that they were able to forge and perpetuate their own political alliances. They frightened the traditional majorities in many of the largest eastern cities by changing the ethnic mix and taking political control. Initially when the Know-Nothings were still a secret party they had refused to open their membership roles to public scrutiny, but once having grown large enough to win public support, they found it more in their interest to open membership roles to the scrutiny of outside observers—and when, finally, these roles were opened, few were surprised to discover that a plurality of members had been former "Cotton Whigs."

By mid-century, the Know-Nothings had become a political force to be reckoned with in California, with unusually large memberships in San Francisco, Sacramento and the northern end of the Central Valley, as well as throughout the Oregon Territory. Wherever large blocks of northern Europeans congregated one was sure to find the Know-Nothings actively seeking to increase membership—in California, however, they found it prudent to dampen their anti-Catholic rhetoric. They voted to drop from their original lists of unacceptable immigrants German and Irish Catholics, and by the time of their first official meeting in June of 1855, they were willing to welcome into "[the] brotherhood [all] white native born citizens of good moral character who are loyal to the United States." "White" and "native-born" represented the limit of their generosity, however, for true to their founding impulse, they were not without the requisite dark-skinned ethnic enemies in California. A new collection of "foreign enemies" were identified—expressly, eastern and southern Europeans, along with the usual "Negroes, Indians," and "Mongols."

On June 24, 1855 an orphaned faction of Whigs and Southern Democrats packed the First Congregational Church on Sixth Street in Sacramento. They gathered to establish the American Party (Know-Nothings) as a political party in California. They decided to compete openly for public offices against the state's entrenched parties. There was the interminable list of speakers, some impassioned, some dull, most a little of both. But when David Terry arose to speak his address was neither dull nor interminable. His "Preserving the Union" speech so moved the congregation that ex-governor Foote of Mississippi urged Terry's immediate nomination as the party's candidate for governor. Other delegates, however, not as overcome by Terry's speech as Foote, argued that his judicial talents made him a much more sensible choice for the state Supreme Court—and thus the group agreed that Terry would be nominated for the state court. Even Terry agreed that his preference was for the court. The following day, this pre-convention convention was recessed with a decision to hold the party's first official nominating convention two months later. On August 7, 1855, 379 designated delegates met to nominate a slate of candidates for the November election—"men of temperance," they were to be called. Terry's name was included for a short-term position on the Supreme Court. He would run alongside the controversial but effulgent Hugh Murray, who was running for a second term as the candidate for chief justice. J. Neely

Johnson, state senator from Sacramento, was the eventual gubernatorial nominee for the Know-Nothings, while Robert M. Anderson of El Dorado was chosen the nominee for lieutenant governor. The staunchly loyal Democratic newspaper *The San Joaquin Republican* was not impressed with the nominees, calling them "a mongrel hybrid ticket that can be easily beaten." The paper was particularly incensed that Terry had, yet again, switched parties, and it predicted that come November, his perfidious nature was certain to lose him the election.[33] By contrast, *The San Jose Tribune* called the Know-Nothing's gubernatorial nominee, Johnson, a "gentleman of prime manhood with a brilliant well-cultivated mind," while of Terry they wrote, "He was a man of honor [because he had] bolted [the corrupt] Democratic Party]."[34] The *Fresno Expositor* later was to declare Terry "both brilliant and learned."[35] Satisfied that they had nominated a ticket that the other state parties could not ignore, the delegates adjourned their convention after passing the hat and collecting $860 to finance their entire November campaign.

By election time in November, with the traditional parties daily falling into more and more disarray, the Know-Nothings sailed into office, winning every major political position in the state. This outcome, however, surprised no one more than Terry. He had defeated his Democratic opponent, Charles H. Bryan, by a slim 3,000-vote majority; but ever true to his style, he told friends that he had been lucky to win. Once elevated to the position, however, he admitted that he had "fondly [but secretly] aspired, to it, [it was an honor he had come to] by accident, [but it was] welcomed with pleasure." At the time, few voters knew that they had elected to the state's highest court a "most common sense, but meteoric judge," one who could not abide the pretentiousness of his judicial colleagues and, especially those who he considered to be "corrupted pretenders." (Although it was a common practice for judges to take money from those seeking favorable opinions, Terry made it clear that he considered this practice morally unacceptable, and would himself refuse all such offers. He announced that he would hold any judge who took these bribes up to public scorn.)

The election of 1855 was notable because it would be the last time that any conspicuously pro-southern, pro-slave candidates would ever be elected to a statewide California office. In point of fact, southern candidates would not return to California politics until the Civil War had passed into history. During the decade of the 1860s, most Californians were loyal Unionists. This was best illustrated by the election of 1859, when all the "nativists" were turned out of every high public office in the state. "Federalism" had returned during this election cycle and had reached new and durable levels of loyalty among Western voters. (Single-issue parties in the U.S., of course, have had a history of burning brightly, but not long. Political zealots soon run short of devoted disciples who are willing to prove themselves zealous enough.) Parenthetically, Terry's biographer Buchanan maintains that in Terry's case his switching back and forth from party to party should not be interpreted as unprincipled:

> [I]f [Terry] were making his moves purely for personal advancement, he accomplished little. When he left the Democrats in 1853 they won, and when he rejoined them [again in 1854] they lost. [Unquestionably] one of the reasons for his shift in party allegiance was the desire for [the Supreme Court post], but there were stronger forces that prompted his action. Uppermost was his intense interest in furthering the cause of states' rights and of Southern sectionalism. [Terry had felt, as did others] that the [Know-Nothings] would be a convenient vehicle in which to ride into power. Once before, when not seeking office, he had deserted his party when he felt that its leaders were not working for the political goals he sought. Terry had numerous faults, but they did not include exorbitant self-interest or ambition.[36]

Assuredly Buchanan is correct in one sense: Terry was a bona fide ideologue. But when the occasion was right, he could also be an opportunist. Whether Buchanan gives Terry more credit for meritorious behavior than he deserves is open to debate, but it is doubtless true that without the endorsement of the Democratic Party in 1859, Terry would have had no chance to be reelected to the Supreme Court. He was perceptive enough to know that an endorsement by Know-Nothings in 1859 would mean the end of his Supreme Court career. While no record is available that state his reasons for returning to the Democrats, later actions and attitudes make it understandable that his tenure on the California Supreme Court, which he perceived to have been holding with "dignity and honor" and "without pride or ostentation," unquestionably had become, in his mind, the pinnacle of a public career that deserved to be continued.

In the summer of 1857, California's Chief Justice Hugh Murray suddenly died, and with the convening of the fall court, Associate Justice Terry took Murray's seat at center bench as chief justice of the state's highest court. At his side sat Associate Justice Peter H. Burnett and the newly elected Associate Justice Stephen Field. Terry and Field served together on the court for only two years, from 1857 to 1859; but during those years they had a remarkably stabilizing influence on the fledgling court. While on the bench, both men proved themselves to be intelligent, productive and ambitious; but more importantly, both were inclined to measure self-worth in terms of the influence they held over colleagues and public circumstances. Inevitably, this obsession to direct the course of events and lives of other people would bring them together in a protracted conflict that would become ever more spiteful as years passed. Their deeply rooted cultural diversities were to play no small part in keeping this shared narrative alive.

In the following two chapters the text will assess the changing legal environs in which each judge found his *métier* as California moved from one national government to another and from territory to state.

NOTES

1. Carl Brent Swisher, *Stephen J. Field: Craftsman of the Law* (Washington, D.C. The Brookings Institute. 1930). 9. For synopsis of these early days see "Stephen J. Field of the Supreme Court." New York *Sun,* April 25, 1880.

2. —— *Craftsman.* 9.

3. Henry Martyn Field. *The Record of the Family of the Revered David Field* (New York: Private Printing). 40. Also see S.J. Field. *Biographical Notes.*(1892) Private Printing.

4. Charles S. Potts: "The Romantic Story of a Great Texan." *Southwest Review,* (spring 1934): 296.

5. —— *"The Romantic Story . . ."*296.

6. D.S. Terry to Cornelia Terry. June 30, 1856. D.S. Terry MSS, The Huntington Library, San Marino, California.

7. A. Russell Buchanan. *David S. Terry of California: Dueling Judge* (San Marino CA. The Huntington Library Press, 1955). 8.

8. A.E. Wagstaff, *The Life of Ex. Chief Justice of the Supreme Court of California: David S. Terry* (San Francisco: Continental Publishing Co., 1892). 42.

9. Buchanan. *Dueling Judge.* 19.

10. —— *Dueling Judge*. 8.

11. Stephen J. Field, *The Personal Reminiscences of Early Days in California* (New York: De Capo Press, 1968). Reprint of 1898. 13. See also Mead B. Kibbey *Sacramento City Directory, 1850.* California Library Foundation, Sacramento CA. 2000. 105. Sacramento was the jumping off place for gold miners. It boasted of two thousand residents plus forty-five wooden buildings that included seventeen restaurants, nine saloons, and 600 tents and open-air camps. On the down side the citizens were dying of cholera at the rate of twenty a day.

12. —— *Reminiscences*. 14.

13. —— *Reminiscences*. 16.

14. —— *Reminiscences.* 30.

15. Carl Brent Swisher. *Stephen J. Field*. 36.

16. Stephen J. Field. *Reminiscences.* 25–26.

17. —— *Reminiscences*. 27.

18. —— *Reminiscences.* 49.

19. —— *Reminiscences*. 55.

20. J. Edward Johnson: *History of the Supreme Court of California 1850–1900* (San Francisco: Supreme Court 1963). 67. At the time The San Jose *Herald* wrote:

"Some of the best timbers of the new government structure are the handiwork of Mr. Field. The Criminal Practice Act with over 600 sections was passed without reading."

21. Field, *Reminiscences* 65. Also J. Edward Johnson, *History of Supreme Court of California.* 68.
22. Benham v. Rowe. 2 Cal. 387 (1852). Also cited in Carl Brent Swisher: *Craftsman of the Law*, 60.
23. —— *Craftsman*. 75.
24. —— *Craftsman*. 61.
25. James O'Meara. *Broderick and Gwin: Pioneer Senators* (San Francisco: Bacon and Company, 1881). 160.
26. Buchanan. *Dueling Judge,* 8.
27. *Dueling Judge*. 12.
28. May 31, 1852. Cited in Buchanan. *Dueling Judge.* 13.
29. Wagstaff, *Life of Ex. Chief Justice*, 65.
30. *Life of Ex Chief Justice*. 53.
31. Davis, Winfield L, (*History of Political Conventions in California: 1849–1892*). Sacramento, 189, 42–50.
32. Payton Hurt: "The Rise and Fall of the 'Know Nothings' in California." *California Historical Society Quarterly.* Vol ix (1930) 16–49.
33. Aug. 7, 1855.
34. Aug. 15, 1855.
35. May 26, 1880.
36. Buchanan, *Dueling Judge.* 18.

Chapter Two

A Hasty Footpath to Statehood

In a stretch of time that fell between two national wars in the 19th century, the California Territory became the United States' 31st state. The first conflict, the Mexican War, ended February 2, 1848, with the Treaty of Guadalupe Hidalgo. The treaty settled a territorial dispute that had been smoldering between Mexicans and North Americans since the European Texans had precipitously torn themselves away from Mexico's authority in 1836. When the embers of this remarkably disordered struggle had cooled, two-fifths of the disputed territory was under United States control, and Mexico had been stripped of vast reaches of land north and west from *El Rio Bravo del Norte* (the Rio Grande) to *La Oceana Pacifica.* The treaty provided Mexicans living in the annexed territory U.S. citizenship on the condition that they foreswear all political alliances to their mother country. Fidelity of citizenship, the treaty read, "[shall give] to Mexicans living north of the treaty line the right to retain ownership to all real and personal property within their possession."[1]

The Mexicans were given six months, until July 1, 1848, to decide whether they would remain in annexed lands or move south of the treaty line—six months to decide whether to forsake century-old loyalties and patterns of deportment and become citizens of what could only be, under the best of circumstances, a place with the unfamiliar cultural environment of northern Europe. As to be expected, the nature of retaining, transferring and registering land titles generated interminable disputes, some of which remain unresolved even to this day. Yet treaty or no treaty, for the most part the North Americans rushing west into California treated the Mexicans living north of the settlement line as if they were the interlopers in a land that their Spanish and Indian ancestors had inhabited for more than three centuries.

Fifteen years forward and the North Americans were in the midst of the bitterest of wars—the Civil War. But unlike the Mexican War—which was a battle over territory and racial alienation—this internecine struggle, hallowed by the venerated trappings of social justice, was, deep-down, a battle to perpetuate conflicting regional control and power.

During this 15-year interlude between these wars, fortune hunters, speculators and landholders (i.e., the "squatters and settlers") were, for the most part, only tangentially interested in California's transition from Mexican to American institutions. The focus on transition arose from the immigrants' need for personal independence, or more precisely, "on commercial independence." The territory's legal institutions, however, were worthy of the fortune hunters' attention (i.e., miners) only to the degree that the law enhanced commercial ambitions and private protection. But it was not an easy task to structure a legal system, given the relative disinterest of immigrants, and the nature of Mexico's indigenous legal tradition. Nevertheless, with the ever-expanding influx of immigrants and the continued presence of a sizable number of Mexican inhabitants, these discordant declarations of what was meant by law and order were to become root and branch of California's embryonic legal system.

Prior to 1848, the coastal land stretching northward from Mexico's *Sierra Madres* to the Oregon border, and westward from the *Sierra Nevadas* (the snow-crested mountains) to the Pacific Ocean was fittingly perceived as vast, arid and empty, with most of its agrarian population clinging to the Pacific Ocean's shoreline. In an inexact census conducted in February 1848, it was estimated that there were about 7,500 Mexicans and 6,500 "Americans" (few of the native Indian population was counted).[2] Yet, by December of that year, after news of the discovery of gold had seemingly roused the avaricious impulses of the entire world, the population quickly exploded tenfold. This meant, North Americans from the east and south, Europeans, Australians, Asians and Central and South Americans streamed across the territory's newly drawn "Treaty of Peace" borders. They came first on horseback or by "shank's mare" and proudly referred to themselves as "the overlanders." Many were penniless and pawned possessions, even their horses, in order to buy rudimentary mining gear. So that by year's end, 40,000 pilgrims were panning the rivers and streams east and north of Sacramento as well as south along the hills that bordered the upper and lower San Joaquin Valley. The "gold corridor," as the Argonauts (mineral hunters) called it.

By late winter, however, the overlanders faced the unwanted competition of thousands of travelers who came to California by sea. In a certain sense, these sea travelers were a different breed. Many had money in their pockets—for coming by ship usually meant having a substantial sum of money to pay for a sea voyage. This is to say that seafarers could afford travel tickets from eastern and southern seaports to the diluvia town of Charges in Panama, and once there, they had the price of a mule or boat ride across the Isthmus River. Next would come the price of the 15-to-20-day passage on a shuttle ship, up the Pacific coastline to the bayside city of Yerba Buena—shortly to be renamed San Francisco.

But with the onrush of these more affluent immigrants came greater numbers of "professionals"—entrepreneurs, financial investors, speculators, physicians, dentists, undertakers, merchants and tradesmen. They, no less than their mining comrades, were fortune seekers; but unlike the overlanders, whom Josiah Royce called "rootless wanderers seeking wealth in a peaceful and rapid manner" the "shippers" tended to be more *emigrants* than immigrants.[3] They were inclined to stay put and accumulate their fortunes at a more leisurely pace. Josiah Royce, who grew up in California, the son of a supply-store merchant, well understood the difference between overlanders and sea-travelers. He had witnessed firsthand the poverty of "the diggers" and the shanty and tent dwellers, people who sometimes had only a dense oak tree serving as a roof. "They were," he wrote, "without a sense of permanence or community, without families they were vagabonds—hunting overnight fortunes." Such "fortune seekers "were in a hurry," so civil society (one of permanence and order) was only of marginal concern. In fact, it was usually only when a miner's efforts to find and keep gold were interrupted by thieves that he would call for "law and order." At such times, mining-camp justice, "with Judge Lynch" presiding, routinely proved sufficient for the occasion—never mind how capricious, circumstantial, or immediate the situation might be; rules of legal fairness were never of great concern to foragers. Predictably, miners' law resulted in rapid, irrevocable decisions that were rarely formalized with ink on paper—most "diggers," unencumbered by such notions as "due process," felt no need to replicate their actions. There was, so to speak, a needy and appropriate remedy for every occasion.

Mid-century San Francisco, as the point of entry for ship travelers, was at times even more lawless than the gold fields. It was a town that was populated by footloose fortune hunters, spirited individuals with high expectations, and dispirited and penniless vagabonds with no expectations. Thus, travelers coming by sail through San Francisco's "Golden Gate" saw before them, crowded against the southern and eastern shores, the very ensigns of impermanence—a montage of schooner masts, wooden shanties and canvas tents. The journalist and traveler, Bayard Taylor, seeing San Francisco for the first time, described it vividly:

> The mountains on the northern side [of the bay] are 3,000 feet in height, and come boldly down to the sea. As the view opens through the splendid strait,

> three or four miles in width, the island rock of Alcatraz appears, gleaming white in the distance. [T]here is a small fort perched among the trees on our right, where the strait is narrowest, and a glance at the formation of the hills shows that this pass might be made as impregnable as Gibraltar. [A]t last we are through the Golden Gate—fit name for such a magnificent portal to the commerce of the Pacific! Yerba Buena Island is in front; southward and westward opens the renowned harbor, crowded with the shipping of the world, mast behind mast and vessel behind vessel, the flags of all nations fluttering in the breeze! Around the curving shore of the bay and upon the sides of three hills which rise steeply from the water, the middle one receding so as to form a bold amphitheater, the town is planted and seems scarcely yet to have taken root, for tents, canvas, plank, mud, and adobe houses are mingled together with the least apparent attempt at order and durability.[4]

Observers who had watched immigrants come and go were in the habit of saying that nine of every ten who came hunting gold were next-to-destitute when they arrived and completely destitute when they left. Every man came looking for a fortune for a lifetime, but perhaps only one in half-a-hundred ever found anything worth bragging about. After months of scrabbling the plains and foothills of the Sierra Nevadas, most solitary diggers could barely pay the cost of a fortnight in San Francisco—supplies, lodging and entertainment emptied their gold-dust knapsack *tout à l'heure*. After one, two, maybe three years with nothing to show for their efforts, most stake-miners had had enough disappointment and lethargically returned to their homes in the east. Those who did stay (generally single men), more likely than not drifted into farming, construction labor or the military.

At the same time the merchants and businessmen were having a better go of it. They were three times more likely than the miners to remain in the state, and by the end of the first year, their margins of profit as *entrepreneurs petits* were running twice, even three times, the earnings of most miners—"northern barons," Royce called these merchants, "with a patina of reasonableness and ferocious intolerance for their competitors."[5] Few of these émigrés doubted that there was a bonanza to be discovered in California but rarely was it to be found in the gold fields.

In contrast to the emigrational turbulence going on in California's northern territory, however, the southern territory remained much more as it had been before annexation—a bucolic region blanketed by cattle ranches and orchards, and controlled by a handful of U.S. homesteaders (shipping and cattle magnates) and *Californios Viejos* (Mexican land-grant aristocrats). These Californios dynasties had land-titles going back a century or more, and by 1850, perhaps there were 1,000 Mexican families claiming land-grant titles. Records, however, appear only to identify about 500 *rancheros*—and their titles ran from the Russian River in the north to the Mexican border fifty miles below the 33rd parallel in the south. Mexican law decreed that these grants were not to exceed seventy-six square miles, or about 50,000 acres. Moreover, many of the most powerful families held several grants simultaneously. As conglomerates many ranches grew to be more than 300,000 acres.[6]

When the Treaty of Guadalupe Hidalgo was drawn up and signed in Mexico City in 1848, these muscular aristocratic families were influential enough to demand and receive from the U.S. signatories a concession called the "progenitor's proviso." Called the "Protocol of Querétaro" it declared that "legitimate titles under Mexican law" would be honored. The equivocal word, of course, was "legitimate," and from that moment forward this became a never-ending point of litigious contention between the governments and the citizens.[7] At the time, however, the shared struggle of land owners was to maintain islands of permanence against territorial tides of disorder that were taking place in the mining districts. These land barons could be counted on to be the most steadfast advocates of stability, that is to say, the defenders of "law and order."

When California became a U.S. territory in 1848, Congress placed in charge the commander from the U.S. Army's Department of the Pacific, giving each successive commander the title of Military Governor of California. As the U.S.'s highest-ranking field officer, along with the title of Governor, came the hurried and somewhat vague assignment, "to keep order in the California Territory under the laws of war." But keeping order in desperate towns and villages of so vast a territory also required placing in the hands of local civilian leaders a district's jurisprudence. Only on rare occasions, however, were the military governors called upon to enforce civilian compliance in the districts. In fact, these military governors continued to have, essentially, the same problem—maintaining a viable military presence over California's immense territory in the face of the Army's unending string of gold-hungry deserters. One of the last of these military governors, Brigadier General Bennett Riley, voiced his frustration on the occasion of losing an entire platoon of soldiers in a week's time: "[I am] unable to put a sentinel outside the gate for 15 minutes lest he be gone, musket and all, to the gold mines."[8] Keeping a military presence in the territory to enforce a minutia of civil orders, or to settle jurisdictional squabbles, was never a high priority for these military governors. Moreover, the lack of legal review proved destabilizing, for without a military presence, civilian courts of review were only rarely convened, or even worse, nonexistent. The upshot was that implementing law and order in the California territory led to a hodgepodge of conflicting, overlapping rules and regulations, which had the effect of making the military governor's attention to matters of legal adjudication secondary to matters of military discipline and control. Keeping the peace required more of the military's attention than did any duty to oversee courts of equity. What is more, whenever the U.S. Department of War changed its commanders, territorial policies were sure to reflect the style and character of the new commander, a situation that served to compound unpredictability. This constant instability within the ranks of the military governors led James DuPont, Captain of the USS *Cyrano,* to observe wryly, "[T]he people of California think [we] cannot be much better than Mexico for they connect the appearance of every new commander-in-chief with the result of some new revolution."[9]

These vagaries of government management became so unsettling to the Californios (rancheros such as Mariano Guadalupe Vallejo and Jose Antonio Carrillo) that they made an effort to revive an old land-grant proposal that Mexicans had been pressing for well before the war. They argued that the California Territory was much too large to be controlled as a single territory and would be better managed as two separate, evenly divided zones—a north zone and a south zone. When northern immigrants heard of a proposal to divide the territory there was only middling interest, even though it did elicit some support from the military governors who were anxious to reduce their civilian responsibilities. Mexicans did, however, find considerable support among immigrants from the southern states. Southern immigrants saw the division of California as a way to neutralize the federal government's despised Wilmot Proviso—the 1846 federal anti-slavery proviso that forbade slavery in any of the territories that had been annexed the aftermath of the Mexican War. The southern immigrants argued for the extension of the 1821 Missouri Compromise line from latitude 36 to latitude 30, which thereby would extend slave territories from the Atlantic Ocean to the Pacific Ocean. Expressly, the southerners argued for a provision that would make all land north of Monterey a free state and all land south of Monterey open to slavery, (this concept of a divided territory was given mild scrutiny during the drafting of the state's first constitution in 1850, but the proposal was brushed aside by a majority of convention representatives when they insisted that only the united front of northerners and southerners could secure congressional approval for statehood.[10] Consequently, Mexican ranchers were forced by the changing ethnographic environment and the fear of losing even more political power were to come together with southern immigrants in a common cause—the protection of "property rights," i.e., the protection of both land and commercial ownership.[11]

With the division of California proving to be a dead-letter issue at the state and federal levels, the way was again open for financial powers to push for statehood in a single-minded manner. They turned up the heat by pressuring the military governor, Bennett Riley, to convene a constitutional convention without delay. In reality, San Francisco's business leaders had been agitating for a constitutional convention as far back as July of 1848, and toward the end of the year, even the mining population (increasing tenfold every six months) was paying enough attention to the issue to join in pressing for a constitutional convention. So by the spring of 1849, most major political factions were pressing General Riley to convene a constitutional convention. Despite pressure, however, he failed to act, arguing that without congressional approval his hands were tied. But then for reasons never fully understood, he abruptly reversed himself, and even without articulated federal approval, he dropped his resistance and announced that the California Territory's first constitutional convention would be held in September of 1849.

By way of preparation, Riley declared that the territory was to be divided into ten districts, with each district represented in proportion to its population, and that each delegate be male, at least twenty-one years old and a resident of the district he represented for not less than six months. To this, Riley added that Mexican-Americans by stipulation in the Treaty of Guadalupe Hidalgo also had the right to representation before governing bodies—more specifically, wealthy land-owning Mexicans.

On the first day of September 1849, the delegates crowded into a 30-by-60-foot room at Colton Hall in Monterey, California. Built several years earlier by the first American alcalde of Monterey, the Reverend Walter Colton, it was the largest "pedestrian" building in the township and served as schoolhouse by day and city hall by night. Forty-eight delegates met to write California's first constitution. By any measure, it was a convention of amateurs. The convention's youngest representative was twenty-five, the oldest, fifty-three. Three-quarters of them were under 40, and three-quarters had been in California less than a year. Delegates from the southern section were under-represented, making up 22 percent—eleven delegates in all, six of whom were land-grant Californios. The remaining representatives lived north of Monterey. Perhaps most bewildering of all was the elected delegates from Sacramento and San Joaquin Valley districts who chose not to attend—sending word that they were too busy excavating the hillsides to waste time organizing delegations. When final convened the convention consisted of fourteen lawyers, seven *rancheros,* twelve farmers, eight merchants, four members of the military and one independent delegate, who declared himself in the convention's registration book as, "B.F. Moore, a man of elegant leisure, from the State of Alabama."

Josiah Royce offered an interesting, albeit somewhat problematic political assessment of these apprentice delegates.[12] He lumped them into three proximate political categories. The seven rancheros (Californios) he characterized as "conservatives." They were men who fought to preserve the political and the legal status quo. They were, Royce writes, determined insofar as possible to defend a continuation of the Mexican civil tradition, while laboring to keep the judicial system in the hands of those people who owned the land. They struggled to preserve a civil system that would protect legal autonomy and strengthen local control over land-holdings. It was by all odds, Royce suggests, the primary reason the rancheros chose to attend the convention. Assuring fellow delegates from the eastern and southern blocks that they were loyal to the United States, they set out to persuade the convention that civil law, a system that had been operating in the territory for almost two centuries, would provide, with but trivial emendations, a smooth and orderly transition from Mexican to U.S. jurisprudence. With small adjustments, they insisted, hoary European jurisprudence would serve the new government as competently as it had the old one. It was foolish, the ranchero insisted, to destabilize the country by overturning a legal system now in place with one that is, at best, desultory and uncongenial to the disparate needs of an ethnically mixed population. The civil law still in place, they argued, most readily promotes California's transition from a Mexican territory to a U.S. state, and it is least likely to unsettle California's diverse cultural equilibrium. "The termination of war left an existing government—a government *de facto*—in full operation; and [such a system should] continue with the presumed consent of the people, until Congress [provides a new and permanent] government."[13] The Californios, with their incentive-driven defense of local autonomy, were hoping to strike a sympathetic note in the hearts of the miners, whom they saw as individuals with entrenched fidelity to personal independence. Later events would prove that they had badly misread the miners' avowed commitment to personal autonomy.

Royce's second classification of delegates was those in the political center—the "interregnum," as he called them. This group was made up of northern immigrants, most of whom had been at one time or another miners, but were now permanent residents and homesteaders. The middle, Royce writes, insisted on a strong central government, one best realized by moving the region from the status of territory to statehood as quickly as possible. These delegates saw no need for the typical waiting period that had been applied to earlier incoming territories before statehood, nor for a protracted, destructive debate in the Congress on the wrenching political issue of slavery—slaves and slavery were unwelcome in California.

The overriding judicial issue motivating the interregnum, Royce continues, was the relationship between the land as possessed and the land as inherited. In other words, the miners were interested in pressing the issue of how legal title to property was to be determined. The incentive behind the interests of the "old-timers," as these centrists called themselves (they were merchants and miners who had been in California perhaps for a year or more), was to control the incursion of waves of "squatters" who were flooding all western territories everywhere and demanding title to any parcel of land that they had staked out and worked—just, as it must be remembered, the old-timers had done themselves scarcely a few months earlier. It was a problem exacerbated by the drying up of available federal lands and the encroachment onto deeded private property. The conundrum for centrists was finding a legal conception of land titles that excluded the squatters but did not go as far as strengthening the pre-treaty land-grant claims of the rancheros. Such moderates, Royce writes, regarded newcomers as "transient fortune-seekers," miscreants who gutted the hillsides, scraped the surface of the land for gold and then moved on in search of new land to plunder—just as the rancheros, with their inestimable and ancient land-grants, had earlier vanquished alien immigrants. Moderates pressed for a statutory restriction that would insure for themselves, as "true settlers," something called "natural possessory rights," in contrast to what they describe as the "naked possessory claims" that aided "squatters" and Mexican-Americans. In a rudimentary sense, the interregnum sought to prevent ownership of the land, either by virtue of occupying and working it or by inheriting it, and to that end they pressed for a land-distribution policy that would survey and then permanently record the ownership of *all* territorial land that had fallen under dispute since the immigration of Anglos into the territory. The serious question remaining, however, was how these "parcelers," as they were called, were to go about establishing the size and location of their claims—that is, how conflicts were to be settled when a dispute arose between individual settlers, and how, and to what degree, sanctions were to be imposed if "squatters" and rancheros chose to ignore legal directives. Moreover, once the parcelers' "law of distribution" was enacted, it would remain unclear what was to be done with the Mexican-American ranchers and farmers whose land had not been in dispute.

Finally, Royce's third designation of the convention delegates reflects his own misgivings about specific immigrants. He does not mince his words. He calls this third faction "the radicals on the left"—individuals whom he perceived as hard-core southerners who hid their seditionist's goals under the terminological guise of "political autonomy." The influential and talented former congressman from Tennessee by the name of William M. Gwin led these individuals. The self-assured Gwin, having been in California scarcely three months, was elected as the convention's first delegate from San Francisco, and on the convention's opening day he confidently announced plans to be elected California's first senator (as it turned out, the soldier-explorer John C. Fremont would be California's first senator, but Gwin's declaration had not been far off; he became the state's second senator). According to the Roycean exegesis, Gwin and the southern radicals were clandestinely planning the creation of one gigantic western territory stretching eastward from the Pacific Ocean to the Texas-New Mexico border, northward to the Mormon encampment on the Great Salt Lake and westward again through the Oregon Territory to the Pacific Ocean. They were pushing for this massive territory, Royce declares, as a way of disrupting the northerners' efforts to turn California into a free state. Congress, Royce points out, was unwilling to ratify statehood for so large a region and would, therefore, divide California into several smaller states.—And in keeping with national congressional policy, it would vote to maintain a systematic balance between free-soil and open (slave) states—all the way to the Pacific Ocean.[14]

If Royce's immigrant-categories reflected, even in part, the political warfare of the conventioneers gathering at Monterey, then it would not be surprising to find delegates in the first few days taking the measure of each other's intentions and goals—for once these first impressions were sorted out, then alliances should fall into various political factions. But evidence never shows alliances breaking up into blocks of inclusion or exclusion—as would have seemed predictable according to Royce. Radicals and conservatives, for instance, were able to find common ground in their mutual effort to prevent the centrist majority of northern commercial and mining representatives from controlling every strategically important committee at the convention. And despite a variety of alliances, power plays and political payoffs, the moderate center's majority retained control of the political agenda—a circumstance that served to draw the radicals and Californios more closely together. It was a point of view, Royce declares, that otherwise would not have had a voice.

Paramount to this radical/conservative alliance, he writes, was its opposition to statehood unless the new state was open to slavery—expressly, this alliance found common cause in the concept of political autonomy. This is to say that the southern radicals wanted a state open to slavery while the conservative rancheros wanted a continuation of a jurisprudential system that had been in place before annexation. Many southern merchants and suppliers, for example, united with rancheros to urge statutory protection for land-grant rights as uncontested *proprietas plena* (title and exclusive use) under the ancient civil law conception of *possessor bonae fidei* (none having a greater right). In exchange, Royce argues, radical southerners were to get the rancheros' support for expanding California territory into regions so vast that Congress would be forced to create numerous states throughout the entire western territory—half of which would then be designated slave states (assuming that the U.S. Congress continued its pre-Civil War policy of trading off territories in its quest to keep the Union together). In actuality, the rancheros' support for expanding and dividing the territory was public and active, while southern immigrant support for the traditional system of Mexican pre-Treaty civil law, if it existed in any more than silent agreements, was more assent by not opposing.

While the alliances at this constitutional convention held all the intrigue that might be expected between factions coming together from hither and yon to form a new state in the Union, historians and writers coming after Royce are not persuaded by his divided-state analysis. Most critics found little evidence to support the existence of the ideological factions that he insisted controlled the convention. Particularly unconvincing for them was the assumption that the southern delegates were hatching a plot to force slavery into the southwestern United States. This notion appears to have no basis in the accounts and records of the convention, and Royce's critics insist that such an interpretation is merely a rehash of Royce's mentor, Herbert Howe Bancroft. In spite of the elegance of Royce's presentation, later writers argued that he had fallen too much under Bancroft's spell. As a member of the University of California's first class, Royce had access to Bancroft's superb collection of early California manuscripts, which would be one of the major sources for Bancroft's massive *History of California*—undeniably the most exhaustive 19th-century reference collection on early California. These manuscripts and Royce's close and loyal relationship to Bancroft make it difficult to distinguish their positions when it comes to evaluating the character and intentions of California's constitutional separatists. Bancroft's sympathy for the northern financial barons and his suspicion of the south's transplanted politicians has been well documented.[15]

J. Ross Browne's *Debates* (for which he was paid $10,000) indicate that a good part of delegate time and attention at the convention were concentrated on four issues. There was a protracted dispute over the state's boundary (see, Chapter Two, Note, 31), second, the nature and status of slavery in the new state; third, the formulation of a stable political and legal system flexible enough to meld cultural strangers into a community of institutional patronage; and fourth, the acceptable fiscal procedure for generating state revenues. The conventions' resolutions of issues of slavery and taxation, for instance, need further explication, that is, a glimpse into the latent inequities that laced the social and political notions of California's constitutional elders should not be ignored.

The Virginian and U. S. President, Zachary Taylor, shortly before his untimely choleragenic death, made it clear to California politicians that only a vote against slavery would secure the territory's status for statehood. It was a declaration that brought from the convention delegates, by now eager for statehood, a unanimous constitutional amendment declaring California a free state. In fact, all fifteen southern delegates supported the anti-slavery declaration. Yet it would be a misreading of the delegates' social perspectives if one were to conclude that their unanimous vote against slavery meant that they held a progressive view of racial equality, or that as an assembly they had somehow risen above the age's racial stereotypes, or that they were determined to condemn slavery at some lofty moral level. Quite the opposite was true, of course: resistance to slavery in California in 1850 for most delegates was a simple matter of political expediency. Perhaps there were on the convention floor a half-dozen abolitionists from New England who were fully determined to make a morally enlightened case against slavery.[16] But a large majority of delegates were opposed to slavery, by and large, for political and economic reasons and not for any ideals promoting social equality. This pragmatic vision of race was a viewpoint shared by the majority of northern and southern immigrants—idealistic arguments defending the natural parity of race do not appear in the convention's records (most northern delegates were every bit as truculently "anti-Negro," "anti-Indian or "anti-foreigner" as any southerner). The common element of agreement among conventioneers was economic. For example, the expressed fear of mining delegates was that slave-manned southern mining cartels would drive the independent miners from the gold fields. Mining on a large scale, they argued, would include the importation of thousands of slaves into the state by speculators—a circumstance that inevitably would make it impossible for the individual miners to compete. Financial investors, they argued, were sure to control acres of mineral-rich land and turn slaves loose to sluice the hillsides into pebbly creek bottoms. Stories of ruthless mining cartels had been making the rounds in the mining camps for months. Conversations with bankrupted private "surface-diggers" were more than enough to convince those miners who might need further persuading. As a matter of fact, from most miners' perspective, mining was meant to be "manly and solitary labor."

Robert Semple, a one-time Missouri printer, summed up the apprehensiveness of fellow conventioneers on the economics of slavery as well as anyone. There was a great deal of wealth to be had by speculators who had the money to spend, he said. To prove it, he offered the following calculations: It would cost mine owners somewhere between $50 and $200 to buy a slave and an additional $700 to bring him to California. But for the effort, owners stood the chance of making a $2,000-to-$6,000 profit per slave per year mining the company's gold. In no time, Semple warned, large southern cartels would turn the "noble" occupation of mining into a chattel industry.[17] That said, Semple took his seat, with most listeners sympathetically supportive. But one delegate arose to question Semple's assumptions, arguing that southerners would never bring their slaves to California, for they knew that once on California soil, the slaves were sure to do "what they have always done;" they would run off and dig their own claims and steal the gold of the independent miners, which were certain to lead to even greater calamities. There is no recorded reaction to this exchange, but doubtless fresh on the minds of delegates was an account of a Texas colonel who had been arrested earlier that summer for successfully mining gold on the Yuba River with his own slave gang.

O.M. Wozencraft, a physician from San Joaquin, was next to enter the debate. His was a metaphysical explanation that apparently brought no rebuttal: "The Negro was created by the Creator to serve the white race and since they do not serve [our needs], they should be returned to the boundless wastes of their native land. [Otherwise] the 'capitalists' [the southern slave owners] will fill the country with these living labor machines, [and the rest of us will be helpless to compete]."[18] Wozencraft's interpretation was followed by that of a pettifogging delegate from Wisconsin who insisted that the definition of a "free slave" was a slave that was "free to stay home."

Further confusion then engulfed the debate when individuals rose to change the direction of the argument. They insisted that "only white citizens were qualified to vote on the slavery proposals." It was a shift in the discussion that, not surprisingly, was not well received by the dark-skinned Californios. The intrusion of the skin-color conundrum had the effect of drawing the delegates into a somewhat muddled and murky discussion that led them down a meandering trail of ancestry and a definitive denotation of "dark-skinned." Seemingly a fruitless hour later, the debate was abandoned after most members agreed that defining the color shades of white men was well nigh impossible, except, as everyone agreed, at the extreme ends of the spectrum.

Thereafter, the debate shifted from determining when a citizen had a right to vote to whether "racial inferiority" was an appropriate reason for withholding voting privileges. Eventually a majority of the delegates reached a partial solution: Don't settle on a definition for including people, the argument went, just find a reason to exclude those that the majority had, from the outset, wished to exclude. One northern delegate was prepared to offer the following list: "Negroes, Indians, and *especially* the Chinese, were *primitives*" and, therefore, should not be allowed to vote. Again the Mexican-American ranchers were uncomfortable with this proposal. They reminded delegates of their ancestral Indian roots. Then, delegate William Gwin, always looking for the political advantage, recommended that the vote be based not on color but on one's ownership of property. The question of how much property arose. S.C. Foster of Los Angeles started the bidding modestly: "For the voting privilege a man ought to have at least $100 in his pocket," But L.W. Hastings of Sacramento deflected the debate when he reminded the convention that every male Mexican-American citizen, no matter his skin color or wealth, was already eligible to vote by virtue of the Hidalgo treaty. But he unfortunately stumbled over his own argument when he then declared that "tribal Indians" should be excluded because "[they and women] were too easily led astray by demagogues."

The Treaty's restraint now set the delegates off in a new direction: searching for a definition of "tribal." How many generations must pass, one New Yorker wanted to know, before they no longer would be able to distinguish between tribal Indians and wealthy landowning Indians, or, in other words, "Indians who read, write and pay taxes?" To this question another delegate gave an answer. He suspected, that four generations would be enough time [to] civilize the Indian before he would be allowed to vote.

Eventually, however, under Gwin's prodding, the convention agreed that taxes, not skin color, should decide which men would have the franchise. What finally emerged after several additional hours of debate became Article II of the new constitution.

> Every white male citizen of the United States, and every white citizen of Mexico who should have elected to become a citizen of the United States under the treaty of peace exchanged and ratified at Queretaro, on the 30th of May 1848; and of the age of twenty-one, who has been in residence six months, by next preceding election, can vote. The Legislature by a two-thirds vote can admit suffrage to Indians and the descendants of Indians.[19]

But then, a puzzling rider was attached to the Article I that revealed the underlying conflict that still burned in the hearts of delegates—a proposal that left the entire question irrelevant and therefore unresolved. It began, "Men are by nature free and independent, and slavery is not to be tolerated, [nonetheless] 'free persons' of color are prohibited from settling in the State." In other words, people of color, in the minds of white Californians, were "free but not free to live in California." Sanity was restored when the southerner Gwin again had the foresight to insist that a law of this magnitude should not be written into the permanent record of the constitution, but left to public sentiment to resolve through elected representatives. With this, Gwin was able to persuade the delegates that the specious clause should be dropped from the final version of California's first constitution.[20]

Next the convention turned its attention to other matters of social orderliness (notwithstanding the remark by L.W. Hastings concerning a woman's vulnerability to demagogues—a remark that could not have represented a more exquisite example of 19th-century paternalism). On the question of social responsibility, many of the delegates found themselves riding a national wave of financial progressivism. The issue of equal rights for women, for example, an issue that first emerged on the southeastern seaboard in the mid-1840, became in California's constitutional convention a full-fledged battle for gender rights. As a result, the state's new constitution contained some progressive fiscal provisions concerning a woman's right to property and financial representation while concomitantly including what seemed to a few delegates a scandalous provision against the abridgement of rights for divorcees. Nevertheless, it would be another forty years before the law recognized the right of property distribution earned by a divorcee if her former spouse was still alive.[21]

Not all the delegates were sanguine about placing these items in the constitution. A heated debate broke out on the issue of gender rights. C.T. Botts of Monterey (formerly of Virginia) lamented vociferously over property rights for women. His distress made the Victorian age palpable:

> In my opinion there is no provision so beautiful in the common law, so admirable and beneficial, as that which regulates this sacred contract between man (husband?) and wife. Sir, the God of nature made women frail, lovely, and dependent; and such the common law pronounces her. Nature did what the common law has done—put her under the protection of man; and it is the object of this clause [a woman's right to own property] to withdraw her from that protection, and put her under the protection of law. I say, sir, the husband will take better care of the wife, provide for her better and protect her better, than the law. He, who would not let the winds of heaven to rudely touch her, is her best protector. When she trusts him with her happiness, she may well trust him with her gold. [The] only despotism on earth that I would advocate is the despotism of the husband. There must be a head and there must be a master in every household; and I believe; this plan by which you propose to make the wife independent of the husband is contrary to the laws and provisions of nature—contrary to all the wisdom, which we have derived from experience.[22]

Botts' complaint brought from San Francisco delegate F.J. Lippitt's mouth a countervailing French aphorism: "The world is divided into two classes [Sir], those with better appetites than dinners, and those with better dinners than appetites." In France, he continued, "where the civil law prevails, there is no greater example of domestic disunity, [and where] raising the wife from the position of head clerk to partner is not [regarded as] against nature!" Botts responded, "A doctrine of woman's rights is the doctrine of mental hermaphrodites—[it is the scheme of] husbands of rich wives [who] would make Prince Alberts of us all." No additional exchange was recorded—only that Potts announced himself unwell and withdrew from both the dispute and the chamber.[23]

The convention was winding down and it had come time for the delegates to face the issue that had been brewing from the first day. It was time to deal with the rancorous problem of taxation. It had been the intended purpose of the convention to leave the topic open until the various committees had a better sense of what the costs would be for financing an annual budget. Under the best of circumstances, delegates recognized that the issue of government costs was going to be divisive—even irreconcilable, perhaps—given the disagreement among legislators on the matter of how citizens should be fairly taxed.

In what had turned out to be a relatively concordant convention, the matter of taxation certainly became the most discordant of issues that they faced. Nonetheless, after considerable dissonance, the convention's tax disagreements were finally resolved with a cranky-voiced vote, a vote that left an important minority frustrated and not assuaged. It was a disagreement that caused a rift in California's emerging political parlors, a division for which delegates would never find an adequate solution. In fact, the debate on taxation became contentious on Monday of the third week of the convention and continued to be a roadblock until the day the constitution received final approval before the full assembly.

During the debate there were two positions: A small faction of delegates insisted that the revenues collected from port duties and charges to exporters, shippers and local service fees would meet the state's operating expenses, and no additional taxes would be necessary. One cheerful delegate even went so far as to declare that it was a fortuitous balance of nature that the state's needs and its costs were commensurate. He was so resolute about it that he dubbed it a "state of nature tax." Notwithstanding this delegate's confidence, a more sober block of delegates acknowledged that the current taxing policies would, in all likelihood, be insufficient to meet the continually expanding financial needs of a burgeoning state—a situation, they argued, that would worsen even more once the congressionally mandated territorial funds were discontinued. In the end, however, a majority of the conventioneers were resigned to the reality of establishing an extendable tax base. During the protracted debate, and over the loud objections of southern land owners, a coalition of San Francisco and Sacramento businessmen, along with delegates from the northernmost counties, pushed through the convention a landed property tax—to which was later added a personal property tax—in an effort to secure the durability of a revenue base.

A property tax was the only "fair tax," argued this northern coalition, for it was the one taxing procedure that could accurately assess a citizen's true wealth and would more properly, therefore, measure and collect taxes reliably. The hopelessly outnumbered southern California delegates, in responding, insisted that a property tax was nothing more than a garnishment masquerading as a fair tax. A fair tax, they insisted, would be a common tax that was to be applied equally to every citizen. The matter was eventually put to rest in the last draft of the constitution, where the taxing provision simply reads, "a value tax of real and personal property shall be the basis of taxation."[24]

Making property tax the cornerstone of state revenues, however, was, for the rancheros, tantamount to imposing a class tax, and it severed whatever consonance northern delegates had hoped to draw from their southern compatriots. When the final roll call was finally taken no delegates from the southern section of the state cast a vote supporting the personal and property tax provisions. The upshot was, that it strengthened the resolve of some of the southern ranchers to continue fighting for the north-south division of the territory. However, promoting a division of the state was not so much a matter of making room for slavery, as Bancroft and Royce asserted, as it was a reaction to what the Californios, particularly in the southern parts of the state, believed to be a confiscatory tax that had been placed on land owners' backs by the northern mining interests. Taxation, not slavery, was the prevailing unresolved problem in the southern territory. Rancheros acknowledged that the business-rich northerners would pay a tax, but by comparison with the land-rich southerners, wealthy northerners, living in a territory overrun by vagabonds and squatters who daily extracted unknown quantities of gold from lands of disputed ownership, would pay a far smaller share of tax—because it was untraceable.

It was land owners, they reminded their antagonists, that made it impossible to levee statewide taxes in an equitable fashion. They were, of course, arguing the obvious; titled ownership of *real property* was measurable, while the taxable assessment of *personal property* was easy to hide, and even easier to misrepresent. (The Mexican-American ranchers insisted that if land were to be the basis for tax assessment, then it should be assessed from county to county and not statewide. Their position would prevail when a State Board of Equalization was created.) In floor debates, however, many land-poor delegates made no attempt to disguise their expectation that a land-taxing policy would eventually force the land barons to sell off their holdings, parcel by parcel.

Within the year, the ranchers' predictions proved to be true—citizens in the southern territory paid in taxes, on average, $2.65 per person, per month, per annum, while citizens in the agricultural counties in the middle of the state paid $1.65, and their northern brethren paid $1.00. As a corollary, by the early part of the next century, almost every large ranch had been broken up or sold off, either to pay delinquent taxes or to benefit from the soaring profits that were to be made from real estate speculating in the boom years between 1880 and 1938.

October 13, 1850, the day the convention drew to a close, was a cloudy, soggy day, but that was not unusual, for it started raining early in the fall of that year and seemed to rain off and on throughout the 40 days and nights of the convention. For their efforts, the self-congratulatory but weary representatives from the 10 districts produced a constitution that turned out to be better than critics predicted. During convention days, newspaper representatives who covered the sessions ridiculed the efforts of the delegates. Journal consensus was that the delegates did not have the good sense to produce a workable document of which the state might be proud—that the only thing likely to come from their effort would be increased revenue for the political careers of an otherwise unemployable class of people. Newspaper writers reminded the convention of one of their benighted delegates who had objected to the proposed constitutional phrase "a jury of one's peers," on the grounds that the United States was a democracy and had no "house of peers." But he was only one of numerous delegates who were held up to ridicule by "intellectually superior" newspaper critics. Observations of this order were not uncommon and seemed to give credibility to the reporters' general opinion of the entire enterprise.

However, taking a later and wider view, most of these criticisms appeared to be petty and contrived. True enough, there were delegates who spent more time in the saloons than on the convention floor, but there was also a sizable number of accomplished representatives who were able to produce a document that brought a progression of continuity, where before there had been only disarray. Bancroft wrote, "in the last analysis, the mistakes [they] made were more of circumstances than of judgment."[25]

Of course, in retrospect, it made sense to argue, as did its critics, that California's first constitution was a document of "shreds and patches," a mélange of the immigrants' favored home-state politics and constitutions. That is, passages appear throughout the document that had been extracted almost verbatim from the constitutions of New York, Ohio, Texas, Iowa, Alabama and Florida; notwithstanding the jerrybuilt quality of their founding document, however, it would be a full three decades before Californians would find it necessary to return to the state capitol at Sacramento and write a second version of their constitution.[26]

Before adjourning, the delegates were mindful to increase the number of state districts from ten to twenty-seven, thereby tripling the size of the state Legislature and assuring themselves greater political opportunities. They justified these increases as the only practicable way to handle the additional responsibilities that an exploding population was sure to place on state government. The cynical onlookers, however, rejected this position, insisting that district increases were meant solely to secure greater bureaucratic influence and political patronage for themselves (a majority of the delegates ran for the district offices that they had represented at the convention).

On November 13, the newly drafted constitution was ratified. The lassitude of the citizens seemed to match the gloomy weather. In all, a paltry 12,061 votes were cast. Of these, 811, took the occasion to merely opposed ratification even though no such question was asked (770 were miners). In the southern section of the state, not surprisingly, only seven hundred eighty-five citizens bothered to vote.[27] Politicians blamed the weather for this outcome, but historian Franklin Tuthill seems more astute:

> There was a stronger reason [than weather], it was the case that the majority looked upon politics as a matter of small account, in the midst of such a harvest of gold, especially as they expected to return soon to their old homes, taking their fortunes with them, and leaving the state and its politics for others, of different tastes and more modest expectations, to regulate.[28]

With the election one month behind them, the elected representatives assembled in San Jose on December 15 to organize California's first Legislature—the "Legislature of a thousand drinks," one disgruntled journalist called it. Peter Burnett, the territorial governor of Oregon, who initially, had come to California to hunt for gold, was elected the future state's first governor, while John McDougal became lieutenant governor, while John C. Fremont and William M. Gwin became its first senators. Fremont was declared the first senator, having drawn a greater number of votes, but he was also to serve a limited two-year term for having drawn the shortest straw in an informally devised appointment lottery. Gwin, openly delighted at his good fortune in gaining the six-year term, declared himself humbled by the "fortuity of events," and publicly pledged himself to represent the interests of "every Californian," not merely the interests of his brethren from the southern states.

It now had come time to find a permanent location for the state capital, and there were occasions when the search for a capital seemed more vexing to the legislators than drafting the constitution. Early on, most representatives assumed that it would remain in San Jose, but political factions in various communities, who had envisioned the trade and commerce that a capital city could lure, lobbied for the advantages of their respective districts.[29]

When, however, the Californios General Mariano Guadalupe Vallejo donated 156 acres of land, plus an additional $370,000, to construct the capitol building at the mouth of the Sacramento River—conveniently accessible to San Francisco, Sacramento and the mining districts—a majority of the legislators shifted allegiance from their provincial neighborhoods to the dusty village of Vallejo. In a matter of weeks, though, inadequate accommodations and mosquito-infested tide pools from the swampy lowlands north of the bay drove the lawmakers back to the more commercially welcoming streets of San Jose. But then, months later when a powerful northern block of legislators found San Jose too far south for their convenience, they voted a return to Vallejo, and back they traipsed to the stagnant marshes of San Pablo Bay. Yet, even then the traveling legislators were still not ready to settle in. The next group to make a bid was Sacramento's struggling business community, eager to induce commerce away from San Francisco. Once again, lured by various emoluments, the legislators moved east to Sacramento. But they were hardly settled and back they went to Vallejo, then grudgingly on to Benicia and, eventually, with the Sacramento legislators putting together a firm, unfaltering majority, they returned to Sacramento—this time for good, a five full years after they had first begun looking for a location on which to build the state's capitol.

Californians now had a constitution, and a capitol city.[30] They had elected leadership and they had two senators-elect haunting the District of Columbia's federal halls importuning the United States Congress to ratify California's entry into the Union as the 31st state. But nothing in the federal capital moved in that direction, because congressional attention in February 1850 was not to be diverted from the incessant struggle to balance the admission of slave and free-soil populations into the western territories. In fact, at the outset there were not even enough votes in Congress to muster a majority necessary to bring the petition for statehood onto the floor for debate. Stymied and frustrated, senators-in-waiting Fremont and Gwin sent word home proposing that California carry on as a state, with or without congressional approval. State legislators agreed. Fremont and Gwin remained in the United States capital as senators without portfolio; they continued to lobby in the federal hallways until they received congressional approval for statehood.

It was inevitable that these first steps toward statehood would be slow and difficult, caught as California was in the middle of the most self-destructive political conflict in the nation's history. Legislators in the U.S. capitol, both northern and southern, saw little in the far West that suggested that they should rush this untamed territory into statehood. From eastern and southern perspectives, the territory was an eccentric mixture of miners, vagabonds and speculators—a region that held very little future promise. What these congressmen observed from their east coast vistas was an immigrant population that was anti-foreigner, albeit infiltrated by foreigners, and anti-slave, albeit without room or tolerance for Mexicans, Native Americans or "Negroes" (Mexican and Native American populations made up more than two-thirds of the country's inhabitants).

The only ones favorably disposed to permanent statehood, reasoned many in the U. S. Congress, were the eastern and southern transients who would eventually lose interest when they returned to their homes in the east and south. It was, for the most part, a land made up of settlers and squatters who showed little interest in establishing social and political institutions in California. That is, it was a land made up of a plurality of scattered parts with little prospect for homogeneity.

But where politicians east of the Mississippi River saw only *disject membra,* western immigrants saw an estimable union bound together by political and legal institutions. These were incipient institutions, to be sure, that sometimes, even unbeknown to the immigrants themselves, they had packed along with their material belongings on the way to "their land of golden promises." Yet it was with these entrenched English aspirations of law and order that they meant to build an Arcadia on the Pacific shore despite aboriginal resentments.[31]

NOTES

1. See Richard Griswold del Castillo, *The Treaty of Guadalupe Hidalgo: legacy of conflict* (Norman, OK. University of Oklahoma Press. 1990).
2. For a contemporary account of native Californians during this period, see William S. Simmons "Indian Peoples of California," in R. Gutierrez and R. Orsis. Eds: *Contested Eden: California before the Gold Rush* (Berkeley: University of California Press. 1999). 48–77.
3. Josiah Royce. *California: From the Conquest in 1846 to the End of the Second Vigilance Committee in San Francisco* (Boston: Houghton, Mifflin Co. 1892).
4. Bayard Taylor, *Eldorado* (Lincoln NE: University of Nebraska Press. 1949). 41.
5. Royce. *California,* 181.
6. See Robert Glass Cleland. *From Wilderness to Empire:* A History of California 1542–1900 (New York: Alfred A. Knopf. 1944).
7. Richard Griswald del Castillo, *Treaty.*
8. Elisha Oscar Crosby. *Reminiscences of California and Guatemala, 1849–1892* (San Marino CA: The Huntington Library Press. 1945). 33.
9. Bean, Walton, *California: An Interpretative History* (New York: McGraw-Hill Book Co., 1965). 125.
10. The divided-state proposal eventually reached the floor of the U.S. Senate, but by the time it did, the nation's Congress was so precariously balanced between anti-slaves and pro-slaves that the prospect that either side might gain an ideological advantage brought the entire enterprise to a standstill. (When the proposal finally reached the Senate, each of the three titans of the Senate—Daniel Webster, Henry Clay and John Calhoun—had their say, but nothing changed. In fact nothing would change the prospects for or against a divided state until war was waged.)

11. In the arena of commerce, for example, the rancheros had their roots in the monetary and investment practices that were a part of *Romanus Jus Civitatis*, that is, the rules of trade and industry fixed by the hoary *Corpus Juris*. By comparison, the immigrants' commercial heritage had been immersed in *Common Law*—a codex of ordinances, sanctions and penalties whose origins were traceable to the first common law document of cases, the 1516 printing of Sir Anthony Fitzherbert's *La Grande Abridgement*.

12. Kevin Starr. *Americans and the California Dream* (NY: Oxford University Press 1973). Starr writes that Royce sets out to describe the formation of the state as it truly was, not as the pioneers had romanticized it. 155.

13. J .Ross Browne, *Report of the Debates in the Convention of California on the Formation of the State of California in September and October, 1849*. 38.

14. Considered briefly, the extrapolations that Royce (Bancroft) employed. He argued that William Gwin, the most influential of the Southern delegates, arrived in Monterey expecting to offer a motion on the floor of the convention that would divide California's immense territory into a balanced number of free and open states. If his thesis were correct, then it is to be expected that elements or hints of such a strategy should appear in convention notes and records—but constitutional records are lacking such evidence. Some years after the convention, Elisha Crosby, who had been a delegate to the convention, wrote that Gwin had promised southern colleagues that, if elected senator, he would propose, on the floor of the United States Senate, a plan to divide California. Yet, Crosby's claim lays silently unconfirmed by anyone else, and congressional records do not indicate that Gwin made such a proposal.

15. In point of fact, what meager evidence there was for the Bancroft-Royce thesis had seemed to have arisen from a speech given by delegate John McDougal from the floor in the midst of a lengthy debate on the question of setting the state's borders. McDougal, shortly thereafter the state's first lieutenant governor, in a rousing speech made midway through an extended disputation on state size, declared that: "[the conservatives and southerners] want a constitution presented to Congress so objectionable that it will be thrown back for another convention. "Gentlemen I have a risen on this floor and stated that they had received letters from the South; and that they knew of many who want to bring their slaves here, and work them for a short time period in the mines and then emancipate them. If this constitution is thrown back on us for reconsideration, it leaves them with the opportunity of bringing their slaves here. It is what they desired to do; to create some strongly objectionable features in the Constitution in order that they may bring their slaves here and work them three months."(*Debates* 48). Viewing the controversy with fewer presuppositions, McDougal's charge seems to be little more than hyperbole. Were his observations even remotely accurate, then the southerners were truly fomenting a sagacious plot so much so that it had become well-nigh ineffable, and contradicts Gwin's publicly stated goal, *viz*, to be California's first senator for "all the people." But more inimical to the Bancroft-Royce thesis is the fact that in convention records support for dividing the territory never fell along regional lines. The record shows that there was only a single southern delegate that ever voted to enlarge the territory, and by convention end every delegate supported a motion to ban institutional slavery in California. Moreover,

almost all support for expanding territorial boundaries came from the land-grant ranchers who were soundly defeated twenty-eight to seven when the issue was put before the entire convention. In fact when a final vote on state boundaries was taken, no delegate could be found who supported the larger boundary thesis. Voting unanimously, the convention delegates declared that the state's boundary on the east was to be drawn on a diagonal line from the center of Lake Tahoe southeasterly to the Colorado River, and from the point where it reached the river it was to follow the river's course south to the Mexican border. Heading north the boundary was to proceed from the middle of Lake Tahoe on the 120th meridian northward to the Oregon territorial line. As the debate wound down, one representative seemed to capture the feelings of most when he declared that "all" land east of the Sierra Nevada to the Great Salt Lake was much too harsh and miserable to ever be settled by anyone. Franklin Tuthill. *History of California* (San Francisco: H.H. Bancroft & Co. 1866). 271.

16. J. Ross Browne. *Debates*. 48, 95, 256. For an analysis of specific aspects of the law by topics, see Gordon Morris Bakken, *The Development of Law in Frontier California* (Greenwood Press: Westport *CN*, 1985), e.g. contract laws, real estate law, finance law, seller's law.

17. Robert Semple Slavery *Debates* 48–49.

18. J. Ross Browne. *Debates*. 49. See also Walton Bean, *California*, 130. On Slavery.

19. Articles of California Constitution. 61–76.

20. J. Ross Browne D*ebates*. 51–54, 259.

21. Goldberg, Charlotte K. *A Cauldron of Anger: The Spreckels Family and the Reform of California Community Property Law* (Western Legal History vol. 12, Number 2, Summer-Fall, 1999).

22. J. Ross. *Debates* 259–261.

23. —— *Debates.* 260.

24. State of California Constitution 1851, Article XI, Sec. 13. This tax resolution was settled decidedly in the favor of the northern territory. Northerners could do much more tax manipulating than could the southerners. For example, the amount of gold extracted from the northerner territory from 1860–1865 ran in its favor over the southern territory at about 4 to 1. See *Mineral Resources of the United States*: Browne and Taylor (Washington D.C., Government Printing Office, 1867).

25. Hubert Howe Bancroft. *Political Tribunals* (San Francisco: The History Company. 1887). Vol. II. 24.

26. 2nd California State Constitution, September 1889.

27. Walton Bean. *California.* 133.

28. Franklin Tuthill, *History of California* (San Francisco: Fords Howard & Hubert, 1866). 284. See: *Debates,* 137–138, 142, 145, 149, 305 331, 337–339.

29. Walton Bean. *California.* California. See also A.A.Gray. H*istory of California From 1542* (San Francisco: D.C. Heath and Company. 1934). 309–310. Robert Glass Cleland. *History of California*: the American Period. (New York: The Macmillan Company, 1922). 343.

30. The state seal was original although cluttered. It contained the goddess of political wisdom Minerva, a grizzly bear, a cluster of grapes, ships on the Sacramento River and a miner with pick, bowl and rocker.

31. For discussion of such topics as: dueling, state boundaries, taxing, compensation, limits on the judiciary, African-Americans and people of color, Common v. Civil Law, a wife's property claims, and per-diem, See: 95, 123–124, 137,140–145, 163, 170, 225–230, 247–255, 256–57, 259, 26330. For a provocative and helpful discussion of early days of transition see: John W. Caughey with Norris Hundley. *California* (Engelwood NJ: Prentice-Hall Inc. 1982; Don Antonio Franco Coronel 1817–1894. *Tales of Mexican California,* Editor Doyce Nunis. Santa Barbara CA. Bellerphon Books, 1994); Oscar Lewis. *This was San Francisco* (NY: David McKay Company Ine.1962); Kevin Starr. *America and the California Dream 1850–1915* (New York: Oxford UniversityPress1973). For rebutting Bancroft's southern strategy thesis *s*ee Edward McGowan's *Mogowan v. Vigilantes.*

Chapter Three

From Roman Law to Common Law: *Juris Civilus* of Use and Custom

In the two years that California was a United States territory, merging cultural pressures worked against the establishment of a coherent system of jurisprudence. Immigrant miners, for example, with neither time nor interest in producing a coherent legal system, would turn to territorial law only when they found that they could not recoup loss or injury in any other way. Yet, even after time and interest were no longer impediments, when, so to speak, the state had accumulated more *settlers* than *squatters,* the Mexican civil system continued being perceived as both inefficient and quixotic by the Americans. Cultural differences, during this era, made acceptance of the land's legal traditional slow going. The protagonists of this book: Terry, and Field, were to find themselves together on California's highest bench during the incipient stages of this transition from Mexican to American law, from *civil* to *common* law, so to speak.

Henry Campbell Black's dictionary of law defines European Civil Law as "the codes of social action and order for a nation, a commonwealth or a municipality, whose origins are traceable to Roman and Justinian jurisprudence." In juxtaposition, Black defines common law as the social "use and custom" affecting persons and property originating in English or Anglo-Saxon jurisprudence.[1] In a panoptic sense, civil law descends from the religious doctrinal and secular traditions of the European countries lying north of the Mediterranean Sea. Laws of society in this region had been inoculated with large doses of religious piety and Aristotelian rationalism—hence, it seems fair to argue that the individual and his or her state were legally bound together by a system of *paternal formalism.* By contrast, proponents of common law understood the law to be the basic instrument for balancing, not binding, the relationship between the individual and his or her government.

The struggle between these two traditions is described in the celebrated quotation of Oliver Wendell Holmes, Jr: "The actual life of the law has not been logic; it has been experience. The felt necessities of the time, the prevalent moral and political theories, intuitions of public policy, avowed or unconscious, even the prejudices which judges share with their fellow-men, have had a good deal more to do than the syllogism in determining the rules by which law shall be governed."[2]

Beginning with United States' formal annexation of California in 1848 at the Treaty of Guadalupe Hidalgo it was not surprising that civil and common law systems would generate a territorial quagmire. After annexation, the territory's vast regions became a battleground where southern and northern émigrés bickered over the merits of Civil and Common Law. Many immigrants, carrying a visceral dislike for all things Latin, began campaigning to remove every vestige of the Civil system with England's system of Common Law—never mind that Civil Law had been a part of Mexico's California for generations. Nonetheless between 1849 and 1851 rampant North American "nativism" successfully undermined the civil tradition, depicting the civil system—often correctly—as a legal system that nursed confusion, inefficiencies and ethnic subordination. It was agreed that the new state needed to establish some legal form of order as soon as possible, for not only was there legal confusion, there were also thousands of newly authorized Mexican-American citizens struggling to assimilate culturally new expectations. The dysfunctional nature of the legal system was summed up in Hubert Howe Bancroft's cryptic account of the disarray prevailing in San Francisco in 1849: "[It had become] a city of a hundred thousand voters, of 538 homicides, and but one conviction!"

Perhaps the only positive note was that the confliction of the judicial traditions enabled freelance, and often ill-prepared American lawyers, to get work.[3] Lawyers that, in more than a few instances, were semiskilled in common law, and wholly in the dark when it came to Mexico's civil procedures. Many of these lawyers, whose sojourn in California had begun unsuccessfully in the gold fields, ended up in new or growing townships, where they scrambled for the opportunity to return to their former profession. But where there are lawyers inevitably there will be judges, and in keeping with the standard of its lawyers, California quickly assimilated a brotherhood of judges. Some were good, but many were as deplorably lacking in an understanding of law as the ragtag lawyers who stood before them in court.[4] And implementing the wishes of these judges and lawyers was a coterie of cantankerous constables whose policing authority originated in towns and villages they inhabited, and worked its will as far and as wide as their pistol and rifle shots would allow.

Meanwhile Mexican landowners, fearful of the growing confiscatory retaliation that the immigrants' political and legal power was producing, urged the preservation of the Spanish civil system that had been in place for almost two centuries. It was, they pointed out, easily adaptable to common law. Any hope of mixing these two jurisprudential systems was destined to fail, however, for as the immigrant population grew, so also did their power to make California's legal system the total instrument of common law.[5] From the newcomers' perspective, that is, from the perspective of the immigrants with legal training, they had little knowledge and even less interest in the Mexican legal system. The sentiments of the third justice of the California Supreme Court, Nathaniel Bennet, summed it up: "[Civil Law is nothing less than] disorganized custom and tradition [operating] at the outskirts of civilization."[6]

The heart of the immigrant-miner's complaint was that California's land, and everything *on it* or *in it* was free for the taking—for it is not be forgotten that California was "conquered" territory. The land belonged to those who staked and worked it—the Mexican War had established sovereignty in the *Norte American's* favor, and *prima facie* the "labor of mining it" settled the issue of ownership. In his final chapter in *Law and Community of the Mexican Frontier*, legal historian David J. Langum describes northern sentiments thusly:

> The expatriates were unable to adapt well to Mexico's legal system in California. The older residents, those who had arrived before the overlanders, had become naturalized citizens, had married California women, and had otherwise worked themselves into positions of prominence, nonetheless, distrusted and deprecated the formal judicial structure. Although they were thoroughly assimilated into the California culture and had a significant economic stake in the current system of government, subconsciously they would measure the worth of Mexican law in terms that seemingly corresponded to common law practice. That is, these early settlers were usually merchants or sea captains, who by preference, tended to settle their disputes among themselves.[7]

When, however, prejudices were set aside, a dispassionate investigation of the Civil Law reveals that it was not as superficial and as useless as immigrants claimed it to be.[8] It was, in fact, an intricate patriarchal network whose roots extended as far back as Spain's 11th-century ecclesiastical *Siete Partidas*—the Roman Catholic Church's *Seven Certifications* of life: birth, coming of age, adulthood, marriage, parenthood, old age and death.[9] For when Americans moved beyond generalities and actually articulated their dissatisfaction with Civil Law, by far and away, their greatest objections were leveled against the haphazard fashion in which sanctions were administered and reviewed—which came down to the issue of how penalties and punishments were to be enforced. Because the traditional *Alcalde* (i.e., the mayor-judge) weighed off penalties and compensations against what was perceived to be the community's welfare, it made it impossible for litigants, even in the most trenchant or trivial of disputes, to expect fair settlements. When, for example, a merchant won a judgment against a thief he expected his loss to be made whole by equivalent compensation. Yet, the alcalde, more often than not, would take the community's general welfare into consideration when assessing penalties. If the alcalde did not consider the thief's effect on the community, then the community itself might suffer unjustly (e.g., a wife, children, aged parents, or even the entire community might be penalized unfairly.)

In the Civil law, the alcalde would administer sanctions incrementally, or, perhaps, he might postpone them altogether, thereby harming the plaintiff who was expecting his circumstances to be made whole. How then, the Americans wanted to know, can contractual agreements ever be trusted as reliable documents, or how can trade and commerce be expected to flourish under the judicial ambiguities of civil law that will not enforce fair compensations, that is, cash-value compensations, so to speak? What is more, what assurances are there that tradesmen would ever collect on defaulted debts?

Next in the order of complaints, one frequently heard from shopkeepers concerned the scarcity and trustworthiness of legal records. Court records, if they existed at all, were generally incomplete and/or inaccurate. This paucity of record-keeping typically gave way to anecdotal accounts of outrageous delays and inequities on both sides of a litigated issue.[10] Émigrés were not in the least reluctant to draw newly arriving immigrants aside with all manner of hyperbole. Criminals, so the stories went, might serve six months for murder or be hanged—depending on who had murdered whom or on what surreptitious arrangements had been made under the cloak of judicial privilege. *Surety* contracts (bail bonds), for example, that had been subjected to pretrial agreements were forever prey to the arcades' power of *forfeiture*—a process whereby the judge might dismiss the defaulting penalties in interest of a community welfare if he judged the guarantor's investment of lesser social importance than a defendant's service of penalties. (In fairness, in so far as records can be depended upon, immigrants suffered no more under the civil system than did their Mexican counterparts.)[11] For these reasons, and many more, in the early months of 1851 the state Legislature decreed that the codes of Common Law were to replace the Mexican Civil Codes in all state courts. But, outside larger population centers, this legislative-driven transition was barely noticeable for almost a decade. A title shift from the alcalde (generally the same person) seemed to be the only discernible difference. "[The alcaldes continued] to gather evidence and trust their own sense of justice. [T]hey followed the devices of their hearts," wrote Royce.[12] The Mexican government, in fact, wanting more centralized control over legal proceedings, reduced the alcalde responsibilities to that of being the mayor and not the legal officer, as far back as 1837, even while alcaldes in Upper California were still serving as legal as officers well past the treaty date of 1849.

It was inevitable that the patriarchal system would crumble once the North Americans were in full control, yet often these men, many of whom were North Americans, earned the respect of the local citizenry as district mayors, judges and sheriffs—presiding over courts, making arrests and, when necessary, even serving as camp or village wardens. These alcaldes were popular with many American miners because their decisions were uncomplicated and swiftly implemented. Characteristically alcaldes presided over a loosely structured system of rules and penalties unburdened by the interminable checks and balances that were so much a part of Anglo-Saxon law. As one miner expressed it, "In the camps you'll find no law books laying about." What miners wanted above all else was predictability. But it was a particular form of predictability—conflict resolution, so to speak, that settled disagreements on the spot. A judicial judgment was meant to be swift, resolute and permanent. A mining camp banality summed it up: "If we have no lawyers, then we have no need of law"—for without the swift acts of an alcalde, miners' law would tolerate vengeance killings, long-running feuds and manifestly more unfair punishments. Argonauts knew full well, for example, that banishment as punishment was difficult to enforce, whippings rarely deterred, and reliance on hangings merely served to increase a cycle of vengeance. While reporter-traveler Bayard Taylor's curious accounts to his eastern newspaper readers stated that "miners' common goals fostered common trust so that even their property is safe [in unsecured tents]," Most miners' accounts were to the contrary—camps were being forever rifled.[13] Reality suggests that miners were powerless to prevent camp theft—a circumstance that led to the continued escalation of penalties for thievery. If a miner's livelihood was threatened or if his gold cache or horse were stolen, for example, the penalty might very well escalate to hanging. Yet if equipment or supplies were stolen, punishment was usually a fine or banishment—or perhaps both. Charles Shinn writes that miners were fined one to three ounces of gold—plus a three-ounce court fee—for the theft of pickaxes, lanterns, sleeping bunks, tables and tents, while murder and mayhem at times, oddly enough, might not be prosecuted. Rather it was expected that miners who had suffered offence could count on friends to settle scores by taking matters into their own hands. Miners believed, or perhaps feigned the belief, that those unable to defend themselves on the frontier were better off living the "soft-handed" life of easterners.

But it was also true that where jurisdictions were unclear or traveling alcaldes unavailable, many miners organized themselves into camp-wide meeting or *folk moot* to settle camp disputes.[14] In these circumstances, a lack of jails made lynching the punishment of choice, and with few lamentations, miners dealt out hanging as punishment that had the proficiency of irreversible consequences—with barely a hint of a trial, cattle thieves, horse thieves and bandits were hanged. The overlander-historian Franklin Tuthill offers an eyewitness account of this lawless form of miner-justice:

> When a robbery was committed, they rallied from all the camps about to hunt the culprit, and when found, to try him. These juries wanted no part of long trials. The examinations were sharp and brief, the questions apt to be leading. When the jury found a verdict of guilty, the miserable prisoner was run up by the neck to the limb of the nearest tree. The very swiftness of justice saved them from being called into frequent requisition. Lynch law knew no delays, and made some terrible blunders, which while it scared the evildoers, nonetheless, brought border law into disrepute.[15]

Yet migrant miners were not the only ones to suffer this form of patchwork justice. In his book *The Wild Frontier,* William M. Osborn reports that after the arrival of the gold seekers, between 1849 and 1861, more than 2,000 American and Mexican Indians were killed by immigrant miners and settlers; presumably some of them had faced the swift veto of the *folk moot,* "the rule of all."[16]

In an era of migration and legal turmoil, it is to be expected that the state's judicial history would be replete with rulings rendered by mediocre, ill-prepared alcalde-judges, many of whom were completely at a loss when it came to understanding how either Mexican or American legal proceedings were to be conducted. It was a condition aggravated by a lack of written sources and references (which, even when written, were often in a language that a newly arrived judicial manager could not read, or more likely, would not read). As a consequence, a litigant and his lawyer might not always know what to expect when facing a judge in his courtroom. It is irresistible, therefore, not to offer some bewildering albeit entertaining examples of "sage-brush" justice in some of California's earliest California-American courts. One such case concerns a hard-drinking judge by the name of Redman, who had the habit of intoning when he was about to render an opinion, "If the Court knows itself, and the Court thinks it does. . . ." On one stifling hot afternoon, dumbfounded spectators heard the judge end his standard legal admonishment with, "If the Court knows itself, and the Court thinks it does, it will now adjourn for five minutes and the Court will take a drink."[17] And then there was the account of a jurist by the name of Almond whose habit it was to rush through his court docket. On one occasion, he brought a verbose young lawyer up short with the remark, "Yes, sir, you are a remarkably fine talker and you know a great deal of law, but the Court has no time to hear you unless you insist upon it. For the Court has already decided this case, and directs the clerk to enter the judgment."[18] But one would have to look far and wide to match the performance of Judge Andrew Blackburn who executed a thief "[because] the 'calaboose' was in disrepair and prospects for preventing the [man's] escape too precarious," and then followed this decision with an order to execute a prisoner before getting the required approval of the governor. Once the prisoner was executed Judge Blackburn cheerfully appended to the execution document a note requesting permission from the governor to execute the "dead" man. Several weeks later, however, he outdid himself when he ordered a *vaquero*—whose cow had run down a pregnant woman, causing a miscarriage—to "restore the woman to her pregnant condition" at the same time he was ordering the woman's husband to pay all court costs.[19]

But eccentric legal judgments were not exclusively the province of obscure rural judges. Idiosyncratic opinions were to be found at every level of the judiciary—even within the solemn walls of the newly established Supreme Court. Justice Peter Burnett is remembered no less for being the author of the famous *Archie* opinion he rendered, than as he was for being the state's first governor and the Supreme Court's fourth chief justice. In this opinion, a Texas rancher had moved to California but failed to free his slave "Archie" as required by the recently drafted state constitution. Six months passed and the state filed suit against the Texan for failure to comply. But he resisted and went to court to get a variance. Eventually the case made its way up to the state's high court where Chief Justice Burnett opined that he would find in the slave-owner's favor, even while acknowledging "[t]hat the facts support Archie's release, [but because] this is the *first* case that has occurred under the existing [new] law [we] are not disposed to rigidly enforce the rule. [But] in reference to all future cases, it is our purpose to enforce the rules laid down strictly according to their true intent and purpose."[20] Why the first case was dismissed by virtue of being the first case, without setting precedence for dismissing the second case, seemed a mystery to almost everyone but the chief justice. Perhaps in Burnett's defense, it should be reported that at the time the slave was due to be dismissed, the slave-master was ill and unable to get along without assistance.

Early on, while the advent of common law in mining camps was still tangential, its role among California's urbanities was in place and essential, particularly among people in the trades, and commerce and transportation. City and town folk welcomed its appearance, for without it, business was persuaded, commerce could not be conduced profitably. "Only common law is business law," it was said. Granted that a great deal of North American dissatisfaction with the civil system was xenophobic; but the criticism also uncovered a vital disjunction between Mexico's patriarchal conception of *justa causa* (social justice), and the Anglo-Saxon notion of *stricti juris,* "a right granted by law." Proponents argued that tort and contract law was ineffectual without the foundational principle of *stricti juris.*[21] Put another way, North Americans were fond of characterizing litigants in Mexican civil courts as tongue-tied bystanders, expressly, because of the "inquisitorial" nature of civil law the parties were turned into spectators, not participants at their own trials. The alcalde's "unregulated" judgments, so to say, were meant to serve as the government's political interest. Whenever an alcalde determined that a greater community good was served by setting aside the trial evidence in a case, the judge was free to do so. That is, the plaintiff's case could be abrogated in favor of a higher sense of communal or social justice. As one disgruntled plaintiff of common law observed, "the [civil] court can put an arbitrator's interests before the plaintiff's rights," that is, once a legal judgment makes room for the interests of non-litigants, codified sanctions as a tool for compliance is greatly weakened or disappears.[22]

The disparity between civil and common law judgments generated a crescendo of complaints from immigrants, particularly when social justice, although undeclared *prima facie*, was treated as *prima facie* in Mexican courts. It became problematic that a plaintiff could get equity in a commercial case when the line between the *welfare* of a society and the *rules* of a society could be erased. Such an amalgamation violated the hallowed ground that necessarily stood between judicial and executive separation.[23] Defenders of Anglo-Saxon jurisprudence maintained that the courts must settle commercial disputes between parties according to rules of commerce in an open and unfettered adversarial contest. Under these circumstances, the welfare of a third party (non-litigating party) was deemed unfair for the Code must be *prima facie,* not the King. (According to Americans, Mexican legal institutions were there expressly to advance government policies.)

Frustrations of the Americans toward the patriarchal system were manifested in numerous ways. Americans, for instance, resented the practice of installing judges without consent of a voting public. It was a situation that frequently placed judges on the bench without much legal training (many Mexican alcaldes were wealthy community leaders without a trace of legal education).[24] Parenthetically, Americans preferred common law practice of rotating judges rather than the civil law practice of allowing judges to serve seemingly term-less appointments under the "meddling" influence of overseers.[25] Immigrants also objected to the practice of interrogating witnesses outside the presence of the defendant. Confronting one's accuser in open court was "quintessential to the law court." David Langum cites an 1837 procedural statute that underscores Mexican government's lassitude on the matter. "[The] confrontation of witnesses with the culprit shall only be practiced when the judge considers it absolutely necessary to find the truth."[26] What is more, the civil court's indifference toward careful record keeping acted as a nullifying practice. It was a habit that gave substance to the accusation that Mexican courts decided cases unhindered by codes, precedence or evidence—"Nothing is predictable, nor is there any constancy of expectations" opponents complained. A litigant's claims might easily become fortuitous or ancillary, which is to say that these ancient fraternal courts had been the messengers of governmental rulings for so many decades that acquiescence to their authority *de novo* was endemic to a Mexican citizens' expectations in the court.

The entrenched racial arrogance of the migrants reinforced the perception that traditional civil courts were not to be trusted. Americans commonly believed that these courts operated in the shadows and existed for the sole purpose of imposing the government's will on citizens. Consequently, immigrants treated these courts as "courts of last resort." Langum writes that when well-positioned Americans could not avoid courts altogether; they were likely to appear *in propria persona* (unrepresented). By not using a court's officers, they believed, they were not endorsing the court's authority. Two accounts of the 1858 *California Senate Committee of the Judiciary, Report on Civil and Common Law,* laid bare the disdain that the Americans held toward Mexico's civil system:

> [In countries that operate under common law] you perceive the activity, the throng, the tumult of business life. [The] boldness, the impetuosity [of] advancing knowledge and civilization. [In contrast, civil law nations] drift toward stagnation of trade, [f]eebleness of intellect, [and] timidity of spirit.[27]

In another flummery comparison, critics asserted that "self-reliance" was the benchmark of common law while paternalism was the inevitable consequence of the civil system:

> [In common law] when trade is fairly consummated the rights of the parties are fixed, and it becomes too late for retraction. In other words, the common law allows the parties to make their own bargains, and when then they are made, holds them to a strict compliance; whilst the civil law looks upon men as incapable of judging for [themselves], and assumes the guardianship over [them], and interpolates into contracts that which the parties never agreed to.[28]

Langum's account adds that such notions confirm De Tocqueville assertion that "the Americans [owe] nothing to anyone, expect nothing from anyone, and stand without anyone, [for the] gains or losses rest squarely on their own shoulders."[29] An immigrants' idealized vision of proper court proceedings was of one structure, an entity bound by procedures that adjudicate disputes openly, equitably, and, above all, promote personal autonomy. So to say, a common law court was meant to orchestrate an adversarial contest, to decide a winner and a loser, and then administer civil or criminal penalties in accordance with evidence and rules of law. It was meant to implement sanctions without modification, delay, postponement or forgiveness. It was the judge's responsibility to act as referee, to be a neutral observer applying the rules as legislatures intended. On the austerity of sanctions, Langum's offers *The United States v. James* (1894) as representative of the jurisprudential differences between civil and common law:

> From the earliest times the governmental systems of Anglo-Saxon and Latin races have been widely different. Among Latin people, the chief thought has been for their welfare, and advancement as a collective entity. [While among the Anglo-Saxons] the individual always remained the prominent purpose in governmental conception. [T]he progress of the English-speaking people at the highest form of civil and religious liberty is not adventitious or accidental, but is due to this ennoblement of the individual in the conceptions and practices of the English law."[30]

Hovering over the entire process, however, was the conviction that civil law's lack of a jury posed the greatest threat to one's autonomy. In the eyes of the new Californians the publicly appointed jury was a birthright that dated from the *Magna Carta.* Even as the standard explanation offered for serving on a frontier jury (excluding, perhaps, the desire to collect a jury fee) was the individual's intent to assert legal autonomy over the government. In a manner that has diminished only in degree from the ambiance of the 19th century is the public's obsession with self-image. As Langum put it, frontier common law courts adjudicated conflict "by letting the chips fall where they may, so as to gain whole hog or none; it was [the] apogee of rugged individualism."[31]

In the 19th century the right to a jury was a wellspring that nourished the troublesome doctrine of *jury nullification*. Particularly in the west, was jury nullification sacrosanct. American citizens saw it as the quintessential act of freedom from government tyranny. The practice was common in the western territories where it represented independence from the sectarianism of government. Immigrants, rather grandiloquently, described jury service as "the priority of conscience." Only in the jury box, jurors insisted, was the government forced to yield to the citizen. "Law must serve citizens, not citizens the law."[32]

Hence, it was not surprising that a large segment of rootless immigrants, faced with an equivocal legal system and transitory economic prospects, became fertile ground for a host of political hacks and their oft-times dubious schemes of deliverance. Most of these prophets were disillusioned fortune seekers and partisans who had drifted into the state's urban centers to run, and sometimes win, elected office amid the expanding opportunities that were a part of California's growing county and state government. Many were dilettantes with an immoderate but generally fleeting influence on the oftentimes-disorderly politics of the western territories. Living on a financial margin, some of these new bureaucrats embraced variations of populism. Antebellum politics offered a tangled web of populism and *laissez faire* traditionalism. In this mixture was found agrarianism (e.g., Grangers), pro-slavery southerners agitating for western territories congenial to slavery, and urban and rural laborers (more often than not ex-miners, or ex-soldiers) seeking collective co-operatives to protect them from the consequence of California's increasing use of cheap foreign labor—particularly Chinese labor. In addition, there was a class of urban anti-slavery northerners devoted to enlarging their earnings from the easy flow of labor and products.

As a result, the makeup of California's first legislature was in good part an assortment of these transient newcomers: ranchers and homesteaders, city laborers and wranglers, shopkeepers and small-town professionals. It seemed to many that they were in a lifelong battle with others who were, by good fortune or chicanery, the recipients of privilege—barons of industry who, by moving into the western territories, tripled their profits (railroading was the investment *du jour*), plus a handful of land-rich Mexican-Americans with ample reason to fear the approaching penury from an Anglo-Saxon majority. This collection of legislators—privileged white men and their descendants—controlled the state's political fortunes, and were for the most part men with middle-class sensibilities and a dogged self-image as independent frontiersmen.

The push and pull of a counter force, *viz,* democratic populism, had its beginnings in the southern states' workers' suffrage movement, a movement that first made inroads in statehouses as early as 1840. In many respects it was a remarkable era. It was a decade when legislatures were establishing commercial rights for workers living under the restraints of the most limited of means. As a result, workers' suffrage began to elevate the political power of the working classes. Property rights, for example, for both men and women were approved (including a provision shielding a woman's property even after the disillusion of her marriage). Debtors' prisons were disappearing, and for the first time, statutory exemptions on executions became legal. Un-collateralized homesteads were instituted at both federal and state levels for those (white) men who declared themselves willing to settle the west and improve modest patches of a scabrous land. (This policy raised expectations with California miners that finally the despised *sovereign's domain proviso* of the 1848 Treaty of Guadalupe protecting Mexican landholders would be abrogated. It was not to be, however, for only confiscatory taxation would finally separate Mexican-Americans from their land holdings.)

It was also an era when legislatures finally did away with property ownership as a voting requirement, even as Latin and other foreign languages began to fade from courtroom proceedings.[33] Of just as great a moment for the working class was the legislation adopted protecting the purchaser as well as the seller. Many of these reforms owed their origins to the fact that for the first time a debtor class was beginning to take control of the organs of legislation.[34] By mid-century, populist legislators had gained sufficient political numbers to challenge the voting pluralities of even the most hide-bound political institutions.[35] More to the point, a foundation was finally being laid for "workingmen's" unions, that is, it was the beginning of legislative protection for the boycott and the strike—nascent weapons of approaching labor wars.

Two decades later all traces of civil law jurisprudence had disappeared from California courts. It was the culmination of the constitutional directive that first appeared on April 13, 1850. The directive read: "So far as it is not repugnant to, or inconsistent with, the Constitution of the United States or the Constitution or laws of the State of California, [English common law] shall be the rule of decision in all the courts of this State." The directive became Section 4468 of California's Political Code, with statewide enforcement penalties in place by 1873. By then, campsite juries, *ad hoc* juries that satisfied the local community's sense of fairness or retaliation became a thing of the past. But there were other fall-outs as well; thereafter, the California Code declared that the interpretation of law would be restricted to the legal skills of state judges, even as the citizen's responsibility (jury member) would be limited to the "finding of facts." It was a legislative policy, of course, that was fully on the way to blunting the frontiersmen's cherished attachment to the concept of jury *nullification.* It had become a public obsession that later legislatures would conclude had done enough mischief.[36]

In reality, most immigrants had little or no knowledge of their legal institutions, for whatever exposure they might have had of the law's workings was when it intruded into their own lives. For instance, some people might be familiar with promissory notes, or equipment consignments, or travel loans, or marriage contracts—but only on special occasions when they were suing or being sued, or being arrested, or seeking assistance, were they ever likely to see the inside of a courtroom.

By the close of the first decade of statehood 1850–1860, California's exploding agrarian and working classes had become easy converts to various forms of populism. These "laborers' had cultivated a deep mistrust of bankers and industrialists, and the lawyers who represented them. These "workers" had developed a resistive skepticism toward state law and lawyers that ministered its "theoretical" assumptions. Particularly mistrusted were those lawyers who were prolix and obscurant, i.e., lawyers who manifested a "rehearsed obtuseness." Such confusion, so the argument went, was intended to make the lawyers and their clients indispensable. Yet, as the doggerel of mining camps went, "[n]o law was necessary until lawyers appeared." A skeptical migratory population looked upon lawyers, especially those who had labored through legal apprenticeships, not so much as men prepared to serve public interests, but as strangers who were likely to swindle them. From an immigrants' perspective, a "good" lawyer was a person of strong moral character, and the better a lawyer's moral reputation the better his lawyering—moral rectitude was a character trait more likely to be praised than any legal education. Even among legislators there was a propensity to mistrust well-trained lawyers. It was an attitude that, in part, was instrumental in formulating the constitutional provision requiring judicial appointments to be of "short duration and of meager compensation," for "modest compensation," is the test of a truly trustworthy lawyer.

But as common law replaced civil law doctrine, the effect of short governmental terms and modest means proved to be an even greater deterrent to competent judicial candidates than the attorney-phobic legislators could have ever imagined. From the court's inception in 1850, for 15 years the Supreme Court judgeships were caught in a revolving door: Governors were continually called upon to make judicial appointments to replace judges who had more likely resigned than had retired or died. In the state's first decade, for example, there were no less than 10 different chief justices on the California Supreme Court, even as associate justices averaged less than three years *per* appointment. It was a situation that produced a court lacking cohesiveness. The public's preference for common law and untrained lawyers, however, did produce one salutary result—it hastened the day when the state would codify its laws. Codes were essential if there was to be anything resembling a workable state court system. State codes, said its advocates, would "increase the preservation of evidence," the "assessment of predictable adjudication" and "public protection from autocratic judges."[37]

Immigrants, before they had become migrants, wanted a legal structure with limited powers that could be called upon when needed but otherwise ignored; they yearned for what they conceived to be the common law's consistency, replication, permanency, and above all, its limited intervention—for populists and traditionalists alike, the fewer legal restraints in their lives the better. The mid-20th-century legal scholar Roscoe Pound summarized the components that attracted the frontiersmen's veneration of common law. The common law, he said, is its supremacy over the sovereign, its predictable and consistent implementation, and, most of all, its subjection to the authority of an independent jury. Obviously, most emigrants would not have formulated Pound's bookish description—but a desire for personal freedom and limited legal intrusion would have led them to embrace his summary enthusiastically. Pound's analysis was an exact account of why so many immigrants on the western frontier embraced the common law with such fealty.[38]

By joint resolution, both houses of the legislature elected the first three judges to serve on the state's initial court.[39] The chief justice was Serranus Clinton Hastings and the associate justices were Nathaniel Bennett and Henry Augustus Lyons. Hastings, before arriving in California, had practiced law in Iowa and had been its first congressman and first chief justice. (He was just one of innumerable Iowans to find his way to California.) After sitting on the court as chief justice for two years, he resigned to become attorney general, and then solidified his name in California's legal history by establishing the state's first school of law in 1887. Justice Bennett, who began his legal career in the legislature, was acknowledged to be the most productive member of the first court in addition to being the common law's strongest advocate, he was also the most prolific opinion writer. By contrast, Justice Lyons offered a limited number of opinions, but did take over as chief justice after Hastings' resignation. The next year, Bennett resigned and Governor Peter H. Burnett appointed Hugh Murray to serve in his place. Murray was brilliant but quixotic, appointed at age 26 and dead of alcohol poisoning by 32. Yet during his brief tenure, he was the court's most avowed enemy of the "landed-interests" and friend of "migrant miners." Next came the Alabamian Solomon Heydenfeldt, who in 1852 became the first judge to actually earn a seat on the court by winning an election (He succeeded Hastings), as its fifth associate justice. His "workman-like" judicial habits brought a much-needed stability to the sometimes-quixotic court. Sadly, his first appearance in the state was without wife and son, who had been lost to typhoid fever while on the journey to California. The sixth associate justice, Alexander Wells, who came to the bench in 1853 at the age of 59, died a year later, leaving no published legal mark on the court. The seventh associate justice, David Smith Terry, joined the court in 1855 and became the next chief justice upon Murray's death in 1857. He resigned in 1859. The eighth justice, Peter Burnett, born in Tennessee, was elected to the court in 1857 and resigned a year later. Burnett had been the state's first elected governor, but he gained an unfortunate yet enduring reputation on the court with his famous *in re Archy* opinion discussed earlier. In 1857, Stephen Johnson Field joined the court as its ninth associate justice, and in 1859, he became its fifth chief justice. Field was the first college graduate on California's highest bench, and in 1863, he was chosen by Abraham

Lincoln to become the first westerner to sit as an associate justice on the United States Supreme Court. Scholars agree that Field was the most gifted jurist on the early state court. Moreover, he was the most important U.S. justice California produced in the 19th century, and he became the federal bench's most brilliant and effectual legal conservative in the latter half of the century. He held the federal appointment thirty-four years, making his length of service on the nation's highest court, at the time, unsurpassed.[40]

When judging the legal and political influences of the two justices (Terry and Field) whose legal tenures make up the remaining pages of this book, it is fair to say that each man was endowed with the temperament and training that is most congenial to common law jurisprudence. That is, each had a disposition toward reinforcing a doctrine of *settled* law. Each was disposed to assess information analytically with an eye to *stare decisis* (deciding the present case with intent to adhere to past cases), and both men were masters of logical discourse—the indispensable tool, if legal opinions were to carry the important aura of finality—this notion of finality brought to California's superior court a reputation for stability and permanence. But Field, much more than Terry, was more inclined to see the historical importance of protective continuity between civil and common systems as California passed from a Mexican territory into a U.S. state. On the other hand, Field was given to convoluted though brilliant argumentation in an effort to reach a specific ideological destination, while Terry—who was described by the press as a "bundle of logic and brevity"—was inclined to characterize opinions in practical terms, and his colleagues as a bit too pompous. However, the one trait that both judges shared equally was a consummate faith in the wisdom of their own conclusions—each regarded his decisions on matters of the law as legally and morally trenchant. Working together, the two men supplied opinions that strengthened the fledgling court, particularly during the year of 1857 and less so in 1858–59. And even as their opinions become more conflicted their decisions played a germinal role in establishing judicial boundaries for California's inferior courts.

Terry, however, under no illusions when it came to comparing legal skills, often yielded to Field's superb forensic mind even while maintaining a cautious distance from him as a colleague. Field's true feelings regarding Terry, on the other hand, were guarded, notwithstanding his published statements that often praised the chief justice's legal dexterity. Records of conflicting opinions on the court betray Field's uneasiness—his choices of words in published opinions that oppose Terry's decisions were sometimes unnecessarily harsh.[41] Early on, it was Field's recorded traits of Terry's character and temperament that revealed how incompatible these men truly were, even though at the time they shared the bench Field could not have imagined how prescient his comments would prove to be. In Field's *Personal Reminiscences of Early Days in California,* prepared in 1877, he wrote, "Terry was a man of vigorous mind, of generous nature and of positive will, [but he] also had the virtues and prejudices of the extreme South. [H]is contact and larger experience since, with men of the north, have no doubt modified many of [these] prejudices, and his own good sense must have led him to alter some of his previous judgments."[42]

To summarize, at the vortices of conflicting social perspectives that defined California's march toward political and legal stability, were the lives of these two influential jurists. Each man found himself temperamentally drawn to social movements and allies that were in conflict with the other man's goals and allies, and each found it impossible to remain sanguine at the prospect that his adversary's preferences might prevail. Both had lived through the legal and social transitions leading up to statehood, and both would witness the viciousness of the Civil War. Yet most importantly, each was certain that his own view of political and legal institutions was anchored on the moral high-ground—therein one can clearly witness two judges driven by the excesses of zealotry while on a mission to teach the other a lesson.

NOTES

1. Henry Campbell Black. *Black's Law Dictionary*, Fourth Ed. (St. Paul, MI.: West Publishing Co).

2. Oliver Wendell Holmes Jr. *The Common Law* (Boston: Little, Brown, and Co. 1881).

3. By no means were all judges and lawyers incompetent. See: *Law in the West,* David L. Langum, Editor, "Western Lawyers and Judges: Image and Reality."

4. Wunder, John R. *Inferior Courts, Superior Justice: 1853–1889* (WestPoint CT. Green wood Press.1979).

5. Shinn, Charles Howard. *Mining Camps: A Study in American Frontier Government* (New York: Charles Scribners & Sons. 1885). 119.Also, John Wunder in his *Inferior Courts, Superior Courts* makes the case that a distinction is to be drawn between lawless individuals and the lawful procedures of Western courts. Expressly, that embellished folklore of the West as a cauldron of mayhem, must not be confused with the legal system that was in place. Insofar as the Western courts were concerned they were as efficient or as inefficient as courts anywhere in the country. 169ff. Of the 100 or so lawyers who organized the state's first legal society in San Francisco 80 percent declared themselves unwilling to practice "any form of law but common law," the remaining 20 percent (generally southerners) declared only a lukewarm willingness to practice a hybrid form of law under special circumstances. One who was quite prepared to defend a hybrid version of the law was the state's first Governor Peter H.

Burnett. See. Peter H. Burnett. *Recollections & Opinions of an Old Pioneer* (New York: D. Appleton and Company, 1880). 329. Southerners lawyers were less inclined to reject the civil system because many of them had been exposed to it in courthouses along the Mississippi delta (courts under French influence). What is more, it was endemic to southern culture to express distaste for the confrontational rudeness of the English court system, "[these] procedures and behavior in the English courtroom are unduly vulgar and confrontational." In its place, many sons of the south, expressed a preference for "procedures conducted in an honorable and noble fashion, [w]here civility is to be expected from one's judicial adversaries." Of course, northerners were quick to return the insult, mocking southern lawyers as ostentatious patricians. It is this perception that caused northerners to tag southern adversaries with the sobriquet "Chivs" (slang, intended to taunt chivalrous posturing).

6. Nathaniel Bennett. Associate Justice of the California Supreme Court, 1849–1851.

7. Langum, David L. *Law and the Community of the Mexican Frontier.* (Norman OK.: University of Oklahoma Press, 1987). 268–277.

8. In David L. Langum's article, "Californios and the Image of Indolence." *The Western History Association*, vol. 9 1978, points out that it would be misleading to argue that dislike of Mexican [civil law] by the Europeans was solely the result of "racism, imperial ism, or Manifest Destiny". Rather, Mexican lawyering was considered by many as merely "indolent."

9. During the Mexican Revolution of 1810, under the military dictatorship of Miquel de Hidalgo, Mexico established its own new-world version of *Siete Partidas.* By 1824 each district had a magistrate, a *Prefect* (usually called the *alcalde,* (mayor-judge), a sub-prefect or *Juez de paz* (Justice of the Peace) i.e., day-to-day legal administrator. *El Paga dor* (tax collector), and *El Escribano* (town clerk). Overseeing these operations, larger ci ties and towns had councils called *Los Ayuntamientos.* By all measures, however, the most important political officer, from the smallest hamlets to the largest cities, was the alcalde for he was expected to maintain "order and tranquility, and to settle civil and criminal disputes." Litigants in the courts were represented by two community leaders called *Los Hombres Buenos* (trustworthy men—not lawyers). These men were either appointed by the alcalde, or met with his approval. They shared simultaneous duties; and were expected to represent their client, as well as protect the general welfare of the community. The process was a precarious balance of conflicting interests. The losing Hombre Bueno assisted his client in finding a "tranquil face-saving" form of restitution. In cases where the dispute remained unresolved, the litigants' Hombre Bueno prepared a *certify cate of irresolution* enabling the disputants to come before a court of review. At this level, first appeals passed through a district court called the *second bench*, and, if necessary, on to the *first bench,* or *Superior Tribunal.* The Superior Tribunal was Mexico's highest court. It held the label of *the Governor's Court* and consisted of four judges, and the district's Attorney General. In Mexico's California courts these procedures were standardized to include one appeal for a criminal case, two appeals for property claims for less than four thousand dollars, and three appeals for larger amounts.

10. These legal procedures are traceable to Moorish Spain where pleadings before the Alkaldi (alcalde) were settled with one trial. Rarely were these trials appealed. When an appellate hearing was ordered before the Spanish *Court of Records*, the chances that the appeal would be lost or forgotten were not uncommon. Charles Shinn, writes in his popular book *Mining Camps* (1885), that theses courts are deservedly mocked in a refrain from an ancient Iberian play: "Yonder stone wall will rot ere thy law suit ends." Such cases could meander through appellate courts, only to find that the initial oral arguments had been distorted, or even worse, forgotten altogether.

11. A footnoted observation by Langum is worth repeating. "The Mexican period of California [law] has been neglected by historians, perhaps for two reasons." First, the difficulty of reading the hoary Spanish language documents, and second, reading them from [ema- ciated] manuscripts. 44. See also David L. Langum, *Community,* 138–139.

12. Josiah Royce. *California: From The Conquest in 1846 to the End of the Second Vigilance Committee.* (Boston: Houghton, Mifflin Co. 1892). 59.

13. Bayard Taylor, *El Dorado* (Lincoln NE: The University of Nebraska Press. 1949). 76–79.

14. Charles Shinn, 83–84. *Folk-moots.*

15. Franklin Tuthill, *History of California* (San Francisco: Fords Howard & Hubert. 1866). 339.

16. William M. Osborn. *The Wild Frontier* (New York: Random House. 2000). 195.

17. See Charles Albro Baker, Ed. *Memoirs of Elisha Oscar Crosby: Reminiscences of California and Guatemala from 1849–1864* (San Marino CA. Huntington Library Press, 945). 112.

18. Oscar Crosby 112.

19. —— Crosby. 113.

20. *In Re Archy,* 9 Cal., 147 (1857). (Terry supports Burnett).

21. For a comprehensive account of civil and common law see David Langum's, *Law and Community of the Mexican Frontier*. Chapter 5. Also. O.K. Murray, "Seventy-five Years of California Jurisprudence," *California Law Review* XIII no.6 (1925): 445–467. David Bodenhamer. *Fair Trial Rights of the Accused in American History* (New York 1992). Christian G. Fritz. *19thCentury Courts in San Francisco.* "The American Constitutional Tradition. Revisited: Preliminary Observations on State Constitution-making in the Nineteenth Century West." *Rutgers Law Journal,* 25 (1994).

22. David Langum. *Community*. 270–271. See reply to the common law attitude.

23. —— *Community*. 37.

24. —— *Community*. 42.

25. —— *Community*. 36.

26. —— *Community*. 71–73.

27. Cal. State Commission on the Judiciary. Report on Civil and Common Law. 1 Cal.588 (1859). Cited in Langum, *Community* 140.

28. Cal. State Commission. 1 Cal. 595 (1850).

29. Langum 142.
30. U.S. v. James. 60 F. 257, 262 (D. Ill, 1894). Cited in David Langum, 271.
31. David Langum, *Community.* 271.
32. See David M. Gold "Reforming the Civil Jury in the Nineteenth Century." W*estern Legal History*, Vol. 15, November 2, 2002. Gold writes that after 1860 civil juries pressed to determine jury size and render unanimous verdicts. In criminal cases the unanimous verdict of twelve impartial men was expected. Even in civil cases this was often the practice.
33. O.K. Murray, *California Law Review* XIII no. 6 (1925). Obviously not all early legislative reforms were successful; many were unenforceable if public sentiment lagged too far behind legislative directives. For instance, the 1850 constitutional ordinance against dueling had only marginal affect during the state's first decade-and-a-half. For as long as a majority of the community considered "[l]ife's risk, the defense of honor," the dueling restrictions would exist only *de jure* not *de facto*. Usury laws were another area where statutory injunctions outran social practice, little was likely to change so long as there were rapacious lenders available to make loans to stone-broke debtors, note: the legislative act of 1851 that licensed gambling houses even while making lotteries illegal. The celebrated twentieth-century Supreme Court Justice Benjamin Cardozo offers a vivid description of the relationship between behavior and effectual law: "Life casts the molds of conduct which will someday become fixed law. [Yet] it is the law that preserves the molds which have taken the form and shape from life." *California Law Review.* XIII, no. 6, 447.
34. Ibid. 451. Also, O. K. Murray, *An Historical Sketch of the Supreme Court of California:* San Francisco: Bench and Bar, 22–39. J. Edward Johnson, *History of the Supreme Court Justices of California, 1850–1900.* (San Francisco: California Bar Association, 1963. Richard R. Powell, *Compromises of Conflicting Claims: A Century of California Law. 1770–1860.* (1977).
35. —— *Compromises.* . . . 447.
36. By the sixth decade of statehood the courts had accumulated a sizable amount of procedural documentation—codes and cases, digests and proceedings—that greatly improved a citizen's willingness to trust the state's canonical resources as a way of settling grievances. The advent of published rules and records defined the judges' role more precisely; and, as an aftermath, judging became more procedural and less controversial (it became more predictable and less idiosyncratic, which engendered a greater respect for the law).
37. As the power and prestige of the state's judicial branch increased, so did the legislators' misgivings about courts increase. For fear of a diffusion of political power, legislators were determined to reduce the judiciary's growing potency. They established oversight committees and passed innumerable regulations designed to throttle judicial power. The judges' constitutional role, legislators declared, was to decipher the legislative intent of statutes and codes, interpret judicial procedure, render rulings on the admissibility of evidence—but they were not to have any additional oversight role to play. These restrictions also hastened the legislators' authorization of the California Codes of Civil Procedure, and with its final completion and publication in 1873, the last vestiges of the Spanish and Mexican civil law disappeared—as did

the Mexican alcalde and his ancient and "mysterious" rules of civil order. If one were to describe the weakening and final disappearance of civil jurisprudence in California in a word, it would be 'diversity, i.e., too many people with too many legal viewpoints rendering too many directives from too many competing jurisdictions. For the battle with the California Legislature over the right of the California Supreme Court to judge the constitutionality of California Legislature, see *Fowler v. Peirce,* 2 Cal. 165. April 1852; People *v. J. Neely Johnson,* 6 Cal. 499 Jan. 1857; *Johnson v. Fall* 6 Cal. 359, October 1856; *Billings v. Hace* 7 Cal. 1, Jan. 1857 (D.S. Terry dissenting).

38. Murray, O. K., *California Law Review* XIII no. 6 (1925). 451.

39. Article VI, sections 1 through 4, and 10, 15, 16 of California's 1850 constitution consolidates the structure and function of the high court. It declares that the Supreme Court shall consist of a chief justice and two associate justices. Justices will run for office at six-year intervals and the terms of office will be staggered at two-year intervals. The court is to convene for three eight-week sessions, beginning on the first Mondays of March, June, and December. It is responsibility of the Court to affirm, reverse, or modify the actions of lower courts. It is to have appellate jurisdiction over cases exceeding $200, and where the legality of any tax, toll, impost, or municipal fine is under dispute. On criminal matters it is to review felonies where questions of legal interpretation are raised and to hold a power to issue writs of *habeas corpus* (personal liberty writs) as authorized by the legislature—it is a writ that removes a resolution or dismissal of charges against a prisoner. (Americans cherished the common-law writ of *habeas corpus* as a guarantee of freedom from interminable confinement). The state's highest court is also authorized to issue lesser writs of restraint whenever peace and tranquility are threatened, and to maintain court records through the office of a permanent clerk-of-the-court that shall be appointed by the justices. The state is to provide the financial assistance necessary to preserve a printed record of all official proceedings.

40. Carl Brent Swisher. *Stephen J. Field: Craftsman of the Law.* (Washington: Brookings Institution 1930). 449.

41. See. *Hyman v. Read,* 13 Cal. 144 (1857). *McCracken v. City of San Francisco,* 16 Cal. 591 (1860).

42. Stephen J. Field. *Personal Reminiscences of Early Days in California* (New York: De Capo Press. 1968). 101.

Chapter Four

A Judicial Activist

Long after the illusion of overnight fortunes had become for most immigrants a mournful memory, the "Golden State" continued to attract more than its share of drifters—from Europe, Australia, Asia and South America; *Los Filibusteros* (freebooters) the regional Mexicans called them. Some were French, German or Latin American mercenaries biding time until they could march south across the territorial border and take control of what they were convinced was a feckless Mexican government. Others, who came west, were rough, tough English and Irish expatriates from Australia looking for a fortune by the quickest means possible. Editorializing on this steady stream of vagabonds, *The San Francisco Daily Herald* frustratedly declared, "[These] motley restless adventurers ought to return from whence they came."

By mid-decade, however, the glut of freebooters was being replaced by another form of fortune seeker—the "nester," the speculator, merchant, farmer or entrepreneur; people who, no less than the freebooters, were looking for a quick and generous return on their time and effort. Yet, the nesters had a character trait not generally found in California's first wave of "diggers." These were people with a sense of permanence, that is, people with an inclination to put down roots. Initially lawlessness or vigilantism controlled the remote areas of California, but as the mining camps grew into permanent villages and the central valleys' cow-towns turned into shipping hubs for farm and ranch produce, the nesters began to agitate for greater political and judicial stability. "As the gold rush subsided," wrote California's Judge, Earl Pomeroy, "the settlement of California took on a more permanent shape, and self-interest drew men [away from seeking fortunes in the hills] and into public affairs."[1]

However, it must be remembered that the social and political life that emerged in California in the middle "fifties" under the influence of the diggers and nesters had a certain tang to it; expressly it was made up of excessively young males. That meant that while they were ambitious, hard driving and self-serving, they could also be immature, impatient, impulsive and transient. Nine of every 10 members of California's first state Legislature, for example, were under 35—most had been residents for three years or less. In 1855, Governor J. Neely Johnson was an earnest but immature 27; his secretary of state, David F. Douglas, was 35; and eight of the first twelve justices to the state's highest court were in their 20s and 30s. The first chief justice and the catalyst behind the state's first law school, Serranus Clinton Hastings, was 36, while the third chief justice, Hugh Murray, was 29; and the associate justices, Alexander Wells, David Terry and Joseph Baldwin, had barely reached their 30s. Stephen Field, as the ninth justice, was the court's oldest judge at 39. Youthful leadership, of course, has compensations, including vision, zeal, ambition and tireless energy; but it also has its liabilities: impetuosity, intolerance and, most of all, a consummate self-confidence that made thoughts of compromise with one's adversary's seem, at times, almost profane. Public leadership in the hands of youthful visionaries made the prospects for unbridled success or dismal failure hang by the thin reed of impulsive behavior. Early on, maintaining stability in a territory where its youthful inhabitants expected unfettered independence made the conventions of social order seem only as safe as the resolve of the nearest military encampment. As one journalist put it, "[O]ut West [our disputes] are settled by mob-ocracy, and [conformity to] the letter of the law was [the exception, never the rule]." True enough, there were small and growing coteries of lawyers and judges in the larger towns, and in fact, in the largest city in the state, San Francisco, there were enough attorneys to establish a legal society. But there were never jurists enough to represent the many disputants who continued to settle their differences privately on the city streets or in the remote and unknown valleys that ran eastward from a seemingly endless seaboard.

The groups, of many stripes and inclinations—ethnic, religious and financial—that were flooding San Francisco were people who found security in their own diverse and lively parochial enclaves. Seemingly overnight they were able to turn hillside camps of wood and canvas into neighborhoods. But unlike New York City, where a moderately well-established police force had finally become strong enough to impose order across the ethnic boundaries of the boroughs, San Francisco's communities, at mid-century, were generally laws unto themselves. The enforcement of boundaries on the urban encampments fixed territorial limits by parochial fiat, but also created territorial gaps between encampments where armed gangs had room to flourish. One of the most notorious of these roaming gangs called itself the Regulators. In large part, it was made up of cashiered New York military volunteers.

Without asking, it appointed itself San Francisco's constabulary, and because it was considerably stronger than the ill-recruited and understaffed city police force, for a time it answered to no one. Soon, without restraints, its members were able to turn their efforts from "watchmen of the streets" into extortion thugs. They exacted protection fees from small merchants and vendors, and shopkeepers who refused to pay for these unwanted services were quickly driven out of town after witnessing their shops and homes burned to the ground. Cudgels and fires at midnight were their methods of control. They evoked from San Franciscans the sobriquet "Hounds," for, like excited dogs running in packs, the Regulators "hounded" their adversaries until they left town—dead or alive. And as to be expected, their favorite targets were those least able to fight back or least able to pay—poor Mexicans, Native Americans, escaped or released slaves and, above all, the Chinese. In less than a month's time, the Regulators had gone from maintaining a semblance of vigilante order to extorting small merchants, particularly Catholic shop-keepers, and to looting, robbing and killing the powerless.

Eventually, however, it became an unbearable situation, even among established business coalitions. These groups, who were beginning to feel the pinch of economic instability, in a two-month period organized a counterforce called the Committee of Vigilance, whose task it was to drive the Regulators out of town. But unlike most of the hurriedly organized citizens' enforcement groups, San Francisco's Committee of Vigilance had a complex paramilitary structure to it. It had weapons, uniforms, even a motto: *Fiat Justitia Ruat Coelum* (let justice prevail though the heavens fall). It was a motto that seemed to add just the right amount of transcendence to their resolve. "Vigilante" (watchman) committees prior to 1856 were far less productive. One organized in 1851 by William Tell Coleman, a young building-supply and patent-medicine merchant, had a paramilitary cadre that, in a period of three months, produced ninety arrests, twenty-eight deportations and uncounted whippings, banishments and hangings. The principal targets of the 1851 Committee were the "Hounds" and their partners in crime, a gang of Australian ex-convicts called the Sydney Ducks. The Ducks, thinking that there were quick and easy profits to be made, had foolishly followed the Hounds into the maelstrom.[2]

Five years passed, and the disbanded Vigilance Committee of 1851 had become a part of the city's saloon folklore. But by 1856, when things again began to sour for San Francisco's commercial interests, city leaders called for the committee's revival. The merchants and traders were suffering the most serious financial downturn since statehood—and because misfortune always finds an offender, the merchants looked for, and found, a suitable scapegoat in San Francisco's political and judicial establishments.

These two city institutions, disorganized and admittedly corrupt, became a convenient target. Everyone agreed that local political leadership had come to power by stuffing ballot boxes, buying votes and paying thugs to drive off competitors. Corruption, however, was as much a part of the parochial neighborhoods as it was a part of city hall. It began with the local political factions that controlled neighborhood elections and perpetuated private constabularies. In many ways, the citywide institutions had become haplessly ineffective entities while neighborhood wards protected their own interests with internecine agreements that encouraged graft and violence. Indeed, all of San Francisco was being stifled by brawny gangs of thugs who imposed order in their wards for a price—both on the street and in jury boxes. Visiting San Francisco for the first time, Rudyard Kipling's famous regimental sensibilities reflect these conditions when he writes that "the saloon keepers and the Irish immigrants control politics in San Francisco."[3]

But, when it came to corruption, the merchant class was hardly blameless, for in an era of competitive excesses many merchants and tradesmen engaged in reckless financial gambles that were well beyond their reach. These engagements were so tenuous, in fact, that when in 1854 a recession struck San Francisco, many merchants were ill-prepared for the falling revenue that unfettered commercialism had produced. Prospectors and homesteaders in the state's interior had become accustomed to these erratic "boom" and "bust" cycles, but city merchants had enjoyed only a steady growth of prosperity since the Argonauts began arriving in 1849. The trade and supply industries, for example, had become increasingly more speculative, even while commodities and real estate buying on credit increased—and more often than not the collateral posted in buying and selling remained risky or unsecured. But chasing profits with promises rather than collateral was dangerous business, and without the usual legal restraints, prudence disappeared as a virtue, and eventually only the underwriters could depend on making money. It is fair to say that a lack of restraints on investment and inadequate financial stabilization had as much to do with the misfortunes of San Francisco's merchants as did the corruption that infected the city's political and judicial establishments.

San Francisco's merchants, however, had no inclination to direct their energies toward reforming a shaky financial system. On the contrary: they focused resentments on political adversaries, on a graft-ridden police force, an inconsistent and unjust court system, a 4 percent commercial tax, encampment squalor and, above all, "the foreigner drifters and shell-game artists that were flooding town." The Harvard philosopher Josiah Royce, who had spent his early years in San Francisco, had a better grasp of the community's situation than did most of its citizens. "[It was a] businessman's revolution," he wrote, "That needed to deal less with violence and more with corruption. [I]t had less need for brawny policemen and more need for commercial statutes, financial detectives and investigators."[4] Royce was primarily interested in overcoming the area's selfishness, says one contemporary analyst.[5]

The 1856 flashpoint for the return of the vigilantes (*posse comitatus*) was not, however, financial mismanagement or even political and legal chicanery. Rather, it was the death of two of San Francisco's most prominent citizens. The first to die was William H. Richardson, U.S. Marshal for the District of San Francisco. Richardson was shot and killed by Charles Cora on November 19, 1855. Details of the killing were conflicted by partisanship, but there was enough agreement among bystanders to enable San Franciscans to draw whatever conclusions they wished. Newspapers reported that on the evening of the 18th of November, Cora, a 130-pound, grandiloquent gambler and miscreant, had escorted Arabell Ryan, one of San Francisco's most nefarious madams, to opening night at the opera. Cora and Ryan (or, as she was known, "Belle Cora"), as it turned out, were sitting in choice and expensive seats directly behind General Richardson and his wife. The Richardsons, visibly annoyed with the "profane" couple at their backs, became ever more so when Ryan and Cora, having lost interest in the musical offerings, began making rude, loud, disrupting remarks. It was reported that it all started when Richardson's wife objected to being stared at by Belle Cora.[6] At one point the Marshal had had enough—he made his feelings known to the pair, but the gambler and his demi-rep remained unrepentant and seemed eager to double their clamor in an effort to further annoy the Marshal and his wife.

The following evening Richardson, whom the news journalist James O'Meara describes as a morose man of low stature, dark complexion, black hair and a bulldog look, was to be found in the city's popular Blue Wing Saloon, bemoaning to listeners his night at the opera, when who should step through the barroom door but the prurient Cora himself. Sensing that cheap brandy had put Richardson in a dangerous mood, Cora attempted an apology, but the general refused to accept it and challenged Cora to take the disagreement to a more corporeal level. Friends and patrons intervened and drinks were poured to sooth frayed nerves, but later that night, after extra alcohol had served only to make the situation worse, Richardson, still unmollified, again demanded that Cora step outside and settle their differences. This time, without the intervention of erstwhile friends, the two men went outside alone. Each carried a derringer—but it was Cora who would fire a single unwitnessed shot into Richardson's chest. It was reported to have happened in front of the well-known Fox & O'Connor Liquor emporium.[7]

One evening later, the rabble-rousing *Evening Bulletin* offered an incendiary and one-sided account of the episode. The *Bulletin*'s editor, James King of William (William, so as not to be confused with the other Kings living in

San Francisco) railed against Cora, claiming that the gambler had shot an unarmed man (most knew that Richardson always carried two loaded derringers). Citizen agitation only grew greater the following day when San Franciscans learned that Cora's consort, Arabell Ryan, had hired some of the best lawyers in town "to get her companion off." It was rumored that Cora's lawyers would argue that Cora was defending himself. A trial quickly ensued but it proved to be a messy affair, with both sides accusing the other of jury tampering (both sides were correct). When the verdict to hang was handed down, most city residents seemed to be satisfied and quickly turned their attentions to other matters.

Almost six months had passed when the *Evening Bulletin's* bombastic King again stirred up the news business; he himself was shot to death by County Supervisor James P. Casey. Casey's penchant for ballot-box stuffing as a "shoulder striker" and "election bully," and the heavy-handed treatment of his enemies had made him one of the most disliked supervisors in San Francisco.[8] King argued that Casey should be run out of town because he was a supervisor not be trusted, and to that end, he felt it necessary to remind his readers that Casey, a former New Yorker, had served eighteen months in Sing-Sing Prison for first stealing and then selling the apartment furniture of a one-time girlfriend. An aggrieved Casey, who believed that "what was past was past," confronted King in his office on the morning of May 14, 1856, demanding a printed retraction and apology. King turned his back on the supervisor, refusing even to discuss the matter.

At day's end, as King was preparing to leave his office, the silhouetted figure of Casey appeared in the shadows striding rapidly along Montgomery Street toward King. Casey, it seemed, still in high dudgeon from the morning's humiliation, was determined to shoot it out with King. Moving into the middle of the street about forty paces from King, Casey challenged him to draw his pistol and settle the matter (King had often stated in his newspaper that he never went anywhere without his five-barreled pistol). As he had in the morning, again King chose to ignore Casey's challenge, and hoping to avoid any further confrontation, ducked into the open doorway of the nearby Pacific Express office, at the corner of Montgomery and Washington Streets. By this time, however, the enraged supervisor would not be put off. He rushed toward King, leveling his pistol as he ran. The weapon discharged, sending a single bullet slamming into the newspaperman's shoulder just above the heart. The bullet's force staggered King and he fell backward into the doorway of the Express office. Startled express workers hastily dragged him to safety, while the now anxious Casey, having regained his wits and fearing reprisals from a surly crowd, hurried off to Sheriff David Scannell's office and turned himself in—more for protection than for compliance. Back at the express office, it was decided that King was too seriously wounded to be moved, so a makeshift convalescent station was fashioned in the rear of the building. A doctor was called, but to no avail, and two days later King was dead. Many believed that he died not from the bullet but from inept medical treatment of the physician. The bullet, the rumor went, would not have been lethal on its own, for it had spent itself passing through King's heavy tunic, printer's coat, waist coat and wool shirt.

With the death of King, the city was ablaze with calls for righteous recompense, and if these were not met, then insurrection. It was a state of affairs that the *Bulletin,* whose masthead ironically proclaims, "YOU CAN'T DODGE THE BULLETIN," was more than eager to foment. The paper demanded that the Vigilance Committee be reactivated. It was time, it declared, for the city to avenge the deaths of Richardson and King. "[The city leaders must] immediately call a halt to the disorder and lawlessness that was making San Francisco unsafe for [us] respectable citizens."

William Coleman, the 32-year-old former leader of the Vigilance Committee of 1851, was eager to answer the call. "Duty and justice demand that I convene the Vigilance Society straightaway," he announced grandly. At the urging of the *Bulletin* (now being edited by King's brother), Coleman drew together prominent San Francisco businessmen—"the group of thirteen" the newspaper dubbed them—men of means who overnight were able to raise enough money to finance the committee for almost two months. With money in hand, Coleman then appointed an "Executive Committee of Forty-one," who were charged with the task of appointing an officers corps and recruiting the troops necessary to control the city. Finding volunteers did not prove to be difficult. Within twenty-four hours, the committee had 2,000 volunteers, and by the end of the sixth week, their ranks had swollen to (a disputed) 7,000 disillusioned miners, financially depressed workers and ex-soldiers who had either retired or had been cashiered.

Only one task now needed attention—finding an appropriate headquarters. This was resolved when the committee rented a string of second-floor rooms above shops in a block of brick buildings called the Truitt buildings. They were located on the southeast corner of Front and Sacramento Streets and ran an entire block along Sacramento Street. These buildings were to serve as the committee's headquarters. Displayed prominently over the entrance of one of the buildings was a banner that harkened back to the days of the now ennobled 1851 Vigilance Committee. "Let justice prevail though the heavens fall," it declared, and above the banner was stenciled a large mythic "All-Seeing Eye"—a reminder to all passer's by that the laws of governments were temporal but true justice was eternal. Finally, as a means to call the citizen-militia to arms in an instant, the committee suspended a gargantuan metal triangle on the roof at the tallest point (it was a gift from a nearby fire department). When the triangle was struck, citizens claimed, it resonated across the misty bay as far as the hills and canyons of Oakland. The outside walls of the fortress were stacked ten feet high with a breastwork of sandbags—thick enough to repel any bomb thrower. Members of the committee soberly referred to their bunker-like relic as "Fort Vigilance," but its detractors had a less estimable term for it: "Fort Gunnybags."

Once organized but fearful of reprisals, an initial policy of the committee was to keep volunteers' identity secret by issuing identification numbers and passwords. But this precaution was soon discarded by many recruits who demanded, for financial reasons, that their names appear "unencoded on payroll records." Being a secret militia was of little concern to the volunteers who knew that they were easily identified by their next-door neighbors. Payroll records confirmed the obvious—the majority of the volunteers were Northern Europeans, with a smattering of Irishmen. There were, of course, no Mexicans, no Chinese and no "fugitive" African-Americans. Finally, the matter of acquiring arms and ammunition did not prove to be much of a problem, for most volunteers either had their own arms or had brought rifles with them from the state's armories when they deserted the militia to join the "citizens'" crusade.

Initially a large majority of San Franciscans welcomed the return of the Vigilance Committee, even though several factions in the city publicly opposed it—specifically, members of the legal and political establishments and members of the policeman and fireman guilds. There was a sizable number of southerner "Chivs" who had been active leaders in the Vigilance Committee of 1851 who also opposed its return. Led by southerners, they formed a competing organization called the Law and Order Society—a name they had taken from the city's original Law Officers' Society of 1849. This Society was made up mostly of members of the police and fire departments and the southern members of the state militia's officer corps, most of whom had been members of the Vigilance Committee of 1851. The protesters included men who had been in southern politics or had been veteran officers in the Mexican War (in contrast, the Vigilance Committee proudly proclaimed that "no politicians, judges, or lawyers are to be found in [our] ranks").

In point of fact, both sides eagerly recruited, but the Vigilance Committee had much the easier time filling their ranks—more than two-thirds of those who volunteered signed up with the vigilantes. It was a disparity of numbers that virtually rendered the Law and Order Society constabulary powerless as a countervailing force.

The boyish governor of the state, J. Neely Johnson, facing the vigilantes with an undermanned militia and little more than the impatience and abrasive vocal support of the Law and Order Society, did not flinch from his duty—he did what he believed he must do. On May 16, 1856, the afternoon steamer from Sacramento brought him to San Francisco where, with much fanfare, he rode the governor's carriage to Turnverein Hall in the center of the city.[9]

When Johnson met the vigilante's "Commanding General," William Coleman, he was optimistic about the meeting, for they had once been friendly business rivals in Sacramento. Johnson told Coleman that he was ready to bargain. He offered Coleman the heads of Cora and Casey in exchange for a pledge to disband the Vigilance Committee—he was, he declared, even prepared to concede that Cora and Casey were dangerous malefactors and deserved to be executed. All Johnson asked was that the two be tried in a proper fashion before the appropriate state tribunal. "Find them guilty, then hang them," it was reported that Johnson had said.

Coleman appeared to be interested. But, by noon of the next day the peace agreement had vanished. In reality, Coleman was unable to convince his comrades that such an accommodation with the governor was in any manner a bargain that would work in the committee's favor. Most of the Committee of Forty-one refused to support any agreement that declared that once Cora and Casey were disposed of, the vigilantes would disband—the Committee believed they were just getting started.

Reasons for this are convoluted, but one of the major factors was their conviction that the committee leadership would be unable to persuade the street troops and their leaders to accept such compromise. The troops, who were now well organized and clamoring for a fight, were in no mood to strike a bargain with the feckless young governor.[10] As a consequence, on the evening of May 17, Coleman knavishly insisted that Johnson had completely misunderstood their discussion the day before; he denied that he had ever consented to turn over Cora and Casey to the state (notwithstanding the testimony of a number of witnesses, including a statement from the yet-to-be-renowned William Tecumseh Sherman). Insofar as the street commanders were concerned, there was no misunderstanding—with two divisions drilling in the streets and their ranks swelling 50 recruits a day, they saw no reason to strike a bargain with the governor. The next morning, to underscore their point, the troops, 2,500 strong, marched to the barricades of the city jail and demanded that Cora and Casey be released into their custody—even aiming brass cannon at the jail door and holding a lighted wick aloft above it. Sheriff David Scannell, powerless to resist, turned over the prisoners to a street captain and his soldiers and retreated into his ever-constricting jailhouse with an accumulating sense of rage.

This episode served as a metaphor for the endemic weakness that lay on both sides of the conflict. For his part, the governor was naive to think that he and his undermanned militia had any bargaining capacity with San Francisco's financially powerful business community. Yet on the other hand, it was equally gullible for Coleman and his cadre of businessmen to believe that the mercenaries they had so eagerly and indifferently recruited would be willing to be totally submissive to their control. Unfortunately, the governor was being squeezed from both sides. The Vigilance Committee judged him to be immature, flaccid and obstructionist (even as his own state militia and Law and Order Society considered him irresolute and disorganized). To a degree, the critics were right. At 27, Johnson suffered alternately from credulity and suspicion. In retrospect, however, he suffered more scorn than he deserved, for one might easily judge him to be decisive and courageous—at times acting almost alone. In San Francisco, a town choking with "codfish aristocrats," Johnson's attempt at compromise was maligned as either meddling or mollycoddling, or both, but for the most part, he took the only course of action he had open to him—there were times during his dealings with the vigilantes when his title as governor was the sum of his authority. Moreover, his enemies had never thought him capable of the job, convinced that his election to the office had been wholly a mistake of "the political times."

Thursday, May 22, Cora's and Casey's fates were sealed. A public trial was held in front of Fort Gunnybags that was nothing short of theater—debatably a half step above lynch law. Coleman began the proceedings by assuring Cora and Casey that they could expect a fair trial because no lawyers were present (much laughter). But justice and fairness were hardly the order of the day. It was a *trial de novo*, a trial without the legal protections of a bona fide court—without due process, or defense witnesses (who would be so foolish?), or a *writ of clemency*, or a *review of extenuation* or a change of *venue*. But above all, it was a trial without any possibility of appeal. The prisoners were forbidden to raise a plausible argument of self-defense, and they were not allowed to plead for imprisonment—to be convicted was to hang. The trial took two days to find them guilty and on the third day they were hanged without provisions "for the dying" many said. Although as Roman Catholics they were the offered the rites of absolution, they were not offered the comfort of their families. At 1 p.m. on the 22nd of May, the two were twisting from ropes strung from a second-floor window beam at Fort Gunnybags. Afterward, the "party" onlookers agreed: Coleman knew how to slake the thirst of a mob looking for a moment of amusement.

On the day Cora and Casey were hanged, a cortege of eighty carriages wound its way through the streets of San Francisco on its journey to Lone Mountain Cemetery, where James King of William preceded Cora and Casey into the ground. He had died at 34, the father of six children, while Cora and Casey remained in the heart of city, buried in the cemetery at the Mission Dolores.[11]

Having "hanged somebody," Governor Johnson hoped that the committee would disband—but it did not. The hangings only whetted the street soldiers' appetite for more "hasty justice." The euphoric mobs had convinced the governor that these two executions were just the beginning of the committee's effort to purge the city of "undesirables." If he were ever to get San Francisco under control, Johnson reasoned, he must convince Coleman that his refusal to disband would close the door on amnesty for the committee's leadership. To this end, Johnson turned to his officer in charge of the state militia, William Tecumseh Sherman.

After the Mexican War, in which Sherman had been a junior logistics officer, he had come to California to manage the San Francisco branch of his family's Saint Louis banking company. Sherman was a brilliant but moody—and at times a bit fey—36-year-old executive whom Johnson had coaxed into the position only days before. Initially, Sherman showed little interest in the job, insisting (correctly) that the state was much too short on both ordnance and troops to face down the Vigilance Committee. But he delayed a final answer until he had talked it over with his wife, Ellen, for, as he said, he was worried that without a show of force, the state could easily degenerate into a scattering of vigilante-run townships—a state of affairs he knew full well would be bad for the banking business. His wife eventually gave him lukewarm support, and so he accepted the governor's offer. Oddly, Sherman insists that it was mere accident that Johnson had appointed him to the rank of Major General of the California Militia one day before King was shot.[12]

Immediately Sherman discovered that his suspicions had been well-founded—no amount of coaxing or inducement seemed to make a difference in the size of the state's militia. For every soldier he signed into the militia, another resigned; or, what was worse, signed up with the vigilantes. After Sherman's best efforts, he had only about three hundred troops—and San Franciscans were scoffing at the ineptitude of his militia. Most considered it little more than a "bluff and bluster" drilling club. But not only were the ranks of the militia minuscule, so too was the supply of ordnance in the state armories—there was a disheartening handful of rifles, many of which lacked parts or were likely to misfire, and at best, a three or four days' supply of ammunition.

Acknowledging Sherman's assessment of the ordnance problem, Johnson proposed that he and Sherman seek out General John E. Wool, commanding general of the federal ordnance base at Benicia. (Wool had served as Zachary Taylor's second in command in the Mexican War and was now commandant of the United States Army of the Pacific, headquartered at the northern end of the San Francisco Bay). Together Johnson and Sherman traveled to Benicia to meet with Wool. After considerable discussion, the two men came away with different versions of what Wool had said. Johnson believed that Wool had pledged federal help in fighting the vigilantes. Sherman did not. Apparently, each heard what he expected to hear, yet the confusion was not entirely of their making. Wool's response was so ambiguous that contradictory interpretations were easy to draw; "no person," he told them, "except the President of the United States could grant arms or munitions to a State in case of an insurrection, but a case might arise when a General of a division might take the responsibility and that this situation might be one of them."[13] In the governor's mind, this meant a commitment, but Sherman remained unsure, unable to shake off the ambiguity of Wool's use of the verb "might."

With everything very much up in the air, Chief Justice David Terry decided that it was now time for him to step down from the Supreme Bench and join the fray. It was time, he reasoned to support Governor Johnson's jurisdictional fight with General Wool and the Vigilance Committee. Terry and Secretary of State David Douglas had been urging toughness with the vigilantes from the outset. Both men were champing to mix in the melee publicly—in particular, Terry's sense of southern honor required open allegiance to Governor Johnson. From the outset, Terry had overseen the state committee raising money for the militia's assorted deficiencies. He was now yearning to confront "these renegades face to face"—"to face them down," he often said, "to charge them with treason," for both Terry and Douglas were convinced that all that was needed was a show of strength "[and] these cowards would cave."

Terry goaded Johnson to confront Wool, to insist that the general stop equivocating and declare publicly that the Vigilance Committee's actions were seditious. To that end, Terry proposed a plan to force the General's hand. He would send a writ of *haebus corpus* directing the Vigilance Committee to release Billy Mulligan, one of the city's jailors, whom they had been holding in a cell at Fort Vigilance for more than two weeks. Mulligan was a tough-talking, combative, southern plug-ugly whom the *San Francisco Chronicle* once described as "a bully, a ballot box stuffer, and a shoulder striker." Mulligan, who was a member of the Law and Order Society, had been arrested by the Vigilance Committee's investigative unit on charges that the committee described as "subversive activities." Terry had chosen to make Mulligan an issue partly because they had been comrades in arms during the Mexican War and partly because he knew Mulligan's defiant attitude would make him a difficult man to release. If the committee chose to ignore the writ, Terry reasoned, then Wool would have no choice but to intervene on the governor's behalf or face the charge that he was deliberately ignoring state and federal law. As Terry hoped, the committee ignored the writ and even went so far as to publicly declare that Sheriff Scannell had no legal authority to serve such a writ. On cue, Johnson wired Scannell asking him if he "required a military force [to] execute any process, civil or criminal." The Sheriff replied (as Terry had predicted), "I do, there is a combination [of armed men] here to resist the law, which cannot be put down without exercising the military power of the State." In response to Scannell's warning, Johnson exacerbated the situation by proclaiming that "all of San Francisco was in a state of insurrection," and that "members of the state militia living in the region [were to report to their armories] and await orders from Major General William Sherman."[14] As much as Sherman's loyalties were with San Francisco businessmen he also saw a greater threat if the Vigilance Committee was left unchecked. For unchecked they could become a fixed institution, and "a part of common law in California."[15]

In so far as General Wool was concerned, the committee's refusal to accept the chief justice's writ changed nothing. On June 5, Johnson received word from Wool that he was planning no action against the Vigilance Committee. It was, Wool wrote, a matter between the state and its citizens. The federal government had neither the jurisdiction nor the inclination to intervene. "Only the President has the authority to grant such a request, [and] I shall act only on orders from the President of the United States," Wool declared. At least this time, thought Sherman, Wool has declined Johnson's request for assistance without ambiguity. Speculating (without evidence) on the circumstances that unfolded, at least two events may have solidified Wool's intransigence. On the one hand, subsequent to the Johnson and Sherman visit, Wool and his naval counterpart, commodore of the Pacific Squadron and commander of the Naval Base on Mare Island, Captain David G. Farragut, were reported to have met with the Vigilance Committee's representative John Farwell over tankards of ale. Farwell reassured the commanders that the Vigilance Committee would be careful not to appropriate or destroy any federal properties or installations. "The federalists have nothing to fear from the Vigilance Committee, but they do have a duty to remain neutral," Farwell insisted. Guardedly, he reminded the senior officers of what they faced were they to attempt to intervene: "[A] majority of citizens support the Committee," and it would be unwise and precipitous for the small federal force to challenge the committee's 5,700 troops who were "standing at the ready."

Meanwhile, the governor, despite bad news from General Wool, was still unwilling to accept the matter as settled. Terry and Douglas insisted that the governor had not been forceful enough. Eventually, if enough pressure was put on him, General Wool would "honor his promise," they reasoned. Wool, on the other hand, continued to resist, while openly declaring that Johnson's passions were causing him to deliberately misunderstand his position. Johnson was, Wool insisted, driven by the "secret desire of the heart"[16] In contrast, Sherman, having been pessimistic about Wool's support from the outset, now seized on the moment to get out from under the entire mess by resigning. Nevertheless, Johnson insisted that Sherman meet him in Benicia at General Wool's headquarters where they would discuss both Wool's edict and Sherman's plan to resign.

They met in Benicia the following day. Their meeting became a series of meetings, beginning in Wool's headquarters, then later moving on to a room above a tavern a block from the headquarters, and ending in two spontaneous meetings on the wharf while various participants awaited steamers that would take them west to San Francisco or east to Sacramento. When Sherman showed up he was accompanied by a half-dozen businessmen who were not members of the Vigilance Committee. These men made a proposal that they believed would resolve the standoff between the governor and the vigilantes: The governor would be well served to publicly acknowledge support for the Vigilance Committee's actions "thus far," they insisted, thereby assuring the committee leaders that no legal repercussions would follow once matters were settled. In return, the committee would publicly pledge to begin the process of disbanding their forces.[17]

Thus were the circumstances when two dozen disgruntled men (including some of Terry's Texas friends) crowded into Wool's headquarters—a cramped meeting room over the well-worn hotel lobby that was Benicia's only traveling inn. "Controlled disarray" best describes what followed. Recriminations went in many directions. Johnson and Sherman were angry at Wool for having reneged on his "promise" to support the militia (the governor refused to answer any questions on this matter except in writing). Wool, for his part, was angry at Johnson for intentionally choosing to misunderstand their initial conversation. On the one hand, Sherman and the business delegation were angry and mistrustful of Johnson and Terry, and Terry's volatile Texas interlopers. On the other hand, Terry and his friends were angry at the business delegation for its insistence on amnesty for "traitors and renegades." Terry and the southerners—in particular Volney Howard and E.D. Baker (Baker was the lawyer who had produced a hung jury in the Cora trial)—were opposed to any compromise that rewarded the Vigilance Committee for what they had already done. Sherman recounted the edgy affair:

> All were talking furiously against Wool, denouncing him as a d— liar, and not sparing the severest terms. [Then the discourse] broadened to include the Vigilance Committee. David Terry took part in the discussion and was vehement in his utterances [characterizing] the members of the Vigilance Committee as a "set of damned sour flour and pork merchants" who had become frightened [of the rebellious mobs] and were in collusion with General Wool to bring the state into contempt.[18]

It is noteworthy that, on earlier occasions, Sherman had praised Terry, applauding his "courage and honesty." But on this particular day, he attached most of the blame for failing to reach a compromise on "the Texans" and, in particular, on the at-times-sullen and at-times-contentious Terry. Sherman characterized the chief justice as a petulant stumbling block—sitting, he wrote, with his hat over his eyes and his feet propped upon the conference table, scowling and protesting loudly whenever the subject of compromise was raised. Sherman's final assessment of Terry (one suspects properly) was that he was a heroic fool, who had completely misjudged the strength and resolve of his adversaries. Conversely, the suspicious Terry believed that Sherman and his business partners had been cut from the same cloth as the contemptible Vigilance Committee, and that their appearance in Benicia was no less than an effort to save their own corpulent hides—in other words, this was an effort to rescue their businesses from the growing threat of street anarchy. Terry argued that the businessmen had become fearful that looters and thugs might soon cause them to lose money. When, as was inevitable, these discussions ended in failure, Sherman did what he had intended to do from the outset. He resigned. Wool's refusal to support the militia had made Sherman a major general without an army; and Johnson's refusal to accept a compromise had made him a bargain-maker without a bargain.

Perhaps the governor was hoping for as much; perhaps he and Terry had discussed replacing "Cump" Sherman on the trip down from Sacramento to Benicia. For without protest or further discussion, the governor accepted Sherman's resignation and straightway appointed the Texan Volney E. Howard to take command of the state militia.[19] (Howard had been a southern congressman and would later become a politically successful lawyer in southern California.) Sherman was relieved to be out from under the confusion and a helpless command, for he was now free to return to San Francisco and concentrate on managing the banking business. He was anxious to return and patch up his differences with the commercial community. For many San Franciscan businessmen, however, the damage had been done, and they would never forgive Sherman, believing that he had betrayed his "own class." The historian Hubert Howe Bancroft would later write that the Vigilance Committee was quite prepared "to string him up as [one] would a dog [if he continued to interfere with the] crusade."[20]

Years later, after Sherman's fame had been secured by his exploits in the Civil War, he wrote in his memoirs that a "soldierly sense of honor and loyalty" had prevented him from condoning the Vigilance Committee's lawless behavior, no matter what the personal cost might have been. Nevertheless, his very brief incursion into California politics had angered many and pleased almost no one. In point of fact, only the vigilantes seemed to benefit from the combustible meeting in Benicia. Everyone else was at loose ends, and the governor, almost powerless, was left searching for a way around Wool's neutrality.

A fortnight later, Terry, poring through law books, offered Johnson what seemed to be a way out of his predicament. He proposed the implementation of a rarely used federal emergency-powers statute requiring the federal government, upon a governor's request, to turn over to a "state or commonwealth" a proportional allotment of the arms and munitions that were being housed in the state's armories. The next day the newly appointed commander of the militia, Major General Volney Howard, sheltered with this obscure directive, appeared before Wool and informed him of his legal obligation. Wool, who, along with Farragut, was by now beginning to steer a studied neutrality between the warring sides, agreed to release a modest cache of weapons and ammunition to General Howard. And modest is an understatement—Wool released 113 rifles and one saber.[21] The federal naval agent in San Francisco, Dr. R. Porter Ashe—another of Terry's Texas comrades and a member of the Law and Order Society—was assigned the task of transporting this paltry cache from the ordnance center in Benicia to a state armory in San Francisco. He chartered the private schooner *Julia* for the 50-mile round trip from San Francisco and ordered militiamen James Reuben "Rube" Maloney, James McNabb and John G. Phillips to bring the rifles south into the city.

Somehow the Vigilance Committee got wind of the plan (perhaps through Wool) and dispatched John Durkee and a squad of 12 bay-going vigilantes to intercept the *Julia* as she lay anchored off San Pablo point, 15 miles north of San Francisco. Each boarder was armed with a "Colt" and quickly subdued the three-man Law and Order militiamen. Thus before dawn, on June 21, the *Julia* was firmly in the hands of the vigilantes.[22] At noon, Durkee and the victorious boarding party marched the three captives to Fort Vigilance where, with great fanfare, troops were turned out, and Maloney, McNabb and Phillips were publicly declared prisoners of war.[23] However, after several hours of pointless interrogation they were judged of no further use and released. No sooner had they been released, however, than the committee sent orders to have them re-arrested. The re-arrest order declared that they had been heard slandering the committee in the local bay-front saloons (which was doubtless true), and hence had become subversives. A more plausible explanation for the committee's change of heart was suggested in Sherman's memoirs. Maloney and McNabb, Sherman wrote, as members of the state militia, were qualified to file a complaint before the federal District Court claiming that the committee had pirated U.S. property—an act that would give Wool an excuse (if he wanted one) to intervene on the governor's behalf.

Apparently someone at committee headquarters, recalling their promise to Wool not to expropriate federal property, alerted committee authorities of their possible predicament.

While rumors swirled in the downtown saloons that the committee was looking for the three militiamen, the commander at the fort ordered Sterling Hopkins and members of its newly formed vigilante constabulary to find Rube Maloney and Jim McNabb and bring them again to vigilance headquarters. Hopkins, celebrated as the one who had sprung the scaffold door beneath the feet of Cora and Casey, had a reputation as a hard-bitten, foolhardy drifter. But Hopkins knew where to look for Maloney and McNabb—at Colonel Ashe's office at the Palmer-Cook Bank Building. This office served as the headquarters of the Law and Order Society. Finding Maloney at the Law and Order Society's headquarters was easy, but arresting him became another matter. When Hopkins reached Ashe's office, he found himself facing a dozen militiamen who straightway made it clear that they were not prepared to turn Maloney over to the Vigilance Committee. In the office that afternoon there was Ashe and Ashe's business partner, Hamilton Bowie, and the chief justice of the California Supreme Court, David S. Terry. The tough-talking Hopkins, imbued with a mindless courage that sometimes crossed the line into recklessness, moved quickly toward Maloney, but he was intercepted by the equally unyielding chief justice, who identified himself and demanded that the constable produce a warrant for Maloney's arrest.

Hopkins, surprised by the chief justice's presence and realizing that he was out-numbered, retreated into the street where he commandeered a horse and set off for reinforcements. As he rode off he ordered a companion, Horace Russell, to stay behind and keep an eye on Maloney. The Ashe crowd, sensing that Hopkins was off in search of reinforcements, armed themselves and made for the safety of the Jackson Street Armory—the militia at the armory, the Marion Rifles Brigade, was one of only a handful of militias in San Francisco that had remained loyal to the governor. A few minutes later, as Ashe and Terry and their henchmen approached the armory, they were overtaken by Hopkins and a squad of well-armed reinforcements from the fort. This time, with decidedly more at stake, the constable renewed his demand: "Hand over Maloney; I'm placing him under arrest." Again Terry refused, insisting that Hopkins produce an arrest warrant. "Without it," he snapped, "you have no authority to arrest anyone." Hopkins, sensing that he must act before the convoy reached the security of the armory, ignored Terry's challenge and waved his partners forward in an effort to push by the militiamen and take Maloney forcibly. Leading the assault, Hopkins singled out Terry, and the chief justice, knowing what was coming, raised his rifle chest-high to brace for the attack. In an instant the two men were chin to chin. Hopkins grasped Terry's rifle with both hands and pushed the barrel down and away, but at the same moment—whether by accident or design was never determined—Hopkins' companion, Horace Russell, discharged a pistol. The weapon sent a bullet hissing past the chief justice's left ear. It was all that it would take to set off Terry into his well-know trigger-quick rage. Releasing his grip on the rifle, he drew his Bowie knife from his shoulder scabbard and thrust it forward into Hopkins' neck. Instantly the policeman dropped onto his knees clutching his neck howling in pain as a spasm of blood seeped through his fingers. His comrades, so unnerved by the vision of their bloodied leader, retreated into the Pennsylvania Engine House, dragging the caterwauling Hopkins with them.

The retreat gave Terry and his men enough time to reach the armory. However, once behind the walls of the armory, they quickly realized that they were hardly better off than they had been on the streets. A crowd of irate vigilantes surrounded the armory calling for the hanging of everyone within the armory—Terry and Ashe and a band of seven, plus 16 exceedingly surprised and frightened militiamen. Sherman captured the scene: "[It was] such a tumult as I have never witnessed. The Vigilante bell pealed forth its wildest clangor, and men ran, calling hang him, hang him! [C]rowds of people with muskets and swords and pistols poured up Jackson Street, and a dense mass of men filled the street from Montgomery to Stockton."[24] Later, word passed through the crowd that Hopkins had died (he had not), and the anger of the mob grew—they began battering at the doors, even as they called for a hangman. Trapped and without a chance of escape, Terry and Ashe sent word over the parapet that they wanted to surrender. Shortly, William Coleman appeared on the scene and agreed to the surrender, but only after getting the concession that all city armories under the control of the Law and Order forces were to be turned over to the Vigilance Committee. Without the governor's approval but with few options available, Ashe and Terry agreed. Word of their capitulation seemed to calm the mob, for minutes later the anxious militiamen walked out of the fortress into a cacophony of cursing, but becalmed, men and into the arms of a full company of vigilantes. Terry and Ashe and their companions were quickly transported down Sansome Street to Fort Gunnybags, having traded surrender for their lives.

That evening, the *Bulletin* was jubilant. "[T]he rowdy judge [is behind bars], and if Hopkins dies, Terry will and must be hung. If he lives, which is extremely doubtful, Terry must be banished. His doom is unalterable; justice requires it. *Salus populi suprema lex*—THE PEOPLE'S SAFETY IS ABOVE THE LAW." Two days later, editor Tom King, still savoring the chief justice's arrest, hyperbolized, "The malevolent Terry, a man-beast, who had come to gloat over the gore of blood running in the streets of San Francisco, was now finally [to be removed once and for all]."[25] In the inner offices of the fort, however, not all of Terry's antagonists were pleased. Many executive members of the committee were fearful that they had "hooked too big a fish." Many committee members were beginning to feel that they were moving toward unmanageable boundaries—in particular, moving toward provoking the federal authorities into retaliation. Joining these members was also a growing chorus of business leaders who were urging the committee to release the chief justice and begin to disband.

Yet, not surprisingly to those who knew the Terry family, it was Terry's wife, the genteel but resolute Cornelia Terry, who had as much to do with changing public sentiments as anyone. On the evening of Sunday, June 22, Cornelia Terry was at her husband's side, determined not only to bolster his spirits, but also to prod him into standing fast. The following morning, after some mendacious editorializing by the *Bulletin*, the committee was bulldozed into forbidding her return to Terry's jail cell "lest [she] be conspiring to help him escape." The *Bulletin's* laughable charge, however, only worsened the situation by adding to the growing resentments of those who were pressing for the judge's release. Two weeks earlier, a majority of the public had been prepared to believe the newspaper's characterization of Terry as "a monster with uncurbed rage, consumed by guile and malice," but now such sentiments were being replaced by sympathy for his wife.

With these changing sentiments, the *Daily Herald*, the single pro-Terry newspaper in San Francisco, found its voice and began publishing letters from Cornelia that cast her husband in heroic proportions. This effort did not go unrewarded. Slowly public perception of the chief justice began to change. The decorous "Neal" portrayed her husband as an honorable, honest, courageous, albeit uncompromising man—a man willing to stand for principles even in the face of overwhelming dangers. Cornelia's literary sensibilities had the effect of smoothing Terry's rougher edges, and eventually her importuning reached the ears, and then the hearts, of many of San Francisco's socially conscious organizations, particularly groups with strong female influence, such as philanthropic and historical societies, even as she was reaching out to the traditionally hide-bound southern church congregations. As this softening toward the chief justice grew, it annoyed the historian Hubert Howe Bancroft, who wrote condescendingly, "God bless [these silly women] with their warm hearts and credulous heads; who would have them otherwise? [They believed in Terry] no matter how dastardly [his] deeds."[26] Even the heretofore-silent Senator Gwin began to speak up in Terry's favor once the city's mood began to change in the chief justice's direction.

But changing sentiments or not, the bank and railroad-controlled newspapers continued to demonize Terry on the streets and in the boardrooms. Led always by the bombastic *Bulletin,* his enemies continued to call for Terry's execution if Hopkins were to die. Amazingly as this journalistic crescendo swelled around him, the usually imperturbable justice appeared to flinch, for in a low moment, and just for a moment in Neal's presence, he insinuated that he was willing to forfeit his seat on the high bench in exchange for his life. Cornelia, however, would have none of it. She made it clear that she was shocked by the mere suggestion, and pointed out to him that swapping life for honor would be a humiliation that the family was not prepared to invite—she would rather see him hanged. The steeliness of her response was enough to put an end to the judge's talk of compromise—somehow his wife had fortified his resolve—and thereafter he let it be known that only unconditional release would be acceptable.

The trial awaited and the Justice, considering the possibility that he might be hanged, set down in a letter to Cornelia the reasons for the crisis he was now facing—he put them on paper, he told her, for his sons' future understanding. Cornelia, seizing the moment, incorporated her husband's reflections in her letters to the sympathetic *Daily Herald.* The most famous of these letters has remained in the records of *The Sunday Herald*. It appeared on June 30, and was read by many San Franciscans:

> I acted [from] a desire to prevent the consummation [of an act] which was a violation of the Constitution of this state which I had sworn to support as well as the Constitution of the United States to secure the blessings of which to their posterity both my grandfathers fought & bled & toiled & suffered. [The] meanest criminal is under that instrument guaranteed the same rights as the noblest citizen & cannot without a violation of its provisions be deprived of his liberty, except by legal process—It was at this holy principle and the obligation of my oath that I looked upon, and not at the demerits of the man who I knew to be a bad man [Maloney]. [So] my darling don't fear that I will falter. I believe that if I am permitted to live out my three score years and ten I have those elements in me which would enable me to be of service to my country and to leave a name of which my children would be proud. I cannot doubt this when I look back in the past & see what I have already accomplished with so little effort.

Several days passed and executive committee members, feeling the pressure of the community's shifting sentiments, began to have second thoughts about their actions. The executive members were not unmindful that reprisals might very well follow once the state was again in control of the city (some members, of course, talked of beginning "The Republic of the Pacific," but most knew better; and they were aware that once the insurrection was over it would be the leaders of the Vigilance Committee upon whom the axe would fall). Executive member John Dows expressed his uneasiness when he lamented, "[W]e started to hunt coyotes, but we've got a grizzly bear on our hands, and [we] don't know what to do with him." But not all committee members had misgivings. The bellicose C.J. Dempster was not one to flag (at least not verbally) in the face of adversity. "[S]hould Hopkins die and the entire Committee acquits [Terry], I would, myself kill him." One thing all seemed to agree upon: Hopkins' life or death was the critical element in everyone's future.

But now events began to surface that were to move the committee leadership toward termination of the struggle, even though the troops in the street and the field commanders made it clear that they were in no mood to disband. Naval Commander Captain David Farragut's neutrality, for instance, had begun to wane and he made his thoughts public. Complaining that the situation had gone on much too long, Farragut put pressure on the committee to finish their mission. To show that he meant business, he ordered naval Captain E.B. Boutwell to anchor the United States frigate *John Adams* within cannon range of Fort Vigilance, "[just] for the moral effect," Farragut would later say.[27] (For some time Boutwell, an outspoken "states-rights" advocate and a friend of Terry's, had been prodding Farragut to intervene on Governor Johnson's behalf.) Then, for whatever reason, on July 1, the naval commander's patience came to an end. He wrote the executive committee, reminding them that Judge Terry had constitutional protections that the committee was in no position to abrogate. "The release or trial of Judge Terry," he wrote, "in accordance with the Constitution of the United States, would be the readiest mode of attaining the great object we all have in view. [I]t is my sincere hope that some satisfactory arrangement may be made for the release of Judge Terry [posthaste]." While the committee was still dithering about Farragut's use of the word "release" in his letter, a second letter arrived. In it, the naval commander declared that he had become dissatisfied with the pace of the trial and expected that action to release the judge should take place within the next few days. "[Captain Boutwell]," Farragut wrote, "was prepared to receive on board Judge D.S. Terry, for his personal safety, should any arrangement be accomplished to that end." Farragut's salutation in the first letter made it clear how he was expecting the matter to end (release Terry).

Unquestionably, Farragut's changing outlook gave members of the executive committee pause, but their spirits were not altogether dashed, for a few days later, word arrived that the president, Franklin Pierce, had decided not to intervene on Governor Johnson's behalf. Pierce, speaking through the nation's Attorney General Caleb Cushing agreed with the governor's assessment—the Vigilance Committee was indeed violating state law. But only two conditions would be impelling enough to warrant intervention by the president—first, a majority of the state Legislature must request it, and second, there must be a violation of federal law or the destruction or seizure of federal property. The

Cushing letter was definitely bad news for Johnson, for it ended any hope he had of getting assistance from Washington, D.C. He knew that he dare not ask the legislators for support, for it would be lucky for him to get the support of one-third of the legislators.

Terry, on the other hand, unlike Johnson, was not at all disappointed. He was not surprised by the president's response, for word had come through Cornelia that his cause was becoming an issue of public discussion in Washington. Moreover, he had become *cause celebre* throughout the country for the southern doctrine of states-rights (Terry seemed to believe the entire nation was taking sides.) The Texas Legislature, under the urging of Sam Houston, presented a petition to the U.S. Congress demanding Terry's release, just as the Texas Rangers announced their readiness to "force-march [to California] if need be to fight for the Judge's release." On the floor of the U.S. Senate, legislators from Tennessee, Louisiana and Mississippi called for federal intervention, and the entire congressional block from the Southern states warned of countrywide unrest should Terry in any way be harmed.

As tensions mounted, the Vigilance Committee, as a whole, urged the executive committee, with no more delay or further consideration of Hopkins' health, to begin the trial. Taking note of the pressure, on June 27th the executive committee began Terry's trial in a cramped, sultry, makeshift courtroom off the main hall at Fort Gunnybags. Influential executive committee members were chosen to fill the positions of the court—judge, jury, prosecutor and defense counsel. (Initially Terry was to face seven charges, five of which had been resurrected from old charges that had been adjudicated years before. But as the trial progressed and a hasty resolution became a vital consideration, even the most implacable members of the jury agreed that only the two new charges could properly be prosecuted.) The charges read as follows: "In the People v. David Smith Terry: Charge *one* resisting, by violence, the officers of the Committee of Vigilance, while in the discharge of their duty. Charge *two* committing an assault with a deadly weapon, with intent to kill Sterling A. Hopkins, a police officer of the Committee of Vigilance, on the 21st day of June, 1856."

With the charges established, the trial began. Executive committee member J.P. Manrow was elected the committee's "judge advocate." Manrow was devoid of legal training—two years earlier he had been working in New York State as an engineer's assistant.[28] Setting aside Manrow's limited juridical potential, however, Terry knew that his welfare lay in the judge advocate's hands, and hence he curbed his professional resentments and deferred to the advocate's oftentimes perplexing procedural quirks.

Manrow opened the proceedings by inviting Terry's defense counsel, Miers Truett, to enter a plea, but by prior agreement, Truett deferred to Terry, who had insisted from the outset that he could defend himself. Rising after Truett's nod, Terry walked to the bench, where he leveled his gaze at Manrow and, leaning forward, brought his face as close to Manrow's face as prudence would allow. He then asked, in the most sonorous tones, whether the charges against him truly represented the position held by the Vigilance Committee, or were they merely the opinions of "newspaper editors who had been caged by the mob?" Manrow was ready for him and did not blink. He declared that the charges reflected the executive committee's point of view, and that they would never be engendered by the fear of street mobs. In effect, Manrow said, staring back at Terry, they were drawn up in a state of cool and calm reflection. "Then," said the Justice, returning to the counsel's table, "I plead not guilty of any crime whatever!" It was obvious that Terry wanted to make it transparent to all who witnessed the proceeding that he had no intention of admitting any culpability before this quasi-judicial court. With this point of protocol in the record and the battle lines drawn, Judge Manrow announced that the trial was officially open, whereupon the prosecutor, Thomas J.L. Smiley, stepped before the jury and began. Smiley introduced to this attentive but perspiring jury, 21 eyewitnesses who, in sequence, depicted Terry's attack on Hopkins. Smiley concluded eyewitness accounts with a bedside document from Hopkins himself. Many witnesses offered slightly differing versions of the same story. Terry, in unprovoked anger, had attempted to prevent Hopkins from arresting Maloney, but when it became clear that he could not prevent the arrest, he fell into uncontrollable rage, which terminated in a final act when he stabbed the surprised Constable Hopkins.

After each eyewitness finished his testimony—portraying the judge's behavior in greater and ever greater portraits of savagery—the prosecutor turned to the jury and asked rhetorically, why was the chief justice not on the bench in Sacramento where he belonged? "Is it not the chief justice's duty to punish criminals, not defend them?" Of all people, should he not have been the very last one to "drag the judicial ermine in the mud?" Then Smiley answered his own question—Terry's presence in San Francisco on June 21 was no mere coincidence. He was there fully intending to provoke a riot "in order to subvert the wishes of the People's Tribunal!" The prosecutor concluded his performance by placing in the record the spoken and written testimony of twenty-five additional witnesses who had faced Terry in times past, each one carefully chosen to bolster the notion that the judge was a "vengeful renegade" with "the strength and voraciousness of a wild beast"—a man without capacity to control a malevolent temper.

Next, the defense attorney was invited to offer rebuttal. But once again the court's defender, Miers Truett, deferred to Terry and allowed him to present his own defense. (Truett and Terry had grown to trust one another, for Truett had been a produce merchant in Mississippi before coming to California, and he and Terry discovered comfort and conviviality in each other's southern ways). Chief Justice Terry began his defense with a request that the judge advocate remand the entire matter to the duly authorized state court, where, he announced with just a trace of condescension, he would be willing to abide by the verdict imposed without further protest—adding with hauteur that if found guilty by the state court, he would resign as chief justice—"For I would have been proven unfit to continue serving." Perhaps the committee was bemused, but it was hardly persuaded to grant his request. How a corrupt court system could convict *the* chief officer of that system, they were left to ponder. Doubtless the judge had not forgotten that the fundamental reason for the committee's revival was to do away with the corrupt courts that were currently in control of the state's legal system. Terry, of course, did not belabor this request. In reality he knew that the committee was the only barrier there was between himself and the *hoi polloi* in the streets who were anxious to hang him. The true intention of his request, surely, was to place on the record his opinion that the executive tribunal was without legitimate judicial authority. From the outset, however, Terry was careful to plead his case in a solemn and deferential fashion, making no conspicuous effort to raise the issue of the court's usurpation of state authority. It is difficult to offer a precise explanation of why he chose to take this approach. In particular, it is difficult to separate his legitimate concern for his well being from his opinion that the legal charges against him were without merit, particularly within the limits of the committee's own proceedings. He understood that a hostile press and an angry street mob would interpret any attempt he might make to question the committee's authority into another display, on his part, of arrogantly defending "the corrupt law above the people."

His defense began, nevertheless, with his feigning sympathy for what the committee was doing. Its goals, he proclaimed, were "a praiseworthy undertaking, [and] candor forces me to confess that the evils you arose to repress were glaring and palpable, and that the end you sought to attain was a noble one."[29] Yet, he continued, "do these ends justify the means you employ?" "I too was concerned with political chicanery, [h]ad I not resigned from the party of my birth, because so many [of my fellow Democrats] had come to office through corrupt means." "[To sum up] the [Committee] condemns in others that which it willingly condones in its own ranks—[do you not have your share of] shoulder strikers and ballot-box ruffians?" Terry then engaged a commonplace legal maneuver. He ignored the issue that had most outraged him, the issue that had fostered his deepest resentments—the committee's impudent usurpation of judicial authority—and embraced the *lex generalis* defense (as opposed to a special pleading). "Hopkins," he insisted, "had no right to arrest me for he had no authorization [e]ven under the Committee's [o]wn seal."

When the prosecutor, Terry reminded the jury, put Beverly Cole, the physician who had attended Hopkins' on the witness stand, Cole testified that he had found a bloody arrest warrant in the policeman's coat pocket. Yet, when Terry pressed Cole to put the document into evidence, neither the physician nor the prosecutor would produce it. Without such a writ—and "indeed there was no such writ," Terry insisted—he had no choice but to defend himself against an unprovoked attack from unidentified street ruffians—any "manly citizen," he shouted, must act against unauthorized assailants.[30] With this line of attack, Terry believed he could avoid overtly challenging the committee's right to serve the writ. That is, by comparison he believed that he could draw a distinction between his illegal arrest without a writ, and the legal writ that he had served upon the committee on behalf of the citizen Billy Mulligan—a writ that the committee had so publicly and defiantly dismissed. "It stung [me] to the quick when that modern Areopagus, (as Terry termed the Vigilance Committee) treated a writ of *habeas corpus* with silent contemp[t]."[31]

In response to the prosecutor's next charge "that he had been in San Francisco making mischief," Terry countered that his presence in the city was mere coincidence. He was not in town to make trouble, he said, but to restrain any precipitous acts that the Law and Order forces might foment, should, in fact, the committee disband as had been rumored.

The prosecutor, of course, never accepted Terry's explanation, convinced, as he was, that the justice was in the city plotting an attack against Fort Vigilance—once Wool's arms delivery reached the state armories.[32] Nonetheless, whatever his reason for being in the city, Terry's next argument was to become his most persuasive line of defense. He had no choice but to defend himself against personal threats, he declared, when these unidentified ruffians attacked him on a public street: "As a man of honor only one course [is] available—to defend himself—anything less would be abject cowardice." As an officer of the court, he said, "I am duty-bound to resist unlawful acts." The essence of the common law, he lectured listeners, is adherence to the basic conceptions of protection and restraint, but in the hands of a mob, these notions are no more than symbolic pretension, [and] the Committee shows a venial contempt for moral fairness—(although he admits that perhaps his own motives may not have been completely free from pride and obstinacy).[33]

Moreover, he continued, the jury had provided no method for ferreting out dishonest witnesses—and as the defendant he was forced to listen while people from his past with unsettled grudges bore false witness against him. (In point of fact, there was a spate of libelous and slanderous words coming from both sides of the courtroom—individual jury members received letters daily from citizens challenging the reliability of both the witnesses and the members sitting in the jury box.) Nor, Terry continued, had the committee been in any manner reluctant to pick and choose the testimony that it wanted to support and to ignore.[34] He then concluded his didactic exercise before the increasingly impatient jury with a somewhat attenuated defense of his own public attacks on the committee-at-large—attacks that appeared in the *Daily Herald.* The ridicule of the Vigilance Committee in published letters, he declared, was not directed at "jury members present," since he had had no personal relationship with any of them and therefore had no basis to assess their moral behavior. Instead, these letters were intended to be an attack on the illegality of the Vigilance Committee's deportment as a political entity. Perhaps the jury could not be faulted if it saw his justification, *lex generalis,* on this elusively drawn point as a distinction without much of a difference. Yet, in fact, Terry was more sympathetic toward the jury than might have been expected, for in a letter written on June 30, 1856, but not revealed until some years later, Terry wrote to his wife, Cornelia, "I have tried with great anxiety to read the characters of those who are once my judges [and I] think that a majority of them are men who desire to do right, but considering the infirmity of human nature, they are assuming an awful responsibility in sitting in judgment on a man against whom so much has been said to excite their prejudices."

True to character, his summation was conflicted. It was at times a diluted mixture of bland acknowledgment of human frailty, deflected guilt and manly exoneration—conceding that he had acted in haste—but he claimed it was his nature to be "excitable and impulsive [yet only when provoked by] outrages, insult or dishonor." Moreover, Terry insinuated sagaciously, the jury must consider the conundrum Prosecutor Smiley presented on opening day, "[that] to put [me] on trial, [is] to put the Committee on trial, for were [I] to be found innocent then the Committee must be guilty, but if you [the jury] are guilty then it is [you] who deserve to be punished." "[B]ut you will never be punished, so this Tribunal is not [a] search for truth but only self-justification."

With this charge, Terry ended his portion of the trial. He then took his seat at the defense table, and Miers Truett concluded for the defense by extracting the testimony of "eight neutral and objective" witnesses who supported the premise that Terry had done no more than defend himself. These eight witnesses were followed by the oral or written statements of more than 70 character witnesses from throughout the country. The essence of their wide-ranging testimony could be summarized as follows: Justice Terry is a man of integrity, free from the common vices of most frontiersmen,—not a user of strong drinks or prostitutes—a brave, generous, honorable man, [not quarrelsome by nature], yet, whenever unfairly challenged, one who could be impulsive and [on rare occasions] out of control.

By now the patience on both sides was wearing thin and the political consequences of the entire saga of Vigilante justice had become uncomfortably obvious: If Hopkins were to die, the street mobs would take over and Terry would be lynched; if he lived, then the committee faced an equally touchy situation—satisfying the passions of the mobs while finding both a verdict that fit the crime while exonerating their own behavior. For once the city had returned to normal status, it was quite possible that the committee leadership would have to answer for their behavior. But whatever the verdict, the executive committee was prepared to defend its own behavior—its mission was to restore efficient and trustworthy political and legal institutions in San Francisco. Hopkins' welfare, of course, was central if the street rabble was to be kept at bay, and after Terry's initial arrest, tensions ran high because the hearsay on the street was that Hopkins was already dead, or in a state of dying. But shortly thereafter, the rumors concerning his survival changed from hopeless to grave, and then evaporated altogether when the truculent deputy walked into Fort Vigilance on wobbly legs demanding compensation for injuries.

The jury now faced a far different problem—what to do with their outspoken constable? It came as no surprise to committee members, however, that Hopkins would demand compensation for his injuries—his mother had been overheard telling her daughter-in-law that "should Sterling die, she would become a very rich widow." On two occasions while convalescing, moreover, Hopkins had demanded compensation, but on each occasion the committee had chosen not even to respond to his request. Now the time had come, however, when the committee was no longer in a position to ignore his demands, for once the constable was back on his feet sharing his woes with patrons in the city's saloons, a reckoning had to be faced. His imploring became more alarming to committee members when he suggested that he and Judge Terry could negotiate a settlement directly, since they were "worthy combatants."

Eventually the *Bulletin's* constant effort to lionize Hopkins turned sour when the public began to interpret his demands as no less than common extortion. The matter was finally put to rest when the committee agreed to pay Hopkins $17,000 at $100 per month. (If Hopkins envisioned a monthly pension for the next decade, he was quickly disabused when the committee walked away from their pledge three months after they had disbanded—having paid him a trifling $450.)

Well aware that public tolerance had come to an end, even as the angry mood of the street soldier remained unrequited, the executive committee hurried toward a verdict. They recognized that it was impossible to wash their hands of the matter (although some jurists suggested as much), and that it was necessary that they convict the chief justice of "something," and the sooner the better. But a verdict did not come easily, for a divided jury quickly fell into extended squabbling about the nature of the judge's crime.[35] And while some information was getting out to the public about the committee's personal deliberations, most information had dried up, for the jurists knew full well that reprisals might await the leaders of the committee if their enemies regained control of the city's legal system. As a consequence, members of the jury extracted from one another "[a pledge] of their sacred honor to God and themselves not to divulge their votes to any living being outside the jury room."[36] Therefore, what little can be corroborated about private deliberations comes from a handful of unsigned and undated sketchpad doodles that survived their discussions. These notes suggest what one might expect—that their discussions were wholly free of judicial protocol. For instance, arguments *tu quoque* abounded (e.g., what Terry did was much worse than anything that the Committee is doing). "[Terry] had ignored [the law] throughout his career whenever it was convenient for him to do so, [so, what now] gives him the right to call us lawless?" "Terry's 'laws of the state' are irrelevant because [we] are implementing a higher law—the public will." The notes also indicate that there was an impetuous faction of jurors who constantly challenged their more timid brethren to summon the courage to hang "[this] vile pettifogger [who is so] eager to provoke a bloody collision—up until now [it has taken] no courage to hang the poor, ignorant rabble from the streets." Some of the more cautious jurors, on the other hand, shifted ground and charged the chief justice with incendiary but superfluous behavior. For example, "[Terry was merely] working to force slavery onto a State whose Constitution and citizens had explicitly rejected." One hard-to-fathom objection declared that Terry's aggressive response to Hopkins "[offered] undeniable proof that [he] had *not* acted in self defense."[37] The jury ultimately reached unanimity on one issue—that the street mobs might find Terry's hanging a satisfying blood sport, but after the deed had been done it would be "us" (the executive committee) who would answer for any missteps.

The deliberations dragged on. Troops in the streets agitated for a decision, even as support for strong punishment of the Justice began to dissipate among members of the executive committee—a few members threatened to resign if the jury voted to hang Terry. One member, J.W. Brittian, fearful of reprisals, told fellow jurors that he had taken to "carrying a loaded and cocked pistol while walking home at night."[38] He argued that Terry should be released and be done with it, "for had [we] been attacked as the Judge was attacked [we too] would have taken the course of action he has taken." Defense Counsel Truett supported Terry, insisting that "any man threatened as he was would act as he did." Many bystanders to the skirmish who had not testified before the jury let it be known privately that Terry's response to Hopkins' police squad was no more than an act of self-defense.

The changing mood of San Franciscans had the effect of pushing the shopkeepers on the jury toward a more lenient verdict, even while many of the anti-slave ideologues continued to call for harsh punishment (death, banishment, or at the very least, resignation from the court). When the verdict was finally rendered, however, it was obvious that the shopkeepers held the upper hand, for on the first charge the jury was in agreement—Terry was guilty. His insistence that he needed a warrant of proof to submit to Hopkins' arrest was a hoax, they decided, for he was challenging the committee's right to arrest him. And hence, at no time did he honestly believe he was being accosted by thugs—in other words, his purported ignorance of the situation was disingenuous. However, in contrast to the first charge, the second charge generated disagreement among jury members that was never resolved. The shopkeepers were inclined to hold Truett's position—Terry was defending himself, therefore the attack on Hopkins could not be considered premeditated. The ideologues, on the other hand, insisted that Terry's history as a violent man was the issue and that there was ample proof that on that bloody day, he was a violent man bent on malevolent intentions.

Because opinions pertaining to Terry's motives were so sharply divided it was difficult to reach consensus, but eventually Truett was able to forge a slim majority—yet as sometimes happens with consensus, most jurors were eager to disavow it once it had become public knowledge. Did Terry intend to kill his tormentor or not? A three-fifths majority was needed to settle the issue, and the concessions necessary to hold the majority together were tenuous. These came only after the jury reworded the second charge. In place of the sentence, "Terry intended to kill Hopkins," the charge was rewritten to read, "Terry intended to assault Hopkins."[39] But now, as critics pointed out, the jury had convicted Terry of something for which he had not been charged. Changing the charge meant changing the punishment, but changing the punishment became the most contentious issue for San Franciscans to swallow. Many were astounded and confused when the jury announced the verdict—Terry would be released because the jury had not been authorized to punish him for what they were now charging him to be guilty. Yet, in order to soften the absurdity of the verdict, the jury attached the caveat that "he must forthwith resign from the Supreme Court"—but how they expected to enforce this provision was an enigma to outside observers. (Terry insisted that as chief justice he had a legal right to resist Hopkins.)[40]

Not surprisingly the troops denounced the verdict. For weeks, committee leadership had worked up the passions of the street soldiers at the prospects of hanging "a big fish," but when it was learned that the jury intended to throw the big fish back—convicted but virtually unpunished—anger on the docks and in the saloons intensified. On the morning following the verdict, 100 members of the Board of Delegates (the inner circle of the committee's non-jury members) hurriedly convened and rebuffed their own jury. By now most delegates agreed that it would be unwise to hang Terry—Hopkins had survived—but they did insist on a penalty that would assure his removal from the court, for most delegates continued to insist that Terry had "intended" to kill Hopkins. For five days the troops in the field waited for a change of verdict, yet, surprisingly, on the sixth day the executive committee announced that the verdict would stand as it had been rendered.

William Coleman and the committee's senior leadership had convinced the Committee of Forty-one that any attempt to punish Terry more harshly could easily make the entire Committee of Forty-one more vulnerable to federal and state retribution. Farragut and even Wool, he argue, had made it unmistakably clear to anyone listening that the military commands expected Terry to be released unharmed. On August 6 the Committee of Forty-one convinced that a stern verdict would produce consequences they might not be able to control reversed their own reversal, and by a margin of ten votes supported the original verdict, i.e. Terry should be released and step down from the court—much to the relief of the senior leaders and the jury. Blame for any charges of a *coup d'etat* would now be shared. The trial had lasted twenty-five days (from June 22 to July 27) with the court in session both mornings and afternoons. Frequently the jurors had other obligations, e.g., businesses to attend to, or trips to take—hence, not all jurors were in attendance all the time, and what made matters worse, at the height of the trial each side was leaking information daily that was either favorable to its own side, or, unfavorable to the other side.

A special session of the executive committee was then hurriedly called to discuss how best to release the chief justice. Some members didn't seem to think it presented a problem, but many were fearful that his release might lead to his assassination—who could be sure that his release without escort might not provoke a lynch mob, or produce a lethal shot out of the crowd? Coleman presented a plan that he said would both save Terry's life and satisfy the street soldiers' mood for retribution. He proposed that the entire Vigilance Committee muster 10 battalions at noon the next day on Front Street facing Fort Vigilance. On a trumpet command, they would march a shackled Terry from his cell to stand before the assembled troops. Then with appropriate fanfare, the guilty verdict would be read to the battalions after which Terry would be admonished never again to intervene in the affairs of the city—for were he to do so, he would be arrested and executed. As a final humiliation, Coleman added, the entire command would then parade him through the streets to the dockside where, still in chains, he would be put on a steamer bound for Sacramento.

The business members, particularly the "Inner-Thirteen," however, were troubled with Coleman's plan. On the one hand, they found it far too self-aggrandizing, and on the other, they believed it increased a madman's opportunity to shoot the prisoner, or even worse, it might give Terry an opportunity to sway the sympathies of the mob. But while Coleman and members of the committee continued to debate their options, Meirs Truett and about a dozen members of the executive committee spirited the justice under cover of darkness to the home of Terry's friend, Duncan Perley.

When news reached the streets the next morning that Terry had disappeared from his cell, the fears of wary committee members were confirmed. Hundreds of frustrated troopers began door-to-door searches for the justice. Fearful that Terry's discovery was imminent, Truett and jury members hustled the justice and his wife from Perley's house and placed them securely aboard the *USS John Adams*. By the time the sun was above the yardarm Terry and Cornelia were safely concealed aboard the *Adams* under the protective custody of their old ally, Captain E.B. Boutwell. Later the couple was successfully transferred from the naval vessel to the commercial steamer *Helen Hensley* bound for Sacramento. By early afternoon, as the *Hensley* steamed north and east past the *Adams*, Boutwell could not resist the impulse to fire a salutatory shot before the *Hensley's* bow honoring what he perceived to be the chief justice's convincing victory over the Vigilance Committee.

In its own small but permanent fashion, memory of the conflict between Terry and the committee acted as a flashpoint between northern and southern factions in California for years to come. A quarter-century later some committee members' hearts were still carrying the scar of that shot. It was a cultural divide, writes the northerner historian Bancroft, between the "soft, plausible [but deceptive] speech of southerners and the coarser [but more] honest reforming language of New Englanders."[41]

If such distinctions in tenor and tone of the language are as Bancroft says they were, then it was time to take a more careful look at this "coarser but more honest" speech of New Englanders. Clearly this is not the place to assess the language of New Englanders generically, but it is possible, at least, to weigh the language of *one* New Englander—expressly his words and also the events that played so critical a role in fashioning Stephen Johnson Field's judicial life in California. After deporting a few more Irish Catholics from San Francisco the Vigilance Committee of 1856 disbanded on August 18.[42] James Meyers writes, "Fort Gunnybags was made a museum for [a] holiday; and, [p]eople brought children there to fondle, among other souvenirs, the ropes which had strangled four men."[43]

NOTES

1. John Norton Pomeroy, "California 1846–1860: The Politics of a Representative Frontier State." California Historical Society Quarterly 32. (Dec. 1953).

2. Walter Bean. *California: An Interpretive History.* (New York: McGraw-Hill Book Co., 1968), 140. See also Cardinal Goodman, the *Establishment of State Gov. in Calif.* 1846–1850. New York: The Macmillan Company, 1914.

3. R. Hal Williams. *The Democratic Party and California Politics, 1880–1896.* (Stanford CA. Stanford University Press, 1973). 6.

4. Josiah Royce, *California, from the Conquest in 1864 to the Second Vigilance Committee in San Francisco: a Study of the American Character* (New York: Houghton Mifflin Co. 1886). 335. Also, see Richard Maxwell Braun. *Historical Studies of American Violence and Vigilantism* (New York: Oxford University Press 1975).

5. Kevin Starr, *America and the California Dream 1850-1915.* (New York: Oxford Press 1973). 155.

6. Roger W. Lotchin, *San Francisco 1846–1856: From Hamlet to City* (New York: Oxford Press 1974), 198.

7. Robert George Bxybee, *Another View of the San Francisco 1856 Vigilance Committee* (Los Angeles: Zamorano Club 2000) Introduction by Doyce B. Nunis. 10.

8. One wonders why King would want to deal with Casey in any fashion. Casey was a dangerous man. He had engaged, it was reported, in the bloodiest street fight that San Francisco had ever witnessed. Five men ambushed him in 1855 and before the struggle was over he had stabbed one, shot another, and ran three others off. John Myers, *San Francisco's Reign of Terror* (Garden City: Doubleday & Co., Inc. 1966) 97.

9. River travel between San Francisco and Sacramento was an active commercial enterprise. There were nineteen steamboats making the trip. The New Orleans was the largest at 800 tons and the Missouri next at 27 tons. Mead B. Kibbey. *The Sacramento City Directory 1850,* California State Library Foundation: Sacramento CA. 2000, 105.

10. For Johnson's view of the dispute see Herbert G. Florcken's California Historical Society Quarterly. XIV (1935). "The Correspondence of Governor J. Neely Johnson."

11. L.H. Woolley, *California 1846–1813* (Oakland CA. Dewitt & Snelling 1913) 14.

12. William T. Sherman, *Century Magazine*, December 1891, Letter from W. T. Sherman to Hon. Thomas Ewing, May 21, 1856.

13. Letter to Thomas Ewing from William T. Sherman, June 16, 1856. See also *Sherman and the S.F. Vigilantes* and Dwight L. Clarke, *William Tecumseh Sherman: Gold Rush Banker.*

14. A. Russell Buchanan. *David S. Terry of California: Dueling Judge* (San Marino, CA. The Huntington Library Press 1956). 27. Sherman would write years later in his memoirs that Johnson's decree was precipitous and that he had overplayed "a very weak hand."

15. Herbert G. Florcken. *California Historical Society* Quarterly. Vol. XIV (1935). 351.

16. A Russell Buchanan, *Dueling Judge*. 29.

17. W. Sherman to T. Ewing, June 16, 1856. *The Century Illustrated Monthly Magazine*, XLIII (1891), 303. Later it was revealed that Johnson was not alone in his disappointment. In a letter to his father-in-law, Thomas Ewing, Sherman portrayed his own frustration with Wool's behavior. "I was thunderstruck, as I could look nowhere else for arms, and the idea of enrolling the militia without arms was an absurdity."

18. A. Russell Buchanan, *Dueling Judge.* 30. See also W. T. Sherman letter to Stephen J. Field, *The Overland Monthly* vol. 12 February 1874, No.2. Should the Governor not accept such a compromise, Sherman warned, it might precipitate civil rebellion. To reinforce this notion Sherman handed the Governor a copy of the evening Bulletin in which the new editor, Thomas King (brother of William) vowed to lead San Francisco and the northern districts of California into secession from the United States. King had editorialized that the northern Californians' patience was wearing thin, and that they were not reluctant to establish "an independent country" which they would name "The Pacific Republic."

19. Sherman, Letter to T. Ewing, June 16, 1856.

20. Hubert Howe Bancroft, *Popular* Tribunals (San Francisco: The History Co.1887). 31.

21. A. Russell Buchanan, *Dueling Judge*. 34.

22. John D. Gordon, *Authorized By No Law*. (San Francisco: The Ninth Judicial Circuit Historical Society and the U.S. District Court Northern District of California Historical Society 1987). 17–18.

23. —— *Authorized.* . . . 19.

24. Sherman letter to Lucas Turner, July 2, 1856.

25. A. Russell Buchanan, *Dueling Judge,* 43.

26. Hubert Howe Bancroft, *Popular Tribunals*.Vol. II. 486.

27. Loyall Farragut. *The Life of David Glasgow Farragut* (New York: D. Appleton & Co. 1872). 172, 184.

28. John M. Myers, Reign of Terror. 186. Parenthetically, in a randomly preserved note in committee records, one is offered a glimpse into Manrow's potential qualifications as the judge advocate. "Resolve," he wrote, "that the Ex. Committee concur, with the Delligates in relation to the perade on Monday next."

29. John D. Lawson, *American State Trials* (Wilmington DE: Scholarly Resources, 1972). XV, 140.

30. —— *American.* . . . 141–142.

31. A. E. Wagstaff, *The Life of Ex. Chief Justice of the Supreme Court of California: David S. Terry* (San Francisco: Continental Publishing Co. 1892), 102. There is evidence to suggest that Hopkins had sought a writ from the committee's Secretary, the infamous, I. Bluxome. But Bluxome was not at headquarters when Hopkins set off in search of Maloney. It was Bluxome (committee member #33) who had issued so many foreboding "proclamations of custody" during the Vigilance Committee's four-month reign.

32. A. Russell Buchanan, *Dueling Judge,* 36. Terry's reason for being in San Francisco on June 21 has never been fully explained, Buchanan's interpretation seems as plausible as any—Terry, he says, was there along with Secretary of State David Douglas and Major General Volney Howard to map out a new strategy now that it was clear that federal assistance would not be forthcoming. While any explanation remains problematic, it is apparent that Terry could not have known of John Durkee's raid on the *Julia*, for he was either *en route* from Sacramento or already in the city when the news of the raid reached the streets. Nor was he planning to stay in town for any length of time, for in his pocket, when arrested, was a return-trip ticket on the 4:00 p.m. steamer bound for Sacramento. See, John D. Lawson, 142f.

33. Lawson, John. D. *American State Trials*, "The Trial of Judge David S. Terry for an attempt to Murder and for other Crimes, San Francisco, California, 1856." Vol. XV, 143–145.

34. Lawson, John D. *Trails,* 143. The Huntington Library, Terry MSS, March 14, 1870. In a letter to Cornelia, Terry compares the Vigilance Committee's legal practice to zealots who selectively chose Bible passages that suit their purposes. The Bible and the law are of one piece, he argued, "to choose them selectively defiles them both." Later, when Cornelia laments that the law has abused him, he scolds, "I don't like you slandering the law—you say law is not always just. I know that the law is always just and if one fails to get justice done it is because [his] cause is not properly managed or the witnesses lie." (Terry seems to have been persuaded by the hoary Thomistic adage—that unjust law is no law at all.) The law, he goes on, is inviolate, blameless. To be blamed are its misusers—those at whose hands innocent people suffer unfairly—"the libelous, ultra-abolitionist, licentious tabloids [that have] prostituted themselves into an anti-southern frenzy [at my expense]."

35. A. Russell Buchanan. *Dueling Judge.* 66. Bancroft, *Tribunals.* 468.

36. —— *Dueling Judge.* 65.

37. Notes from 1856 Vigilance Committee, The Huntington Library, San Marino CA.

38. George W. Frink. *Statement,* MSS, Bancroft Library, Berkeley CA, 17.

39. A. Russell Buchanan. *Dueling Judge.*65, Hubert H.Bancroft, *Tribunals*, Vol. II 468.

40. Terry. MSS, 1856 Vigilante Committee Jury Notes, the Huntington Library, San Marino California.

41. Hubert H. Bancroft, *Tribunals* Vol. II, 484.

42. Robert G. Byxbee, *Vigilance Committee,* Another viewpoint, 9.

43. John M. Meyers, San Francisco's Reign of Terror. (Garden City: Doubleday & Co. 1966). 200–202.

Stephen J. Field, U.S. Supreme Court. 1890.

David S. Terry. Central Valley Squire. 1823–1889.

Josiah Royce. Judges the political factions of California's first delegates.

William Coleman. President of the Businessman's Revolution, 1856.

James King of William. Editor of the Daily Evening Bulletin, 1856.

Wm. T. Sherman. Former San Francisco Banker, 1864.

John E. Wool. Oldest Union general in the Civil War, c. 1855–1865.

Captain David G. Farragut, c. 1860–1865.

Chapter Five

Justices of the Supreme Court of California

The adoption of California's first constitution in May of 1850 brought Stephen J. Field's tenure as the alcalde of Marysville to a close. His termination coincided with the installation of William Turner as presiding judge of the Eighth District Court in Marysville. Turner was an irascible old Texan, with a well-earned reputation for spending more time in saloons than in chambers. It was inevitable that Field and Turner would clash, for Field, as the former alcalde of Marysville, resented Turner's appointment as the area's presiding district judge. Turner was the highest legal officer in Yuba County, California, but Field considered him an interloper, and an unlettered one at that. Nor did it help matters when Field took to belittling Turner's legal abilities publicly. In his book *Reminiscences,* Field insisted that it had always been his plan to befriend Turner, but that he found it impossible because the "old judge" was an implacable judicial bully who ran an unruly court.

Their troubles really began, Field wrote, when he sent the Texan a parcel of *New York Evening Post* newspapers. The *Post* was filled with anti-slavery oratory that offended Turner's southern sensibilities, but Field insists that he never meant to offend. He assumed that Turner would accept the newspapers as "a gesture of good will and respect."[1] But whether this was true or not, it appears disingenuous for Field to imply he was surprised that Turner was offended by the abolitionist newspaper. It was only a question of time before the two men would fall into persistent controversy.

That day came when, as an active lawyer, Field appeared in Turner's courtroom—their first encounter took place on a Wednesday morning in early June 1850. As it happened an attorney for the gold rush's famous John Sutter was reading a preliminary motion seeking to set aside a suit that had been filed against Sutter. In mid-sentence Judge Turner cut the attorney off and denied his motion. This galvanized Field and without an invitation or permission from the bench, Field, who was acting as Sutter's co-counsel, rose to his feet and began reading aloud a provision from the newly adopted statutory code of California that appeared to be in conflict with Turner's ruling (presumably Field assumed that Turner would be unaware of any new statutory provisions). The district judge interrupted Field and told him to sit down and be quiet. "The court knows the law and the mind of the court is made up," Turner snapped. But the truculent Field was not to be put off. He continued standing and he continued reading. When finished he added, "Should [Turner] make an unfavorable ruling it would be appealed to the state Supreme Court."

The magistrate knew insubordination when he heard it and barked at the bailiff, "Fine that man two-hundred dollars." Field reports his response to Turner's outburst as a "very well" or "well sir." The record is unclear, but barring selective inflections, either response seems harmless enough. But Field remained standing and Turner without delay increased the fine, "three-hundred dollars, then four-hundred dollars," and finally "five-hundred dollars and forty-eight hours under house arrest." The confrontation eventually ended with Field calling Turner "a damn old jackass" even as he was being ushered through the courthouse doors into the street.

When the county courthouse opened the following morning Field was in County Judge Henry Haun's courtroom seeking a writ of *habeas corpus*. Turner, he explained to Haun, had held him illegally overnight without a proper "writ of custody." Without delay Field had his writ from Judge Haun, who clearly shared Field's poor opinion of Turner. That same evening Field and two legal associates, Sam Mulford and Jesse Goodwin, plus a few other onlookers (including some saloon patrons and town layabouts) organized a mock hearing on the courthouse steps. At their meeting they ostentatiously proclaimed the irascible Turner unfit for the job and demanded his resignation. Then some of the more exuberant members of the crowd gathered in the town square and burned the judge's effigy. Later Field made it clear that he was not among the mob that burned Turner's ectype, but conveniently for these "friends" he was on hand to pay their $290 bar bill.

Two days passed and Field was again in Turner's court. He presented his writ, but the judge, having been informed about the "tomfoolery" two nights earlier, dismissed the writ and without further discussion disbarred Field, Mulford and Goodwin on the spot, and then, just for good measure, placed the three under a 48-hour house arrest and fined the colluding Judge Haun fifty dollars for having the effrontery to issue the writ in the first place. This action quickly brought a fighting Field and his friends before the California Supreme Court justices in San Francisco where they sought to vacate Turner's order with a recently enacted writ of *mandamus* (overturning, in this case, a writ of a lower court). Chief Justice Nathaniel Bennett of the Supreme Court was quite willing to oblige. He declared that a judicial officer had no right to disbar a lawyer without first holding a hearing of review, whereupon Bennett invited Turner to accept from Field "a reasonable apology and move on"—adding that "should the Judge fail to comply he would be fined $1,000."[2] But Turner ignored Bennett's order, and then lamely defended himself by insisting that the district courts were not under the jurisdiction of the state Supreme Court. After which he reaffirmed the original disbarment order and announced that, should Field, Mulford or Goodwin attempt to practice law in the "Eighth," he would "cut their ears off."[3]

Field, of course, was not likely to be put off. He again returned to the Supreme Court seeking Chief Justice Bennett's advice. "My advice" said the chief "is to buy a pistol and get off the first shot." Small comfort, thought Field. His tenacious discontent, however, led him to take Bennett's advice. As a "New Englander", he wrote years later, "I [was] inclined to settle [these] matters without violence, but, given Turner's [southern] nature I [heeded] Bennett's advice."[4] He returned home, and acting in no small measure, purchased a Bowie knife, two pistols, and a heavy muslin coat with pockets large enough to conceal the weapons. With his hands tucked in the coat, he practiced discharging the weapons through holes cut in the bottom of the pockets. In no time at all, he wrote, "I was proficient enough to hit a target [the size of a man's hat] from across a street."[5] What happened next depends on who is telling the story. According to Field, the old judge became so terrified by Field's newly acquired martial dexterity that he did all in his power to avoid the lawyer. In fact, Field writes, Turner was so fearful that he took to ducking out the back door of a saloon whenever Field appeared at the front door. Turner's friends' versions do not square with Field's rendition—it was Field who fled the saloons when Turner appeared, they insisted. But no matter where the truth lay, Field had every reason to fear Turner, for when the judge was drinking, he was a man pushed to violent behavior by a quick temper.

Field's next occasion to rankle Turner's disposition was a petition he distributed with one hundred forty-three signatures of prominent Marysville citizens demanding that Governor Peter Burnett fire Turner for incompetence. Yet because the governor was a friend of Turner's nothing came of Field's complaint, and he was forced to instigate his own strategy for removing Turner. He published a notice in the *Placer Times* newspaper describing Turner as a "man of depraved tastes, of vulgar habits, of an ungovernable temper, reckless of the truth when his passions are excited, and grossly incompetent to discharge the duties of his office."[6] Turner returned the compliment. He disbarred Field for a third time declaring him "a perjured damned villain." Again Field was back before the state Supreme Court pleading his case, and again the court directed the curmudgeonly Turner to lift his sanctions. This time the censure brought results. The three attorneys Field, Mulford and Goodwin, returned to the Eighth Court District and resumed practicing law without further hassling from Turner.

Yet, insofar as Field was concerned, the matter was far from over. When he joined the California Assembly as a legislator a year later, his first order of business was to guide through the assembly a bill protecting practicing attorneys from the tyranny of heavy-fisted judges. His *Bill of Judicial Reform* provided statutory relief for lawyers and set jurisdictions for courts of appellate review. The legislature had no trouble supporting his bill, insofar as it was intended to protect lawyers from unruly judges. Yet when he turned his attention to settling a personal score with Turner, his effort began to lose the support of most legislators.

Partially under the pretext of efficiency, Field proposed expanding and rearranging the state's judicial districts in such a way as to disguise a reprisal he intended for his old nemesis Turner. He proposed that the eight judicial districts in the state be expanded to eleven—essentially it was a plan to add two additional districts and divide "the Eighth." The old eighth district would represent Yuba, Sutter and Nevada Counties, and a new district, "the tenth," would be made up of Trinity and Klamath Counties along the Oregon border—so far so good. The legislature went along with his plan, but when he proposed four new judges to fill the district judgeships, most legislators balked. Field argued that the state needed three judges to fill the empty districts, and a fourth judge to replace the incompetent William R. Turner on "the old Eighth bench." The assembly, of course, had no disagreement on filling the empty positions, but they resisted his effort to remove Turner. They proposed a compromise—pack him off to the farthest reaches of the north county, for there, as the presiding judge of the "tenth district, he would do the least damage. This, of course, did not satisfy Field. He continued to badger the legislators, but to no avail. The best they were willing to do was to hide Turner away on the Oregon border.

Although they were in no mood to impeach Turner, Field continued his importuning until the legislators grew weary and began to publicly chastise Field as vindictive. One legislator responded, "Field, what's the use of pressing this matter? You have sent [him] where there are only grizzly bears and Indians; why not let him remain there? He can do no harm." Indeed, neither the assembly nor Field would do more harm to the judge, but the actions they had taken over time would prove destructive enough to slake even Field's vengeful impulses. Several years after banishment, Turner, having lost whatever interest he had in law, died a bitter, ineffectual and dipsomaniacal old man.

Turner, however, was not the only one upon whom this very public battle left its mark. It also established a perception of Field among fellow legislators as a vituperative and vindictive man. Field's biographer, Carl Brent Swisher, wrote "[Field] was a bit too lordly and suave in his manner, and too sublimely confident of his own rectitude, to be acclaimed a hero by the rougher elements of pioneer California."[7]

An anecdote, offered by Field himself 30 years later, was illustrative of why so many of his acquaintances found him in personal dealings too clever by half. While Turner was enduring his seventh year of banishment on the Oregon border, he brought before the Supreme Court a compensatory claim. The year was 1858, and Field was by then an associate justice on the California Supreme Court. When Turner appeared before the court, he was quite convinced that Field would see to it that the appeal would fail, but Field recused himself from the case and Turner won his claim. "Overwhelmed by my fairness," wrote Field shamelessly, "Turner sought me out to make amends for past differences, but I refused to accept an apology, [u]nder no circumstances would I ever [speak] to him [again]." Puzzled by the rebuff, Turner returned the following day and tried again to speak to Field only to receive an even harsher stare and more silence for his effort. "[Had I] yielded one inch I should have lost my self-respect and been for life an abject slave," he wrote.[8] This explanation leaves unexamined why calling off his resentments would have destroyed self-respect and enslaved him. Perhaps it is helpful to remember that Field's *Reminiscences*, from which this anecdote was drawn, was written in 1877, and Field was playing to a much larger audience by then—one that he hoped was politically attentive.

A second event from these exhilarating inaugural days that was interpreted through Field's lens of self-aggrandizement was a sketch concerning a running disagreement he had with Judge William T. Barbour. In 1851 both Judge Barbour and Judge Gordon N. Mott ran for Turner's vacated position on the Eighth District Court. Mott won the election, but before he could be seated, a dispute arose over the length of the term he was to serve. The governor, John Bigler, settled the matter by ignoring Mott's election altogether and appointing his friend William Barbour. Naturally, the governor's solution was unacceptable to Mott and he refused to drop out. It was an action that eventually forced the attorney general to take the matter before the Supreme Court. Field, representing Mott before the court, lost his client's appeal.

Forward two years. Barbour was running for reelection, and Field, still smarting from the earlier legal denunciation, campaigned vigorously against him. In no time at all, the campaign degenerated into a series of personal attacks: Field against Barbour and vice versa. In fact, campaign tactics became so rancorous that eventually a challenge was issued to settle the dispute on the dueling field. Which man actually initiated the challenge has remained a matter of dispute. As was the custom, the one challenged had the right to choose the weapons, but, according to Field, Barbour insisted on setting the terms for the entire event regardless of protocol. Absurdly, Barbour announced that they should fight to the death "with pistols and Bowie knives, [i]n a room twenty-foot by twenty-foot." Almost everyone considered Barbour's challenge a ridiculous bluff, but Field, wasting no time accepted all of Barbour's demands. It was a bluff indeed, and from that point on the ruse unraveled as Barbour began modifying his proposals, first by dropping his demand for a 20-foot room, then the Bowie knives, and finally the fight to the death.

What happened next, according to Field's friend Judge Mott, who was acting as Field's second, confirmed Field's version. A week after Barbour's bluff was called, the two men agreed to meet at an isolated spot on the banks of the Bear River, south of Marysville. It was a remote but convenient place to meet as it was adjacent to the stagecoach that ran from Marysville to Sacramento. On the day appointed for the duel, Field and Mott arrived at the agreed upon time, but Barbour did not appear until a full hour had passed. When the Marysville stage finally did arrive, it stopped on the well-traveled stage road several hundred yards from where Field and Mott were waiting. Barbour dismounted from the coach, but he did not walk toward the two men waiting at the dueling site; rather he lingered on the road under a spread of oak trees until the eastbound stage arrived. Then without a word, he mounted the coach and returned to Marysville. What had begun as a potential for tragedy, Mott later wrote, "ended as a farce." Everyone agreed, Field later commented, that Barbour's bluff had run its course and in the end he had come off looking like the "coward he was."

What occurred the following day ended the saga but remains in dispute, for excepting the two protagonists, apparently there were no witnesses (Field claims there were at least ten witnesses to the incident). According to Field, while he gathered firewood, Barbour crept up from behind and pressed the cold barrel-tip of a pistol to his ear, demanding that he defend himself. Whereupon, Field writes, he wheeled about and said, "You infernal scoundrel, you cowardly assassin—you come behind my back and put your revolver to my head and tell me to draw; you haven't the courage to shoot; shoot and be damned."[9] Barbour, Field insists, confronted by such courage skulked away in humiliation. Barbour and his friends, of course, offer a different version of the event. There was, they said, no pistol involved and Barbour used his boot "where it would do the most good." It was Field, not Barbour, they insisted, who fled the scene, locking himself in his office for the remainder of the day. Both versions of the encounter were given without additional declarations from witnesses so the truth of either, or neither, lay with an outsider's sympathies.

Months later, Barbour sought Field out hoping to settle their differences amiably, and surprisingly Field was agreeable—but only on the condition that no effort be made to explain each other's earlier behavior. Barbour cheerfully agreed and the two men sealed their reconciliation in a Marysville saloon. Obviously, Field's pledge of silence did not hamper him from putting his version of the episode in a published book twenty-five years later. But the mystery remains as to why Field was able to set aside his differences with Barbour but not with Turner. Perhaps in his own mind, his personal sense of complicity in the Turner incident was more equivocal.

The legislature that had met in San Jose in the winter of 1851, a legislature in which Field was to play a significant role, was, in Swisher's words, a "frontier legislature, [a collection of] rugged sun-tanned, bewhiskered frontiersmen with guns strapped around their waists." It was during such a burly state of affairs that the Legislature eventually passed a rule requiring legislators, while in legislative session, to remove their pistols from their waistbands and place them in their desk drawers. And such was the situation on that spring morning in 1851, when Field rose on the floor of the assembly determined to once again press his attack on Judge William Turner's character. Field had been pressuring the legislature for more than a week when one of Turner's friends, a much vexed legislator from Alabama by the name of B.F. Moore, had heard enough from the prolix Assemblyman Field on the character of his friend Turner. Ostentatiously, before Field's gaze, Moore withdrew a pistol from his desk drawer and placed it on top of the desk. In an instant Field had received Moore's message. He fumbled his words and cut his speech short in mid-sentence, after which he took a seat without further comment. Later in the afternoon, after fretting about how he had appeared to his comrades in the Assembly hall, and believing that he had been made the fool by seeming weak and ineffectual when challenged, Field decided to draw Moore into a duel. He contacted friends, requesting that one of them act as his emissary and carry a note to the Alabaman demanding a public apology or satisfaction, but his friends declined, citing the newly drafted constitutional prohibition against dueling.

Unsure of where next to turn that evening, Field wrote, he wandered downcast into the Senate chamber where he confronted David C. Broderick, who at the time was president of the Senate and would soon be California's fourth U.S. Senator. Broderick looked up from his desk, noticed Field's demeanor and asked for an explanation. Field recounted the morning's showdown, and with not a little hyperbole added, "I have not a friend in the world." To which the president of the Senate responded, "Ah, my dear Field, I will be your friend in this matter; go and write at once a note to Moore, and I will deliver it myself."[10]

Field's letter, however, evoked in Moore neither apology nor acceptance of the challenge, for as others before him had done he pleaded that legislators were prohibited from dueling. But, not wishing to be thought a coward, Moore declared himself quite willing to settle the dispute with "fists." To which Broderick responded, "That is unacceptable, [for] gentlemen do not settle these matters with fist-fights." Then concluding that nothing had been settled, but that nothing more need be said, Broderick announced that Field fully intended to continue making his charges against Turner the next day on the assembly floor. Moore's friend, Drury Baldwin, however, who was standing within earshot of the Broderick-Moore exchange, interrupted and warned Broderick that if Field were to continue to denounce Turner in the assembly he could expect "to be shot in his seat." "Field would not be the only one shot," was Broderick's instant persiflage.

The next morning when Field entered the chamber, he claims that he was surprised to notice that Broderick and nine of Broderick's somber friends were seated in the back row, "armed to the teeth." Moore, fully aware of what was going on, quickly jumped to his feet and offered a public apology before Field could rise and resume his monologue on Turner's failings. The apology defused whatever resentments may have been generated, but it did not change the feelings of the legislators toward Field and his calumny of Turner.

As an epilogue to this episode, six months after the event, Field and Broderick were conversing in a popular San Francisco haunt, when over Field's shoulder, Broderick noticed, in the vaporous recesses of the saloon, the glint of a pistol barrel pointed directly at Field's back. Without hesitation, Broderick shouldered Field onto the floor and, as it later proved, out of harm's way. The two men would discover that the weapon had been in the hands of Vicesimus Turner, one of old Judge Turner's revenge-seeking brothers.

These two events, Field later told his readers, left him with a durable sense of "gratitude and admiration" for Broderick, "even though [Broderick's] habits and companions were so much coarser than my own" (this assessment of Broderick's character only appears in an early draft of Field's *Reminiscences*). Unfortunately, however, their friendship was to falter several years later when Field refused to stand with Broderick in his patronage fight against the U.S. President James Buchanan. It was a rift that became even more rancorous when Field ran for election to the California Supreme Court against Broderick's handpicked candidate. In the campaign for the Supreme Court, Broderick would refer to Field as "a disloyal, ungrateful scoundrel." But Broderick's efforts notwithstanding, Field won election by a wide margin and joined David Terry on the State Supreme Court in October of 1857.

The two years that Terry and Field served together on the California Supreme Court (1857–1859) were invaluable foundational years in the history of California case law. Paul Kens, in his exhaustively researched study, *Justice Stephen Field*, writes that during Field's first year on the court, Terry and Associate Justice Peter H. Burnett teamed up to frustrate Field's judicial preferences; but this claim, while true, is also, to a degree, problematic, for Field's silence did not always imply disfavor.[11] For example, in close to 150 cases, the Texas populist Terry and the Massachusetts patrician Field wrote and supported each other's legal opinions, and more often than not, one or the other of the justices' concurring signature accompanied the opinions. Only in a relatively few cases did the record indicate that they were on opposite sides of an issue, but when they were, it proved to be a reliable barometer of their culturally rooted differences. In other word, when they declared their differences publicly, in each man's mind they were never minor differences, and in ensuing years the differences would produce between them vexation, indignation, bitterness and eventually palpable hostility. At the time of their court tenure, of course, they had no way of knowing that these moments of shared service would set the tone for perpetual mistrust, disrespect, suspicion and public hatred that would fulminate within each man's breast for a lifetime.

When the quality of their work on the California bench is assessed, comparisons are odious, for at every turn Field is by far the more gifted judge. He offered brilliantly complex, groundbreaking opinions, some of which continue even today to exercise influence over both federal and state courts. By comparison, Terry wrote overly austere, commonplace opinions, always with an eye to solving the momentary problem directly in front of him. There was no sweep of precedence, no minutely structured sense of philosophical coherence that was intended to stand the test of time—he never wrote with an eye to historical permanence. Perhaps, in a fundamental sense, they were comparable only in structured style, that is, their opinions were conceptually balanced, logically tight, and almost always imbued with a self-annointed sense of moral certitude.

In the remaining pages of this chapter the following cases are presented as fitting examples of the conflicting sensibilities that were both precursor and epilogue to the rancor that each man harbored toward the other. One of the earliest disagreements between them, and in many ways one of the most interesting, arose in a case called Ex Parte Newman, cited in the State Report of April 1858. It was an example of how each judge understood the intrusive yet necessary role that religion plays in the country's law and politics. The occasion was the review of a legislative statute entitled *"An Act to Provide for a Better Observance of the Sabbath."* The act was meant to forbid merchants from engaging in commerce on "the Christian Sabbath." In this particular instance, an "Israelite" clothier by the name of Newman (referred to *only* as Newman in the court opinion) had been arrested for desecrating the Christian Sabbath day. As a result, Newman had been given the option of paying a fifty dollar fine or spending thirty-five days in Sacramento's city jail. He chose jail and immediately filed a writ of release. When the case eventually reached the Supreme Court, Field, in an opinion that was to foreshadow his later judicial ingenuity, offered an effulgent defense of the statute.

It would be a mistake, he wrote, to think of this event as raising First Amendment issues pertaining to the freedom of religion. The legislature is not violating the "free-exercise clause of the First Amendment; [rather the California] statute should be read as a simple issue of civil restriction designed to protect social order." The legislative result, whether the legislature was aware of what they had done or not, Field insisted, had the consequence of placing restrictions on the country's rampant commercialism. That is to say, by initiating a law requiring "the cessation of labor one day in seven for good and natural reasons" it protects those who labor with their hands from exploitation. Unabated manual labor without a resting time is contrary to "nature's law," he argued, and if left unaccommodated would eventually ravage the working class. Without a day of rest in every seven, a worker's health and moral stability would dissipate, for in any master-servant, employer-employee or owner-worker relationship, there must be civil laws that protect the "controlled from the controllers and the powerless from the powerful." In this case, Field continued, the legislature had stepped in to prevent the destruction of workers "by restraining [the obsessive] power of capital to work them until they fall ill."[12] Moreover, it is irrelevant that the day of rest coincides with the Christian Sabbath for this is mere happenstance. True enough, the act supported the religious preferences of Christians to the inconvenience of non-Christians, but setting aside any day of the week would have its "critics and inconveniences." The court, Field concluded, had to determine whether this act is equitable and uniform and leave the question of its "abusiveness," if there was any, to a vote of the people of California. Field's finished opinion, of course, was all that the legislators could have asked for and was a remarkably canny legal defense of the community's religious preferences, aspirations and biases.

In contrast, the act held no such hidden "natural agenda" for the majority. Chief Justice David Terry and Associate Justice Peter Burnett. Contrary to Field's assertion that it was not an example of a violation of the First Amendment's "free exercise clause" Terry and Burnett saw the statute as a clear-cut violation of the free exercise clause. True to his independent southern Baptist polity, Terry began the case for reversal with the charge that "even the title was unequivocal [the Legislature would impose penalties on those who did not observe] the *Christian* Sabbath." The act, he wrote, was on its face unconstitutional in two fundamental ways. "[*P*]*rima facie,* it prevented a 'free exercise of religion' and 'a right to acquire property.'" By compelling individuals to observe the religious preferences of the society's majority it was in violation of the church-state Doctrine of Separation. One would err, Terry declared, to assume that the Constitution was designed to be a mere treatise on "religious toleration." It implies much more, he continued—the authors devised it intentionally to protect both religious freedom and religious liberty. To judge the act as Justice Field did was to create a slippery slope that eventually will only slide into *"an establishment* of a state religion." The state's intent was unambiguous, Terry insisted. It is meant to impose "the Christian day of worship on its citizens," and it was disingenuous to believe that the act was a civil order meant to advance the general interests of state commerce. By interpreting the act as a civil rather than a religious document, Terry insisted, Field had given legal protection to a new form of law—a law promoting "majoritarian intolerance." In point of fact, Terry concluded, how could such a statute ever sensibly assess the amount of "rest" individual laborers needed from their labor?

On the record, Terry showed no hesitancy to admit that Field's "Sabbath law" opinion might appear to be a well-reasoned and farsighted piece of social legislating, but privately he was convinced that Field knew better. It was no less than an ingenuous legal device that supported what Field could not bring himself to oppose, namely, the whims and wishes of politically powerful people. With the religious freedom case, Terry began for the first time to formulate the notion that his colleague Field was dispositionally incapable of writing opinions contrary to the interests of his wealthy and well-placed friends. Field was, said Terry darkly, "bought by the church and reversed by the federal courts."

Justice Field's propensity for protecting the aspirations of businessmen and entrepreneurs, in contrast to Terry's march toward anti-monopolist populism and the defense of miners' and the workingman's interests (never mind the injustice of any particular case), played an increasingly wider role in a growing distrust that the two men were to have for each other. It was a division that manifested itself most indelibly in a series of major "property rights" cases, more particularly in the interminable conflict that arose between landowners' "rights" and a miner's intrusive "claims." In short, miners wanted assurance that the law would protect their proprietary rights to the gold they extracted from the land *wherever* they might find it! As a consequence, an entirely inadequate attempt to determine which land was the government's and which was a private citizen's was made by the state legislature in the Land Act of 1851, but the responsibility for sorting out the complex exceptions and differences inevitably fell into the hands of state court judges.

State legislators, well aware that a large segment of the population would find one solution or another unacceptable no matter how the issue was settled, were all too willing to sweep this mare's nest of legal ambiguities off their own desks and onto the desks of courtroom judges.

The state's fifth Supreme Court justice, Solomon Heydenfeldt, was one of the first of the judges who dealt with the subject in a significant fashion. In *Hicks v. Bell*, pressed with an ever more demanding public call for the resolution of the "entitlement problem," Heydenfeldt searched for a legal remedy that would protect the miners' rights by virtue of their "seeking and finding."[13] In his seminal opinion, Heydenfeldt reached back three centuries to the conception of *ownership* as it appeared in English common law. In common law he singles out the doctrine of *first possessor.* Under this formula, he argued, a miner had a "right of ownership" over all that he had mined. It was a right secured by the sovereign who owned the land as *first possessor,* for as first titleholder, the sovereign had the sole power to authorize the transfer of the deeds to whosoever [he or she] would. "[T]he King has the right of distribution thereon and therein. [He] has a claim on the forest covering the surface of the land, or a claim on the harvest of the minerals within it—and even when the land has been deeded to subordinates, the crown's first-claim continues to prevail." Under the rule of *first possessor*, Heydenfeldt concludes, the state of California has the right to authorize boundaries, because its ownership was transferred by the continuity of *absolute legacy* from the U.S. government's treaty with the Mexican landholders back through time to the Spanish monarchs *jura regalia* (royal privilege). Now insofar as the miners' mineral leases were concerned, the state, as first possessor, had agreed to share the land's mineral wealth with the extractors for the price of "royalty due,"—that is to say, for a taxable percentage of the value of the minerals mined. The miners' legal rights, therefore, were secured as *subordinate possessory*, and were protected by toil and taxed payment, *jura signa* (against all other parties).

Unfortunately, Heydenfeldt's 1853 version of *Hicks* hit a snag immediately, for he had chosen to remain silent on the essential matter of private ownership, i.e., the connection between the *first possessor* and the common law principle of *prima facie* title to private land. The omission, quite obviously, left vast amounts of unsurveyed land without legal relief, and it also left in limbo the matter of illegal or disputed grants or deeds (that must necessarily flow form the problem of ill-defined or overlapping boundaries). Much of California's land was without judicial immunity, having been methodically ignored or left legally uncovered by overburdened or ineffectual land assessors. "In the first years of frantic activity," wrote Carl Swisher, "most of the mines were located either on public or on private tracts which were so large that the use of the land brought no great loss (or at least no noticeable loss) upon the owner."[14]

By mid-decade, however, expectations and activities had changed. Mining was proliferating in every rivulet, creek or gully, and the congestion drove ranchers, speculators and homesteaders into the state's legislative offices, demanding that the lawmakers deal with the problem. Homesteaders, in particular insisted that boundaries be accurately drawn so that legal ejectment of squatters and fortune-seekers who "continued to despoil California's hillsides with impunity [could be run off]." Two years later, Heydenfeldt, finally acknowledged that the omission between public and private land in *Hicks* was a howling misjudgment when he attached an *obiter dicta* (an, "oh by the way") to the original opinion—declaring that the *Hicks* decision was applicable only to public land.[15]

It now remained for Terry and Field to face the problem of public-private land rights that *Hicks* had only begun to solve. And it was not surprising that any judicial consideration of Mexican land-grant rights, private ownership and possessory claims by the miners was sure to nourish legal dissension between two intransigent justices.

An illustrative example of the continuing dispute was to be found in *Ferris v. Coover.*[16] Ferris, representing the plaintiff Captain John Sutter, brought into court the defendant Coover seeking to eject him from land that Sutter owned—land that Sutter had purchased from the Mexican government in 1844. Coover's defense was to insist that Sutter's original land deed had "floating boundaries" and did not, in fact, cover the land Coover was occupying. Moreover, even if it could be shown that the property occupied by the defendant was within the original 11 leagues purchased by Sutter from the Mexican government, Sutter should relinquish his ownership, Coover said, because he had never acknowledged ownership during the three years that Coover was occupying and improving the land. In other words, just in case it should prove to be Sutter's land, the toil expended improving the land qualified Coover as its *first possessor*.

Coover's first argument had been rejected when a lower court jury determined that Sutter was the *bone fide possessor* by virtue of a pre-treaty Mexican map confirming the deed's ownership. However, on appeal in the spring of 1858, the defendant stood before Chief Justice Terry and Justices Field and Joseph G. Baldwin with his first possessor claim as his first line of defense. Justices Field and Baldwin straightway upheld the jury's ejectment of Coover, while Chief Justice Terry supported him, insisting that his toil had indeed made him *first possessor*—"[p]ossession should prevail over title," Terry argued. Coover, still unwilling to give up, therefore moved on to the federal district court in San Francisco where he filed a *writ of error* seeking to overturn his state Supreme Court defeat. With Coover's action Terry was squeezed into a jurisprudential box. He was forced to face two conflicting principles: Coovers's right of first possessor and California's jurisdictional right over the federal government. Ever the southerner he found himself deliberating on the other side of his own Coover decision. He defended the autonomy of the state Supreme Court's action even though he had opposed the original decision. He contended that the federal district court had no legal authorization to file *a writ of error* before the state's highest court. The Tenth Amendment to the U.S. Constitution, he maintained, reserved to the states "powers not delegated" to the federal government—citing Alexander Hamilton's famous declaration of "first attachment." State and federal jurisdictions, it said, hold the "power of coordinated tribunals."

To make his argument, Terry recited with approval Heydenfeldt's opinion in *Johnson v. Gordon*: "The Court of first attachment is the final and conclusive reviewer."[17] By which Terry meant that Coover had no legal basis for appealing a losing verdict suffered at the hands of the state's court on the grounds that state courts are inferior to federal courts—which, Terry insisted, they were not. The U.S. court was, Terry concluded, *scoram non judice* (a prostituted jurisdiction), for the right to settle controversies "[is] an essential element of sovereignty, which is possessed by each State before the adoption of the Constitution, and is not surrendered by that compact." Therefore only agreements by "common consent of both governments" meet the American constitutional standard for the determination of superior jurisdictions. Terry then acknowledges that the only two examples where state government must acknowledge federal jurisdiction were national treaties and interstate commerce. He then concluded with his approval of Heydenfeldt's declaration "[that the subordination] of the States' courts to the federal court under the guise of uniformity is the chimera of an unhealthy brain."

Again, Terry's northern protagonists, Baldwin and Field, found Terry's position implausible. They laid down as settled law the Federal Judiciary Act of 1789 that years earlier had determined the matter and created "[the] doorway of appeal." Federal law was sovereign over state law, they wrote, in response to Coover's *writ of error*, and hence had "standing" before the United States Supreme Court. Chief Justice Terry, Baldwin explained, had ignored the explicit authority granted the federal court, and had covered himself with the mantle of anachronous *constructionism* in an incorrigible effort to misread the "reserved to the States or to the people" clause in the Tenth Amendment. On the question of state and federal authority, therefore, Terry and the associate justices' constitutional interpretations were irreconcilable, said Baldwin, for at the center of the disagreement lay each judge's perception of "state autonomy." To be sure, on numerous occasions Field had defended the venerable southern doctrine of "states' rights," but when it came to appellate review at the federal level, Field and Baldwin would never concede that the state court and the national court were coordinate tribunals.

Twenty-five years later, Terry's and Field's notions of superior and inferior jurisdictions would again produce irreconcilable differences between the two men, but this time it would take place in a federal court room.

The most famous, far-reaching and interesting case on private ownership, however, that Terry and Field shared was *Biddle Boggs v. The Merced Mining Company.*[18] It was a dispute that was once again to pull the jurists in opposite directions. Field, eager to strengthen California's law on land entitlements, plunged into the *Boggs* case with his usual intellectual fervor. He envisioned a more serviceable replacement of *Hicks'* frontier or agrarian populism, one that would bind "a miner's right of land entitlement" to the secure foundation of contractarian law. Conversely, Terry felt no need to adjust his perception of the issue or his populist sympathies that lay for him with the miners. He continued supporting Solomon Heydenfeldt's original interpretation in the early *Hicks*.

Eventually, thanks primarily to Field, *Boggs* would become one of the earliest and most frequently cited and effectual opinions, on "frontier property law" in the United States. The *Boggs* case began as a gigantic tangle of overlapping issues entailing property boundaries, property transfer, treaties, and civil penalties, but eventually it came down to a definition of "caretaker" and "protector" when applied to California's doctrine of private ownership. It is difficult, and perhaps even misleading, to condense the circuitous story of *Boggs,* but the essential points of dispute are these: California's first senator, John C. Fremont, had leased to a man with the euphonious name of Biddle Boggs a portion of an estate that he had purchased from Juan Alvarado four years prior to the 1848 Treaty of Annexation (Mexico's version of the treaty of *Guadalupe Hildalgo*). This vast tract of land had come into Alvarado's hands by deed of the Mexican governor. Alvarado called the land "Las Mariposas (the butterflies)," and, as was typical of so much property at the time, the Mariposas was a gigantic "floating land grant" whose exact boundaries had never been adequately surveyed either by the Mexican or U.S. authorities.

Prior to Boggs' lease, the Merced Mining Company had discovered a giant deposit of gold ore embedded in the bulky, resistive veins of quartz rock that ran through the northern end of the Alvarado estate. Everyone agreed that it would be an expensive project to extract the gold from the earth, for not only did the quartz have to be blasted from the ground, but it also had to be transported to a mill that had the costly crushing machinery that could extract the ore from the quartz. Prospectors agreed that the project would require many speculators with a good deal of money to invest. (Conventional wisdom also insisted that the Merced Mining Company had not been digging on the Mariposas but on land adjacent to it).

Once the size of the gold cache had been determined, however, Fremont decided to make a significant adjustment to the original story he had been telling. Contrary to what he had stated in his initial report, he now insisted that the Merced Mining Company was mining not adjacent to the Mariposas, but on it, and hence, owed him compensation for the gold ore they were extracting. In the earliest litigation of *Boggs*, the quartz vein had been excluded in the Land Commission's survey, but by 1855, when the case reached the United States Supreme Court as *Fremont v. United States,* a revised survey was presented in the federal court that supported Fremont's assertions to a tee. The gold-rich northern region, the second survey declared, was indeed on the famous explorer's property. (It was, however, in the eyes of attentive cynics, not by accident that the new survey included as part of Fremont's estate much of the gold-rich property, for it was common knowledge that the District Court's appointed surveyor, Texas Ranger John C. Hays, "Texas Jack," had been a long-time friend and comrade of Fremont's.)[19] Justices Burnett and Terry, collaborating on the state court's first review of *Boggs*, found in the Merced Mining Company's favor. That is, consistent with the original *Hicks*, they wrote that Merced had the right by land entitlement, and also by discovery, as *first possessor* of the minerals. The plaintiffs, Fremont and Boggs, therefore, were not entitled, nor had they earned compensatory relief. The newly elected Justice Field may have disagreed with Terry and Burnett, but if he did he kept his own counsel for he wrote no concurring or dissenting opinion.

A year went by and the makeup of the court changed. Burnett resigned, as did Baldwin, who had been one of Fremont's original attorneys before another court replaced him. Yet, no one was astonished when a motion was filed to revisit *Boggs*. Field granted the motion, and Baldwin, as Fremont's former counsel, recused himself, thereby making it necessary for Terry and Field to hammer out the decision between themselves. Terry's position did not change; he remained the constant populist. He supported the original *Hicks,* to wit, the government had transferred the right to dig for the minerals to the miners. The government as the sovereign had the authority to "license" the miners to extract the gold, and thus it was not a relevant matter whether the mine lay within private or public boundaries.

Terry's opinion, however, would prove to be neither of interest nor an impediment to Justice Field. Field decided that he need only write an opinion that pleased himself, knowing full well that in the end he could depend on Baldwin's support. Field went to work. First, beginning where Heydenfeldt had begun, he sought the somewhat rarified historical confirmation of 16th century English jurisprudence, but in contrast to Heydenfeldt, his argument was meant to stand the *Hicks* case on its head, and therefore critics were quick to accuse him of being swayed by Fremont's and Baldwin's interests. Yet, whether these accusations were true or not, it became inconsequential, for his analysis had the authentic ring of his long-held perspective on the absolute sanctity of private property. Heydenfeldt's opinion, Field began, "[failed to enforce] the imperative between public and private land [thereby destroying the legal relationship between *meus et tuus* (mine and thine)], between appropriation and the [*prima facie*] i.e., priority of ownership [the unchallenged act of mining another's private land]." As Heydenfeldt had clearly stated, Field continued, the 16th century common law doctrine of *first possessor* properly defined the relationship between private and public ownership. There was, and still is, a "right of the sovereign doctrine," he wrote. But while the sovereign's ownership doctrine applies to "all public lands," it fails when these "attributions" are transferred to private possessors, that is to say, "the deed to property is relinquished by the sovereign [into the hands] of the private owner[s]." Under these conditions, the sovereign turns over the right of possession to the private owner. And in *Boggs*, everyone must agree, entitlement of the land is *prima facie.* At the Treaty of Guadalupe Hidalgo, Field argued, the federal government acknowledged "the right of private ownership and the transfer of [attributions] contained on or within the land, [and had, thereafter, given up any controlling authority] to permit mining on what was deemed private land." As long as the government is the owner of the land, it controls the entry and removal of its attributions.

> [But] there is something shocking to all our ideas of property in the proposition that one man may invade the possessions of another, dig up his fields and gardens, cut down his timber and occupy his land, under the pretense that he has a reason to believe there is gold under the surface, or if existing, that he wishes to extract and remove it.[20]

Well aware that the chief justice would never support his version of *Boggs*, Field did not press his case before the court, nor did he enlist Baldwin's support. And, of course, he was right about Terry; as a southern populist, the chief justice remained loyal to the wishes of the independent miners and settlers who were united in their demands that the profit of their labor had produced a right to it. The immigrant miners had a verifiable claim to the minerals of state land, Terry declared, because California's sovereignty "holds [in perpetuity] the attribution, [u]pon and within its domain, [both public and private]."

However, by September of 1859, circumstances were such that Terry had resigned from the court and a new associate justice, Warner Walter Cope, had taken his place (an associate justice that voted with Field), and so it was that *Hicks* I was overturned much to the anguish of the "stake miners and settlers," and much to the satisfaction of land owners and speculators. The repercussion of the reversal, of course, produced unfettered gossip against Field who, after Terry's resignation, had become the chief justice. Charges of legislative and legal corruption erupted throughout the state, with many of these accusations arising from within the state legislature itself. Shortly after the decision, the slanderous chatter, commonplace in San Francisco and Sacramento, took on a statewide life of its own with the appearance of a published pamphlet inelegantly titled, "*The Gold Key Court: or the Corruption of the Majority of It*," by an "Ex Supreme Court Broker."[21]

The consensus was that it was the work of James A. MacDougal, who, at the time of the first *Boggs* decision, was Attorney General of California. MacDougal would later continue his political career as a U.S. senator from Oregon. The pamphlet charged, among other things, that Fremont had given Associate Justice Baldwin a $100,000 bond secured on the value of the Mariposas to see to it that *Hicks* was reversed; that Field was given a wedding present of $25,000 by a grateful Fremont for writing the brilliant reversal, and that Field and his new bride, Sue Virginia Swearingen, would honeymoon on the East Coast until public rumor on the subject had blown over. Moreover, the pamphlet continued, when the Fields returned to the state the couple was to be given an additional $25,000 to get their marriage off on the right foot. Evidence of such a nefarious arrangement, of course, was next to impossible to prove, but miners and settlers were quite willing to believe it, given their losses and the order of the so-called "coincidences."

While it was not unusual for litigants to buy favorable decisions in the 19th-century courts, Judge Terry was outspokenly opposed to the practice, and needless to say was quietly pleased when the pamphleteer declared him to be "presently the only honest Judge on the court." In contrast, Field, by saying nothing about the charges, only fanned his critics' belief that he had been accepting money for crafting legal and statutory opinions, not just on this occasion, but from his earliest days in the Legislature—accusations, of course, that were only hunches without hard evidence. From Terry's perspective, however, the charges were substantiated when one of Fremont's attorneys approached him with cash if he would vote in a manner that supported Fremont's interests. The bribe failed miserably when the chief justice, in one of his well-known rampages, was said to have chased the terrified courier out of his office and even down the street.

Field's motives aside, however, it would be a mistake to minimize the importance of his opinion in *Boggs,* for almost single-handedly Field's interpretations hastened efforts to fix accurate boundaries of ownership that in turn, played a primary role in stimulating a century of booming land speculating throughout the western territories. Field's effort was in reality one of the earliest constructive attempts to settle the problem facing landowners, land speculators, miners, immigrants and settlers. It also became a forerunner to many of the statutes drafted thereafter that were to provide "land titles" procedures—procedures that are to this day in place, with only transitional emendations. It is fair to argue that Field did more than any other individual to initiate stability in California's land claims. Moreover, he was also one of the chief architects of mining and water law—strategies that, twenty-five years later, would imbue the federal government's mining and water laws.

Boggs was the most important and best well-publicized land-title controversy in which Field and Terry found themselves in serious disagreement, but second to it in influence and interest was a drawn-out controversy known to San Franciscans as the "water-lot" cases. These cases appeared well before either justice had joined the court and carried with them into the era of both justices' innumerable accusations of judicial conjuring.

The trouble began in the first year of statehood when San Francisco's "Commissioners of the Funded Debt" (the Board of Supervisors) made available to the public bay-front marsh land for launching and docking private boats. This largess became possible only because the commissioners believed that the marshy land was good for nothing else. The land in question was adjacent to the warehouse district, stretching along Fourth Street from the China Basin south to a water inlet know as the Central Basin. Years later the land would become invaluable, located as it was in proximity to the city's expanding commercial district, but in 1852 it appeared to most San Franciscans as worthless swamp land.

A year later, however, when city engineers argued that a landfill and a breakwater would easily convert the tidelands into valuable commercial property, the commissioners withdrew their offer making the land available for docking. Within weeks of the reversal the board began selling these slips at auction as business venture property. The commission's perfidy was amply rewarded when the auction reaped considerable profit—in excess of $1,200,000, which was a sizable amount in 1853. But it also provoked litigation from the citizenry, particularly from those people with money tied up in dockside commercial services. Charging fraud, irate investors and speculators took the commission into court, seeking both a policy change and financial redress. During preparation for trial, however, as experts for the defense began questioning the economic feasibility of reclaiming the marshy land, the commissioners again changed their minds. But the matter had dragged on for so long that public inattentiveness had allowed the litigation to fall into the conveniently languorous state of postponed court dates. Ultimately, the case lost the public's interest altogether, and became a litigious exercise devoted to rescuing the financial investments of wealthy speculators who had participated in the initial offerings.

The high-profile San Francisco attorney, Joseph Baldwin (later to join the state's Supreme Court), was engaged to find a legal loophole whereby investors might recoup the value of their original investments. Baldwin's solution was straightforward and uncomplicated. He argued that the commissioners had no authority to sell the water-lots in the first place—that only the state legislature had the authority to sell California's shoreline property. Hence, the city's 1853 "Water Lot Act," giving the city commissioners the right to sell the property, was in violation of the state's constitution. When the case eventually found its way to the California Supreme Court in 1857, Terry, after reading Baldwin's *brief of title*, reacted in predictable fashion. He dismissed Baldwin's argument out of hand calling it "without merit." "The law," he declared, "is a tool for resolving social problems not for doing mischief through legally contrived technicalities." "The aldermen," he went on "had [every] authority to sell the city's property and to expect the purchasers to honor their contracts."

At this 1857 review, Field, who had just joined the court, remained silent on the issue, and therefore led most court watchers to believe that his silence meant agreement with the chief justice. But three years later, he had either changed his opinion or was now ready to declare his true feelings on the matter.[22] Terry's time had ended on the state's highest bench by 1860. He was no longer chief justice, Burnett had retired, and Joseph Baldwin, who had been the plaintiff's attorney in the initial water-lot cases in 1852, had become a gifted and influential member of the state's Supreme Court. Baldwin's former law firm judged it now time to ask for a review of the case, and Field, as the court's new chief justice, granted it without a great deal of discussion. As the first step Baldwin, with public fanfare, recused himself from the case, so that once again the task of review fell upon the capable shoulders of the chief justice.[23] With the freedom to do it the way he wished, Field wrote a stinging reversal of the original opinion—including a gratuitous slap at the former chief justice. Terry's initial argument, Field declared, "was completely erroneous."[24]

In order to reverse it, however, and with Baldwin again recusing himself, Field needed to turn to the newest member of the court, Associate Justice

W. Walter Cope. Unfortunately for Field, Cope was unwilling to support the opinion unless Field was prepared to make certain textual modifications. Field agreed to the changes but not without publishing his vexations. In Field's first draft, he had argued that the city fathers had no right to sell the lots because the contracts were not theirs to sell. Therefore, he reasoned, the city contracts were worthless. Thus all investment money must be returned to the plaintiffs. Plus, he ventured for good measure, "the costs they have lost [in] interest payments. But Cope rejected Field's interpretation, arguing contrarily, as Terry had two years earlier, that Field's position was protecting defaulting investors who were *bona fide judgment creditors*. The city council, Cope insisted, had acted in good faith. They had met their obligation as sellers, and therefore had a right to reclaim all land titles by *reconvention* (counter suit). The annoyed chief justice conceded Cope's point, but did, so it seemed, only to avoid another judiciary stalemate.

Later he would publish a logical objection to Cope's reasoning: "[if Cope] is correct, then the court has found in favor of the plaintiffs (the commissioners) who have voided their contracts by reneging on them."[25] Exactly! Cope must have thought.

Once again Terry's efforts were brushed aside while Field's legal sagacity prevailed, and once again, Field faced the charge from a contentious public that his opinion had been written not on the merit, but with an eye to reaping a profit and ingratiating himself with the state's business establishment. Concerning this episode, Attorney General MacDougal reported that Field had received $10,000 plus the title to some prime San Francisco property. *The Bulletin* commented bemusedly that it would be wise if the commission did not rush to carry out the Supreme Court's latest legal verdict, "[f]or in time this Court will change as it frequently does and eventually there will be an honest court that will render a fairer ruling." From all the evidence available, Field seemed unconcerned with these charges and never offered any public explanation. This was unlike his predecessor, Terry, who continued to cherish his public image as an honest judge, and went out of his way to cultivate the image. Indeed, shortly after stepping down from the court, Terry was publicly praised for a circumstance that was in sharp contrast to his colleague's public image.

In the incident, well known to the public, Terry had ruled that the 1858 legislators were acting unconstitutionally by spending money that exceeded the $300,000-per-year limit as stipulated in the state constitution. As a result, California had become four million dollars over budget. What, in retrospect, was remarkable about Terry's judgment was not so much that he had stated the obvious—the state was indeed over budget, but rather it was the public's awareness of a relatively inconsequential personal event that followed. A colleague of Terry's, knowing that the chief justice held a sizable portfolio of state bonds, encouraged Terry to trade them off before he made his judicial opinion public. The chief justice bristled at the suggestion. "What do you take me for, a damn thief? Do you think I would be a Jew with what I have declared worthless? No sir! I'll take my chances with the other creditors of the State for their redemption. Never come to me with such a proposition again, sir."[26] Of course, his colleague never brought up the matter again, at least not in his presence.

In April of 1859, as Terry's elected term on the court was drawing to a close, an event occurred between Terry and Field that offered outsiders a rare glimpse into their relationship. To set the context of the incident, it was a time when the legislators and the justices were not on the best of terms. From the state's inception, legislators had been diligent in their effort to "reign in" what they exaggeratedly called the excessive power of the judiciary. Because of this concern the legislators, during that spring of 1859, imposed on the Supreme Court a rule that the court would see as yet one more trivial restriction undermining their authority. The state senate took from the justices the responsibility of interviewing and hiring their own court reporter and handed the task over to the governor.

What had started out as an incidental policy change then became a public indignity when the Sacramento newspapers played up the episode and sided with the legislators (the newspapers had been for some time complaining about the long delays between the announcement of judicial decisions and their public documentation). The transfer of responsibility got off to a rocky start, however, when Governor J. Neely Johnson chose to replace a popular court reporter, Charles S. Fairfax (the last English Lord Fairfax), on the pretext that only an American should hold the job. The indignity was then compounded when Johnson appointed to the position his political associate and friend Harvey Lee. Lee had earned the animus of all the justices when he failed to return to Chief Justice Hugh Murray's estate books he had borrowed when Murray was alive. Rumor had it that Lee (Murray's part-time aid), always financially strapped, had sold Murray's books and pocketed the money. Not surprisingly, therefore, the justices, incensed by Lee's purported conduct, were wholly unprepared to accept his appointment as the court's reporter. Field, particularly indignant, was determined to make his displeasure known. The following morning a "card" (public notice) appeared in the *Sacramento Bee* from Justice Field stating, among other things, "that the Supreme Court Judges did not want [Lee] nor would they allow him to be [their] reporter, because he was a thief."[27]

A day later, a fractious coterie of Lee's friends paid Field a visit and presented him with an ultimatum: withdraw the charge or be prepared to face Lee in a fight. Field, fully aware of Lee's violent reputation as a knife-fighter, offered to retract his comments but asked to do so privately, Lee's compeers, however, made it clear that only a public retraction would be acceptable. Field sent them away, then vacillated for a day, but eventually agreed to offer the public retraction they had insisted upon. His public notice appeared in the *Bee* on April 29:"[I] applied to you [Lee]" he said. "an opprobrious epithet—[it was misinformation] given to me by another. [I] did you an injustice. [An] injustice to you as well as to me, for I believed the man [unnamed and now deceased] (did he have Justice Murray in mind?). [Therefore] I have availed myself of the first opportunity [to] withdraw [the] epithet used."[28]

The denouement of the melodrama was even better. Terry had been out of town, but returned just in time to read Field's public retraction. Without delay he went to Field and chastised him for publishing such an unprincipled letter. By capitulating, he insisted, Field had demeaned both himself and the court. "Never should [you] have written the retraction, for what [you] said [about Lee on the first card] was correct!" Lee's behavior, Terry went on, "deserved the condemnation leveled at him, but your belated retraction ha[s] made [you] and the Court look weak [and ineffectual]."

Apparently Field absorbed Terry's rebuke without protestation. Yet, just as quickly, he sought out someone other than himself to blame even as he had done in his letter of retraction. It would seem that Justice Baldwin standing nearby was conveniently accessible, so Field turned to him and protested, "see what you have made me do, Baldwin; see what you have made me do. If Terry had been here he would not have let me [be] disgraced. It was all your fault Baldwin; you have said worse things about Lee than I."[29]

One can only suppose that when Field reflected on this curious confrontation years later he would be inwardly uncomfortable by his pusillanimity and the chief justice's all-too-public disdain for what he regarded as Field's mealy-mouthed, blame-shifting performance.

NOTES

1. Stephen J. Field. *Personal Reminiscences of Early Days in California* (New York: De Capo 1893). 33.
2. *Mulford v. Turner,* 1 Cal. 143, (June 1850. 3. July 27, 1850).
3. Stephen J. Field, *Reminiscences* 43.
4. —— *Reminiscences*. 44.
5. —— *Reminiscences*. 44.
6. Carl Brent Swisher. *Stephen J. Field: Craftsman of the Law* (Washington D.C.: Brookings Institute. 1930). 42.
7. Ibid. 49.
8. Stephen J. Field, *Reminiscences,* 107.

9. —— *Reminiscences*. 90.

10. —— *Reminiscences.* 67.

11. Paul Kens. *Justice Stephen J. Field* (Lawrence KN.: The University of Kansas Press, 1997). 74.

12. Stephen J. Field, *Some Opinions and Papers of Judge Stephen J. Field U.S. Supreme Court.* v. 2, pamphlet 20; also, Ex parte Newman. 9 Cal. 502, 9 Cal. Rep. 518. (1858).

13. *Hicks v. Bell,* 3 Cal 219, July 1853.

14. C. B. Swisher, *Craftsman,* 83.

15. *Stoakes v. Barrett,* 5 Cal. 36, January 1855.

16. *Ferris v. Coover,* 10 Cal. 589, October 1858, and *Ferris v. Coover,* 11 Cal. 182, October 1858.

17. *Johnson v. Gordon,* 4 Cal. 368, October 1854. See also, *Gunn v. Bates,* 6 Cal. 263.

18. *Biddle Boggs v. The Merced Mining Company,* 14 Cal. 279, October 1858. See also, Field. *Some Opinions. v.*1 pamphlet 24, Jennison v. Kirk, October 1878, 98 U.S. 453. Review of common right of mining and water by same claimant.

19. For a detailed, enjoyable account of this legal battle see Paul Kens, *Justice Stephen Field*. 70ff.

20. 14 Cal. 279.

21. The Huntington Library MSS (San Marino CA.) (1861).

22. Stephen J. Field, *Some Opinions and Papers of Stephen J. Field.* The Ninth Circuit Court of the United States, v. III, pamphlet 1, Also, *McCracken v. the City of San Francisco,* 16 Cal. 591, and Grogan v. San Francisco, 18 Cal. 590, (July 1861). Also, S. J. Field, *Some Opinions,* Beard v. Federy, December 1865, and 3 Wallace, 478. Field reviews all private claims by Board of Commissioners of March 3, 1851 that were generated by the Spanish or Mexican Governments. His conclusion: that all claims must be treated as abandoned title after the above date, and thereafter becoming part of the public domain.

23. *Hyman v. Read*, 13 Cal.144. 1857.

24. *McCracken v. the City of San Francisco*, 16 Cal. 591. (1860).

25. 16 Cal. 6.

26. Overland Monthly, Oct. 1889. Vol.14, No. 82, 343.

27. *Sacramento Bee*, April 3, 1859.

28. C. B. Swisher, *Craftsman*. 108.

29. A.E. Wagstaff. *The Life of the Ex. Chief Justice of the Supreme Court of California David S. Terry.*

Chapter Six

Persona Non Grata

The year 1859 meant the end of Terry's elected term on the state's Supreme Court. If he were to return to the court, something he most earnestly desired would happen, he needed to be nominated again; but unfortunately the Native American Party that had nominated him in 1855 was now in shambles, having lost all semblance of statewide influence. They had blundered through a series of calamitous gubernatorial and senatorial mistakes and by election time were on the verge of disappearing. In fact, by 1860, almost all of their state leaders had been defeated for political office. Not surprisingly, the "Know-Nothings" were going the way of splinter parties. The issues that had given them a public voice had either lost political appeal or had been absorbed into the major parties.

Justice Terry, aware that the Know-Nothings were on their way out, returned to the Democratic Party for the second time in two years. He hoped that they would forgive his prodigality and nominate him for a second term as chief justice of the state court. But the Democrats, in the midst of their own ideological schism, had fragmented into two factions.

In point of fact, by the summer of 1859, these factions found it necessary to hold separate conventions. The southern faction "states'-rights," or "Lecompton" Democrats (a name taken from the town of Lecompton, Kansas, where the pro-southern Democrats first organized), held its convention in Sacramento in June with Senator William Gwin as its leader. Terry joined the "Lecomptonites" asking for acceptance as the prodigal, but principled, son returned. On the other hand, Northern Democrats were lead by California's other senator, David C. Broderick, who publicly supported Stephen A. Douglas. Douglas had become a leading critic of President James Buchanan, who he believed was exacerbating the division in the party by granting too many concessions to southern Democrats. Southern Democrats in California, by contrast, were convinced that Broderick's anti-Buchanan sentiment was moving him closer and closer to the abolitionist views of the newly emerging Republican Party. At mid-century, by every political measure, Senators William Gwin and David Broderick were the two most powerful Democrats in California. Broderick, with his abolitionist leanings, led the Northern wing of the party, while Gwin, a Mississippi "Chiv," led its southern bloc.

Broderick was a young ambitious and rancorous politician, the product of impoverished beginnings and a ghetto street-life. He was a man of irrepressible energy and perseverance, living at times, said his enemies, just on the edge of civility. He was suspicious, quick tempered, easily offended and unpredictable, yet he was also a man who had cultivated loyal friends and followers.

The first 14 years of Broderick's life had been spent in Washington, D.C., where his father labored as a stonemason. When his father suddenly died, the family moved to New York City to be near relatives. In New York Broderick pieced together a modest living as a part-time fireman and a Tammany Hall apprentice. At 26, however, with most family members gone, he and a cousin moved to California, determined to become rich and famous. As it happened, making money came easily to him. By 30 he had made a sizable profit turning gold dust into gold coin, and two years later he ran for office and was elected president of the state Senate. In 1857 he became California's third United States senator. He had just turned 37 years of age. In a certain sense, Broderick had become the senator from California by creating his own west coast version of Tammany Hall. He surrounded himself with a coterie of political militants, abolitionists, longshoremen, firemen, policemen and city service workers. Taken together they were a formidable, but, at times truculent lot.

The ex-Mississippian William Gwin, by comparison, had grown up with the advantages of wealth and position, having been trained as a physician and a lawyer. He was a man of a cultivated demeanor with a subtlety of verbal expression that made the younger Broderick seem even more unpolished than, in fact, he was. Gwin had come to California with an active ambition to be elected a member of the U.S. Senate—Mississippi had made him in every respect a polished, and electable southern politician. On arriving in California he promoted slavery as a moral institution, he was a strong advocate for the primacy of states-rights, and he claimed his support for dividing California into two states.

Yet once having been elected to the California Legislature, he modified his stance on slavery, becoming, much to Terry's annoyance, an opponent of dividing the state into a "free-soil" north and a slavery-tolerant south. In other words, Gwin, unlike Terry, had proven himself practical enough to recognize that slavery-politics was rapidly losing whatever political appeal it might have had in pre-civil war California.

To be expected, Gwin and Broderick became political adversaries, yet, also to be expected, as a second term drew neigh; Gwin found it necessary to ameliorate his differences with Broderick. In fact, to win a second term in the U.S. Senate in 1860, Gwin recognized that he needed Broderick's endorsement, if he were to have any chance against a field crowded of influential candidates. After hesitating, Broderick agreed to support Gwin on the condition that should Gwin win, he would turn over all political patronage to Broderick. Gwin did win, and he knew that Broderick's endorsement had proven decisive, but when it came time to turn over his patronage he equivocated. Moreover, he was able to get the president, James Buchanan, to support him. Buchanan, in an effort to keep the party together, refused to side with the abolitionist posturing Broderick, but instead offered all federal patronage to Gwin's southern friends. In return Gwin made no effort to honor his promise nor even discuss it with Broderick—he remained silent, forcing Broderick to return to California a frustrated, bitter politician determined to weaken southern political influence in the state.

The slavery controversy had made the election of 1859 one of the most vituperative in California history, and while the California election did not become quite as publicly brutal as it became on the east coast, it had its share of ever-festering ideological brawling.

Terry, now firmly identifying with the Lecompton Democrats, grudgingly accepted Gwin's leadership, even though he remained adamant that were the legislators unwilling to support an open policy on slavery he would continue to fight for the state's division. He wrote:

> I was born and reared in a southern state, and believed in the doctrine of the ultra states' rights men of the South. I desired to see the government of the state in the hands of those whose political opinions coincided with my own. [I] desired to change the Constitution of the state by striking out that clause prohibiting slavery, [or] failing in that, to divide the state and thus open a portion of California to Southerners and their property (slaves).[1]

For the present, however, Terry prepared himself to accept Gwin's leadership, for there was now no place for him to go if he were to retain any chance of reelection to the California Supreme Court. With the option of winning as the Know-Nothings candidate no longer a possibility, and a portion of traditional Democrats siding with the abolitionists, he knew that if he were to have any chance of reelection, he must learn to get along with Gwin and the Lecompton Democrats.

And so it was that on a warm Sunday afternoon in June of 1859 Terry stood before the state's southern democrats and offered a fiery speech attacking Broderick and extolling the virtues of the Lecomptons. He spoke before a curious but enthusiastic crowd of conventioneers in Sacramento's First Congregational Church. Although he was well received, when it came to selecting a nominee the delegates rejected him and placed in nomination the name of the considerably more conventional 30-year-old Judge Warner Walter Cope. Terry was decidedly more disappointed than he was willing to admit to anyone but his wife and closest friends.

Two circumstances seem upper-most in causing his disappointing loss. First, too many of the delegates packed into the church hall that Sunday evening had felt the sting of indignity that Terry foisted on them with his humiliating victory over the Vigilance Committee of 1856. After all it had been Broderick that had stood with Terry in that fight, not William Gwin. Moreover, many of the delegates in the hall had been members of the Vigilance Committee and clearly had never considered the Committee as lawless. Obviously, these ex-vigilantes were in no mood to return him to the Supreme Court where he might again interfere with a legitimate reform movement. The second circumstance adding to the convention's suspicions of Terry were southern delegates who had taken offense at his silence on pro-slavery issues while on the bench. Many knew him personally to be a southern loyalist, but during his time on the bench, so they believed, he had been relatively quiet on issues that mattered most to a southerner's heart.

Nevertheless, his endorsement speech before the convention on that evening enthusiastically praised southern virtues and the southern "Chivs," and also leveled an attack on Broderick's northern Democratic leadership, describing the Senator as the man most responsible for dividing the Democratic Party.

Terry began by declaring Broderick is an abolitionist in the guise of a moderate who opposes all of us. His is:

> A party based of no principle, except the abusing of one section of the country and the aggrandizement of another; a party which has no existence in fifteen States of the Confederacy; a party whose principles never can prevail among freemen, who love justice and are willing to do justice. What other, is it? [A] miserable remnant of a faction sailing under false colors, trying to obtain votes under false pretenses. They have no distinction they are entitled to; they are the followers of one man, the personal chattels of a single individual, whom they are ashamed of. They belong, heart and soul, body and breeches to David C. Broderick. [But] they are ashamed to acknowledge their [true] master. They call themselves Douglas Democrats, but the best that can be said is that they are sailing under the banner of the black Douglass whose name is Frederick not Stephen.[2]

After loss of the nomination, it was a short but painful trip through the deserted streets of Sacramento to the Supreme Court building where he would no longer be the chief justice. He had no illusions, he would be gone as the state's highest jurist in six weeks. What is more, Stephen Field's tenure as the chief justice would begin in October. Terry's tenure as chief justice had been the most self-confirming four years he had ever had in government, and to think that it was his long-time southern comrades who had deprived him of a second term! Later events in life would prove that the Supreme Court judgeship had been the most important and satisfying civic success that he would ever enjoy and more than a quarter of a century later he and Cornelia would say as much.

> The morning after the close of the convention, David Broderick, eating breakfast in San Francisco's International Hotel, read an account of the judge's speech in the *Sacramento Union*. Aware that Terry's good friend Duncan Perley was sitting at an adjacent table, Broderick leaned over and whispered to Perley, "I see your friend Terry has been abusing me. That damned miserable wretch after being kicked out of the convention [m]ade a speech abusing me [even after] I ha[d] defended him when all others had deserted him [during his battle with the Vigilance Committee]. [During that affair] I paid three newspapers $200 dollars every week to defend him." His complaint ended with one remark too many, a remark that Terry later would be unable to overlook. "I have hitherto spoken of him as an honest man, as the *only* honest man on the bench of a miserable corrupt Supreme Court, but now I find I was mistaken. I take it all back. He is just as bad as the others [Justices Field and Baldwin]."[3]

Perley, whose short fuse rivaled Terry's, wanted to know if the senator were calling the judge a "wretch." Broderick assured him that he was. Perley responded that the senator would not dare use that language in Terry's presence, but were he to do so, the judge would demand a retraction or satisfaction. Broderick, however, had said all he wanted to say on the subject and dismissed Perley curtly, pointing out that his status as a senator forbade dueling, and were he to face everyone who wished to challenge him he would have no time for anything else. "What is more," he added with condescension, "I have no intention of dueling someone *beneath* my station." (Some later commentators have argued that Broderick believed that Gwin lay behind Perley's challenge, so that the comment on his status was meant to force Gwin out in the open, in other words, to force Gwin to offer the challenge. No evidence has turned up that supports this interpretation, although it is true that Broderick would have eagerly awaited any such challenge. He had survived a duel once before when his watch fob deflected a bullet, and he believed himself now to be the best pistol duelist in the state.

Terry read the senator's remarks in newspapers the next day, and as expected, he considered that his honor and reputation had been questioned. It is certain that he would not allow any remark about his honor to go unchallenged—especially when it came from such a lofty state leader. However, since Broderick was in the middle of an election campaign it would be inappropriate for him to demand satisfaction; he would wait, he declared, until the election was over. Yet, Broderick should not think that he would forget or forgive.

The waiting, however, gave his wife Cornelia and friends an opportunity to urge the judge to drop the matter. Broderick's insults, they argued, were as common and as unreflective as they always had been, and thus, were not worthy a reply. (Now, it is true, there are many husbands and fathers whose devotion to family and career would have been enough to heed a wife's counsel, but this could hardly be expected of Terry. At one time or another, he would insist on a public apology from the senator.) But the judge did seek to calm his wife's fears with the admonition that once the election had passed, the senator's partisan ardor would abate. That he would most certainly offer a retraction. After all, Terry declared, "Am I not the Chief Justice of the Supreme Court?" (In fact, the remarks that Terry made at the convention against Broderick were relatively mild by comparison to remarks that had been made by Gwin and others. Moreover, from the outset of the stir-up, Terry did not believe that his comments were in any manner personal (i.e. unlike Broderick's remarks toward him).)

If, however, Broderick would not retract them, he told Cornelia after several weeks of brooding about the matter, he would have no choice but to defend his honor, for his honor was a question of social approval. At one point, he explained to Cornelia, he might have been induced to drop the matter early on, "[b]ut when it reached my early home, and had been read by those whose good opinion I prize above all things I could not endure that those friends should hear of the slander and not hear also that it had been retracted or atoned for."[4] Texans, he added, would rate "Broderick's accusations as an insult not only to me but also to them and to the entire South."

On September 8, 1859, the day after the election, with Terry's letter of resignation from the Bench now public, Broderick and his friends knew that Terry meant to have satisfaction. In one sense Terry viewed resigning as a relief, for it meant that court business was out of mind. He no longer would be forced to endure the quiet smugness that he perceived his colleagues Field and Baldwin to have been enjoying at his expense. When the fall court convened, Field would be the new chief justice, and as far as Field was concerned, Terry's populist impulses and moralistic posturing would be a thing of the past. The portentousness of the event for the sake of honor would now begin to crowd the stage.

The next day Terry prevailed upon two Oakland friends, Thomas Hayes and Calhoun Benham, to ferry to San Francisco and deliver his message to Broderick demanding an apology. When Hayes and Benham eventually found the senator, he was still fuming about the elections, for both he and the Republicans had taken a political thrashing from Gwin's Lecompton Democrats. Terry's friends sensed immediately that Broderick was in no mood to be conciliatory, and these suspicions were confirmed when the senator chose to feign ignorance of the effrontery that the chief justice professed to have suffered—Broderick wanted it explained to him just what "particular remarks offended the Chief Justice." The following day, in a letter that exhibiting forbearance on Terry's part, he responded. He wished a retraction "of any words which were calculated to reflect on my character as an officer or a gentleman."[5] Significantly, Terry made no mention of the word "wretch," the word that had so incensed Duncan Perley. From the judge's perspective, words driven by passion do not dishonor a man; only those words of guile made in moments of cool, calculating reflection are to be challenged.[6] Broderick, however, would not retract a single word. "Terry is a dishonest judge," he reiterated, thus making it impossible, in Terry's mind, to withdraw honorably. From Terry's perspective he had been lumped together with the incorrigible Field and Baldwin, two judges who were well deserving of their reputations as dishonest dealers. Terry pressed his challenge for he believed that such an accusation now had been unpardonable! Broderick delayed his answer one more day and night and then accepted the challenge—and thus began an episode that pleased both men's enemies, delighted nugatory friends, but troubled all those who genuinely cared for the senator's and the judge's welfare.

Two days later the rules of the duel were drawn up. Colonel J. C. McKibben would represent the senator and Calhoun Benham the judge. The accord stated that the protagonists would square off at the northern end of Merced Lake, southwest of the city within a mile of the sea. Each man should bring two aids and a surgeon. Broderick, the one challenged, chose the weapons. They would be dueling pistols at ten paces. Terry's friends suggested that if the judge had chosen the weapons they would have been Bowie knives or rifles. Those close to Broderick knew that the senator would insist on ten paces because he could get off a shot as fast as anyone could and he didn't want to miss, and he certainly didn't want to give Terry a second chance should he be wounded but not fall.[7] Each dualist would bring a set of matching pistols and a coin toss would determine which set would be used. The signal for engagement would be "Gentlemen are you ready?" It would be given by one of the seconds, also chosen by a coin toss. Broderick's representatives then proposed a perplexing modification: after each man had declared himself "ready," McKibben said, the count would be as follows: "fire, one, two." On the command to "fire," each would bring their weapons from the ready position (pistol arm hanging at the side, barrel pointing earthward) to the target position and fire, but after the count of two "firing would be discontinued." Terry's representative, Calhoun Benham, objected to the uncharacteristic firing count. "Why" he asked, "was not the customary three count to be used?" Broderick's representative made no attempt to explain, yet held firm. The count would be "one, two." The judge "[should] accept or decline the proposed terms." The next day, without seeking an explanation, Terry agreed to Broderick's unusual dueling count. Many observers thought that Broderick wanted the "short count" because of his rapid, accurate marksmanship. A coin then determined whose second would count off the engagement, and whose second would have the choice of positions on the field. Finally, when all terms were agreed to, the time and date were set—5:30 in the morning on Monday, September 12, 1859. Amazingly, just five days after Broderick's disappointing election defeat and Terry's resignation from the Supreme Court these two men would face each other in a life threatening fight.

A cold, ocean fog had settled over Merced lagoon on the morning of the duel, and gathered in a damp ravine just east of the lake were more than 70 friends and curious bystanders. It would turn out, however, that on that Monday one of the bystanders was Martin Burke, the Chief of Police of San Mateo County. As preparations got underway, Burke stepped out from the crowd and served each side with a warrant that placed Broderick and Terry under arrest for violating the state's constitutional ban against dueling. By noon they were both ushered before District Judge Coon who had come to office three years earlier during the reign of the second Vigilance Committee.[8] Judge Coon dismissed the charges, declaring that since both men were standing in his court they could not be violating the dueling ordinance. This was a sure signal to witnesses present that those with the power to stop the fight were not in likely to do so.

The next morning the fog had returned to the swampy moor and so had the participants. It was later, 6:45, and this time the sheriff had stayed home. Terry won the all-important first coin toss. They would use his weapons! His weapons were lightweight French dueling pistols with hair triggers and barrels a foot long. When Terry's second handed the pistols over to Broderick's second, remarkably, Terry was seeing the weapons for only the second time. Two days earlier the judge had borrowed the pistols and had fired them for the first and only time, commenting as he did: "[They] seem to discharge the bullets below the line sighted."[9] Having lost the weapons toss, Broderick would now have his choice of positions. He chose to have the sun, should it break through, at his back, and it would be his second, David Colton, who would count the firing pace.

The reporters described stark and surprising contrast in the demeanor of the two men. One bystander wrote that "Mr. Terry's lips were compressed, his countenance darkly sallow, and his whole appearance betrayed that of a man without fear, as well as without religious constraint."[10] Newspapers reported, less metaphysically, that Terry was expressionless, stolid, and from all appearances calm. On the other hand, onlookers described Broderick as quite the opposite. He was tense and befuddled, even to the point of appearing catatonic. Doubtless, reports declared that he was fighting to gain control of his emotions. Witnesses were astonished, for many had expected that Broderick would be the cooler man under fire, being the better marksman and having gone through a duel once before.

A day earlier, *The Morning Call* had expressed such a sentiment when it wrote that Broderick could hit a grapefruit-size target at 30 feet 200 hundred times in a row, whereas Terry was a close-in knife-fighter or an accurate rifleman at long distances.[11] Many of Terry's enemies, having heard stories about his instability in moments of stress, believed that passion would get the best of him and he would be immediately at Broderick's mercy. It was obvious to the lakeside witnesses, however, that it was Broderick who was struggling to keep his composure. Broderick's surgeon, Dr. Loehr, moreover, did not help matters. He paced back and forth at the senator's side with a satchel of rattling surgical paraphernalia that included a long saw protruding ominously from the top of his medicine bag.[12] As time drew near for the count, Terry remained motionless, arms to his side, while Broderick fingered his alien pistol, fidgeting for a comfortable grip. Then disconcertingly, Terry's second, Calhoun Benham, interrupted the proceedings to protest that the senator's pistol barrel was not in the proper position "groundward." Broderick's second stepped close to remind the senator of this, but he did not respond. Finally, Colonel McKibben approached Broderick and forced the weapon into the correct position, which unfortunately pulled Broderick's body out of the dueling posture and into a three-quarters face-on stance, thereby making the senator a larger target. There he stood, a helpless combatant, frozen in position, unable to focus his thoughts or realign his target. Next, each man's garments were checked for protective armor, after which Terry's second, Benham, approached the judge and whispered that he should pull his hat brim down to shield his eyes from the shaft of sunlight that had burned through the fog and was slowly climbing over Broderick's shoulder. He did. The senator's second, David Colton, called out, "Gentlemen, are you ready?" "Ready," Terry snapped. Broderick hesitated, continuing to struggle with the unfamiliar pistol grip. Finally he mumbled, "ready." Colton began the count. According to one writer's description, the count was at the pace of a cathedral clock "fire," "one" and at 'one,' Broderick stiffly fought to draw his weapon to a horizontal position and pull the trigger.[13] The pistol discharged prematurely and a bullet buried itself in the dirt about one pace before the judge's boot (perhaps Terry had it right the pistols seemed to fire low). Colton intoned, "two," and Terry fired. The bullet struck Broderick's right lapel where a "slight show of dust . . . emerged."[14] Convulsively, Broderick lurched face-forward onto his hands and knees even as he continued to clutch his weapon. Friends rushed to his side, gathered him up, and carried him to a nearby tree where they seated him upright with his back resting against the tree. Soon he was in conversation with sympathizers, and shortly thereafter accepted a tumbler of brandy from Dr. Hammond, Terry's physician. His physician, Dr. Loehr, had apparently neglected to bring along a stimulant. Hammond and Loehr found the senator to be coughing very little blood and they announced to the relief of bystanders that "the senator will survive." If the lung had been pierced, Hammond added, he would be coughing a greater quantity of blood, and "there is barely a teaspoon full." A few minutes later, Terry began to worry that Broderick's witnesses who far outnumbered his own might seek to avenge their fallen leader, and decided after fifteen minutes or so that it was time to withdraw from the site. He quickly made his way from the field, climbed aboard a waiting carriage and returned with friends to Oakland.

Four days later the news reached Terry that the senator had never left the tract of land but died nearby at Black Point in the house of his friend Leonidas Haskell. The newspapers reported that the bullet had torn away a greater portion of lung than had been suspected, and that Broderick died three days later of internal bleeding—he died at 40.

On Sunday September 18, he was buried at the fog-shrouded Lone Pine Cemetery in San Francisco, and the next morning the vilification of Terry as a conspirator began when *The Daily News* lead column declared "it is said that Napoleon should have died at Waterloo. Mr. Broderick died not on an inappropriate field. 'The blood of the martyrs is the seed of the church;' and we mistake greatly if the sacrifice of Mr. Broderick's life will not be fruitful of revolutionary results in the popular mind." Even though the aftermath had provoked charges of conspiracy from Broderick's allies, most who witnessed the duel had thought it to be a fair fight. Terry's comment, widely reported in newspapers, that the "bullet struck the Senator's chest too far out," was interpreted by Terry's foes to mean that he was disappointed that the shot had not been closer to Broderick's heart; but his supporters insisted that the judge was only reassuring bystanders that the shot had been wide of its mark, and thus would not do the senator any permanent harm. Other antagonists contended that if Terry had wanted, he could have spared Broderick's life by merely firing to miss. Yet some eyewitnesses disputed this claim, insisting that his shot was fired instantaneously (some pointed out that if there had been a three-count, as Terry had wanted, then he would have had time to collect his wits and spare Broderick). Others charged that Terry's side had manipulated the dueling pistols so that Broderick would be forced to shoot with a weapon that had a faulty trigger. The gunsmith Bernard Lagoarde, who had provided Broderick with dueling pistols, that chance had determined would remain unused, made such a charge at the inquest. But Broderick's seconds, McKibben and Colton, published a "card" in the San Francisco *News* denying Lagoarde's claim: "Mr. Lagoarde did not tell us while on the ground [at the duel], as he testified at the inquest, that there was any difference between the pistols used; [a]nd, that as far as [our] careful examination of the weapons was concerned, there was no perceptible difference in the tightness of the triggers."[15] Unfortunately for Terry, however, as Broderick lay dying he intensified conspiratorial suspicion among his friends by insisting that the duel had been planned by the cowardly Senator Gwin and his southern henchmen, and that it had been from the start a plan to assassinate him under the guise of a private quarrel. The charge was never supported by evidence but there were many who willingly believed it, for it reinforced the perception of Terry as a villainous monster who had been at the task of making mischief since the vigilante days of 1856. As later events would reveal, even three decades would not be enough time to bank the fires of the enemies' bitterness.

This duel that tragically and foolishly took the senator's life and defamed Terry's name until he died need never have happened had the passions of both men not overwhelmed their intellects. Broderick, once having acquiesced to the loutish council of sycophants, while ignoring the advice of his friends, had become dispositionally incapable of backing away from this folly for fear of being perceived as weak. (He confirmed his lifelong habit of mistaking brashness for courage.) Until the moment the senator was struck down by Terry's bullet, he was driven to prove himself the better man. He went into the duel convinced that he was the superior duelist, would win, and would teach the "[s]outhern Chivs a lesson." In fact, shortly before taking the field, Broderick remarked to his friend John White, "Don't you fear, John; I can shoot twice to Terry's once: beat him shooting every time." "It was this supreme confidence in his own expertness with pistols," writes the journalist James O'Meara, "[that] inspired him from the first to the last."[16] It was maintained that the senator had pushed for the 10 pace range because he expected to fire first and wanted to assure himself that he would not miss his target.

Terry, on the other hand, in spite of his obsession to prove his courage and save his honor and rectitude, became for many Californians *oppositio exemplar*, the personification of dishonor and perfidy. Many were convinced that he was indeed Senator Gwin's surrogate, that is, that he was merely playing a role as a crafty southern toady. In the eyes of his northern antagonists he had become the perfect caricature of southern chivalry.

Justice Stephen Field took the opportunity to pour vinegar into Terry's wounds from his snug, sheltered perch on the high bench. Field, who had been traveling in the East when the duel took place, announced that had he been present in California at the time of the duel, it would never have taken place. Maintaining his esteem for each man, and with the power of his office—a power that Terry had so recently and painfully lost—Field proclaimed:

> "I should have exerted all the power I possessed by virtue of my office to put a stop to the duel. I would have held both of the combatants to keep the peace under bonds of so large an amount as to have made them hesitate about further steps; and in the meantime, I should have set all my energies to work, and called others to my aid, to bring about a reconciliation. I believe I should have adjusted the difficulty."[17]

It is not implausible that what Field says is true. Yet in the face of what did transpire, what could Field have said that would have been more demeaning to Terry, for Terry to hear from his judicial adversary that his vaunted professions of honesty and trust would have been publicly reduced to abject compliance, for fear of losing some money?

NOTES

1. David Boden. "Terry's Justification." *The Wasp Magazine* (1933), vol. LV, 3.
2. James O 'Meara. *Pioneer Senators: Broderick and Gwin* (San Francisco: Bacon & Co. 1881) 226. See also, Carrol Douglas Hall. *The Terry-Broderick Duel* (San Francisco: The Colt Press, 1939) and Jeremiah Lynch. *A Senator for the Fifties.* San Francisco. (1911).
3. —— *Pioneer Senators,* 220.
4. —— *Pioneer Senators,* 227.
5. David Boden. *Wasp.* Cited in A. Russell Buchanan, *David S. Terry of California: Dueling Judge* (San Marino CA: The Huntington Library Press, 1956). 97.
6. Oscar T. Shuck. *Bench and Bar in California* (San Francisco: Occidental Printing House 1888). 287.
7. *The Morning Call,* September 13, 1859.
8. James O 'Meara, *Pioneer Senators,* 242.
9. —— *Pioneer Senators*, 240. See also. Shuck. *Bench and Bar.* 291.
10. Oscar T. Shuck, Bench *and Bar.* 289.
11. September 13, 1859.

12. A. Russell Buchanan, *Dueling Judge,* 104.
13. James O' Meara, *Pioneer Senators,* 245–246.
14. —— *Pioneer Senators,* 247.
15. A. Russell Buchanan, *Dueling Judge*, 108.
16. James O' Meara, *Pioneer Senators,* 242.
17. Stephen J. Field. *Personal Reminiscences of Early days in California* (New York: De Capo Press 1969, reprint of 1898). 102.

Chapter Seven

Growing Resentments

The decade of the 1860s was a time of transition for both Terry and Field. Terry returned to his beloved Texas to fight for the southerners' "War of Secession," while Field traveled east with an appointment from President Abraham Lincoln in hand that made him the first United States Supreme Court justice from the state of California.

Terry would fight. For the warrior instincts of Scot-Irish ancestry and the soldierly exploits of revered progenitors made it inevitable. He was the progeny of an insular island population—the offspring of people who had fought the English for more than two centuries. In the end, however, Europe in the 18th century proved to be Britannia's century; and those Scottish and Irish rebels who were unwilling to face martyrdom or accept subjugation were left with a single option: migration. Many migrated to North America and populated the southeastern seaboard of the United States; but when, over time, the coastline became too crowded to accommodate their insular ways, they pushed westward into Tennessee, Kentucky and Mississippi—and eventually into disputed Texas border territory. Years of tribal conflict had nurtured in these Gaelic immigrants a gladiatorial culture. Theirs had been a lifetime in pursuit, at the manifold levels of strife and discord, an intransigent sense of "rectitude and honor." Frequently defeated and thus deeply bellicose and remorse-ridden, they did not recoil from the cruelest forms of warfare: massacre, ambush, even genocide. David Smith Terry was an authentic child of this fierce legacy.

In stark contrast was Stephen Field's ancestral history. It was laced with English ecclesiastics, physicians, lawyers, politicians and successful entrepreneurs—ancestors who were either heir to wealth and power or on the best of terms with those who possessed them. But even as with Terry, in Field's orderly world there was little room for self-doubt or ambiguity—life was a narrow path with no shadow of turning, and personal compromise was either a sign of a vacuous mind or a moral weakness of the will. In the Field household, a successful life was forever perceived as a balance of piety and reasoned obedience.

Such strong family loyalties made ancestral intuitions all-pervading and formative in both men, and at those not-so-infrequent moments when they faced a crisis, both were able to call upon these securely rooted instincts. Yet, as a consequence, both were capable of shameless moral posturing; when under stress, Terry became emotional—bold and aggressive to the point of foolhardiness—while Field was secretive and ratiocinative.

From their earliest days of marriage, Cornelia Terry had urged her husband to let his mind supervise his passions, but not until after the Broderick affair did he begin acting as if he truly believed that prudence was a virtue. That fateful shooting produced such resentment toward Terry—even among friends—that for a time he chose to make himself scarce in the Central Valley by packing the family off to his sister-in-law's farm in Mississippi. Terry was not idle, however, for while the family visited relatives in the south, Terry returned to Nevada's Washoe Mountains and earned money prospecting for silver and gold. It was his plan to combine mining and lawyering. He would work the surface mines while offering legal aid to those miners who found themselves bogged down over land disputes with powerful mining conglomerates. However, four months of difficult labor in the Washoes produced the barest of compensation. Most silver and gold on the land's surface had been reduced to scrabble. Moreover, his outspoken southern sympathies did not make him a popular figure with a majority of miners who were decidedly pro-Unionist. The miners did not trust him, so much so, that by Christmas time of 1861 he was ready to return to his Stockton City ranch with Cornelia and "the boys."

During their thirty-two years of marriage, Cornelia bore six sons, but childbearing and rearing on the frontier left her and the judge with a constant sense of loss and melancholy—friends said that these traits were especially noticeable in "Neal." Their first son, Frank Davis, born in 1853, lived but a year. The second, Samuel, was born in 1855, and died an untimely death after minor surgery in 1885. He had been the family's pride and joy, and his obituary reported that he had been well on his way to a promising career in law and politics (in contrast to his father, "Sam" was known as the "smiling" Terry). The next son, David, born in 1856, accidentally killed himself at 17 while cleaning his rifle. The family's enemies whispered that he had taken his own life, but there was never any evidence that supported the rumor. The fourth son, Clinton, was born in 1858 and proved to be the only child to survive his parents. He died in 1931. He and his father were to have a painful, but inevitable, falling out at the end of the elder Terry's life. The family's Civil War babies were Jefferson and Frank Cheatham. Jefferson was born in the first year of the war, 1861, and was named after the Confederate president. He lived 10 months. Frank Cheatham, the last to be born, survived but 3 months into the year of 1863. In 1865, however, after the death of Judge Terry's younger brother Aurelius, his 10-year-old son, Aurelius Jr., "Reel," joined "Uncle David's" virile family.

It was on the family's Stockton valley ranch that the three surviving sons and nephew Reel grew to manhood, brought up by a humorless and, at times, unduly harsh father and a controlling but loving and protective mother. A story from these formative years bears repeating, for it reveals something about the boys' relationship toward their father/uncle. Theodore Steiny, one of the Terry boys' playmates, first told the story to a reporter from the San Francisco Examiner in 1921. As a 50 year-old reminiscence, it may have suffered from the dimming of details, but the vividness of Steiny's memory has not affected the zest of the account.

On a hot summer's morning, Steiny says, the young teenage Terry boys cooked up a prank to pass the time of day. They began by stuffing clothing with straw until they had produced a good-sized mannequin resembling a man, after which they hoisted it up into the leafy foliage of a large cottonwood tree that overhung a pathway leading from their home into town. Once all the boys were securely hidden in the foliage of the tree, they proceeded to drop their scarecrow into the laps of unsuspecting passersby who were traveling beneath. After several happy minutes of entertainment Judge Terry, on horseback, came into view. As he drew near, Sam whispered to the other boys, "Don't drop it on Pa! He'll raise hell." Ignoring Sam's warning the pranksters released the dummy just as the judge rode beneath them. "Well, sir, I'll never forget what followed," Steiny told the reporter. "Judge Terry's hand flashed back to his pocket, and before you could wink he had pulled a revolver and put two bullets into that straw dummy. [After which] the judge rode on looking neither to the right nor to the left. If the joke was supposed to be on him he certainly didn't show it."[1] Pity the poor mannequin.

A second episode symptomatic of Judge Terry's quiescent aggression was revealed in a menacing, albeit embellished, letter he wrote Cornelia on May 12, 1870. It concerned their son David who was away at an Episcopal boarding school in Benicia. Young David had written his mother complaining of the fate of a schoolmate who had been beaten for dropping a schoolbook on the parade grounds. The elder's response to his wife was nothing short of histrionic:

> I think Dave's indignation at the cruel punishment of the boy in school is just. No teacher should be allowed to administer severe punishment even for a grave offense. I quite agree with you that it would not do to treat one of our boys in the way Dave says that the boy Earl was treated—for such a case if I did not treat the community to a funeral I would at least cut a clerical hide into ribbons with the heaviest mule whip I could find in the State. If when I go down I find the case as bad as stated I shall not send the boys back as I do not wish to take the chances of having [murdered] a preacher.[2]

These tales notwithstanding, after the Broderick killing, Terry successfully kept his aggressive instincts well in check as he plunged into the intellectual and social life of the community, even while adding to his family's financial nest egg. His law practice began to show sizable dividends, as did his investments in real estate, cotton and livestock. Be that as it may, the year 1861 was also to give new direction to the judge's resentments and sense of honor. It was the year when a decade of smoldering social and economic quarreling between the northern and southern states exploded into the most lethal and malevolent, of the nation's wars—the Civil War.

Astonishingly, Terry, the southern firebrand, remained in the San Joaquin Valley, enlarging his law practice and providing pecuniary advantages for Cornelia and the boys that they had never enjoyed before—his newly acquired virtue of prudence evidently in control of his southern passion perhaps for the very first time? Yet, by necessity, this changed the following year when his oldest brother, Frank, suddenly died at the hands of northern forces at the battle of Green River in Kentucky, even as his youngest brother, Clinton, was dying in ambush at the battle of Shiloh on the banks of the Tennessee. Within a six-month span, Terry's brothers had been martyred to southern veneration, but their deaths had made it impossible for him to remain quiescent in the long shadow of filial distress—no longer was he able to ignore the admonishments of his and Cornelia's southern families to stay at home and work his practice.

As had happened just two years earlier, the family locked the farmhouse door, slipped out of California and headed south. Terry left first, traveling due south from Stockton into Mexico and then east across the southern delta region of Texas into Mississippi, where he joined up with General Joseph E. Johnston.[3] In short order, he struck off to the north looking for General Braxton Bragg. Several weeks later Cornelia and the boys followed Terry south where they eventually joined her sister Ophelia on the Mississippi Delta. By then Terry had caught up to Bragg in Tennessee, arriving just in time to fight alongside the popular general at the Battle of Chickamauga. Reports from the battle field declare that Terry had fought bravely but only briefly. For as a battalion commander on the second day of battle, a fusillade of rifle pellets pierced his upper left arm even as his horse was being shot from under him. But unlike brothers Frank and Clinton, his luck held—he survived.

Bragg, however, unwilling to lose another Terry to the war, ordered him back to Texas with the charge to find new recruits to replace the troops that had been lost at the battle of Stone River. The judge, of course, did not want to go, but his reluctance seems to have been assuaged with a Brigadier General's field commission. Once back in Texas he began recruiting troops for a renewed assault on the western front. But the war was drawing to a close and Terry had little success finding recruits, for all the able-bodied Texans willing to fight had long since enlisted and were off fighting, or were wounded or dead. As a result, his efforts proved modest and frustrating, even though he was able to gain a reputation for developing well-trained and well-disciplined troops.[4] In due course, the state of Texas would honor the memory of the fighting Terrys, but during the war their Texan neighbors were not surprised by the family's decimation, for Texans understood that the "Terry brothers" had always found it difficult to locate the line between courage and recklessness.

After General Lee had surrendered his sword at Appomattox in April of 1864, General Terry decided that he would not submit to the disgrace of an occupational army in his home state; as his Scot-Irish ancestors had done four generations earlier, he emigrated to another country. Discharged from the Confederacy on June 25, 1865, he and 600 loyal soldiers repaired to the Mexican state of Jalisco, where, for three years, he and the expatriates cobbled together, on arid land, a marginal living off cotton and cattle. Apprehensive Mexican authorities and a limited number of established markets, however, eventually exhausted Terry's financial prospects, and forced him back into California. In a way it had been anticipated—two years earlier he had sent Cornelia and the boys on ahead so that the "children could resume their schooling in California."[5] It was apparent that Terry's patience in Jalisco was running thin when, in a letter written to his wife on October 11, 1867, he described Mexico as without prospects, "save anarchy, bloodshed, oppression, and outrage."[6]

On July 2, 1868, unannounced but clearly not unexpected, Terry returned to San Francisco on the leaky steamer *Sierra Nevada*—but this time when the family gathered together in Stockton City they were in California to stay. Without delay Terry and his young sons set about rebuilding the family estate.

By the year's end, with the energy that he had displayed in Mexico, Terry had replaced the farm house with a "ranch house," mended fences, cleared and planted land, and set to work trading for livestock.

However, these were not easy times for the Terrys—many of his old law partners had moved on, and he found it difficult to pick up where he left off. During the war he had fought on the wrong side, and many of his neighbors had not forgotten it. A. Russell Buchanan sums up the Terry family's adversity this way:

> [T]he band did not play for Colonel Terry when he returned to California after the war. Not only had he fought on the losing side, but to many Californians the shadow of the Broderick duel and the Vigilante affair still hung over him. [Mrs.] Terry was reduced to sending bills to persons who in past years had become indebted to the Terrys, bills that in normal times probably never would have been sent. Terry found that the prejudices against him made it difficult to rebuild his practice, although he continued the effort for six months or so.[7]

By the end of the year, with family money nearly exhausted, Terry returned again to the silver mines of Nevada. But prospects were no better than they had been on his first two attempts at "mining the Nevadas." Surface mining for silver was much too meager to realize a profit for the effort; for mining to be profitable meant buying equipment that he could not afford, and even his ability to dredge legal fees from the squabbling miners had declined. Miners, mostly Unionists, avoided him, so that by the year's end, he was back in Stockton, his dreams of striking it rich in the ore fields finally laid to rest for good and always. Now at last he was prepared to acknowledge to his greatly relieved wife and family that as a miner he had been on a fool's errand.

In March of 1863, while David Terry was in Texas recruiting soldiers for the Confederacy, Stephen Field was making his way east to the nation's capitol where he was to become the Pacific coast's first Associate Justice of the United States Supreme Court. He would fill a place on Abraham Lincoln's newly created Tenth Federal District Court (six years later the court would return to nine districts). In point of fact, the schismatic Democratic Party made this appointment essential if Field were to continue his judicial career, for there was little likelihood that he would be elected for a third term to the California Supreme Court. The ever-growing numbers of Republicans who were being elected to state political offices were in the process of changing the political landscape in California. For quite some time, the president had been looking for suitable jurists to fill the Supreme Court vacancies that had been created by the resignations of three justices from the southern states. Many Western politicians, including Governor Leland Stanford, were urging Field's appointment to the newly established federal district, and Western political leaders up and down the coast had recognized Field's legal brilliance for quite some time. His familiarity with the issues that mattered most to Westerners had made him the leading candidate of Western senators. On the irksome questions of mining rights, property and water access, unfettered Chinese immigration, and the interminable "range-wars" that festered between the homesteaders and the voracious railroad and livestock companies, Field understood the details and was without peer among legal rivals. Some individuals in the District of Columbia, who were closer to the situation, argued that Field's skills had less to do with his appointment than did his brother, David Dudley's, influence as a major fundraiser for Lincoln. Field's brother Henry writes that when the president was informed that "Dudley" was anxious to see his brother appointed to the highest bench, the president was reported to have said, "If David wants it he shall have it."[8] That is not to say that Field did not do his part in making himself available. As during his run for the California Legislature, for instance, on the Union question he had remained non-committal, but he had become more and more publicly pro-Union when it came time to win Lincoln's approval. Nor was he modest about his appointment. He described the newly created Tenth District as a district created specifically for him. He was to bring order out of confusion to western mining and land-title law.

In most quarters in the west, the news of Field's appointment was welcomed, but support was not unanimous. As a rule, Californians well stationed in life were delighted. "[T]he appointee has not now, nor ever has had his superior on the bench," proclaimed the railroad-financed *San Francisco Alta*. Nor had Field's hometown newspaper, *The Marysville Appeal*, forgotten him—their support was close to exultation: "[T]he appointment of such a man," it wrote, "will be universally regarded on this coast as a wise exercise of appointing power."[9] Joseph G. Baldwin, Field's colleague on the California court, when hearing that Field would be leaving the state bench for the federal bench said: "[California] has been deprived of the ablest jurist who-ever presided over her courts."[10] However, the claim of the *Marysville Appeal* notwithstanding, not all voices on the "coast" were to see the appointment in such messianic terms. The "workingman's" newspaper in San Francisco, *The Bulletin*, warned that Justice Field was under the thumb of his wealthy friends, and therefore would be incapable of "impartiality whenever the interest of the privileged class" was at stake. "No place in the record of his decisions could it be found that he had ever given a judgment for a poor man against a rich one, no matter what the evidence."[11]

But perhaps the most substantive reminder that not every westerner was pleased with the appointment came in the form of a mail bomb that awaited the justice's inaugural appearance in Washington, D.C. During the process of unpacking and settling into his new office at the court, he happened to reach for what he thought to be a package of photographs that his wife had ordered before leaving San Francisco. The package's configuration and weight, however, persuaded an aide to dunk it into a nearby water barrel. Later inspection revealed it to have been a jury-rigged missile of cartridge shells and matches—a makeshift bomb indeed, but a potentially deadly one all the same.

Before Field retired from the federal bench in 1897, he would serve longer than any other person in the history of the U.S. court to that date—34 years, 8 months and 20 days as he was fond of reminding his colleagues. During these influential and distinguished years, more often than not his opinions on specific legal matters became the flash point for much of the statutory law that dominated economic legislation in the U.S. throughout the latter quarter of the 19th century. The heart and soul of the nation's post-war expectations and the essence of Field's judicial agenda were bound together—it was a period that placed before the federal court such highly charged issues as a citizen's loyalty to the nation, the policy toward and treatment of an exploding foreign immigrant population, the growth and power of monopolies, the influence of money-grasping mercenaries, and the distribution or exemption from tax liabilities. In short order, the politically attuned segments of California's citizenry came to form strong opinions about Justice Field. So much so that it does not seem an exaggeration to say that few members of the interested public took any middle ground in assessing his acts of beneficence. In the newspapers, he was both celebrated and vilified. As his long and remarkable career unwound, it was not uncommon to encounter influential institutions and animated public leaders who had been at one time or another both loyal supporters and avowed adversaries of the justice.

One issue in Field's array of legal opinions that westerners felt strongly about was his unpopular stand on the question of a "national loyalty oath." In the unforgiving post-Civil-War era, his opinion on this inflammatory matter came to prefigure a debate that would surface in the state again and again for more than a century. The issue arose in 1862 when a hostile, war-driven Congress passed the "Test Oath Act," stipulating that all federal officials must, under oath, swear that they had never voluntarily borne arms against the United States, nor "given aid, counsel, encouragement, or support, to the country's enemies." During the war, few voices were raised in objection to this attack on civil liberty, but two years after the war was over, with a taste for vengeance lingering in their mouths, the northern Congress extended the act to include the clause "counselors and attorneys practicing before the federal courts [are to be restricted] to those who have been loyal to the United States *throughout* the war." The majority of Congress viewed it as one final effort to eviscerate any sense of political defiance that might remain within the hearts of the southern planter class. But once the war was over, it was inevitable that a man such as A.H. Garland, a confederate congressman, would be denied the right to practice law before the D.C. courts, for he had been in the very inner workings of the Confederacy. On the other hand, it was not so evident that John Cummings, a Roman Catholic priest, should be denied the right to resume his pastoral duties in the state of Missouri after he refused to stipulate whether he had ever been disloyal to the Union's cause.

A Missouri statute of 1865, which was even more repressive than the federal one, had extended prohibitions beyond southern rebels "to [include anyone who had] by act or word, manifested an adherence to the cause of the [Union's] enemies, or [even desired] the triumph of enemies over [the] United States; or [sympathized] with those engaged in exciting or carrying on [the] rebellion."[12] In a border state such as Missouri, the statute was an obvious attempt to stultify the post-war prospects of the pro-southern Missourians. It was a shameless attempt to keep Missouri's northern factions in control and its defeated southern sympathizers in continuing disarray. And as was intended, the statute wreaked havoc on the aspirations of Missouri's southern professionals, for it not only forbade shepherding a religious flock, but it also prohibited pro-southern Missourians from teaching in the public schools, practicing law, holding state office and voting in municipal and state elections. Field, properly, came to the rescue of the southerners by offering unambiguous and progressive declarations on both of these famous test oath cases, *Ex parte Garland* and *Cummings v. Missouri*.[13] He was, moreover, not reluctant to move beyond any perceived textual limits of the Constitution and oppose the cases on ideological grounds—on the basis of what he called citizens' "natural rights." "*Garland* and *Cummings*," he later wrote, "according to Article I, Section 10, [of the United States Constitution] are unconstitutional because they deprive citizens of equality before the law, [taking from them] the right to pursue life-careers without the benefit of a judicial hearing and trial."[14]

The state of Missouri case was especially egregious, he pointed out, because it had explicitly violated the constitutional prohibition against "bills of attainder," to wit, every citizen "has an inalienable right to life, liberty, and the pursuit of happiness unless convicted of violating the country's laws." A test oath statute is therefore an unequivocal example of *ex post facto* law—"[punishing] conduct that was not a crime at the time it was committed." Essential to the justice's perception of a bill of attainder and *ex post facto* law, as the historian Paul Kens points out, is the notion that the statute punishes individuals for committing crimes, not just misdemeanors.[15] If these statutes were not intended to *punish crimes*, Field declared, then the federal government would have no jurisdiction, since no constitutional protection would have been abridged. Field continued:

> . . . all men have certain inalienable rights—that among these are life, liberty, and the pursuit of happiness; and that in the pursuit of happiness all avocations, all honors, all positions, are alike open to everyone, and that in the protection of these rights all are equal before the law. [D]eprivation or suspension of any of these rights for past conduct is punishment, and can be in no way otherwise defined.[16]

Garland and *Cummings,* Field declared, are statutes that administer punishment without trial for an act that is determined to be a crime before the fact. Anticipating what would be ratified in 1869 as the 14th Amendment to the U.S. Constitution, Field wrote: "[N]o State shall make or enforce any law which shall abridge the *privileges or immunities* of citizens of the United States; nor [deprive a] person of life, liberty, or property, without due process of law; nor deny to [a] person within its jurisdiction the equal protection of the law."[17]

But unlike later opinions that accentuated the legal nature of the "due process" and "equal protection" clauses of the amendment, Field structured his argument around the more noetic constitutional conceptions of "privileges and immunities"—ideas that he believed more fittingly rendered a citizen's privileges as "life, liberty, and the pursuit of *property*." The pursuit of property, he theorized, freed the court from the baffling task of defining a chimera such as "happiness." The "life, liberty, property" exegesis had been suggested early on by David Dudley Field when he appeared before the Supreme Court in front of his brother. Later Stephen Field would write that depriving Missouri's Father Cummings of his hallowed profession in the priesthood was no less than a criminal act by the state of Missouri to steal the priest's (intellectual) property.[18] Naturally Field's *Garland* and *Cummings* interpretations were enormously popular among the defeated confederates, and they also proved to be popular everywhere transplanted southerners were to be found, including California where the ties of kinship among southern immigrants were still firmly bound to Dixie.

By contrast, Field's opinion engendered only indignation amongst California's pro-Union populists and northern anti-monopolists. To these people, Field's judgment on loyalty oaths was viewed as an attempt to emasculate the north's hard-fought victory in the Civil War. If disloyal southern renegades and foreign-born rabble were not to expropriate a loyal citizen's political and economic birthright, then, the populists insisted, the southerners must pay the price of defeated and chastised traitors. Field's opinion was seen by Union populists as a calculated effort to weaken and impede the advancement of the state's statutory protection against not only a defeated enemy, but also the ever-growing waves of Chinese immigration washing up on California shores.

Field's ground-breaking attack on "loyalty tests," was, however, only the first of many legal interpretations that fellow Californians would resent. In time, they would discover that his "pursuit of property" opinion was meant to fit neatly into his wider view of "commercial autonomy." In fact, his legal conception of "commercial autonomy" became his most resolute constitutional anchor in defense of the nation's business monopolies. In time these arguments would be fully formed and defended. His defense began with the influential *Slaughterhouse* decisions.

These decisions showed as clearly as any Field's belief in commercial autonomy. They began with what had been an obscure 1869 Louisiana ordinance restricting the dumping of animal waste in the state's streams and rivers. To stop the practice, a state ordinance compelled Louisiana butchers to slaughter and dress livestock in a limited number of state-assigned sites. Butchers in the southern sections of the state, for example, were required to have their meat products slaughtered and dressed by the *Crescent City Livestock Landing and Slaughter Company*, a smallish company with powerful political connections. Louisiana's basic argument rested on the claim that as protector of the public's health it had an obligation to regulate the processing of meat products. For when the public's welfare was at stake, private commercial interest is to be subordinated to public interest. The Crescent City Company and its 17 employees pointed to the state's 25-year contract with CCC to oversee the slaughtering and dressing of all meat products that were sold in the city of New Orleans and the surrounding parishes of Orleans, Jefferson and St. Bernard.

The butchers, however, fought back, insisting that the ordinance had been created not so much to reduce health hazards, but as a way of protecting northern "carpet-bagging monopolies"—the interlopers, as it were, who enriched themselves at the expense of Louisiana's meat-cutters and butchers. Paul writes:

> What actually galled the citizens of New Orleans was the means that their legislature chose to carry out the plan. [I]t had an odor of the kind of exclusive privilege that would have raised the hair on the back of an old Jacksonian's neck. [This] is not a health measure, New Orleans newspapers charged; it was a monopoly pure and simple. [A] central slaughterhouse as a monopoly granted to outsiders who had no experience in the slaughtering industry.[19] The price of meat would rise, they predicted, while speculators grew rich.

When in 1873 the case finally reached the U.S. Supreme Court, Field supported the independent butchers and meat-cutters. It was, he wrote, "[a] naked restraint of trade [without] public considerations, where a right to pursue a lawful and necessary calling, previously enjoyed by every citizen, [has been] taken away."[20] The ordinance was unlawful, he declared, for the nation's constitution prevents the states from creating commercial monopolies that abridge the "privileges or immunities" of private citizens. The state has no right to restrict the preparation of meat to a single location under the control of a single processor. To support his argument Field returns to his "loyalty oath opinions, and the citizen's right to pursue a life-career free from the controls of state ordinances. (By 1873, the Fourteenth Amendment had been ratified, and Field declared that "privileges" include the pursuit of economic self-interest free from intrusive government-appointed regulators.) In response, Field's sometime legal adversary, Associate Justice Samuel Miller, and five other justices on the Supreme Court, dissented. The "privileges and immunities" clause of the Fourteenth Amendment, Miller wrote, had a narrowly designed singularity of purpose. Its intent was "to bring relief to slaves who had been deprived of life, liberty, and property."[21] Therefore, individual states, not the federal government, had the authority to establish business and communal restraints. "This authority—called the [state's] *police power*—is based not only upon the principle that every person ought to use his property so as not injure his neighbors, but also upon the principle that private interests must be made subservient to the general interests of the community."[22]

Not surprisingly, Field insisted Miller's reading of the amendment was far too narrow. "The 'privileges and immunities' clause encompasses an application far wider than slavery—a person's race is not at issue, these privileges and immunities concern the right of everyone of whatever skin color to pursue the 'ordinary avocations of life'." If Justice Miller's narrow reading was correct, Field warned, "then Amendments [Thirteen, Fourteen, and Fifteen,] were 'vain and idle enactments which accomplished nothing."[23] "The citizens of a free government have a natural and inalienable right to pursue lawful employment in a lawful manner, without any other restraint than such as equally affects all persons." The country's political institutions are the natural receptacle of "inalienable rights," in pursuit of happiness, "all honors, all positions, are alike open to everyone, and that in the protection of these rights all are equal before the law."

With the exception of some well-born southerners in the California Legislature who judged the slaughterhouse cases as an attack on the cherished doctrine of "states rights," and some entrepreneurial northerners who found Field's tone "all too Jacksonian," most mining and laboring Californians responded with indifference to the decisions. However, if there were any populists and anti-monopolists who might have hoped that Field was preparing the country for a new theory of distributive justice they were straightway disabused. Field's interpretation of the constitutional "privileges and immunities" clause was never meant to be a formula for protecting the general citizen from institutional power or for the redistribution of wealth to the deprived or the meek and modest. Quite the contrary—it was an uncompromising defense of a "doctrine of personal autonomy, [and the primacy] of private [personal] ownership." His opinion was astonishingly far-reaching—and it was meant to be. "[T]he moment the idea is admitted into society," he wrote, "that property is *not* as sacred as the laws of God, and that there is not a force of law and public justice to protect it, anarchy and tyranny [will] commence."[24]

When Field first rendered this famous opinion—"the right of property [is] a natural right, an inalienable right"—not many 19th-century critics could have foreseen how pervasive this notion would become in his later preachments. His railroad opinions in the next decade, however, would make all too clear to what lengths he was prepared to go to promote the power of federalism under his favored dictum of "privileges and immunities." "Field's right to choose a profession or trade would eventually evolve into a much more sweeping doctrine that he [designated] the liberty of contract." "[F]rom the last part of the 19th century to the 1930s it would give the Court a virtual veto over a wide range of state economic legislation."[25] (Parenthetically, Field, being a product of these paternal times, was not prepared to apply these sweeping privileges to attorney Myra Bradwell, who petitioned the court for the right to pursue a career in law before the Illinois bar. Her attorney, the renowned Matthew Hale Carpenter, argued before Field that if citizens had a privilege to pursue a profession, then it most assuredly applied to the profession of law, and thus to Mrs. Bradwell as an attorney. Field, however, deferring to his colleague Joseph Bradley's majority opinion, concurred with Bradley's assessment without comment. Included in the Bradley opinion was the following oft-referenced sentence) "[T]he practice of law is not peculiar [to] the characteristics, destiny, and mission of women, but is the calling [of men, whose] energies, responsibilities, [and] firmness predominate in the sterner sex."[26]

In the last quarter of the century, the conflation of Field's undeniable judicial gifts and hypnotic attraction to wealth and power made him one of the most influential legatees for *laissez faire* capitalism on the high bench. Not surprisingly, therefore, the societal pages of the country's newspapers were not infrequently filled with accounts of the justice and his young wife, Sue Virginia Field, enjoying unrivaled personal friendship with the most prominent money barons in the country's entrepreneurial class. Field, or Field and his wife, could be counted on to make an appearance at the most private of gatherings—banquets, weddings, funerals. Nor was the justice reluctant to take advantage of these hospitable benefits even while his wealthy friends had litigation pending before the United States Supreme Court. The attention that the rich and famous bestowed on the justice was perhaps only paralleled by the allegiance he gave them in return—whether the favors generated the fidelity or the fidelity the favors could not always be separated out, but undeniably the justice's most seasoned and indelible opinions inescapably favored men of the nation's highest station of wealth and privilege.

In one disputed account that was published in the *San Francisco Chronicle* and eventually made its way into national newspapers, the lawyerly David Colton, president of Santa Fe Railroad, fearing the growing strength of the labor movement in California, wrote to his colleague C.P. Huntington, president of the Central Pacific Railroad, indicating that Field could be counted on to "save the country from communism." "[I] have had several long talks with Judge Field and the hope of the country is the Supreme Court if the nation is to be saved from disgrace."[27] In a letter from Colton to Huntington dated September 20, 1878, Colton lays bare Field's compromising ties to the railroad barons. "Judge Field [will] reserve himself for his best effort (I have no doubt) on the final termination of the case at Washington before the whole bench." (The court was reviewing The Thurman Act, the federal statute introduced in Congress by Senator Allen G. Thurman requiring railroads to set aside twenty-five percent of their net earnings to pay off on-going debts to public lenders.) "I think it wise that [Judge Sawyer, not Judge Field, hear the case before the San Francisco Circuit Court], [for when] Judge Field takes [up] our view of the case on final argument before the [U.S.] Supreme Court, it would have more weight with that court than if he had not rendered a decision before in our favor in California." A returning letter on September 20 from Huntington concurs.[28] The tenor of the Colton letter suggests that Field had already made it clear to his wealthy friends, even before the court review, that he expected to find in their favor.

It was inevitable, therefore, that Field's railroad decisions would not be inconsistent with his notions of judicial restraints and private autonomy. The concept of judicial restraint and personal autonomy was foundational to all of Field's legal decisions, one he had been defending for years. In a series of remarkable railroad decisions, he delineated with greater care what he had argued more than a decade earlier in the slaughterhouse opinions. What he wanted was statutory protection for his concepts of personal liberty and private property. But, as might be imagined, these ratiocinative devices only made his California critics all the more resistive, convinced, as they were, that his decisions were the product not of merit, but of desire for approval and self-aggrandizement. It was hard to find any decisions in Field's California railroad opinions that the state's populists and anti-monopolists could embrace. To the contrary, populists perceived Field as always promoting the interests of "his revered corporations." However, the populists did not take him lightly; they knew him to be a most difficult adversary—nor was he one that could be ignored, His enduring critic Malcolm Clark summed it up this way: "He had the brains of Webster, the nature of a monkey and the vanity of a woman."[29]

One exacerbating example appeared in August 1882, when Field, serving a summer term as presiding judge of the Circuit Court of Appeals in San Francisco, wrote a memorandum to his colleague, Lorenzo Sawyer (presiding district judge of the court), laying out in detail how he intended to rule on *San Mateo v. Southern Pacific* should the case reach the U.S. Supreme Court.[30]

In brief, the circumstances surrounding *San Mateo* were these: Toward the end of the second decade of statehood, Californians, amounting now to nearly a million inhabitants, many of whom had actually had children born in California, were eager to put behind them the state's smudgy beginnings. Because the homesteaders were beginning to outnumber the fortune seekers, there was emerging a strong public sentiment for a culture of permanence. The *San Mateo* case arose because numerous towns and hamlets scattered throughout the central valley, in an effort to insure their survival, competed with one another to lure the population-attracting rail lines onto their confines.

To gain proximate train routes, these communities engaged in what would quickly evolve into reckless bidding wars. The inducements they offered were limitless: tax-free land, priority of access, unregulated hauling rates, private depots, seats on local planning boards, exorbitant investment partnerships. It is hardly hyperbole to say that these inland townships were prepared to make any concession to obtain their own railroad spurs. The upshot was that, in the last quarter of the century, the railroad business in California could not have been better—big and ever-bigger profits for years to come. The profits, however, were earned at the expense of these financially fragile towns. Even worse, the bidding wars continued well after town counsels knew it foolish to persevere—fearful that without railroad access they were doomed to vanish. But ironically, even after a railroad had been lured into a town, little was gained. Getting a railroad to stop in a town did not guarantee its survival. True enough, without a rail line a town might wither and die, but with a line it could face mounting obligations that many—many too many—rash promises from the town's officials had engendered.

In the 1870s and 1880s, the average small town community's railroad litigation was crippling—15, sometimes as high as 20 percent of a town's annual budget could be wasted fighting the railroads. What was worse, the smaller cities and towns routinely lost in the state and federal courts to the powerful legal emissaries representing the national railroads. The Union, the Central, and the Southern Pacific Railroads were, more often than not, shielded by protective statutes that put communities at a decidedly judicial disadvantage before appellate review courts. A federal transportation charter, for instance, granting railroads nontaxable land, or access to state and municipal underwriting bonds, or immunity from local financial liabilities, was more likely than not to tip the balance in the railroad's favor both in state and federal court rooms. Understandably, in very little time at all, a town's leadership could only perceive themselves as the indentured partners of some monolithic cartel that had become invincible. As impoverished way stations, most cities and towns had nothing to show for their skirmishes with the railroads, but unremitting indebtedness—a situation that only worsened as larger railroads swallowed up smaller ones—and as the competition dried up so also did a community's ability to negotiate agreements. The railroads would build new lines and add spurs, discontinue old lines, then set rates and schedules to their liking. If a town were impudent enough to challenge the railroad's hegemony, it would find itself subjected to corporate retaliation—increased rates, service cancellations or, worst of all, abandonment.

For these reasons, by the end of the 1870s, public perception of railroads had become radicalized. Once, the "coal-burners had represented survival and growth," but increasingly the state's population, especially in rural areas, had come to look upon themselves as powerless in the face of these financial and political behemoths. The railroads had become the paradigm of corporate zeal—or to use Frank Norris' colorful 1901 metaphor, "[The railroad had become] an octopus bent on squeezing the financial life out of the country and pressing the states and municipalities for all that the traffic would bear."[31] Eventually, the communities began to fight back by imposing selective restrictive ordinances on the railroads within their boundaries, but they soon discovered that they gained little or nothing for the effort. In most instances, these ordinances were quickly dismissed in the courts, and even on those occasions when a community's case managed to reach the highest appellate courts, it was sure to eventually face the disapproval of the powerful Justice Field—a man who had become a vigilant legal gatekeeper unflagging in his defense of corporate advantage. California populists, in particular the anti-monopolists, soon began portraying Field as the government's greatest impediment to their cherished agendas of reform.

The wellspring of *San Mateo* and its later equivalent case, *County of Santa Clara vs. Southern Pacific Railroad Company* (a case assessing the constitutionality of the California taxing system) was a dispute over taxable mortgage rates.[32] Expressly, Central Valley farmers and ranchers who purchased land prior to 1879 had been required to pay taxes on the full value of the property irrespective of the property's indebtedness. That is, the purchaser was required to pay taxes on both the equity and the debt outstanding. Sulky buyers complained that they were paying a "double tax," first on the value of land that they in part owned, and then on the amount of the loan yet unpaid, that was, so to speak, still in the hands of the seller who held the title. Under mounting pressure from homesteaders and ranchers, delegates at the state's constitutional convention of 1878 pushed through a provision in the tax code that did away with this so-called "double taxation." This revised constitution provision was ratified a year later, and thereafter the debtor's share of tax on land purchase was limited to the equity the buyer actually held—no longer would the creditors be able to force a buyer to pay tax on the land's unpaid balance.

The change in taxing policy was the much-desired relief that property owners had been looking for, but because it applied only to individual property owners it shifted a ponderous new tax burden to the railroads and transportation franchises. As a consequence, all manner of corporate business, large and small, took an active role resisting this new tax policy at every turn. The state's Board of Equalization became the focal point of the corporations' attack because, as the agency assigned the task of determining the revised taxable holdings of corporations, it determined what corporations would have to pay. Beginning in 1879, the railroads were no longer to be exempt from tariffs on roadbeds, rails, rolling stock, offices and warehouses. In essence, they would be required to pay the taxes on all properties under their fiduciary control. This meant that there would be a massive shifting of the tax burden from the private citizen onto the backs of the railroad corporations operating in California.

To no one's surprise, the railroads went into the California courts and claimed that the Board of Equalization had exceeded its authority and was acting unconstitutionally. Railroad lawyers argued that the state had no right to impose a tax obligation of this order on the railroads because, as nationwide providers, they operated under the shield of the federal government and were therefore subject only to federal, never to a state's, tax law. In court, the railroad lawyers repeated the very argument that the state's small property owners had used to force a change in the state constitution, i.e., tax on collateral and debt is a form of double taxation that violates the U.S. Constitution's equal protection clause. Also this litigation generated a vigorous response from state agencies and municipalities, who stood to lose a large source of taxable revenues if the railroad arguments were upheld. Roughly 75 percent of railroad holdings were tied up in collateral contracts held either by state agencies and departments, or regional municipalities. As to be expected, however, the disputes bogged down in lengthy litigation, for whenever one side was upheld in the state courts, the losing side brought its complaints before the appropriate federal courts of review. This created serious financial disruption in California's cities and towns. What is more, once the railroad corporations recognized the state's predicament, they compounded the problem by refusing to pay any tax until the matter of liability was settled on all their taxing disputes. The lack of municipal funds became so acute in some counties that the public schools were forced to close for months. R. Hal Williams wrote:

> In desperate need of revenue [v]arious counties brought a total of sixty-three suits against the railroad(s) for recovery of the delinquent taxes. They attempted to keep the matter in the hands of sympathetic state courts. But in July of 1882, Justice Stephen J. Field accepted jurisdiction in the case of *County of San Mateo v. Southern Pacific Railroad Company,* an action to recover $414,150 in unpaid taxes, together with the prescribed five percent penalty for non-payment, two percent per month interest, and attorneys' fees.[33]

Then in a well-structured directive that had been anticipated a decade earlier in the slaughterhouse cases, Field restated his conviction that the *equal protection* clause of the Fourteenth Amendment prohibits a state from imposing unfair laws on its citizens or its commercial enterprises. In *San Mateo*, he wrote, California's Board of Equalization violated a U.S. constitutional restraint when it taxed private citizens and corporations by standards that were not equivalent. Hence, California violated the *due process* clause by assuming that due process applied only to the nation's former slaves. "[Not so,] it is a provision for both persons and corporations, [for in any conceivable legal sense] corporations are persons [when they] unite for some legitimate business—they are therefore [under law] persons in the aggregate."[34] Four years earlier, Field had anticipated his "corporate person's doctrine" in the "sinking fund" cases when he wrote: "the law that protects the wealth of the most powerful, protects also the earning of the most humble; and the law which would confiscate the property of the one would in the end take the earnings of the other."[35] Field summarized: The California Board of Equalization imposed a double tax on corporations by taxing both holdings and indebtedness, and as a consequence deprived the railroad corporations of a constitutional right:

> [a]s corporate persons to life, liberty, property, and the pursuit of happiness, [for] whenever an individual holds property encumbered with a mortgage he is assessed at its value, after deducting from it the amount of the mortgage. [For example] if a private person owns a farm which is valued at $100,000, and is encumbered with a mortgage amounting to $80,000; he is, in that case, assessed at

> $20,000; if the rate of taxation be two per cent, he would pay $400 taxes. [But] if a railroad corporation owns an adjoining tract worth $100,000, which is also encumbered by a mortgage for $80,000, it would be [according to the California Board of Equalization] assessed for $100,000, and be required to pay $2000 taxes, or five times as much as the private person. There is here a discrimination too palpable and gross to be questioned, and such is the nature of the discrimination made against the Southern Pacific Railroad Company[.] Nothing can be clearer than that the rule of equality and uniformity is thus entirely disregarded. [The] power to tax the railroads by the state is the power to destroy the railroads and thereby deprive the overseer [the U.S. Government] of its [vital] instrument of communication through the postal service, and its [military] defense in time of war. The State Board exceeded its authority when it imposed levies on a federally controlled enterprise before receiving legal approval [to do so] from the Federal Board on Exemptions and Sanctions.[36]

When the conflict eventually reached the highest court in the country, the corporations' lawyers were expecting adjudicatory relief from the federal judges—and they were not to be disappointed. The *San Mateo* decision confirmed again what the state's populists and anti-monopolists had argued—that Field had no interest in protecting a poor man's liberty. As had been pointed out many times before, his slaughterhouse opinions clearly were meant to unchain commercialism—his obsession was nothing less than self-promotion through the wholesale approval of wealthy friends. Or, as *The San Francisco Examiner* put the matter, "[in] his ardor to serve the great corporations, [w]herein the people or the state, or a private citizen, has been a party on one side, and a rich corporation the opposing party, [Field] has invariably pronounced opinion or given judgment in favor of the corporation."

The *Examiner* put it this way on October 27, 1879:

> . . . [t]here ought to be such change [in] the Judiciary Department as will place on the bench judges who will not in every case between the rich and poor, between large corporations and the people, so interpret [t]he law that the poor and the people [i]nvariably be cast [to] be in the wrong.[37]

Field's reputation as the defender of the financially powerful produced resentment within the ranks of small business owners, farmers and ranchers throughout the Central Valley; but this anger was tepid in comparison to the acrimony generated by city-dwelling laborers toward him. In urban centers, such as San Francisco, Sacramento, San Jose and Los Angeles, wherever out-of-work white men gathered, Justice Field became the man most responsible for their woes.

No opinions that he wrote, however, were ever to evoke the bile that his legal opinions on the "Chinese problem" evoked.[38] For laborers, Field's well-known legal defense of the "Mongols" was seen by California's white working men as an unbridled threat to their "economic welfare." These populists perceived Field's unflinching loyalty to the railroad barons as the hidden motive behind his ceaseless attack on the laboring classes—what the railroad and business corporations wanted most of all was cheap labor, and everyone knew that the Chinese were willing to work more cheaply than anyone else. In other words, Justice Field's masterful legal opinions never failed to give the "robber barons" what they wanted.

However, whatever the negative insinuation the populists might have had toward Field's wide-ranging Chinese opinions, their one-dimensional charge was more born of passionate characterization than reason. In fact, the totality of Field's Chinese immigration opinions proved to be both progressive and retrogressive, and therefore never subsumable under a single judicial prejudice. Put another way, a balanced scrutiny does not confirm the interpretation so often projected by the anti-monopolists' mercenaries.

Field was still serving on the California court in 1862 when he issued his first important opinion on the "Chinese question." It was engendered by an indecorous act of the California Legislature entitled: "An Act to Protect Free White Labor against Competition with Chinese Coolie Labor, and Discourage the immigration of Chinese into the State of California." The act required Chinese laborers to pay a $2.50 monthly "police tax" for the privilege of mining gold or operating a business in the state (the legislators had self-servingly exempted from the tax those Chinese merchants who dealt in sugar, rice, coffee and tea). Field supported the act's legality while his colleagues, Justices Walter Cope and Edward Norton, favored the appellants. Cope and Norton argued that the state legislature did not have the jurisdictional authority to tax foreigners—only the federal government had the authority to regulate special fees of commerce with Chinese citizens living in the United States.

Field's dissent, by contrast, avowed California's right as a sovereign state to tax its inhabitants as it chose. "California, standing on the autonomy of state government has the right to tax all its residents as it sees fit."[39] What is more, the state's privilege to tax the public was viable even when the tax levied made it difficult, or even impossible, for those taxed to continue working. "Change," he opined dismissively, "comes only from a legislative change of mind. [The] court is not the protectors of the Chinese, nor is it a matter of congressional power regulating commerce; rather, it is an undisguised [statutory] attempt by legislators to prevent the Chinese from flourishing in California." This early 1862 opinion by Field evoked no dramatic stirring amongst either California's legislators or workers, many of whom, being southern, held a strong affinity for any doctrine promoting the "right of states" to establish their own legal boundaries.

Twelve years later, however, looking down from his elevated position of power on the federal bench, Field was to view the Chinese problem in an entirely different light—and the early casualty of this revised perspective was his quixotically employed interpretation of "state rights." In 1874 in *Chy Lung vs. Freeman* and *Ah Fong vs. California* cases, he found his way from his 1862 position to that of his former colleagues Cope and Norton. They had argued from the California bench; that the federal government's Burlingame Treaty with China had established immigration policy between the United States and China, thereby making void state jurisdiction. He offered his *Chy Lung* opinion in Washington, D.C., and read his *Ah Fong* decision from the District Circuit Court bench in San Francisco.[40] In *Ah Fong* the issue was whether the California Legislature had a right to impose a shipmaster's entry tax ($500) on all the Chinese who disembarked in California. In *Ah Fong,* a shipmaster refused to post the $500 bond for Ah Fong because she was, he declared, "a lewd, debauched woman—a prostitute." In response, a writ of *habeas corpus* was filed on her behalf in federal court declaring her right to go ashore under the provisions of the Burlingame Treaty that had been agreed to a decade earlier in *Lin Sing vs. Washburn*. Revisiting the writ, Field declared that the state was in violation of federal law, having interfered with the U.S. Government's responsibility to honor its treaty. In legal prose occasioned by the circumstances, and remarkable for its farsighted cast, Field wrote that the California statute was flawed for failing to acknowledge a difference between the "infirmed, [i.e.,] the deaf, dumb, blind, crippled, or lunatic—and the able bodied. [T]he state can deal with prostitutes by fining them or imprisoning them but it cannot deny them entry that is protected by national treaty." It was Ah Fong's race, he persisted, not her personal behavior, that produced the statute, "[a]nd I have little respect for that discriminating virtue which is shocked when a frail child of China is landed on our shores, and yet allows the bedizened and painted harlots of other countries to parade our streets and open her hells in broad day, without molestation and without censure." A state has a right to self-defense, but this statute, he continues, goes far beyond that right and encroached on the federal government's treaty-making power and its duty to regulate commerce with foreign nations. Since the days when California's "southerner legislators attempted to prevent 'free-negros' from settling in California," he offered, "the state [consistently] has had unjust immigration policies."

Eight years passed, and Field again blocked the California legislature's effort to restrict Chinese immigration. In *Ah Tie v. California* the state sought to prohibit Ah Tie, a six-year resident of California, from returning to the state once he had departed its soil to work as a shipboard waiter. This California law forbade shipmasters from transporting Chinese laborers "from any port or place." Field rejected the state's plea, writing, "[This statute reaches an] unjust or absurd conclusion [and] violates individual liberty." It was no more defensible, he continued, than it would be to prevent one from returning to the United States who had inadvertently strayed into Canada while on his way to New York. "Surely one cannot impose a tax only on those foreigners who [by chance] arrive by sea (or are Chinese)."[41] As it turned out, *Ah Fong* and *Ah Tie* were historically portentous decisions, because they played one of the earliest roles in enlarging constitutional protections for the foreign-born residing in the United States.

However, the opinion on the "Chinese problem" for which Field is most famous, and deservedly so, is *Ho Ah Kow v. Nunan* (1877).[42] The case grew out of a restrictive San Francisco measure dictating the number of people that might live in a single dwelling within city limits. The Board of Supervisors had introduced a complicated cubic-air formula that limited the number of people that could literally inhabit one room—the ordinance was, so its opponents correctly argued, a transparent effort to stop the Chinese from bringing their relatives into California. Ho Ah Kow, who had squeezed as many of his kin into an overcrowded shanty as possible, was arrested and fined $50. He refused to pay the fine, however, opting instead to serve time in the city jail (a practice not uncommon among the Chinese who were facing jail time while residing in San Francisco). City supervisors, however, unwilling to absorb any additional jail costs, attached a proviso onto the original ordinance declaring that "Mongols" choosing jail in lieu of a fine will have their heads shorn "as a hygienic precaution." For Ho Ah Kow this meant suffering the humiliation of having his braided "queue" cut off. Field's opinion stunned San Francisco's establishment. He began by belittling the city's "sanitary ordinance," pointing out that if it were a matter of hygiene then it was surely reasonable to expect that the heads of all prisoners (woman included) be shorn—but this, of course, was not happening. "The Queue Ordinance," Field declared, revealed the true mission of this statute. Its aim was to discriminate against the Chinese and by so doing dishonor their religious tenets. The penalty was intended to shame its victims into complying. "It is not punishment it is torture," Field inveighed, "[w]hy not the thumb-screw or the rack? [Why not require] the Jews to abandon dietary laws under penalty?" The ordinance, he wrote, robs people "of the Constitution's broad protecting shield, [this ordinance is nothing but] an anti-Chinese ordinance. [Punishment and discrimination, not sanitation, are the issues at stake!] It is hostile and spiteful legislation which is unworthy [California's] brave and manly people."[43] Thereafter this masterful opinion was to have an astringent effect on all discriminatory legislation in California. For its time, it was a most remarkable opinion and it effectively tied the hands of the state legislature.

However, surveying the entirety of Field's legal defense of the Chinese, his opinions can only be judged as a puzzling combination of progressive and retrogressive legal analysis. It can be argued, however, that he was more inclined to protect the welfare of the Chinese when state and federal legislation appeared to violate jurisdictions or to intrude on his convictions involving personal autonomy.[44]

Yet, in a basic sense, the catalyst for dismissing liberty-restricting ordinances came not from any personal libertarian virus that he had in his belly, but from what he would characterize as the effort of the many to expropriate the industrial energies of the few—expressly, as a resolution of the status of foreign immigration as it applied to the policies and practices of entrepreneurial enterprises and the privileges of the financially gifted. The indifference that he held toward individual liberty as an overarching constitutional principal was never better illustrated than in his feeling toward African-Americans.

Paul Kens writes perceptively that blacks posed a long term political threat to Field, for they were intent on controlling portions of their own government. This was in contrast to the Chinese, who posed no such political threat at least in the short run, because they were perceived as alien residents without either a right or an interest in citizenship. They were, simply put, people who were willing to labor long hours at low wages. "You know," Field once remarked to his long-time friend and colleague John Norton Pomeroy, "I belong to the class who repudiate the doctrine that this country was made for the people of all races. [O]n the contrary, I think it is for our race—the Caucasian race. [W]e are obliged to take care of the African; because we find them here, and they were brought here against their will by our fathers."[45]

Insofar as the Chinese were concerned, Field would declare, Caucasians had no obligation to "take care of the Chinese" because of the action of our forbearers. On the contrary, he believed, Caucasians had a clearly defined opposing duty. "It is our duty to preserve this land for our people and their posterity forever; to protect and defend American institutions and republican government from the oriental gangrene."[46] It should not be forgotten that Field consistently supported exclusion of African-Americans sitting on juries. What next, he seemed to be saying, the Chinese and women? In a letter to General John F. Miller he wrote, "The immigration of Chinese into California in large numbers is a serious evil."[47] But, it is also clear that Field could be counted on to object to racially discriminatory legislation if he judged it to threaten commercial libertarianism; i.e., he was for advancing legal protection for economic access and freedom, he was not concerned in defending civil liberties. Field's solution to the "Chinese problem" meant putting the issue in the hands of the U.S. Congress, who then should demand that China open all their ports to unfettered commerce. If China refuses then threaten to close United States ports under some form of treaty reciprocity or what Field calls "comparable restriction." In this situation the U.S. could demand a treaty restricting residents v*is à vis* commerce.[48]

Field's influence on the U.S. court between 1865 and 1885 had a bracing and durable effect on the economic welfare of Californians. During those years, he solidified a bedrock legal theory of individual autonomy and unfettered commerce. Field's view of free commercial enterprise led the state's business and commercial leaders to embrace his apologia of commercialism with a bold enthusiasm—a viewpoint not always shared by Californians i.e., the farmers, independent miners, and urban laborers. From the laboring man's viewpoint, Justice Field's ruminations constituted an abrasively punitive attack on the working class. "What made Field so formidable was his skill in translating the featureless generalities of the Constitution into a coherent system of principled standards," writes Charles McCurdy in *The Fields and the Law.* "He had an uncanny ability to diagnose recurrent problem situations [that] accommodated his value-laden premises. [And for] Field these solutions were neither contingent nor variable; they were 'true.'[49] Throughout life it was this candid image of "just government" that systematically sabotaged Field's political aspirations—and presaging these resentments loomed the large, disgruntled figure of Judge Terry.

NOTES

1. A. Russell Buchanan. *David S. Terry of California: Dueling Judge* (San Marino CA.: The Huntington Library Press, 1956). 166. As told to Ernest J. Hopkins, May 13, 1921.
2. David S. Terry. MSS Huntington Library, San Marino Ca. May 12, 1870.
3. Charles Potts. "David S. Terry," *Southwest Review,* v. 19, no.4. Spring, 1934. 317.
4. Oscar T. Shuck. *Bench and Bar of California* (San Francisco: Occidental Printing House 1888). 285.
5. J. Edward Johnson. *History of the Supreme Court of California, 1850–1900,* (San Francisco: California Supreme Court) 1963. 58.
6. David S. Terry MSS. (Huntington Library: San Marino, CA), October 11, 1867.
7. A. Russell Buchanan. *Dueling Judge,* 149.
8. Henry M. Field. *The Life of David Dudley Field* (New York: Private Printing, 1892). 196.
9. Marysville *Daily Appeal,* March 10, 1863. *San Francisco Alta,* Feb, 24–25, 1863.

10. New York *Sun.* "Sketch of the Life of Stephen Field of the U.S. Supreme Court." April 25, 1880. 26.

11. San Francisco *Evening Bulletin,* Feb, 24 1863.

12. *Ex parte Garland*, 71 US 333.

13. *Cummings v. Missouri,* 71 US 277.

14. Carl Brent Swisher. *Stephen* J. Field C*raftsman of the Law* (Washington D.C.: The Brookings Institute, 1930). 149–150. Also Paul Kens. *Field.* 114.

15. Paul Kens. *Justice Stephen J. Field: Shaping Liberty from Gold Rush to Gilded Age* (Lawrence KN: The University of Kansas Press, 1997). 114.

16. *Cummings v. Missouri.* 71 US 277. 16. Cited in Swisher, *Craftsman.* 148.

17. Paul Kens, *Field.* 121.

18. —— 114.

19. —— 122.

20. Stephen J. Field. *Some Opinions and Papers of Stephen J. Field,* The 9th Circuit Court of the United States Supreme Court. *New Orleans Slaughterhouse Cases. v.* 1, pamphlet 24. Field's dissenting opinion December 1872. The slaughterhouses had an odor that was described as able to raise the hair on the back of Andrew Jackson's neck.

21. See, Stephen J. Field to J. DeBarth Shorb. October 27, 1886, DeBarth Shorb Collection, The Huntington Library. Also, cited in P. Kens, *Stephen J. Field.* 119. 21. 83 U.S. 36 (1873).

22. Carl Swisher, *Craftsman.* 417.

23. Paul Kens, *Field,* 121.

24. Carl Swisher, *Craftsman.* 427, 99 U.S. 700,767.

25. 111 U.S. 746 (1884).

26. *Bradwell v Illinois.* 83 U.S. 130 (1873).

27. *The San Francisco Chronicle,* letter dated August 9, 1878, and published on April 18, 1885.

28. *The San Francisco Chronicle,* Sept. 20, 1878. Also Sept. 30, 1878.

29. Clark, Malcolm. Ed., *Pharisee Among the Philistines.* Judge Matthew P. Deady's Diary (1975).

30. Letter of September 20, 1878. Published in *The San Francisco Chronicle,* April 18, 1885.

31. *The Octopus* 1901. Cited in Swisher, *Stephen J. Field.* 240.

32. Stephen J. Field. *Some Opinions.* v. 1, pamphlet 22, 23, September 25, 1882, and September 17, 1883. *San Mateo v. Southern Pacific,* 13 Fed. 722, 1882.

33. R. Hal Williams. *The Democratic Party and California Politics, 1880–1896* (Stanford CA: Stanford University Press, 1973). 34.

34. Swisher, *Craftsman.* 255. Williams, *Politics,* 35.

35. Stephen J. Field, *Some Opinions, v.* 2 pamphlet 16. (129 U.S. Rep. 26). Corporations are persons within the meaning of the clauses in the 14th Amendment. Corporations, even as individuals, have the right to protection through the government's police powers. See also, *The Sinking Fund Cases,* 99 U.S. 700, October 1878. Cited in Kens. *Field,* 223.

36. George Gorham. *Sketch of Stephen J. Field,* included in S.J. Field's *Reminiscences.* (1898).

37. October 27, 1879. Cited in Kens. *Field,* 225.

38. The "Chinese Problem," was not all concentrated in California. See John R. Wunder, Anti-Chinese violence in the American West. 1850–1910, *Law for the Elephant, Law for the Beaver.* Ed. By John Mc Laren, Hamar Foster, and Chet Orloff. Ninth Judicial Circuit Historical Society. Pasadena CA. 1992. 212.

39. *Lin Sing v. Washburn.* 20 Cal. 534.

40. Swisher. *Stephen J. Field. Craftsman of the Law.* 92 U.S., 275 (1875), 3 Sawyer 144, (1874).

41. *In re Ah Tie*, Federal Case 102, Sept. 21, 1874. *In re Ah Tie v California,* 13 Fed. 291.

42. *Ho Ah Kow v Numan.* Federal Case 6546.

43. *Ho Ah Kow v Numan* 12 F. Case 256.

44. Paul Kens, *Field,* 210–211.

45. —— *Field,* 212, 327. See also, Swisher. *S. J. Field: Craftsman of the Law.* 165.

46. *San Francisco Examiner,* July 8, 1879. Also cited in Paul Kens. *Field.* 205.

47. *San Francisco Morning Call,* March 21 1888.

48. Stephen J. Field, "Some Opinions" 9th Circuit Court of the United States, v.3, *San Francisco Morning Call,* March 21, 1880.

49. *The Argonaut,* Aug 9, 1879.

Chapter Eight

Political Dreams

The nation experienced a surge of financial prosperity between 1865 and 1895 unlike anything witnessed before, and doubtless Stephen Field's *judicia dicta* played no small part in this extraordinary commercial explosion. By comparison, David Terry's political time and effort during those years was devoted to resisting the consequences of this "epidemic of capitalism"—even while finding sufficient time to accumulate his own sizable share of it. Terry's successful practice in civil and criminal litigation went a long way toward smoothing out old political rivalries, healing the memories of war and vigilante justice, and the incomprehensible tragedy of the Broderick affair. In the Sacramento and San Joaquin Valleys, especially, he no longer carried the burden of a sullied reputation; he had become a trusted lawyer and a wealthy man. Never one to limit his procurements to the practice of law, he bought ranch land and livestock, owned town and mining property, and even went so far as to reinvest in Mexico's cotton cultivation.[1] At the heart of Terry's rejuvenated status was a court fight that eventually brought him face-to-face with Field's rulings in *San Mateo* and seemed in degree to change his approach to the practice of law, even as it was playing a role restoring the confidence of valley neighbors in his post-bellum persona.

The 1873 legal battle had begun, as a matter of fact, two decades earlier when Stockton City, along with other towns in the San Joaquin valley, was vying to become the shipping and produce center for the central valley. Stockton City had signed a shipping agreement with the Western Pacific Railroad whereby it agreed to provide passenger and shipping service between Sacramento and San Jose. To that end a contract was signed calling for the Western Pacific to lay track on Stockton's eastern boundary connecting it with northern and southern hubs. Included in the agreement was a provision stating that the Western Pacific would provide a loading spur that would enable the city to move its produce from Stockton's inland port westward into the sea-lanes flowing out of San Francisco's Bay. With their topological advantages, it was not surprising that Stockton's city council was counting on increased revenues and dominance as the Central Valley's major shipping hub. At the time of the agreement, the Western Pacific's rail line from Sacramento to San Jose was the most active shipping corridor in California.

In return for this rail hookup, the city promised to make available to the railroad a large sum of investment money—$250,000 in bonds at 8% interest over a 20-year period. The city also agreed to the railroad's request that the track be laid outside Stockton City's township so it might avoid the city's annual land taxes and fees. After the track had been put in place, however, perfidious Stockton officials, ignoring their original agreement, extended city boundaries to include land on which the Western Pacific had laid its track, and foolishly voted to ignore the original exemption agreement, thereby presenting the Western Pacific with *a fait accompli*—an easement tax. Not surprisingly, the railroaders refused to pay the added tax.

Several months later, Western Pacific interests were purchased by Leland Stanford's Central Pacific Railroad, thereby making the Stockton City railroad contract Stanford's problem. Stanford chose to cut off additional discussions with the Stockton city council and deal with it on his own terms. First he laid down a shipping spur that ran ten miles south of the city into the small hamlet of Lathrop, thus effectively undercutting for the time being Stockton's aspiration to become the Central Valley's principal shipping hub. Then he took the city into court demanding money from them for reneging on their original agreement.

Needless to say, the city fought back. It turned to the cash-poor Stockton/Visalia Railroad and worked out a new arrangement. The city offered the Stockton/Visalia Railroad an even more lucrative cash incentive than they had made with the Western Pacific—a 20-year $300,000 loan at 7%. In return, the railroad agreed to lay track from the city's channel port directly to the agricultural hub in the town of Visalia 160 miles south of Stockton. So far so good. However, an obscure "progress clause" written into the contract that initially had raised no undue concern with Stockton lawyers eventually led to Stockton's second failed railroad agreement. The clause stipulated that for every five miles of track laid, the city would pay the railroad $100,000. Without delay the railroad went to work. They first laid a half-mile of new track from the portside wharves, attaching it to old track that ran 14 miles south and east to the town of Oakdale. Then they came to the city council and requested the $300,000, insisting that before laying any more track it wanted $100,000 for each five miles that was now in place. Once again the city found itself in a legal battle with a railroad that had been not anticipated. After several investigational delays, they argued in the courtroom that the S/VRR had not met the terms of the contract. The contract called for 15 miles of "new" track. To this position the railroad countered that the contract had only stipulated that fifteen miles of accessible working track running southward to Visalia need be provided. Each side, thoroughly convinced that the other side had broken the agreement, was in no mood to look for any additional compromise. The railroad never laid another foot of track, nor did Stockton City's frustrated city leaders ever advance the railroad another dollar.[2]

The clash between the city and the Stockton/Visalia Railroad remained moribund until the 1870s when the dispute finally found a litigious pathway onto the docket of the state Supreme Court. At the state's highest court, the railroad, represented by a battery of expensive lawyers from San Francisco, was joined by former Chief Justice Terry—he had been retained to steer the railroad's coastal attorneys through the labyrinth that was the San Joaquin County court system.[3]

In court, the railroad attorneys presented an aggressive case. They contended that the railroad had met the terms of the agreement. It had provided Stockton with a rail line as stipulated in the contract—a line running from the city's waterfront "through the county of San Joaquin in a *southerly direction toward* the town of Visalia." At no time, they insisted, did the contract stipulate that the railroad "[need] provide an airline," (direct route) to Visalia. They were not required to lay another mile of track until the city of Stockton honored the "progress loan payments" as set forth in the original agreement. In reply, the city council called the court's attention to a clause in the contract that stipulated that "the track be laid in a manner acceptable to the Stockton City Council," to which the railroad attorneys countered that the phrase "acceptable to [the Council]" was far too equivocal to hold "any legally promissory merit." After what Stockton City considered an all-too-brief deliberation, the Supreme Court found in the railroad's favor. The words in the document "acceptable to [the Council]" the court declared, ambiguous and contractually worthlesswere as the railroad had said. Therefore they could not be introduced into negotiations as a form of legal "restraint or guide." Again Stockton had been slowed in its efforts to control the shipping industry in the San Joaquin Valley. Yet along with the railroad's victory came handsome retainers and reward fees to Judge Terry and his high-priced colleagues from San Francisco law offices.

But Terry's success did not rest easily upon him. From the outset it had been a case that was alien to his populist and anti-monopolistic sentiments. His true loyalties lay with the farmers and ranchers in the Central Valley, so that in short order he was soon challenging, not supporting, the corporations—especially the railroad barons. As Terry judged the episode, the railroad had won a general appeal it need not have won. Doubtless, he must have concluded, California's Supreme Court was under the ponderous thumb of the state's most powerful corporations. Thereafter he determined to be more selective, more politically engaged with his clients. The preponderance of later litigating was in the service of private persons and anti-corporate clients drawn from the valleys. Very few were from San Francisco. In the single year of 1877 the *Stockton Daily Independent* reported, approvingly, for example, that Judge Terry had won judgments against the railroads that saved the city of Stockton more than a half-million dollars in outstanding bonds and penalties.[4] At the time, close to a quarter of the Stockton County budget was tied up in railroad debt.

Terry's successful legal efforts in the Central Valley had restored his reputation—there was no doubting it—he had become a respected San Joaquin County squire. Stockton parents took the time to point him out to their children as they passed on the streets, while in the valley he was earning a name for himself as a crusading lawyer with a practice that kept the interests of the valley residents foremost in mind. Stockton's citizens took pride in the fact that he was smart and shrewd enough to fight and win legal battles against the all-consuming esurience of the corporation lawyers who lived and worked on the seaboard. In fact, his neighbors confirmed their faith in him a year later, in May of 1878, when they elected him as one of four San Joaquin County Representatives to the Constitutional Revision Convention. When Terry accepted the nomination, he promised his San Joaquin neighbors that it was his only desire to aid in fashioning a constitutional document that would be a credit to the state framers and to its working people.[5]

California's first constitution had served its purpose for more than a quarter of a century, but as a frontier document it had its limitations. It no longer answered the legislative needs of a state whose population was tenfold what it had been when it was written. The constitutional guides and limits of 1850 were hardly adequate for the complexities that had become a part of California by 1879, and the constitution's ambiguity or silence on so many matters had forced a perplexed judicial system to render too many judgments *constructio legis sui generis* (creating law out of nothing). The constitution had become little more than a document of "shreds and patches."[6] In reality, there had been pressure to revise the state constitution since its first appearance in 1851; and by 1878, every political faction large enough to have influence on state policy was urging either a revision or a complete rewriting. William Irwin, who was governor at the time, was initially reluctant to act, believing that any change of the constitution would entail a change in legislative representation, something that many northern Californians opposed. But after six months of mounting pressure from both corporations and labor guilds, he finally agreed to call California's second constitutional convention. It convened in Sacramento on September 28, 1878, and its purpose was essentially to rewrite, not merely amend, the constitution.

The state's political representation to the convention of 1878 was significantly different from what it had been at the first convention in 1850. Unlike representation at the first convention, there were powerful block delegations from the large metropolitan areas of San Francisco, and Sacramento, and the populated areas around San Jose, Los Angeles and San Diego, counties that came to the convention politically well-positioned—many with timeworn connections to state and corporate power. This time, many delegations were controlled by lawyers. In contrast to the regions living south of the Tehacapi Mountains (these delegates represented about 20 percent of the population), San Francisco, Sacramento and San Jose sent large delegations of highly-trained politically-savvy lawyers to the convention, as well as men who made a living, as labor organizers. These labor representatives were usually members of craft guilds, construction and stevedore brotherhoods, and city service workers. Most working-class representatives, moreover, had begun political education on the streets, in the rough and tumble politics of organized labor protests.

The roots of the rural populations of the state was another matter, made up of farmers, ranchers and small business owners who lived in the dusty towns and villages of the central and southern valleys, and, generally were much less organized and ideological. The most radical of the valley farmers were referred to as "Grangers," after the farm cooperatives in the Midwest that were seeking to publicly regulate private utilities. In fact, valley delegates were inclined to support the business corporations when taxes or free access to produce markets were at risk, but they were not reluctant to switch loyalties and oppose corporate interests when transportation costs or the intrusion of Mexican and Chinese labor became a perceived threat to their pecuniary concerns.

By far, however, the most ideologically active delegates at the convention were the urban workers from San Francisco and Sacramento, who were members of a militant political organization called The Workingman's Party. In San Francisco alone, there were more than 15,000 Workingman's Party members, many of whom were surly, jobless former immigrants who had suffered through two decades of financial boom, and bust, and who were by 1878 in no mood for a revised constitution that was intent on maintaining the *status quo*.

These workers were lead by Dennis Kearney, an out-of-work drayman from Dublin, and his somewhat punctilious partner, William Wellock, who in his younger years had been a London shoemaker. Kearney was the Party's firebrand, stump-speech orator and demagogue, while Wellock was its bookkeeper and pamphleteer. Although the demands of workers were not always the same nor, often times, neither clearly articulated or identifiable, most of these men were able to unite beneath the banners that Kearney and Wellock so exuberantly waved: "curb the excessive profits of the corporations;" "[p]lace all railroads under municipal control;" and "stop once and for all the continuing flood of Chinese immigration into the state."[7]

The delegates tormenting California's laborers were the railroad's "Big Four," Leland Stanford, Collis P. Huntington, Charles Crocker and Mark Hopkins. By 1878, 85% of all the railroad track in California was controlled by these "barons," and it was estimated that between 15,000 to 20,000 Chinese, that is, "substitutes and supplanters," were working for them.[8] As the workers saw their plight, one that Dennis Kearney articulated over and again, the principal enemy was "[t]he railroad barons who were hiring 'Mongols' at a dollar-a-day, and prostrating the hopes of working men—no white worker could [ever expect] to keep his family alive on a dollar-a-day!" "[T]he corporations," argued Kearney, "must stop hiring the heathen who are by nature dishonest, diseased and drug ridden (leprosy and opium) and hold utter disregard for the principle of ownership, they'll steal anything." After which Kearney would draw labor's line in the sand: "We give the Central Pacific three months to discharge their Chinamen, and if it is not done Stanford and his crowd will have to take the consequences." "[A] little judicious hanging would cure the blight of capitalism."[9] "The Yellow Pests must go" was a slogan that Kearney could always count on to unite white men, no matter how their spirits might flag or how disparate their unreachable goals might appear to be. Whenever the suspicious and feisty Kearney judged that the zeal of party members was diminishing, he was not reluctant to take to the stump and catch his listeners up short with a menacing promise that "the first man who flags [will] be hung up to a lamp post." "[T]he people [will control] their own affairs. [T]hey will not be stayed by vigilantes, state militia, nor United States troops."[10]

In due course, newspapers took to calling the workers' party "sand-lotters," a name derived from the rallies that were held on the sandy lots adjacent to San Francisco's city hall. It was a convenient place where the protesters would have easy access to the city's bureaucrats who came and went on daily rounds. The Party's confrontational style and political stridency soon earned them the standard obloquy "communists, thugs and anarchists," and, with not a little hyperbole, the railroad-owned *Daily Alta* declared them "an imminent threat to all civilized society."[11] When reporters pressed Kearney on this issue, however, he denied connection or even any interest in Communism, but did acknowledge "that he had some sympathy with French socialists." In time, San Franciscans grew accustomed to Kearny's bumptious rhetoric and began to pay attention to his message—so much so that some of his proposals eventually gained support with larger segments of the population. There was, for example, support for a proposal to convene the legislature once every four years (a Texan's plan) in order to take the power to pardon criminals away from the governor and put it in the hands of legislators. Also, an 8-hour day was a popular recommendation. But Kearney's proposal that every child under the age of 14 be required to go to "public school at public expense" was the most persuasive. (Shortly thereafter, the proposal was adopted by the legislature).

The state's second constitutional convention convened in Sacramento on September 28, 1878. And, as was anticipated, the most powerful block of convention delegates were the sand-lotters—slightly more than a third of the delegates. In fact, the delegation proved to be so large and well-organized that its convention opponents, becoming fearful that Kearney's agenda would logroll the entire convention, united under a loosely organized coalition called the Non-Partisan Alliance. The Alliance, made up of northern and southern Democrats and a block of newly emerging California Republicans, agreed to send the "best candidates" to the convention, regardless of party affiliation. By prior agreement, these "moderates" were determined to outmaneuver and outvote the Workingman's Party whenever they judged a political threat to the "proper" institutions of government. Nonetheless, once these constitution revision proceedings were under way, the various political alliances anticipated before the convention seemed to generate very little loyalty. So much so, that by the end of the second week, these alliances began to crumble. In their place surfaced blocks of delegates who coalesced behind common political or regional goals, even as traditional party loyalties and affiliations were becoming ever more clearly identified and ever more entrenched.

The Democrat David Terry had agreed to come to the convention as a member of the Non-Partisan Alliance, yet he quickly drew rural and urban populists of every stripe to his side once they had witnessed the ease with which he was able to maneuver through the parliamentarian labyrinth—almost overnight his political affiliations seemed to become extraneous. Labor and farm delegates, for instance, found themselves swallowed up in the legislative conundrums of floor debate i.e., in the loquacious arguments of the coastal lawyers who had a knack for manipulating the convention's parliamentary proceedings willy-nilly (a circumstance that occurred on more than a few occasions). They found in parliamentarian Terry the skill and aggressiveness they lacked. As a simple matter of record, during the six months the convention was in session, with the exception of the speeches and comments offered by Judge Terry, floor appearances by the San Joaquin County delegates were nonexistent or unreported.

Terry, as a constitutional delegate, was a different man than he had been as a judge, duelist and soldier. His ambient sternness no longer seemed to be repressing a volcanic personality, and there was less inflexible posturing. Since returning from the war, even his bravado and bluster had become muted. With a single exception, he had not lost his sense of self-righteousness, for on the third day of the convention, he successfully unseated delegate A.C. Peachy "as an unworthy delegate [because he] was living with a woman, who was not his wife." Later Peachy would challenge Terry to a duel for "this gratuitous public humiliation," but the re-born, laconic Terry waved him away, "I have had all the experience I want on that score," he said. Even Terry's message on the divine origin of racial divisions had softened. At one point during an extended debate on Chinese immigration, he reminded delegates that the Fourteenth Amendment protects "[t]he Chinese even as it protects the Negroes," and then added good naturedly, "[and I will not] foolishly go to war on that matter ever again."

On opening day of the convention, Governor Irwin, acting as chairman *pro tempore,* called the delegates to order. There were three representatives who did not answer the roll call and one of the three was Judge Terry. The Workingman members seized the opportunity to call for a vote banning the judge from the convention, for many of the "working men" had not forgotten nor forgiven Terry for his role in the Broderick duel or his service in the Confederacy. During the year preceding the convention, moreover, Terry had been traveling the state making speeches critical of the Workingman's ticket.

Hence, with the first rap of the governor's gavel the Workingman's delegate Beerstecher was on his feet shouting to be recognized but Irwin, having been informed beforehand of Beerstecher's intentions, ignored his gesticulations, ruled him out of order, and then announced "that all duly elected representatives whether in attendance or not" were to be seated as permanent members of the convention. With that brief but, as it would turn out, fortuitous decision, the second California constitutional convention was under way.

Several days later, a sequence of roll-call votes made it obvious to the Workingman's Party that their failure to remove Terry had been a stroke of good fortune; for within a fortnight he had become one of their staunchest allies. His open and unabashed anti-monopoly, anti-railroad, anti-corporation and anti-Chinese perspective made him a kindred spirit. In fact, they could have hardly found a better ally. Moreover, outsiders had clearly understood Terry's importance to the Workingman's Party. As the Oakland *Enquirer* observed:

> In opinions and temper Terry was a good deal like the Workingmen delegates, and having about ten times as much brains as the smartest among them, soon be-

> came their actual though not their acknowledged leader. The man they had so recently execrated and called by all the vile names they could invent, really directed the movements of the Workingmen during that long and eventful session.[12]

From Terry's viewpoint, he welcomed the support, for he considered himself not only a representative of the inland valley farmers and small businessmen, but also a spokesman for "California's struggling workers."

Perhaps, however, more significantly, he was one of a handful of delegates who could actually influence the opinions of others when he rose to speak from the convention floor. He spoke frequently (albeit in his usual economical style), and like him or not, he was one of the delegates who could successfully generate voting majorities. By the end of the first week, delegates had been assigned to standing committees, and Terry was placed on the judicial and legislative committees. His judicial reputation had put him on two of the most prestigious convention committees, and as a former chief justice, he immediately became chairman of the legislative committee.

The Kearneyites soon realized that the Non-Partisan Alliance had the votes to make them a losing minority whenever it had the will to do it. The Kearneyites usual street-bombastic style, moreover, was entirely ineffectual as a persuasive device on the convention floor—and as a consequence, they were without effective majorities on the essential committees. It did not take the workingmen long to realize that what they needed above all was an articulate advocate who could forge strategic political alliances and generate politically winning majorities. On this score, they concluded, Terry would be invaluable to their interests. They particularly admired his ease on the convention floor and his ability to present a case in a parliamentary fashion. Moreover, he could stick to a cause—he would never be bought off nor would he capitulate—and in spite of the positions he might take, the Workingmen delegates sensed that he could be trusted. Soon they began looking to him for support and leadership, even as they grew to sense that, more often than not, his views paralleled their own.

As convention representatives worked their way through the constitutional revisions, rewriting or replacing the old constitution issue by issue, majorities formed, intent on enhancing or replacing ordinances to more clearly reflect the changing interests of California's expanding population. Foremost on the Workingman's agenda was the formulation of an amendment to the constitution that would prohibit the settling of any more Chinese in California. But the issue was far more complex in 1878 than it had been for their forbears at the first constitutional convention in 1850. By 1878, the convention had to comply with a federal provision declaring that foreign-born Chinese immigrants were under the protection of an international treaty established between the governments of China and the United States in 1868—the Burlingame Treaty. The treaty read in part: "[that a man has] an inherent [right] to change his home [through] mutual advantages, migration and emigration [f]or purposes of curiosity, trade and permanent [residence]." Terry, as the former chief justice, had to remind delegates that Justice Field's unequivocal 1874 opinion *In re Ah Fong* had made the restriction of Chinese immigration constitutionally illegal. After three weeks of debate under the restrained admonishing of cooler heads, including Judge Terry's, the delegates settled on a constitutional provision that required the U.S. Congress to revise its treaty with the Chinese so as to include immigration quotas. By 1878, there were about 300,000 Chinese settled in the United States, with about a quarter of them living on *Gum Saan* (gold mountain) that is to say, in and around the San Francisco Bay.

The final report on Chinese immigration was ready to be presented to the convention by the Committee on Chinese Immigration in December 1878. In essentials, it declared that the state of California had a right to protect itself from the "burdens and evils [caused by] the presence of aliens [the Chinese] who are or may become vagrants, paupers, mendicants, criminals, or invalids afflicted with contagious or infectious disease." Gossip was that Chinese immigrants carried a virulent strain of syphilis that was more ravishing and less treatable than the Caucasian variety.

Summing up the debate and the petitions of the Committee on Chinese Immigration, the annoyed chairman of the committee, John F. Miller, president of the Alaska Commercial Company, vented his resentment of the U.S. Congress's procrastination on the "Chinese problem" as follows:

> If the people over on the eastern side will not hear our complaints, if they say this is not an evil, and that the Chinese are as good as any other class of immigrants—that we are making a great noise and confusion about nothing—let us send over four, or five, or ten thousand of these people—those who are dangerous to the well-being of the state—belonging to the criminal and diseased classes; let us send them a brigade or two of these 'Chinamen,' and see how they like it. There would not be a surer way of changing their views upon the Chinese.[13]

There were other committee members who went so far as to propose that the state withdraw its commercial charter from any corporation hiring the Chinese. Under this proposal, violation of the law would result in forfeiture of any state-established corporate franchise. Other emendations poured forth: deny the Chinese ownership of property, citizenship, voting privilege and even the right to sue white men. "All Mongols are to be denied access to legal redress." But it was left to delegate C.C. O'Donnell to reach the nadir of foolishness. He rose to declare that the Chinese should be prevented from coming ashore in California because "they are a hazard to a Caucasian man's health" (a proposal that brought from his hectoring comrades a motion that O'Donnell himself be "quarantined and isolated" from the rest of the delegates because he had the misfortune of residing in San Francisco where the largest population of "hazardous Mongols live—after all, who could be sure that [O'Donnell] is a healthy man?"). Ten years later, the contemporary historian R. Hal Williams notes, resentment toward the Chinese had not cooled in the slightest:

> "It is difficult," said John F. Swift, writing to Republican presidential nominee Benjamin Harrison's headquarters, "for you who have not lived among the Chinese to realize in your mind the whole extent and force of the degradation and outlandish nastiness that is conveyed to our minds [b]y the term 'Chinaman.' On this Coast to compare a man to a Chinaman is more insulting than to compare him to a 'Nigger' by far.[14]

For Terry, driven as he was by a lifetime of racial and economic resentments and misrepresentations, the "Chinese curse" also afforded an opportunity to combine into one proposal both his sense of ethnic superiority and his antagonism toward the "cursed" corporations. On December 1, 1878, Terry offered from the floor the following punitive amendment: "[No] corporation now existing or hereafter formed under the laws of the state, after the adoption of the Constitution, shall employ, in any way, any Chinese or Mongolians. The Legislature shall pass such law as may be necessary to enforce this provision." The federal court's opinion, Terry reminded his listeners, prevented the states from abrogating international treaties, but it did not prevent the states from restricting an immigrant's ability to make a living; and without a promise of work, Chinese immigration would quickly dry up. "I do not propose to fight the federal government on this matter, I tried that once and [was wounded] and whipped, and [I] have had sense enough to know it after it was done" (laughter).[15] His amendment, ill-tempered and foolish as it was, passed by voice vote, and was quickly swallowed up in multiple pages of constitutional renewal, only to be declared unconstitutional by the federal courts within the year.

While all this was going on, however, Terry had not forgotten his valley constituents. Their primary concern was in gaining tax equity and controlling prices. In particular, they were demanding the control of railroad rates and a proportional shift of the tax burden from the shoulders of farmers and ranchers onto what they characterized as "the broad-backs of the gluttonous corporations." To fulfill his mandate to valley residents, and with growing support from the Workingman's delegates, Terry introduced a proposal that, he said, would increase "tax equity." The fairest way to increase tax revenue "is to tax all holdings having a shared indebtedness as property, [expressly], all commercial documents should be taxed as property, viz., [bonds, notes, mortgages, franchises, liens, etc]. The state provides statutory protection for the owners of these financial portfolios; [therefore] they should pay a 'protection tax' on the value of these secured investments." This was Terry's unrepentant response to "[the corporations'] argument that taxing indebtedness as property is unfair." Corporations, he warned:

> [a]ttempt to shift the tax burden to the modest holdings of working people, [while they] live very comfortably on [unencumbered] property, and if I had a few thousand of these conclusions of law, I could quit work and live very easily [on] $100,000 worth of bonds of the State of California. [This is] very tangible property [and] why should I not pay taxes [as well as] my neighbor, who pays upon his land and house. Why should I be allowed to invest $100,000 in bonds and sit down and rent a house or board at a hotel, and make no contribution [to] support the government, which protects me [and] my personal property, while my neighbor is compelled to pay taxes on everything he has?[16]

Once again, the judge was taking on the railroad corporations' legally protected claim that they were agents of the federal government and therefore held a constitutional exemption from state and local taxation. (Shortly after the completion of California's revised constitution, Field would introduce his historic *solvent debt taxing,* or "double taxation," opinions that declared that the Fourteenth Amendment's *due process* clause was *juris privati*, which is to say that the due process clause is there to protect personal property from the encroachment of a state government that, in the name of some theoretical notion of the public good, has falsely sought to tax a federal agency.) Terry, determined to defeat what he believed to be pro-business proposals, introduced into the discussion "the unfair legal advantage that monopolies held over the working class." Time and again he rose to present a stockpile of provisions designed to weaken the "holdings of the rich and the tax-free status of corporations." The original constitution, he declared at one point, never anticipated the rampant threat of exploitative monopolies and cartels that had arisen:

> [So] I propose the following amendments; 'Terry began,' [first], the state may not invest financially in any corporation; [second], the corporation must open its books to public audit; [third], stockholders must be liable for the debts incurred by their corporations and; [fourth], directors and trustees are to be jointly and severally liable to creditors and stockholders [for illegal transactions] such as embezzlement and misappropriation.[17]

Terry and his newly acquired "friends" from the Workingman's Party received overwhelming support for these proposals, and they were hastily inserted into the constitution. (Twenty years later, his third proposal concerning stockholders would find its way to the U.S. Supreme Court when California attempted to take a portion of Leyland Stanford's estate. At his death in 1893, Stanford's estate was estimated at $30 million and the state of California sought $15,237,000 as payment on the ex-governor's unpaid railroad bonds. Relying on Field's 1870 opinion—that the federal government is the overseer of railroads—the U.S. Attorneys General argued that the nation's Pacific Railroad Act provided railroad corporations with substantial amounts of subsidy bonds, but concomitantly did not hold the corporate shareholders responsible for debts accrued by failure of the corporation to pay at maturity. The Supreme Court would subsequently uphold the Attorneys General's argument. The Stanford estate thereby secured a handsome and permanent endowment for the fledgling Stanford University).[18]

The convention had slowed to a crawl during the railroad tax debates. It was a politically explosive issue because a majority of the delegates favored raising the taxes of the railroad monopolies while at the same time reducing their service rates by 20%. In opposition, seated as delegates, were the corporations with strong legal representation. Fearful that interminable squabbles and growing libelous recriminations between factions would deadlock the convention, a small block of influential moderates proposed a compromise. Establish a railroad commission, they argued, and charge it with the task of overseeing railroad access, rates, schedules, fees and taxes. S. M. Wilson, the railroad's great legal and forensic defender, argued vociferously against the proposal, contending that once a commission had the power to reduce railroad rates it would have the power to interfere with the federal government's operations across state boundaries—the railroads' obligations nationwide would be eviscerated. Terry offered a terse, albeit somewhat extraneous, response to the matter: "Well if the railroad companies, by putting down the rates, choose to commit Hari-Kari, for myself I have no objection to it."[19] Initially, Terry had opposed a railroad commission, arguing that it would be impossible to appoint commissioners who could be trusted "[for they would be] tempted beyond the endurance that they could withstand as mere mortals. [W]here could one find three men that could resist the [railroad's] corrupting influences?" he asked. "[The railroads would fire the Chinese laborers] and over time hire white workers who would support the commissioners that the railroads wanted to see elected."

The debate on the merits of a statewide commission, having lasted for better than three days, seemed to be moving toward a stalemate, when Terry decided that the proposed compromise was better than no change at all. He reversed himself and led a handful of holdouts to embrace the notion of a state commission just so long as the commission was to be granted the power to issue contempt orders "in the same manner [as the] Courts of Record do." With the judge and his holdouts, the convention moved the question to a vote and created the state's first railroad commission.[20] The railroad-supporting *Argonaut* newspaper expressed the sentiments of conservatives on December 7: "[Terry, Howard, Timms, Larken]—all democrats, thank God!—are developing themselves into agrarians and communists of a type quite as pronounced, more dangerous, and less respectable than that of the sand lot leaders whom they are anxiously endeavoring to supplant."[21] Terry's prediction about the vulnerability of the commission came about within the year—all three commissioners had succumbed to railroad's blandishments and dutifully voted as the companies dictated. It was a pattern that held true in California, one might say, until the election of Hiram Johnson's reformist administration in 1911. Johnson's commission actually had some success in harnessing railroad interests to public interest.

All in all, the convention's Committee on Corporations reviewed twenty-seven bills pertaining to corporations and presented a report containing twenty-three sections on state corporations, including eight that were explicitly directed at the railroads. The entire deliberations on corporations took over a month to settle.[22]

Through January and February, the argument-weary delegates faced multiple revisions, and amendments to those revisions. Inevitably this created a backlog of unresolved issues which led the impatient and caustic Terry to express his vexations publicly. One such verbal exchange held special interest because it illustrated how the pace of the convention was forging a growing rancor and ill will between the business representatives and the Terry-led anti-monopolists. On a particular day toward the end of February, Terry succeeded in raising the hackles of almost all the coastal business delegates when he took the convention floor and accused the San Francisco Stock Exchange of being nothing but a pack of thieves. Specifically, he announced, amid much commotion and loud protestations, that the business practice of selling stocks on margin was "an immoral practice." Selling stock on margin, he argued:

> composes the principal part of business in these stock boards [and] is the very worst species of gambling that can be indulged in, [for these speculators] do not buy the stock. [It is all] pretense—the seller has no stock [and] buyers don't want it. Speculators [should] be prohibited from buying and collecting profits on paper futures, no man shall sell stock unless he has got it to sell, [speculators should be] required to deliver the stock at the time of the sale.[23]

When he sat down, members of the business delegation erupted. "The Pacific Coast stock-exchange would move itself to Virginia City, if the [San Joaquin delegate] was to have his way on this matter," shot back a delegate. Terry's reply, of course, was hardly conciliatory. "I'm willing to see the whole business in hell—good riddance to bad rubbish [I'd] say." With this harsh reply, the day's work had ended. The convention adjourned. The next morning calmness prevailed; apparently, Terry had decided he had said enough. He did not bring the matter to the floor again.

The convention wound to an exhausted end on March 3, 1878, (Cynical onlookers and unhappy delegates insisted that the new constitution was far worse than the original.) Yet, when the revisions were completed, one hundred twenty of the delegates were sufficiently satisfied to return to their districts and urge constituents to ratify the results. In the end, only fifteen representatives opposed the constitution's passage. Those who resisted were mostly delegates from the financial community. They in turn were supported by three-quarters of the newspapers in the state, who, in their editorial columns, found the revisions to be "communistic." Carl Swisher writes that the limitation placed upon corporations generated most of the statewide press's hostility toward the new constitution.

> [T]his Communistic Constitution must be voted down by the people if investors are expected to return to California. We find the classes who favor the new Constitution are the criminal classes, all of the thieves, burglars, tramps, the men who won't work and expect to be supported in this idleness. [They] are men who cheer the [communists].[24]

When referring to the populists in the central valleys, the business community inevitably used the term "communist" and "valley agrarians" in the same breath. Less bombastic but every bit as antagonistic were the coastal entrepreneurs who supported the sentiments of the influential San Francisco Railroad lawyer Samuel Wilson, when he described the revised constitution as "[nothing but] absurd, unwise, injurious paternalism." Exchanging insults, the populists and the anti-monopolists, while supporting the convention's work, were no less vitriolic in their characterization of the coastal lawyers. "[Those who oppose the constitution] want a continuation of their freedom to conspire, rob, oppress, and grow rich off the toils of other men."[25] Terry and his band of supporters gave the new constitution unequivocal allegiance. [Not until it is approved], Terry said, "will California be free from the rule of corporations, rings, and monopolies, [then] the government for the people, of the people, and in the interest of the people [will have] a new deal and a square one." Terry may have been paraphrasing Lincoln, but of course he could not have been aware that he was also anticipating the rallying cry of the Roosevelts, Theodore and Franklin.[26]

The public approved the new constitution in the spring of 1880, and Terry, the newly born anti-monopoly-populist, once again had found a villain against whom he could rail—the politically well-entrenched privileged classes. In 1879, mining was still the second largest industry in the state; only agriculture was larger, so there remained a sizable population that Terry could rally, and, to whom a resuscitated Democratic Party could appeal. Terry's outspoken opposition to the monopolies on the floor of the convention captured the attention of the state-wide Democratic Committee, and several weeks later, they came to him and urged him to place his name in nomination for elector-at-large at the National Democratic Convention in July.

Warily he agreed. As a rule, recommendations from the state party received scant attention from rank-and-file party members, but, unfortunately for the judge, on this occasion many party regulars made a bitter exception. They had not forgotten nor forgiven him for the role he had played in the Vigilance Committee's humiliation, Broderick's untimely death, and his fighting efforts on the side of the confederacy. Every other name but Terry's was approved for the Democratic National Convention slate. The judge had always been leery of popularity contests, and again his misgivings had been confirmed. The rejection was painful, as it had been when he failed to be renominated as chief justice, and he was not hesitant to rage about it publicly. It was said by friends that rejection by the National Committee "chafed him to excess."

The Democratic National Convention gathered in Cincinnati in July of 1880, but while a brooding, disappointed Terry was not present in the Queen City, his old adversary Stephen Field was. His name was to be placed in nomination at the Cincinnati convention for president of the United States. Field's closest friends had known for some years that the justice had "coveted the presidency." In fact, as far back as 1868, powerful Democrats in California had been mentioning his name as their "favorite son" candidate. Eight years later at the nation's centennial convention of 1876, Field had garnered fifteen votes for president on the first ballot, but his reputation as pro-business jurist had made it impossible for him to attract enough of the rank and file Democrats to mount a serious campaign.

On the other hand, his prospects in 1880 seemed considerably brighter, and so he decided to make a serious run at the presidency with the help of his brothers, David, Cyrus and Henry and the help of their many influential friends. There was a large block of his own wealthy Eastern friends, moreover, who were actively pushing his candidacy, as well many high-placed financial friends from California's railroad corporations.

Many arguments have been offered as to why Field sought the presidency. One is that he wanted to leave the court because he was then too often representing an ineffectual minority opinion. Another was that his brothers David and Cyrus Field had pushed for it in order settle grudges with the 1876 Democratic candidate Samuel J. Tilden. But perhaps as good an explanation as any can be found in Field's insatiable desire for personal power and influence. By June of 1880, he had what was reputed to be the most competent campaign organization of all the candidates running and quite enough money from the nation's leading corporations to stage an aggressive campaign.

Field's organizers arrived in Cincinnati a week before convention delegates were to be there, and they did their best to win the delegates over individually as they arrived in town. Their plan was to inundate the competition with an account of Field's superior qualifications and win the nomination on the first or second ballot. Failing that, they were convinced, they would garner enough votes in the south and west to eventually wear down the opposition and thereby persuade the unpersuaded to throw their support to Field as the inevitable winner. Among his most ardent supporters was a group of wealthy upstate New Yorkers who caught the attention of the print-ravenous reporters when they steamed into town aboard a silver-paneled passenger train that had been funded entirely by Field's wealthy brother, Cyrus—the "silver train" caught everyone's attention. "The Man for the Times," blared street megaphones, while the banners read, "A candidate to protect the nation's commercial interests," a candidate to stem the flood-tide of "radical populism." Field would later write about his own party's campaign failures as brought on "[by] a lawlessness of confiscation [that] had been infecting the Democratic Party [for] over a quarter of a century."[27]

A week passed and this still scruffy river town was inundated with publicity stunts and pamphlets promoting the justice's candidacy. The *Atlanta Constitution* claimed that 12 million copies of Field's *Personal Reminiscences* had been circulated—an assertion that was as difficult to believe as it was to confirm. "[T]he Field movement burst upon [the scene]," wrote one New York journalist, "in all the glory of banners, band wagons and biographies [while] no other candidate has even his name displayed on a poster," "A verbal band of political touters, [all] brag, bluster, and adornments."[28] "Field's legions," said another reporter, offered the uncommitted delegates "beer and bonfires," while his pamphlets made clear to the uncommitted that he was a "constitutional constructionist," the only candidate in the race that had advanced the principles of "state autonomy, the value of hard over soft money, (gold and silver coins over paper greenbacks), and most importantly of all [never] had he ever voted Republican!"

By convention time, his supporters had thrown caution to the winds and were brashly predicting that he would win the nomination on either the first or second ballet. His strategists were convinced that he had solid support in every section of the country. In the south, their reasoning went, he would hold delegate majorities in Alabama, Arkansas, Missouri and Virginia. The conventional argument offered for this support was that the south had not forgotten Field's Missouri "test oath" opinions nor his unwavering defense of state's autonomy over federal intervention—two measures that southerners believed had played a major role in weakening the stranglehold that Northern carpetbaggers had held on the south. In the west, led by the former California Senator William Gwin, Field's supporters were convinced that the western states would support him by virtue of the pride that westerners had in their California son—he was the first *bona fide*, western legal candidate running for the office who had been capable enough to hold a college degree. His bandwagon banner reminded onlookers that in order to defeat the Republicans, "[Democrats must win] the Pacific States," and only Associate Justice Field, the banner read, had the fame and training to finally return the west to the Democratic Party. Insofar as the eastern part of the country was concerned, the campaign expected that wealthy conservatives would support Field because he, above all, candidates had consistently advocated the principle of "hard money" and had steadfastly defended business' notion of "commercial autonomy." Moreover, his handlers added, he was the only candidate, who would be able to draw disillusioned eastern Democrats back to the party. Had he not promised to "cleanse the Temple," of the "Philistines"? (Had he not stood for historical Jeffersonism against the growing tide of Jacksonian populism?)

And perhaps more significant than any news the Field organization received during the first days of the convention was news reporting that Samuel Jones Tilden had withdrawn his name as a presidential candidate. Four years earlier, the Democratic Party's "Grand Old War-horse" had run as the Party's presidential candidate, but had lost in a bitterly contested electoral fight to Republican Rutherford B. Hayes. Tilden had won a paper-thin voting majority in the election. But, as in all close votes, critics contended that voting day had been fraught with ballot irregularities. To sort out the contesting complaints from the various states, the Congress agreed to appoint an electoral commission, (Most citizens believed it would be possible to appoint a genuinely impartial commission—it was, after all, a Republican Congress and therefore it would be a Republican president.) True enough, the much-ballyhooed search for an impartial commission took many months and had many twists and turns but it offered no surprises. When the fifteen-man commission's final vote was taken, the eight Republicans voted for Hayes and the seven Democrats voted for Tilden. The commission's "non-partisan" election of the 19th president of the United States had been settled as everyone had predicted—in the usual partisan fashion. As a consequence of this defeat in 1876, many Democrats believed Tilden deserved another chance. In fact, there was sentiment to nominate him in 1880, in spite of the trepidation many felt concerning the diminution of his intellectual powers. Tilden's general health was tremulous at best.

When nominating day finally arrived, and without Tilden on the ballot, Field's forces could only express shock when it became apparent how badly his political experts had overestimated Field's chances. Only the "old" south came close to meeting expectations. Sixty percent of the votes Field received on the first ballot came from southern states—and by the second ballot most of them had deserted him. What was even worse, eastern and western support was abysmal—almost nonexistent. Moreover, critics later contended that in the east, Field's brothers clearly had been more liabilities than assets. Many rank-and-file Democrats mistrusted his brother Cyrus, whom they believed had undermined Tilden's chances in 1876 when a fight concerning a business transaction between them became public knowledge. What is more, conservative leaders outside New York City resented Field's brother Dudley's continued loyalty to the "Tammany Hall criminals." One Eastern antagonist summed it up: "If one brother did not kill [the justice] the others would. [H]e has worse relatives than Grant!"[29] The political machinations in the west, however, were even more disastrous and did more to sink the justice's chances of winning the nomination than anything that was happening elsewhere in the country. Six of the twelve California delegates openly worked against his nomination. These delegates were composed of central valley friends of David Terry's, prodigal "Kearneyite," and four political allies of the anti-monopolist Stephen Mallory White, District Attorney of Los Angeles. Such anti-corporation, anti-monopolist zealotry gradually overwhelmed the state's timorous pro-Field delegates once the convention was under way. California's anti-corporation delegates made it clear on the convention floor that they would never support a candidate whose stand on taxation, railroads, corporations and Chinese immigration contradicted the state's burgeoning populist majority. Field could never become California's "favorite son" as long as Terry, White and their anti-monopolist ideologues were controlling the Democratic Party in California. As *The New York Times* put it, "Democrats [in the state of California] gnash their teeth at the mere mention of the name Field."

Insofar as the convention's details were concerned, strategic miscalculations, and blunders began for Field from the moment the convention was officially called to order. To begin, it was a miserable day for an indoor meeting in Cincinnati's cramped 100-by-300-feet convention hall. It was hot, humid and smoky, and there was the smell of rotting fruits and vegetables that were stacked up on the shipping docks along the banks of Ohio River "river bottom weather," one reporter wrote—and the delegates' mood matched the stifling weather. Another journalist grumbled, "Beer is the only drink in Cincinnati—there is no drinkable water in this [whole] damn place." On the first day of the convention, Field's managers decided that J.E. McElrath of Oakland would place their candidate's name before the convention. Unfortunately for Field, when delegate McElrath arose to nominate Field he was decidedly not the man for the moment or the weather. Newspapers reported that he was humorless and long-winded, and showed himself to be completely out of touch with California's true political sentiments. He predicted that Justice Field "if nominated [would] sweep California like the winds that blow through her golden gates." Paul Kens writes that Field's California opponents "cackled at McElath's suggestion that Field was a protector of the miner and the homesteader, a founder of the West and savior of Virginia" (Field had supported Virginia's law to keep African-Americans from sitting on state juries.)[30] But if McElrath was a failure, Field's seconder, Coloradan W. Brown, was even more unpalatable to the audience's tastes. When it came to scoffing at the Field campaign, it was Brown who became the reporters' favorite target. He was an utter parody of political gesticulations and pious admonishments, and quickly tried the patience of a restive, sweating audience. Speaking too softly at the outset, he bought on the chanting clamor "louder, louder," which immediately turned to catcalls, hisses, and shouts of "time, time, cut him off" when he finally did raise his voice loud enough for the crowd to hear what he was saying—notwithstanding the clamorous mood, he persisted.

"Lamentably," predicted *The San Francisco Chronicle* after the first day, "Judge Field may be considered out of the race!" The *Chronicle* had it right. After the first ballot, Field faced humiliation—out of 738 votes cast he received 65. Astoundingly, his backers had been predicting from 150 to 200 votes on the first ballot, and on the second ballot victory! But after several additional ballots, he had gained only one-half vote—and by the end of the balloting, only five Californians and thirty-nine southerners were supporting him. Even the five Californians' support had been tainted by stories in *The New York Herald Tribune* stating that delegates had remained loyal only because of promises of patronage—including a place in San Francisco's poshest businessman's club, the Pacific Club on Nob Hill.[31] On June 28 the *New York Times* summarized Field's entire presidential effort dismissively:

> The complete history of the [justice's] Cincinnati campaign would be very amusing. The attempts to touch the hearts of the delegates by means of bandwagons and banners and long biographies have been described, and the drunk-

enness of the delegate from Colorado who seconded his nomination was an incident that will not be easily forgotten. Not much has been said about the lowest manner in which Field's managers scattered their money, and the ignorance of political methods that led them to offer this money to persons who would not take it. Very large sums that had not been earned by the judge on the Supreme Bench were paid for rooms and music and occasions of all sorts, and their lieutenants seemed to have their hands full of bank bills. A great deal of money was spent for wine and costly suppers, and attempts were made to influence local newspapers through their reporters. It is the general impression that there is a large hole in the income of the Field family for 1880."[32]

Having lost the presidency to Republican military leaders for far too many years, the Democrats were determined to nominate their own war hero. They nominated General Winfield Scott Hancock, a northerner and a wounded war hero who had fought at Gettysburg. On Hancock's recommendation, his running mate became W.H. English of Indiana. Hancock and English were nominated by acclamation.

In California, Terry was pleased to learn that Field had been soundly defeated and he enthusiastically endorsed Hancock's nomination. He assured his wife, Cornelia, that Hancock was certain to carry California by a large majority.[33] But the fall election did not bring the change hoped for and Hancock proved himself to be a better military campaigner than a politician. And the state's leading defender of Field, *The San Francisco Chronicle,* was less than enthusiastic when it portrayed Hancock as "any port in the storm."[34] Republican opponents belittled Hancock's war record. "He chased Indians all over the southwest, it had cost the country 9 million dollars, [and all he had to show for the effort] was two dead Indians—an old man and a demented Indian girl."[35]

With Hancock's loss of the general election it was clear that the Democrats had mistakenly forgotten the southern loyalists, who were slowly returning to southern political power, but could never bring themselves to support a Union general. A man who had repulsed the confederate charge at Cemetery Ridge and played such a significant part in the death of General Lewis Armistead at that vital point when Pickett's division had momentarily breached the Union line. Sadly for Democrats the nation's preference for Republican warriors continued into its twenty-first year with the election of James A. Garfield and Chester A. Arthur.

In retrospect, the proceedings in May of 1880 at the State Democratic Convention in Oakland, just a month before the national convention in Cincinnati, should have warned the Field loyalists that the chances at the national convention would be daunting at best. But Field's organizational optimism was engendered, in part, by former Senator William Gwin's fulsome assessment of Field's support in California. Gwin's certitude seemed to nullify whatever public expression of doubt his national committee might have had. At the Oakland convention, on opening day, twenty-five delegates had come declaring allegiance to Field, but after three days of raucous calumny, only two delegates remained loyal enough to support him at the national convention. In addition, given that so many members of the Workingman's Party had returned to the Democratic Party, there were very few Democratic ideologues left in California who would favor Field's candidacy. What remained of the Democratic Party after the Civil War, at both state and national levels, was rapidly being taken over by the "long-haired, slouch-hatted [s]outherners" who "opposed capitalism's oppressive drift toward empire."[36] Conservative Democrats throughout the country were quietly changing party affiliation. They were becoming Republicans, and in California, by 1879, 50 percent of the state was voting for Republicans while only 30 percent were supporting traditional Democrats.

Several days after the Republican November landslide, Field, in a moment of pique, discussed the convention with reporters. He blamed the disloyalty of the California Democrats for his defeat. In the last analysis, he said, defeat at the hands of his Democratic brethren had been a disillusioning experience, and consequently, he declared, "[I] will never go into politics again!"

Months later, after feelings had cooled somewhat, he declared that he meant what he had said earlier about never running for the presidency again. Yet with some dissimilitude, he *might* be interested, "[except] for the prejudices in certain quarters in California." When pressed for clarification, he confessed that he had never heard of "an instance in the history of the country where the nomination of a national convention actually tendered has been refused, and I have no idea that I should prove the exception." Disinterested listeners would have paid no heed to this infinitesimal shift in his position, but his enemies were well aware of what he had said and sensed that this was, by no means, the end of his "presidential obsession." Field's declaration that he would never again pursue the office, but would not be averse to the "honor of the office," if drafted, was to those who knew him well running true to form. He had always insisted that he never sought elected office on his own, but had only consented to run at the public's bidding. But Terry and the anti-monopolists, accustomed to his capricious approach, were determined to prevent any reprise. At the state's mid-term convention in San Jose in 1882, they certified their determination. Terry, as chairman of the convention's Platform Committee, steered a patently anti-Fieldian platform through the convention—it was anti-railroad, anti-corporation and anti-Chinese.

These doctrinal influences reached their nadir at the state Democratic convention in June of 1884 in Terry's hometown of Stockton. The delegates at the Stockton convention wanted their sentiments against Field to be made unmistakably clear at the national convention that was to be held in Chicago in

July. Judge Terry was not in attendance at the Stockton convention, in part—because he had been rejected as a delegate during the 1880 presidential year, in part because he felt betrayed by California's Democratic governor George Stoneman, whom he had helped get elected in 1882; in part because he had become associate council in a divorce case that was requiring more and more of his time; and in part because he was content to exercise influence "just down the street," so to speak, from the convention hall. The convention held in Stockton's National Hall was just a buggy ride away from Terry's home and, moreover, his political allies who were in total control of the proceedings. It would be a long time, Terry reasoned, before Field's presidential aspirations would be resurrected in California. Evidence that he had assessed the situation correctly was confirmed on June 10, when the delegates rammed through the convention a senseless declaration explicitly opposing Field's nomination at the national convention. Because "we view with alarm," the last 'whereas' in the document read:

> the power of the railroad monopoly as manifested in its pernicious and corrupting interference in politics and in its control of officials elected by the people, [w]e resolve, therefore, that the Democracy of California unanimously repudiates the presidential aspirations of Stephen J. Field, [and hereby pledge] ourselves to vote for no man as a delegate to the National Convention of July 8, 1884, who will not before this convention pledge himself to us his earnest endeavors to defeat [Justice Field's] aspirations.[37]

Before the convention adjourned, every California elector had pledged his "earnest endeavor" to defeat the justice's aspirations. The Stockton Convention closed with a public resolution renouncing Field in the platform by a remorseless 453 to 19 vote. The resolution was made personal by an accompanying vow to reject all "free-passes" on railroads traveling from California to Washington, D.C.

Rejection of Justice Field by state's Democratic leadership was now complete. He had been orphaned by the anti-monopolists and the populists and, as it turned out this division between conservative and populist Democrats would weaken the Party in California for over a generation.

Smarting from the state's third repudiation, Field again blamed his defeat on the anti-monopolists even though, with or without their public censure, he had no chance of wresting the nomination from Grover Cleveland at the national democratic convention in Chicago in 1884. He later declared that "there is a radical element in California politics [that has] no regard for property but I have never swerved from my duty not to pander to that element."[38] A year later, when he wrote to a Democratic supporter, it was still clear that he continued to be angry:

> You and other friends may rest assured that no dainty rule of propriety laid down for my conduct by those who seek harm to our state will ever deter me from such effort as I may be able to make to thwart their mischievous purposes. [I] have yet to learn that any office is so exalted that its incumbents may be deprived of the privileges or released from the duties of citizenship. [I am] against the selection of any man whose appointment would seem to commit the Administration to the approval of the communistic rulings of the Stockton Convention mob.[39]

By now, however, Field was resigned to the fact that he would never live long enough to see himself nominated as California's favorite son at a Democratic Party's national convention. He would never again venture into national politics. In fact, his election as a maverick Democrat to the California State Assembly in 1851 proved to be his only successful run for elected political office. His very first try at public office was to be his last. As to be expected, Terry had a ready answer to Field's dismissive observations:

> The judge has no affiliation with the Democratic Party in this State. He [is] a sycophantic tool of Stanford and a paid satellite of the railroad monopoly. The Stockton convention [plainly and simply] rebuked the unhealthy political ambitions of the distinguished Jurist. [T]he entire [convention] was unanimously opposed to Field first, last, and all the time.[40]

Later when Terry was asked to assess why Field was the distinguished jurist that he surely was, Terry answered, not altogether speciously, "Field is an intellectual wizard. [H]e can give the most plausible reasons for a wrong decision of any person I ever knew. He was never known to decide a case against a corporation. He has always been a corporation lawyer and a corporation judge, and as such no man can be honest."[41] Terry's public opposition to Field brought from the pro-business *San Francisco Post* an overly wrought editorial declaring that the efforts of the anti-monopolists had left only five hundred Democrats supporting Field. All the rest had become Republicans, but, more significantly, the editor continued, "if Terry and the southerners" have their way, "northerners and foreigners" had better pack up and move away, for they will never again find political success in California." Earlier Terry had written to Cornelia, "I had no idea that I was as powerful as the *Post* says that I am, calling me the 'Boss' of the Democratic Party."[42] As Terry indicates, he was not the "boss" of the Democratic Party. (More aptly the epithet fits Steven Mallory White, the "little giant of California.") Nevertheless, there was no doubt that by the middle of the eighth decade Terry exuded an intimidating presence that did not go unnoticed by political adversaries.

An encounter with the prolific giant of California history during that era, Hubert Howe Bancroft, was the perfect example of Terry's foreboding public presence. In one of Bancroft's accounts of the vigilante movement, Terry had read a passage describing his role in the episode that he believed had been inaccurately portrayed. Some time passed, and then without warning Terry appeared in the doorway of Bancroft's office demanding that the historian correct the record. "You have," Terry grumbled, "the choice of a bullet or a revision." For one brief moment, Bancroft stared into the judge's expressionless eyes; and then, with no further thought, he revised the offending passage, apparently to the judge's satisfaction.[43]

However, it is important not to forget that Judge Field, in his own fashion, was a man every bit as likely to fulminate over an insult as was Terry. Kens describes Field's response to an article in *The New York Herald* after his defeat for the presidential nomination in 1880. The article's writer alleged that Field had bribed some of the delegates at the convention. The day Field read the article he wrote his brother Cyrus requesting that Cyrus call the *Herald* editor to identify the writer: "[It is my] impression [t]hat the writer is a miserable scalawag in California and, if I am correct, it would be a very easy thing for me to have his political head decapitated or his political nose sufficiently pulled to make him hereafter politically silent." Not hearing from Cyrus, three days later he wrote his brother again demanding "personal satisfaction" and warning that he should not be "trifled with." "I say to you that if they do not give me the name of the man who wrote the article it will be the saddest day for Mr. Bennett [*Herald* editor] that ever has been in his life, and those very men who refuse will before the month goes around, regret it bitterly."[44]

NOTES

1. A. Russell Buchanan. *David S. Terry of California: Dueling Judge* (San Francisco: The Huntington Library Press, 1955) 162–163.
2. For a detailed account of these railroad battles see Carl Brent Swisher. *Motivation and Political Techniques in the California Constitution 1878–1879. (*Pomona, Ca., 1930). See also G. H. Tinkham. *History of Stockton.* (San Francisco W. M. Horton & Co., 1880).
3. Stockton vs. Visalia Railroad Co., 51 Cal. 329.
4. December 8, 1871. Cited in A. Russell Buchanan, *Dueling Judge,* 164.
5. A. E. Wagstaff, *The Life of the Ex-Chief Justice of the Supreme Court of California: David S. Terry* (San Francisco: Continental Publication Co., 1892). 255. Also, A. Russell Buchanan. *Dueling Judge.* 184.

6. Harry N. Scheiber. "Race, Radicalism and Reform," *Hastings Constitutional Law Quarterly*. v. 17, 1989. 13.

7. J .C. Stedman and R.A. Leonard. (*The Workingmen's Party* (San Francisco: Bacon and Company 1878). 83, 87. Also C.B. Swisher, *Motivation,* 114, and R. Hal Williams *The Democratic Party and California Politics:* 1880 to 1896. (Stanford 1973). 16–17.

8. There is some dispute about the number of Chinese in California in the last quarter of the century. For a somewhat different assessment see A. Hal Williams, *Democratic Party*.4–5.

9. Winfield J. Davis. *The History of Political Conventions in California 1849–1892*. Sacramento (1903), 365, See also, *The Workingmen's Movement,* Society of the California Pioneers.

10. J. C. Stedman and R. A. Leonard. *Workingmen's Party*. 44. Winfield J. Davis. *Political Conventions in California*. 369–371.

11. —— *Workingman's Party*. 82.

12. Quoted in *The Mail,* August 18, 1889. Cited in A. Russell Buchanan. *Dueling Judge*.187.

13. E. B. Willis and R.K. Stockton, official stenographers, *Debates and Proceedings of the Constitutional Convention of the State of California.* 1880.

14. R. Hal. Williams. *Democratic Party,* 122.

15. E. B. Willis, *Debates*. 699.

16. —— *Debates,* 807, 808, 809, 867, 873. Also, C.B. Swisher, *Motivation*. 58.

17. —— *Debates,* 517, 867.

18. *United States v. Stanford,* 161 U.S. 412, 1896.

19. E. B. Willis, *Debates,* 396, 403, 443, 516. Hari Kari. The invective of the Convention was transformed into mayhem in the streets. See: Richard Rayner. *The Associates*, (New York: Atlas & Co., 2008) 144–155.

20. —— *Debates,* 443,605, 609, 611. RR Commission.

21. *The Argonaut,* December 1, 1879.

22. Paul Kens. *Justice Stephen Field: Shaping Liberty from Gold Rush to Glided Age* (Lawrence KN.: The University of Kansas 1997). 217.

23. E. B. Willis. *Debates*, 807, 808.

24. —— *Debates,* 471–475. C. B. Swisher, 399.

25. —— *Debates,* 404. See. Gordon Morris Bakken. "California Constitutionalism: Politics, the Press and the Death of Fundamental Law." *Pacific Historian*, 30 (1986).

26. *Daily Evening Herald,* April 10, 1880. Also, cited in A. Russell Buchanan *Dueling Judge,* 188.

27. R. Hal Williams, *Democratic Party*, 54–55.

28. *The New York Times,* June 2, 1880.

29. *The Republic,* April 1880. Also, cited in C.B. Swisher.*Craftsman*. 287.

30. *San Francisco Evening Bulletin*, June 24 1880. See Paul Kens. *Justice Stephen J. Field.* 231.

31. Paul Kens. *Field,* 227.

32. *New York Times,* May 20 1880. On June 25 *The New York Times* reported that the New York delegation failed to give Field a single vote. On June 22, the *New York Herald Tribune,* declared that it was "mortified and chagrined by [Field's] beggarly [vote count]."

33. Terry letters June 24, 27, 1880, Huntington Collection (San Marino CA).

34. *San Francisco Chronicle,* June 25, 1880.

35. *New York Herald Tribune*, June 22, 1880.

36. *New York Times* June 25, 1880.

37. Winfield J. Davis, *political Conventions,* 456–60. Also, Edith Dobie, *The Political Career of Stephen Mallory White,* 1927, 48.

38. *San Francisco Daily Alta,* June 18, 1884.

39. Edith Dobie. *The Political Career of Stephan Mallory White* (Stanford CA.: Stanford University Press, 1927). 58.

40. A.E. Wagstaff. *Ex-Chief Justice.* 396–398.

41. David S.Terry, *Character and Career of Stephen J. Field,* 1889, 2.

42. Terry letter July 18, 1880. Huntington Collection. See also Dobie, *Political Career of Stephen Mallory.* 48.

43. James A.B. Scherer. *Lion of the Vigilantes (New York: Bobbs-Merrill Co).*12, 170.

44. August 23, 1880. Cited in Paul Kens, *Justice Stephen J. Field,* 233–4.

Senator David C. Broderick, California's martyred abolitionist, c. 1855–1865.

Dueling Ground of the Broderick/Terry Tragedy, 1859.

Senator William M. Gwin. Followed by John C. Fremont as California's second senator.

Dennis Kearney: Irish Union Organizer.

Sarah Althea Hill. Mrs. Sarah Sharon, c. 1880–1887.

Senator William Sharon, 1879.

Chapter Nine

Jus et Fraus Numquam Cohabitant (Law and Fraud Never Cohabit)

The vanishing point in the Terry/Field portrait falls squarely on a small-framed Missouri-bred woman named Sarah Althea Hill. "Allie," to her friends, was an entrancing mixture of 19th-century southern decorum and down-country coarseness. When she makes her appearance in A. Wagstaff's classic biography on Terry, the writer's Victorian propensities tumble onto the page: "Dramatic incidents are usually embellished by a woman, and no woman is capable of creating incidents of moment, involving the attention of the public, unless possessed of some extraordinary abilities or peculiar characteristic not in keeping with the usual order of her sex—[Sarah Althea Hill was just such a woman].[1]

Allie Hill was born in Cape Girardeau, Missouri, in 1848. Her father, Samuel Hill, was a prominent attorney and for a time an influential member in the state Legislature. Her mother, Julia Hill, was a socialite and a gifted musician. One of Sarah's uncles had been governor of Missouri, another a senator; and even the family's governess was the sister of a prominent Missouri congressman. By the time Sarah was seven and her brother Morgan five both parents were dead.

This left the two young children under the care of their maternal grandfather, Hiram Sloan. Grandfather Sloan raised the "chicks," said friends and neighbors, "under a very slack reign." So slack, in fact, that by the time Allie had passed through her teens she had acquired an unflattering reputation as an obsessive schemer who generally got her way by flirting, fickleness, or a quick temper. Most young women who knew very much about her found every reason to avoid her, even as young men seemed helplessly entranced in her presence. "Her conquests were numerous, [she] was fast, but her name was never tarnished with scandal. In love affairs [she] was tyrannical and her lovers had to suffer her iron rule and eccentric whims." But even worse, she was inordinately mercenary, "a spendthrift who worshiped money, and gave her attention to those who possessed it." When Grandfather Sloan died Sarah was 23, and the family decided it was time for Uncle William to move Sarah and Morgan to San Francisco where they might live under the sterner and more circumspect hand of Grandmother and Grand Aunt Sloan. It was soon apparent that it was altogether too late in the day to tighten the reins on Allie, and after two years of bickering and petty recriminations with her Grandma and Grand Auntie she gathered up what remained of her evaporating $20,000 inheritance and set out to live in San Francisco on her own.

Allie moved first into the Grand Hotel on New Montgomery Street in the heart of the city. But with her customary profligacy, she exhausted her inheritance by the end of the year. Out of money for the first time in her life, she set two goals (goals requiring her to plan and to wait). She would invest, she decided, in stock market futures, and she would look for a wealthy man to marry. No one doubted that both options were well within in her grasp; she was intelligent and beautiful. Time would prove, however, that Allie's success in both romance and finance would suffer serious limitations; for by the time she was 30 years old she had gone through several agonizing love affairs, including a well-publicized relationship with socialite lawyer Reuben Lloyd. Lloyd had been the man with "prospects." He was the man that both she and Grandma Sloan had been searching for, but lamentably, he also had a watchful mother who detested the sight of her. After the luster of the relationship had faded, Mother Lloyd was to get her way when her son Reuben dropped any plans he might have had to marry the "financially irresponsible" Allie. Broken-hearted, and some rivals said, pregnant with Lloyd's child, Allie turned for comfort to an elderly "octoroon," Mary Ellen Pleasant. "Mammy" Pleasant, as she was known to San Franciscans, knew the Hill family from earlier days in Missouri. She had been head-of-household to a politically influential Missouri family during Allie's childhood, and after the Civil War she moved to San Francisco and prospered as head of household in the home of an eccentric millionaire banker Thomas Bell. When Bell died, she was willed money enough to purchase two boarding houses in the tenderloin, dwellings that became a welcomed haven for the penniless, especially for ex-slaves and poor immigrants. Allie needed and wanted the old woman's help, but she was unprepared to live in a boarding house full of the indigent. Mammy Pleasant agreed to pay her living expenses at the nearby Belmont Hotel and, as Allie promised, "just for a very short time."

Allie always seemed to be persuasive. That is, she was generally able to get people to do what she wanted them to do. The *Chronicle's* jaunty description of "Miss Hill" had it just about right: "Miss Sarah Hill is colorful, headstrong, ambitious, intelligent, vivacious and uncommonly pretty. She is fast but untarnished, with a theatrical mannerism that knows no inhibitions."[2] This lack of inhibitions made it easy for her to borrow money from friends or even mere acquaintances in a determined effort to maintain her luxuriant style of life. However, it had been ten years since arriving in San Francisco and her life seemed to be going in a circle; her hopes were fading and her ambitions unmet. But then in the spring of 1880, at a friend's birthday party, she met an eccentric multimillionaire senator from Nevada, William Sharon, and her life would never be quite the same.

Senator Sharon, a well-known albeit mostly unpopular business figure in San Francisco, had gained a reputation as a shrewd, tightfisted, financially ruthless entrepreneur who, on more than one occasion, had been accused of ignoble business dealings. People insisted on saying that he had become wealthy on the misfortunes of bankrupted silver miners who were heedlessly throwing their savings and effort into Nevada's Comstock Lode (the center of one of the largest silver deposits in the country).

In their entertaining book, *Bonanza Inn*, Oscar Lewis and Carroll Hall describe Senator Sharon as "pale, chilly, and old-maidish," a person who out-of-work "wildcatters" made it a habit to refer to as "the runt."[3] With an endless supply of Nevada money flowing into his pockets from the mines and lucrative real estate investments in San Francisco, Sharon had been living luxuriously in San Francisco for more than ten years, yet all the while continuing to serve as Senator from Nevada. Living in San Francisco had provided other advantages too. He was able to indulge in a mildly profligate lifestyle even as he was investing in some of the most lucrative properties in the city. In short order he had become a major shareholder in such conspicuous holdings as the Bank of California, the (new) Palace Hotel (called by Oscar Lewis "The Bonanza Inn") the Opera House, and the (old) Grand Hotel. On the street, there was speculation about his about his wealth. Some said he was worth $15 million, others said he was worth $30 million or even more—no one was really sure just how wealthy he was, but everyone agreed that he was a very rich man. Moreover, he was just the sort of man Allie was looking for—a very rich widower.

But in spite of his reputation as a shrewd, rapacious businessman, Sharon was able to maintain financial relationships with the political and business establishment primarily because he could be depended upon to deliver on his financial promises. His enduring friendships, however, were with his three adult children. The eldest, Florence Emily, in one of the most publicized events on the city's 1881 social calendar, married English Lord Fermor-Hesketh—the Sharon family, obviously, was not averse to reaching out to English nobility—something that was sure to enrich their social standing. Sharon's middle child,

Clara Adelaide, was married to Francis G. Newlands. Newlands was a successful San Francisco political lawyer who received praise at the state Democratic Convention of 1884 when, before a packed house of hostile conventioneers, he delivered a combative speech condemning the party's disgraceful attack on Justice Field. When daughter Clara died in 1883 Sharon was gravely wounded in spirit, so much so that, within a little more than a year, he had taken to his bed—dying in 1885. Sharon's youngest child, Frederick Sharon, was given the responsibility of holding the family's reputation and fortune together thereafter.

San Francisco has always prided itself for being the home of colorful, idiosyncratic citizens, so it was not unusual that it found Sharon's behavior as "the millionaire troubadour" in no way out of place, despite the *Morning Call's* insistence on calling him "jackanapes." In any case, he had earned a reputation as a skillful all-night card player, with an abiding passion for beautiful young women who were willing to listen to his recitations (always from classical Greek and English verse). Moreover, he was eager to sing and recite classic ballads and verse publicly, with or without invitation.

Carl Brent Swisher wrote of him, "[Sharon's] wealth, like that of other men in California at the time, made him the object of bitter envy and hatred on the part of persons who had been less fortunate in the great gamble of life in the pioneer West. He gained no popularity with these people merely by the fact that he was reputed to have quite a 'way with the ladies'!"[4] Journalists, however, were quick to point out that it was his money, not his recitations, that brought young women to his side.

Several weeks after Sarah Hill's chance encounter with Sharon at the birthday party—plus occasional waves and nods to one another as they passed on city streets—Allie appeared at Sharon's upstairs office at the Bank of California to talk, presumably, she said, about her financial investments. From reports the conversation began superficially enough. "Ah," said he, "I hear you are quite the stock sharp." "I must be cautious," she demurred, "for I have little money to spare." However, after a few more minutes of polite conversation, she reported, Sharon proposed a different sort of investment—would she be willing to become his "love companion" for $250 a month?

From this point forward, there were two versions of what happened next. According to the senator, she was interested, but only if he would raise the ante—she was willing to be his companion, but not for less than $1,000 a month. He would not go that high, he said, but he did double the offer and she wasted no time accepting it. As to be expected, Hill's version of the conversation differed. "That is not what happened, not at all," she reported. "I was completely surprised and offended by his proposal and I made no agreement, rather I whirled about and headed for the doorway, only to be blocked from leaving. Oh! she said, "said he, sadly, you have misunderstood me, I was only teasing." "I have inquired about you and know you to be a respectable woman from a good family." "Well then," she announced (apparently quickly regaining her composure and sense of deportment), "you may call upon me." Days later, after telling her confidante, Mammy Pleasant, about the encounter, Hill accepted an invitation to dine with the senator in his suite at the Palace Hotel. Dinner over, Sharon entertained her with his celebrated recitations, and she did her part to entertain him by playing the piano and singing some well-known southern ballads. When it grew late, near midnight, he invited her to stay in a spare bedroom, so as, she said, he said, not to venture out into the dark and perilous streets. She thought his suggestion wise and accepted the offer, quickly withdrawing to the privacy and circumspection of a separate bedroom.

Once again the stories diverge. As Sharon remembers it. "[M]oments later after retiring to my spare bedroom, she arose and joined me in my bed, without comment or explanation." "I believed this to mean," said Sharon, "that in her own, discreet fashion, she had decided to accept my generous offer of money." "Never," Hill countered. "I was unwilling to be anyone's mistress. Only the man I marry shall ever be my lover." Naturally her version of how the evening had transpired was in marked contrast to the senator's: "[T]he Senator invited me to share his bed, but I was insulted and gathered up my wrap and hat and immediately returned to my rooms at the Belmont Hotel, but when I arrived at my hotel door he was waiting. He pleaded that I accept his apology. I was moved by his apparent sincerity and invited him in, but only after he had agreed that there would be no more talk of forbidden love." He promised there would be none and in its place, she recounted, he offered her more poetry—including Lord Byron's *Maid of Athens,* which he recited in a loud and ostentatious fashion: "Maid of Athens, ere we part—give, oh give me back my heart! Or, since that has left my breast, keep it now and take the rest." Sometime later he left, she said, apparently having left his heart with her.

Yet whatever an honest account of that evening might have been, less than a month later, inquisitive hotel patrons shared the gossip that Allie Hill had moved from the Belmont to the Grand Hotel, adjacent to the senator's suite in the Palace, and that each night she could be seen as a whisper of white chantilly scampering across the street-bridge that connected the Grand and the Palace hotels. Eventually their liaison became public knowledge, and the newspapers, in true Venetian fashion, dubbed the access route spanning New Montgomery Street "the bridge of sighs," and the woman who nightly traversed it the "Rose of Sharon." To observers who might wonder why a woman would move to a hotel adjacent to the hotel in which the senator lived while continuing to insist that she would never be his mistress, the senator had an ungallant answer: "for the money." "Never," countered Hill, "only for love and for love we were married" and "I have the document that proves it." "It's a forgery," a stunned Sharon replied.

The gossip, however, continued. If Hill were married, why didn't anyone else know about it? "Because," she responded, "the senator wanted it kept a secret." "Sadly, he had promised himself to another woman—Gertie Deitz." Rumor was that Sharon had packed Deitz off to Philadelphia when she found herself pregnant with his child. "Knowledge of these events," Hill said, he had explained, "would hurt his chances of winning a second term to the U.S. Senate." "I agreed to keep our marriage a secret until after the Nevada election." Sharon, of course, denied that there was a marriage contract. "We are lovers, true enough, but that was all, and once having grown tired of the arrangement I was determined to end it, [and to prove how determined I was], I offered her $5,000 to leave my bed, but she demanded $10,000, eventually, we settled on $7,500."

Lamentably she took the cash settlement but then refused to leave the rooms at the Grand Hotel even as expenses at the Grand were being charged to the account. Sharon said. "Then I pressed her to sign a 'document to vacate,' [for] I did not trust her," yet, "while I was out of town she returned to my rooms in the Palace and bribed her way past my house boy and destroyed the document that we both had signed." For too many months, the senator concluded, he had put up with this unsatisfactory arrangement, but he was loath to remove her from the Grand for fear that it would make their all-too-public fight an even more unsavory spectacle. Once her expenses became too much for him to bear, putting his misgivings aside, he ordered the carpets and the service cord removed from her rooms. But still she would not budge, so finally he was forced to remove the hallway door to the apartment. An uneasy and sleepless night without the door followed, Hill later admitted, "and I was persuaded that I had no choice but to leave." But no sooner had she moved back to the Belmont than the senator was again overtaken by his erotic impulse and pleaded with her to return—this time he was willing for her to share his rooms at the Palace and let the public be damned.

She did not hesitate. An additional two years of this hectic relationship followed—sometimes hot, sometimes cold—but always open to public scrutiny. By the summer of 1883, however, Sharon's carnal desire for Sarah Althea Hill had run its course—there were no more reconciliations, and the very public squabbles were over, despite the entertainment it had provided San Franciscans over their breakfast menus and newspapers.

Almost a year went by, and on September 8th of 1884, citizen interest revived when Hill filed a warrant in Superior Court for the arrest of "Senator

William Sharon of Nevada for desertion and adultery." The senator, of course, denied both charges and hired some of San Francisco's finest lawyers to defend him. Outsiders recognized that it would have been wise to settle the matter with a reasonable compromise, but neither party was any longer capable of being reasonable—they had been too attached to one another in one fashion or another for too long. Five months later, the former paramours faced each other in a courtroom in the east wing of San Francisco's City Hall. Over the next two years, a court battle would ensue that attracted the attention of the entire city, the state, and eventually the nation. Apparently the public could not seem to get enough of the trial's bathos. *The San Francisco Chronicle* wallboard at Bush and Kearney Streets was five deep with readers getting their daily dose of the trial—it seemed that there was hardly a nuance of prattle that newspapers were likely to overlook.

Preliminaries to the trial opened on Monday morning, March 10, 1884, and a reporter from the *Chronicle* captured the flavor of the time and event with a turgid description of the central players. His reporting style brought to mind pages from the smarmiest of the age's romance novels:

> Sarah Althea Hill [entered the court room] looking demure, innocent and as sweet as the art of toilet could make her. She is undersized but compactly built, and if her shape is faulty she understands the art of making up most thoroughly. Her costume is black silk, over which she wore a brocaded velvet dolman, faced with black fur around the throat which, if the truth be told, is no longer as round and full as doubtless it was not many years ago. The face is shapely and oval, the features are regular, the mouth is well cut, the lips rather full and are the most expressive feature. The look resolute but betrays also that their owner has a temper. The nose also looks spirited. It is cast on the Roman model and is fairly large. The eyes lack the expression of truthfulness. Their color is grey-blue and sometimes a little brown. Their movement is quick: the lids full and well creased. The whole face betrays intense nervousness, quickness of perception and mirrors faithfully all that is going on within the mind. It is marked with wrinkles, many of which have appeared since she first became notorious in connection with this case. Judging by her looks, Sarah Althea, must be nearing 40 years [actually, she was 36] though it is asserted that she is much younger. Her hair is auburn, and if it is not false it is of luxuriant growth. That portion growing above the forehead is devoted to curls and ringlets, which fall in profusion over the dome of thought. In the back the tresses are gathered into a Grecian knot, and on top they are covered by a Hazel Kirk bonnet trimmed with jet passementerie and what appeared to be butterflies with yellow-spotted wings.

Even if one failed to get a seat in the courtroom, the newspapers were ready to offer images suited to the voyeur's predilections. Later the reporter turned his attention to the senator from Nevada. His description was equally grandiloquent:

> William Sharon [makes] a far different appearance, small in stature but erect in carriage, small in waist, but certainly stiff in backbone, he is apparently the least remarkable man in the courtroom. He is clad in sober broadcloth, black necktie; and standing collar. Although a remnant of hair is disposed artistically over the bump which is said to denote will. The front portion is round and full and even. Under it are two piercing brown eyes, which look out unquestionably over a nose that tells nothing. Not even of Greek or Roman descent. The mouth recedes for the lips are thin, while the chin is rather sharp and protruding, perhaps more than it was in the Senator's youth for the increase years though it has added to his store of wealth seems to have taken away from his adipose tissue.[5]

The reporter's descriptions of the participants' appearances made it transparent to most, that no trial was needed to determine who the offender was and who the victim.

The *Sharon v. Sharon* trial began on March 11, 1884, with Judge Jeremiah F. Sullivan of the California Superior Court presiding. Sullivan, educated at San Francisco's St. Ignatius College had come to prominence as a school board reformer. In point of fact, Sullivan's state trial was the second trial between the litigants. Six months earlier, on October 3, 1883, *Sharon vs. Hill* had convened before a federal two-judge panel. Judge Lorenzo Sawyer of the U. S. Ninth Circuit Court of Appeals and Judge Matthew P. Deady of the U.S. District Court of Oregon made up the federal court. Because the litigants Sharon and Hill were from different states, Sharon's lawyers were anxious to get the trial before federal judges. (In the federal court most agreed that the senator would get a favorable ruling. Sharon's Washington, D.C. connections would be invaluable.) It was reputed that Field had once said to Sharon, "[b]ring your suit in our court and you will be alright."[6] Recognizing the advantage the defendant Sharon was expected to have in federal courts, Hill's counsel pushed for and received a series of dilatory pleas that enabled them to postpone the federal trial until after the state trial had been settled. To get this concession, however, the plaintiff agreed to drop adultery charges against the senator (adultery charges had been intended to discourage Sharon from marrying someone else during litigation). The plaintiff accepted the condition, reasoning that a criminal charge of adultery with its difficult burden of proof (beyond reasonable doubt) was far harder to prove than the civil matter of marital abandonment. The civil penalty carried a much easier burden of proof (preponderance of the evidence).

On the second day of the state trial, city newspapers announced that Judge David Terry had joined the plaintiff's legal team as an associate counsel. For his services he was given a $1,000 advance. *The Daily Alta* (the railroad controlled newspaper) ridiculed Terry's appearance at the trial, scoffing that he had been retained as "Sarah Althea's bodyguard," while reminding readers of the judge's notorious past and his Civil War treachery. The *Alta's* characterization notwithstanding, it was Terry's knowledge of the complexities of appellate review that made him an ideal appointment to the plaintiff's legal staff—he was there to guard against legal mistakes that might put the plaintiff at risk of reversal in later state and federal courts (at the time the California Supreme Court was the only appellate court in the state). In point of fact, with the exception of summation, Terry addressed the court only on a handful of occasions—and when he did it was usually to scuffle verbally with Sharon's defense counsel William Barnes on issues of protocol and decorum. Terry had been a political adversary of Barnes for years—first when he confronted the then Major General Barnes in the Vigilance Committee's army of 1856 and later at the state's second constitutional convention in 1879.

The lead counsel for Sarah Hill was a not-all-together admirable character by the name of George Washington Tyler. His balsamic name belied his nature. He was bombastic, confrontational and untrustworthy (shortly after the trial, he was disbarred on charges of graft). Invariably, when performing in the courtroom, Tyler would begin with a bland smile and a mild and affable demeanor, but this was only the calm before the storm, for when facing adversarial witnesses, he was called a "bulldog before the bar." His courtroom tactics brought constant admonishments from presiding judges—"Mr. Tyler, stand back from the witness!" "Mr. Tyler, lower your voice!" "Mr. Tyler, you're out of order!" It was only after a judge threatened contempt that Tyler would make a perfunctory effort to comply, and then but fleetingly, for soon he was again overtaken by his desire to command the moment.

In contrast, Sharon's chief counsel, General William H.L. Barnes, represented a notable dissimilarity in style. In the courtroom he was a sagacious schemer—one of the first lawyers wealthy Californians turned to when in need of legal services. He was an attorney with deep-running political connections. The railroad barons employed his skills whenever possible. Oscar Lewis describes him succinctly as the "conspicuous ornament of the local bar."[7] He was a man known to exert a great deal of influence in a courtroom, and he proved it at one point during the *Sharon v. Sharon* proceedings when he became so annoyed by the spectators' habit of cheering Sarah's lawyers that he demanded that Judge Sullivan empty the courtroom of "this gabbling crowd." He was to have his way, and, but for a few handpicked reporters, the room remained empty of spectators for almost a month.

The two competing counsels, Tyler and Barnes, had faced each other many times before, and during their engagements they had cultivated an abiding distrust for one another. Whenever given the opportunity each would irritate the other publicly. It was generally agreed that Barnes, in his quiet but lofty fashion, was predisposed to get the better of the temperamental Tyler in a variety of these supplemental squabbles. On one occasion, when a defense witness was comparing the senator's signature to a forgery, Barnes remarked that the signatures bore as much resemblance to each other "as a jackass does to a horse." This remark spurred Tyler to his feet where he protested: "Your honor, I move to strike the jackass out," to which Barnes countered, "Well then take your hat and go." "Gentlemen, Gentlemen!" cautioned the Court.[8] However, Barnes did not reserve all his insults for Tyler. He did not miss a chance to goad the foreboding David Terry whenever the opportunity presented itself—in particular Barnes was aggrieved by Terry's incessant, gratuitous attacks on what Terry insisted on calling "the habits of the larcenous corporations being represented at this trial."

As the trial progressed and the sordid revelations of the two protagonists played themselves out in a public forum, family members on both sides of the aisle stayed away, determined to distance themselves from the ever more awkward and unsavory details. It was reported that Hill's grandmother, grandaunt and uncle had, from the beginning, opposed her "friendship" with Senator Sharon; they dismissed his wealth and influence out of hand, and resented his reputation for ill-gotten riches—riches gained at the expense of others. They looked upon him as an incorrigible opportunist, a person, Grandmother Sloan insisted, who did not compare well against her granddaughter's southern heritage—they had expected her "to make a wiser and better alliance." After all, she *was* a child of the southern aristocracy, a daughter of a successful political attorney, and the niece of a governor and a senator.

Sharon's family, however, was no more sanguine about the "spectacle playing out each day before the eyes of San Franciscans." Sharon's daughter, Florence Emily, in particular, found the relationship with Sarah more odious than any of her father's earlier seductions. She feared that Hill had become more than an after-dark pleasure. Unlike the other women with whom the senator had had liaisons, the family recognized that their father did not treat Hill as if she were a hidden consort. She was on his arm at social functions and was seen in the company of powerful acquaintances (even Cornelius Vanderbilt had been introduced to her while he was on a visit to San Francisco). Moreover, the open and easy compatibility of their relationship had given family members additional cause to worry, a concern that was intensified by his flourishing financial success and failing health—for even as his health declined he continued to amass large holdings in banking and real estate, and it was clear that the family was in no mood for a deathbed scene with that "harlot" at his bedside. Florence Emily beseeched her father to pay Hill off and send her away.

When the trial had opened, the plaintiff's case was simple enough. Her lawyers would show that Mrs. Sarah Althea 'Sharon' was a virtuous woman who Sharon had scorned after he had grown tired of their marriage. What is more, they would show that the senator had been a dissembler who had lured her into a marriage that he was fully intending to put aside with no further complications or obligations once his carnal designs had run their course. To make this case, the plaintiff's lawyers brought before the court a sequence of witnesses who swore that they had seen the contract early in the fall of 1880, that it was not counterfeit nor had it been patched together a month or two before the trial—as rumors had suggested.

When Barnes rose to rebut these charges, he began by reminding the class-conscious spectators that the plaintiff's witnesses had no social standing in San Francisco. How, he asked, can we be expected to take the word of this miserable "string of rag-a-tags? We cannot." Then Barnes shifted the attack on the plaintiff, from when the marriage document was written to *why* it was written—a matter of far greater importance, he insisted. But before that question could be properly answered, he insisted, it was necessary for the court to remove the "nefarious document" from the duplicitous plaintiff's possession. Once this counterfeit document is subjected "to the most rigorous [forensic] testing for authenticity," he said, "it will be shown to be a pathetic forgery." Barnes guessed that if Hill had the document taken from her she would react to its loss with dread and rage. Barnes believed that her reactions would seem to the court and witnesses as pathological. Barnes was convinced that all who witnessed her performance would be persuaded that she knew, as did everyone else, that the document was "a fake."

Indeed, Barnes had judged plaintiff well. She resisted anyone coming near to take her precious voucher. "I will not turn over the document for fear that it would be the last I will ever see of it," she said. "If I was ever to see it again its content would be altered to suit my enemies' purposes." It took more than an hour of cajoling by her counsel, by defense counsel, and finally by the judge, to pry the contract from her hands. And when finally she did release it, it was on a solemn promise from Judge Sullivan that he and he alone would have the possession of the document and that her enemies would never have an opportunity to tamper with it. Her lawyers, Tyler and Terry, quite naturally, did not miss the occasion to point out to the court that only the document's authenticity had made her so resistive to surrendering it—it had not been off of her person, nor out of her sight, save for a single afternoon when she had hidden it behind the facing in her bedroom mirror. It was apparent to onlookers that whatever the document's worth, the plaintiff's lawyers wanted the court to understand that Mrs. Sarah Sharon believed it to be the one incontestable piece of evidence in the case—stained with perspiration, folded and unfolded until the seams were splitting. She parted with it only with great mental anguish and physical duress.

By mid-afternoon, descriptions of the celebrated manuscript were on every copy desk in the city, and the next morning San Franciscans were scrutinizing every ink mark and splotch on its surface—and with good reason, for it raised some serious suspicions. The content was awkwardly crafted, the sequencing and spacing of the script was simultaneously formal and informal, with what appeared to be an attempt to cast a quasi-legal tone to it. Some words and letters had been traced over or squeezed into the text at odd angles, and curiously, three different colors of ink had been used. But appearance aside, its content was even more curious. It read:

> In the City and County of San Francisco, State of California, on the 25th day of August, A.D. 1880, I Sarah Althea Hill, of the City and County of San Francisco, age 27 years, do here in the presence of almighty God, take Senator William Sharon, of the State of Nevada, to be my lawful and wedded husband, and do here acknowledge and declare myself to be the wife of Senator William Sharon of the State of Nevada.
> Sarah Althea Hill (signed)
> August 25th, 1880, San Francisco, Cal.
>
> I agree not to make known the contents of this paper or its existence for two years unless Mr. Sharon himself sees fit to make it known. S.A. Hill (signed)

And:

> In the City and County of San Francisco, State of California, on the 25th of August, A.D. 1880, I Senator William Sharon, of the State of Nevada, age 60 years, do here in the presence of almighty God, take Sarah Althea Hill, of the City of San Francisco, Cal., to be my lawful and wedded wife, and do here acknowledge myself to be the husband of Sarah Althea Hill.
> Wm Sharon, Nevada (signed)
> Aug. 25, 1880

Oddly, the defense's unrelenting attack on the authenticity of the document produced little counter-evidence from the plaintiff's attorneys. In fact, the evidence they offered and their rejoinder to the charge that the document was forged was almost nonexistent. Tyler put on the stand a single "forgery expert," whose qualifications for the task had been limited to the reputation he had earned in the Civil War as an expert in identifying counterfeit Union money. In the witness box he was handed the marriage contract and a few personal letters allegedly signed by Sharon and addressed to Sarah. After several minutes, poring over the documents accompanied by desultory note checking and audible mumbling, he announced the signatures on "all the documents were genuine!" The defense, however, judged his performance so ineffectual that Barnes felt no need to spend much time in cross-examination. Even Judge Sullivan dismissed him with the sparsest of questions and comments.

The plaintiff's expert performance notwithstanding, it had been Tyler and Terry's plan from the outset to assume the authenticity of the document without extensive time being given over to debating the matter. Contrarily, they made the *textual* legality of the document the nub of their case. As much as was possible, they were determined not to be drawn into a battle concerning the science of "graphology"—if, as they insisted, it were not necessary to prove a false negative, then, obviously, there was no point in trying. Or to put the matter another way, Tyler and Terry set out to prove that the document met all the legal specifications within the California code and was therefore authentic simply by virtue of its existence. The state and appearance of the document, forged or otherwise was not relevant. Moreover, it would have been virtually impossible for Hill to produce a marriage contract that met the legal requirements of the state code without the senator's help. To focus the argument on the document *authenticum,* Hill's attorneys introduced pertinent sections of California's Civil Code on marriage, in particular, Sections 55, 75, and 76. Section 55 declares that a marriage is legal if it is "solemnized by the proper authority, [or] is declared true by mutual consent *in any other form*." Section 75 asserts that "persons married without the rite of solemnization must present documentation declaring mutual consent" and containing the "fact and time" of the marriage—which is to say, the name, age, and residence of the parties. Section 76 adds that if there is no solemnization, specifically no "documentation," then consent must take place before three witnesses. Tyler insisted that Sarah Althea Sharon's document met legal authorization by virtue of the "in any other form" clause written into Section 55 (critics of the state's constitutional marriage codes have argued that only a legislature composed of fortune-seekers, who could not be bothered with matters of licensing matrimony, would have drafted a document filled with so many legal vagaries).

Tyler and his aids had little to add concerning the authenticity of the bundle of "Dear Wife" letters that allegedly had passed between the senator and Hill—except to insist that these letters were the senator's public acknowledgment that, in some fashion or other, Hill had been convinced that a marriage had taken place and that Sharon had been a willing and all too eager to reinforce this perception. The defense's line of rebuttal to the plaintiff's was predictable and squarely on the mark. Barnes argued that if Sharon's signature proved to be a forgery, then it was irrelevant whether the document met the legal requirements of the code or not. Under this rationale, only two explanations made any sense: either the signature was a forgery or the senator had signed a blank page that had been surreptitiously transferred onto the "so-called" marriage document out of his presence and without his approval. Unfortunately, however, by the time the defense began its rebuttal, most of the interesting witnesses had come and gone, and the lawyers faced a courtroom of bored reporters and spectators—it was a situation neither the defense nor the judge had anticipated. Once this phase of the trial unfolded, the rebuttal strategy of Sharon's attorneys became increasingly time consuming, tedious and repetitious, but worst of all, subject to a variety of ambiguous interpretations.

In earliest interviews with reporters, Sharon had insisted that Hill was merely a "passing acquaintance" to whom he had rarely spoken. But later under oath, and as a result of George Tyler's aggressive prodding, he began to adjust his story in order to make it more believable. Yes, he finally confessed, there had been an arrangement, but it had been a "meretricious" one not a "matrimonial" one, and yes he had had a closer relationship with "Allie" than he had earlier acknowledged. Indeed she had been much more than a mere acquaintance (she had attended too many social functions including the reception at his daughter's wedding to be dismissed as one of his passing mistresses). As Sharon's cross-examination wound down, and at the most auspicious moment Tyler could muster, he leaned forward nose to nose with Sharon and whispered, "[Will] you please list the number and names of women with whom you have had the same arrangement as you had with the plaintiff." Courtroom reporters, stirred by the question from after-lunch doldrums, pressed forward, pencils in hand, anxious to record the details of his answer, but the judge sustained the fulminating objection of General Barnes, declaring that "[The court is prepared to believe] that the senator has had a number of these arrangements, therefore, let us move on." Sadly, reporters and spectators were left to fill in the gaps in this side story with their own imaginations.

The defense's principal line of argument, as everyone expected, turned on the common sense assumption that the contract and letters were patent forgeries, and for them to make this point convincingly was to win the case. However, after four weeks of "expert" testimony calculated to demonstrate this assumption, things were not going as well as they had hoped. Most of the courtroom spectators had already made up their minds on the issue of guilt or innocence and were becoming restless and inattentive. This lack of interest was reflected in a bored press that began its daily type leads with such terse terms as "tedious," "dull" and "unconvincing."[9]

Meanwhile, Judge Sullivan and the lawyers were getting on each other's nerves, and Sarah Hill was doing what she could "to think about other things." It was reported, writes Robert Kroninger, that Hill "seemed to get through the first hour each day in the simple enjoyment of being in a new dress or wearing her hair in a different fashion; but when that palled, she invariably turned to Terry, who, always courtly, joined her in light conversation or politely watched as she smilingly demonstrated her penmanship to him."[10] As the trial moved from the cooler days of spring and dragged into the sometimes warm and sometimes foggy days of summer, it became ever more apparent that Tyler's and Terry's decision to ignore the matter of forgery had become a tactically astute move—throughout the proceedings their assumption that the signatures were authentic and that they need not waste the court's time proving it seemed an unwise maneuver only to the defense. In contrast to the plaintiff's style, the defense lawyers chose to build their entire case around the notion that any objective onlooker would agree that the document was a forgery. Thus they brought to the witness stand three "graphologists" who spent interminable hours talking about the document's "looping W's, crossing t's, dotting i's and *plumbago* [pencil widths]." But sadly for Barnes and the defense, the more his experts talked, the less persuasive they became to the increasingly cynical members of the press and public. They presented page after page of detailed technical material that came across to observers as obscure and repetitious, and what was worse, appeared frequently contradictory from expert to expert.

Eventually after several weeks, in an effort to rescue the situation by establishing a basic line of consistency, Barnes put on the witness stand an unexpected fourth expert by the name of Max Gumbel. He was there to sort things out once and for all. Yet with Gumbel on the stand as their clarifying expert, the defense fell into a trap of their own making that went far beyond what even the plaintiff's lawyers could have hoped. At the outset, Gumbel declared that the documents were forgeries, but two days later after, further scrutiny of the materials that had been spread out on a table before the judge's bench, he shocked attorneys on both sides when he reversed himself and declared the "signatures on the marriage agreement and on the private letters are authentic!" With this revelation, and over the strenuous objection of Barnes, the judge invited Gumbel to take the stand as a hostile witness and state why he had changed his mind.

The public's restored interest with the "science of graphology" was reflected in the ruminations that appeared in the daily papers. The *Alta*, openly sympathetic to the senator, pointed out that Sarah Hill's signature appeared first on the document, and this was contrary to custom that had always placed the man's signature first on marriage contracts. On the other hand, the *Chron-*

icle raised questions about the peculiar position of the senator's signature on the document. The document had been written in longhand on a single piece of ruled notebook paper; but oddly enough, the text began not on the first line below the three-inch horizontal margin on the front side of the page, but at the top of the page on the unmargined underside. Moreover, the script proceeded on consecutive lines to the bottom, but then, when turned over, appeared as text squeezed into the three-inch unruled horizontal margin at the top. It was a happenstance that led many of Sharon's proponents to argue that the text doubtless had been composed "around or below" his signature. One enterprising reporter from the *Daily Call* offered the following interpretation of the document's structure:

> The autograph appears to be written just as a man would write it for a friend's album. It also appears to have been written in consonance with a well-established rule of businessmen and the instinct of rich men particularly, who never write their names in blank, save at the top of a sheet of paper, where it is supposed nothing can be written above it.[11]

Other spectators mused that perhaps Sarah was using a freestanding signature Sharon had given her on a blank notepad that had been intended for her use as an access document for hotel services. On one thing both sides agreed—Sarah Hill had written the document. She insisted that she had written it at Sharon's bidding and that she had put it down exactly as he had dictated. They composed it, she said, in his bank office while he consulted various civil codes in order to make sure that everything had been done in the legally authorized fashion. The defense countered that if it had been a proper document, it would never have appeared as the ill-prepared jottings that were now before the court (words and letters squeezed together, traced over, some changed or added). Were it authentic, they argued, there would have been presented a neatly drafted second copy. It was obvious that the forger(s) possessed only a single signature so that she (or they) was forced to structure the contract around the solitary inscription. Later, in rebuttal, Terry turned the defense's argument on its head. "[T]he strike-overs and corrections," he argued, "prove its genuine nature for had it been a forgery [she] would have presented a 'clean' copy to avoid such a charge. No, it was the work of Sharon's meandering dictation [that] caused its disorderly appearance."

Later when the "Dear Wife" letters were introduced into the discussion, the debate was even more riddled with contradictions. Inspecting the letters' signatures carefully, Sharon acknowledged their authorship but denied that the "Dear Wife" salutation at the top of each letter was authentic. Furthermore, Counsel Barnes pointed out, the contents of the letters were much too work-a-day to be the letters of a husband to his new bride—containing such phrases as "in reply to your kind letter" and "enclosed is the balance of two hundred fifty [dollars]," or "enclosed five hundred [dollars]—getting very extravagant!" It is impossible for a reasonable person to believe, Barnes mocked, that a husband would write such commonplace letters to a bride! In all, there were five "Dear Wife" letters in a collection of almost fifty letters from Sharon to Hill. By contrast, only two letters were introduced that had traveled from Hill to Sharon that appeared to hold any relevance to the dispute. What was apparent to everyone who reviewed the letters was that as Sharon's feelings and moods changed so also did the tone of his letters. There was, in the early notes, an unrestrained infatuation toward "Allie," while at the end they manifested a quick-tempered irritation toward "Miss Hill." The letters, taken as a whole, revealed that the senator's attraction had faded by the winter of 1881, then warmed up and cooled down again intermittently through a series of break-up and reconciliation letters in 1882—yet by the middle of 1882, the senator harbored nothing toward the relationship but ill-will. In the final few letters, he blamed his aggravations on her disloyalty and financial profligacy. In degree his annoyance was well founded, but it was also true that he had grown tired of the arrangement and had begun to direct his amorous energies elsewhere.

When Sharon finally stepped down from the witness box, to most courtroom observers as well as to most city reporters, the cape of the blackguard had been firmly twisted about his neck—during his days in the witness box he had laid out an arrogant, heartless performance with a number of culpatory admissions (including an attempt to choke Hill into giving up any incriminating documents she might have had). He knew he had been all too candid, but he had made up his mind that he was willing to suffer public indignation to rid himself of this woman and her vice-grip demands.

Except for a handful of business associates, loyal friends and jurists, public sympathies lay with Hill in spite of the public's obvious disbelief in her professed innocence. Most San Franciscans believed that Sharon was the "scoundrel and bounder" that Sarah Althea had said he was, although they did not believe that she was the guileless ingénue that she had portrayed herself to be. For the most part, citizens were inclined to believe, as one reporter put it, "[she] was more a fallen dove than a stray cat—less sinner than sinned against." As public sympathy for Sarah grew, Barnes called a list of witnesses who could besmirch her character, and the more witnesses he called, the more disjointed and aimless the trial became—each side offered its set of witnesses, and each side brought into court opposing attesters. Witnesses offered demonstrably contradictory, perjured, changing and purchased testimony that left the courtroom spectators and reporters at times confused but bemused.

These witnesses attracted wide public interest but rarely did their testimony have a direct bearing on the central question—was the couple, in fact, in any sense married? One witness for the plaintiff claimed to have seen or heard about the contract as early as 1880 or 1881; another insisted that she was present when Sharon introduced Hill as his wife. Another testified that Sarah had told her that she was still in love with the wealthy socialite Reuben Lloyd, but "over time had grown to love the old man as well." One testified that Hill had often referred to Sharon as "my beautiful old darling." Defense witnesses, to counter, portrayed Hill as a "fortune-hunting strumpet" who, after having been rejected as the senator's mistress, audaciously engaged in extortion. Some testified that she had never been heard to claim more than an "engagement to the 'Sen'". Others insisted that she was treating her relationship with the senator as an interlude while waiting for Lloyd to work up the courage to defy his mother. One woman claimed to have been present in Lloyd's office when Hill threatened to commit suicide if he refused to marry her; another testified provocatively that she had overheard Hill discussing her chances of winning a "breach of promise" suit with a lawyer that Hill happened to meet while crossing a city street.

The testimony most anticipated by the public was that of Hill's confidant and benefactor, Mary Ellen Pleasant. Many believed that the old woman had initiated the entire plan. The street gossip was that Hill might have accepted Sharon's initial $7,500 payoff had not Mammy Pleasant assured her that much more was available if they went into court. Everyone believed that Mammy Pleasant would get a handsome percentage of the settlement should Hill win the case. Regrettably for the courtroom onlookers, the anticipation of Mammy Pleasant's testimony was more evocative than her actual performance. It was brief and uneventful. She supported Hill's claim that the contract and the date of signatures were authentic; "she had seen the contract." However, when Barnes arose to cross-examine her, he was uncharacteristically brief and docile. The common explanation for his mild performance was that he was not eager to attack her too aggressively for fear that, if irritated, she would launch off into the details of a bitter and incriminating financial deal that Sharon had earlier made with her multimillionaire employer Thomas Bell.

As a matter of fact, the least forgettable aspect of Mammy Pleasant's day in court was her presence. She glided into the courtroom elegantly dressed and accompanied by an entourage that filled most of the front row seats in the courtroom. A newspaper reported that many "gentle" ladies in the audience refused to look directly into her eyes for fear that she might cast one of her infamous evil spells on them.[12]

By mid-July, the testimony had taken on a surrealistic cast. Witnesses began telling of Sarah Hill's reliance on fortunetellers and sorcerers—how she had purchased a "conjure bag" full of smelly potions designed to mesmerize the "Sen" into marrying her. The highlight of these ethereal luminescences came when Barnes produced a mud-stained shirt of Sharon's which he claimed Hill had buried beneath the body of a one-eyed murderer. She believed, Barnes explained to a transfixed audience, that such a talisman would enable her to control the senator's romantic whims. The defense continued to offer more unflattering tales of Hill's behavior. She had bribed Sharon's Chinese "houseboy," Ah Ki, to gain access to the senator's apartment, where she had witnessed a tryst with another woman. On another occasion, Nellie Bracket, a 20-year-old friend of Hill's, testified that she had been secreted behind a bedroom chiffonier while Hill shared his bed—she was there, said Bracket, to record their pillow talk. Later Nellie Bracket testified that she and "Allie" had laughed about the incident.

Another defense witness declared that Hill was making plans to leave California for the East to study music and theater (hardly the action of a newly married wife, one would think). As witnesses came and went, the descriptions of Hill in the daily papers began to contain such words as "extortionist," "blackmailer" and "harlot." Finally, the character witness portion of the trial ended in total disarray when the plaintiff's and defense's witnesses reappeared on the stand to recant or correct their misstatements. Many admitted that they had lied or had accepted bribes to lie. One witness would reverse her story on three different occasions. As the battle of testimonies droned on, discerning spectators began to observe a noticeable change in Hill's emotional demeanor. Reporters witnessed it and wrote of her changing stability—she was becoming more quickly agitated, at times disoriented, even as she became increasingly more unmanageable and self-destructive. On one occasion she shouted that she would shoot Sharon and Barnes on sight; on another she turned on the judge and her own attorneys, insisting that they were conspiring with the defense counsel. No one in the courtroom was immune from this haranguing—opposing counsel, witnesses, spectators, court bailiffs, the presiding judge, even her own counsel. Trembling with rage she would leap to her feet and rush at the adversary *du jour*, shouting insults, vulgarities and threats.

But reporters also noticed something else new. Only Terry appeared able to bring her down from these rages—he alone was able to calm her and restore some emotional equilibrium. Her relationship with him had not always been so. At the outset, she was ill at ease around him—thought him pretentious, humorless and quite old. In court he rarely said much, and when he did, more often than not it was to correct a point of law or scold an opposing counsel for tactless or uncivil behavior. By the end of the first month of the trial, however, the reporters detected that the relationship was changing and by the end of the trial Terry appeared to be her one and only confidant. Observers speculated that it was their common southern bloodline that drew them together. "[T]he Judge is fulfilling his role as special counsel and protector to the plaintiff [with emphasis on] protector," said a reporter form the *Daily Alta*. "[The Judge] had taken his place beside Sarah Althea and they [both] looked pleased." "Whenever a judicial matter raised Althea's interest, she [and] Judge Terry put their heads together conferring on its meaning." *The Daily Alta* added that "Sarah and the Judge had been seen together [outside the courtroom] enjoying each other's company." The comments that Barnes had offered at the beginning of the trial belittling Terry as the plaintiff's bodyguard had proved prophetic—yet now the protection she needed was not so much from Sharon and his henchmen, but from herself.

As the trial crawled into August, amid San Francisco's usual damp morning fog and unusually humid temperature, there were for the first time many empty seats in the courtroom. Newspaper accounts had become noticeably shorter, sometimes reduced to a single column on an inside page. The headline leads read "Dull and Dry," "Sharon Trial in Doldrums," "Judge and Counsels Dozing." But then, with little warning, and without additional witnesses coming forward seeking to change their stories or recant, Judge Sullivan declared the adversarial portion of the trial over, and he invited the litigants to prepare their closing arguments. Three days later, as renewed interest in the trial grew, the lines of spectators squeezed into the crowded courtroom eager to hear the lawyers' summations. San Franciscans' enthusiasm for the "trial of the century" had returned.

Summation for the plaintiff began with William B. Tyler, George Tyler's son, standing apprehensively before the bench. Under Terry's steady gaze, young Tyler took up the tricky question of the contract's legality (as had been true during the trial, the plaintiff's counselors had little or nothing to say concerning the marriage contract as a forgery). Rather, William Tyler began his summation with a history of Greek and Roman marriage and ended it with a discussion of the British influences on Scottish contracts—it took him two days to demonstrate that the plaintiff's contract conformed to the marriage contracts seemingly of the entire western world.

Next to face the court for the plaintiff was the elder Tyler, George. He painted a vivid picture of a philandering mercenary senator. This was not difficult to do, but when he turned to his own client, his task was considerably trickier. Putting her in the light of an innocent victim was not easy. To be sure, George Tyler acknowledged to the court that Hill was not a completely guileless young woman, but neither was she a deceitful or avaricious whore. The defense's attack on her character had been inexcusable. In sum, Tyler's picture of her was as a slightly naive young woman who had become a victim of the senator's worldly-wise venality. George Tyler took three-and-one-half days to tarnish Sharon's persona and burnish his paramour.

When it came time for Defense Counsel Barnes to rebut these charges he performed as onlookers had envisioned. He was alternately theatrical, sanctimonious, and disdainful of "Miss Hill": "[She] had spun a lie of such gigantic proportions that there was not enough time to challenge every false assumption; [but even if I] were to challenge every lie there would still be people among us so disquieted of mind that they would believe her anyway. [Some] will believe such lies—even when most of us can see her for the flirtatious schemer and money worshiper she is. Nodding in Sullivan's direction, as the person that must ultimately be convinced, he offered:

> [F]or those prepared to accept the truth the evidence is incontestable. [Hill] insisted that the $7,500 given to her by Senator Sharon was the product of her stock market ventures, but (*holding up bank records*), the evidence shows that she arrived in California in 1875 with $18,000 inheritance money and by 1880, when she had become the Senator's consort, there remained in her bank account but $11. [And] her affluent relatives were in no mode to give her one nickel more. [Moreover when] her shameful love affair with Reuben Lloyd collapsed she feigned suicide [a ruse that failed to win him back]; she then entered into a nefarious plot, at the urging of Mammy Pleasant, to extort money from my client. [E]ven now, her family is unwilling to come into court and lie for her. [Consider] how silent she is on so many critical issues: why cannot she tell us about her relationship with Sharon before the alleged marriage contract? [H]ow believable is it to think that the Senator would sign a marriage contract and then depart for Nevada for sixteen days and write his bride but once? [And] when the Galindo Hotel in Oakland burned down forcing her to move to the Baldwin what was her response when asked why Sharon was not informed? I knew, [she claimed], when he came down [from Nevada], if he wanted to see me he could find me. It was not necessary for wives to run after their husbands. [I]f he cared so much for me as he pretended to, he would find me. I am not in the habit of running after people.[13]

When the senator was in Washington, D.C., Barnes continued, "why was she not with him, or why, during the two months he was gone, he wrote but once—and not a word of endearment but only words about her financial [profligacy]?" "[Where were the letters from her addressing him as] "Dear Husband." "[And finally], why, in this most important of all personal relationships did she not confide in her family? Why were her confidences limited to those persons beneath her station—why did she repose her head upon the bosom of a Negro woman and shun the bosom of her grandmother?" After six days of speculation and guileful credulousness plus three hundred eighty-one printed pages of the trial record, Barnes turned the defense's concluding remarks over to his associate counsel, Oliver Perry Evans.

Evans performed without Barnes' histrionics—he was a pensive lawyer given to tightly wound, systematic argumentation. The onlookers in the court, having been treated to a week of Barnes' torrid hyperbole, were now confronted by a man of candor and orderly argument. Many spectators found him dull and boring, but not all. Some found him to be the most persuasive of the senator's attorneys. In particular, he impressed newspaper reporters. "How," Evans began, "could a woman act toward the Senator's alleged contemptible proposition, as she says she did, and remain the virtuous woman she claims to be? A virtuous woman who is invited to make a choice between becoming a man's wife or his mistress would straightway depart the scoundrel's presence." "[What sort of a woman would accept such a vulgar combination of proposals]—only a prostitute." "Would a virtuous wife importune, or spy upon her husband, or have friends spy upon him? Or seek the advice of fortune-tellers, or put love potions in his food and drink, or sprinkle magic dust on his bed and reading chair, "surely not, this is the behavior of a harlot—not a wife." Who could believe that she accidentally overdosed on laudanum in Reuben Lloyds' office? "No, she feigned suicide to provoke a change of heart" (some were saying that Hill overdosed to induce the abortion of Lloyd's child).

"Her charms," Evans continued, "had failed to persuade either man to marry her." "Sarah Althea Hill loved Reuben Lloyd and paid for a sorcerer's incantations to rid herself of his mother, and when the plan failed she bought a witches' brew to gain Senator Sharon's name, fame, and money." But why would Sharon consent to marry her when he had the choice of so many lovers? Even more curious, why, after she purportedly had entered into this secret marriage, was she overheard discussing marriage and engagements with other suitors? Moreover, why, if her virtue were not at issue, did the senator feel compelled to write of her "unblemished character" in an introductory letter to the manager of the Grand Hotel? Why was she not invited to the wedding of his daughter to Lord Fermor-Hesketh? Would a virtuous wife hide with a friend in the senator's bedroom, while he lay with another woman, only later to laugh about it? Evans reasoned:

> Your Honor, her faulty memory is a puzzle to us all." She is not even certain that their friendship began with the senator as early as January or as late as June; nor does she remember how long it took him to count the $7,500 she gave him to invest in the stock market, nor does she remember the denominations of the bills." If, as she says, "the marriage was to remain a secret until after the Nevada elections, then why did it continue to be a secret months after the election had been settled? Yet, most significantly, even if the contract were drawn up as she

says it was, "which we do not concede," it could not be legal because "it had been neither solemnized nor witnessed."

"No my friends," Evans concluded, "Sarah's coaxing and pleading was the behavior of a woman who knew she had no legal claims against the Senator, for who of us believes that dodging about hotel corridors is a marriage?"

After two and a half days of argument, Evans was finished. In the court room there was a feeling among many that Oliver Evans, by presenting a broad picture and avoiding pointless rebuttal of what had become contradictory details of scoria, had succeeded in removing the last shred of probity from Sarah Althea's pitiful attempt to practice extortion. The defense's entire case was now in order, and, at Hill's urging, it had been agreed by her lawyers that Terry would be given the crucial responsibility of rebuttal.

Long before daylight, people were lining up outside the courtroom to get a glimpse of the proceedings. By the time Judge Sullivan had taken his place on the bench, every inch of space in the courtroom was jammed with spectators. People were wedged into the doorways, standing in the hallways, and outside on the City Hall steps—hundreds of onlookers had made their way to San Francisco's courthouse eager to see and hear the celebrated Judge Terry. The judicial community was there in numbers; judges and attorneys and their wives, many of whom, 30 years earlier, had fought Terry bitterly as vigilantes. Oscar Lewis and Carroll D. Hall write that Terry sensed the full significance of the occasion. "His appearance, in black broadcloth of fashionable cut, formed a marked contrast to his usual careless attire."[14]

Speaking without notes, the judge began his defense with an analysis of the California Civil Code. "Your Honor." he declared, "a marriage contract need not be a public document. The code does not require an 'open assumption' of marriage. It requires only three things of the partners: 'that they assert their consent in writing, that they cohabit, and that they assume each other's expenses and debts.'" All can plainly see, Terry continued, "that these requirements were met in the alliance that is before the court today." The senator assumed responsibility for this marriage when he provided "Sarah Althea with shelter, food, clothes, household goods, and expense money." Terry then responded to the charge that "the document was too defective to be genuine." "Its very defectiveness proves its authenticity," he argued. It was the product of the senator's dictation given once to Sarah and never revised. Tracing blemishes in their written agreement "demonstrate that she wrote the document precisely as the senator had dictated it to her. Passages were squeezed together because there were no ruled lines to guide transcription; in fact, (pointing to a document) the contract's blemishes are no different than those appearing on these notes of the defendant's handwriting expert, George Hickox—traced over and squeezed together. Terry argued in this summary by Oscar Lewis:

> What's more, if the plaintiff had intended to present a forgery, would common sense not have told her to present as neat a forgery as possible—the document's disrepair confirmed its validity—why would she cling so tenaciously to a document of this sort if she could have offered another one in its place? "Judge Sullivan, she would not!" Yes, she carried this record on her person as the one and only earnest of a promise. Moreover, we should not forget that her delay in making the marriage public after Sharon's defeat for a second term as Nevada's senator was wholly according to the senator's wishes, not hers.[15]

Then, Terry set about restoring a sympathetic image of the plaintiff in words that perhaps even he found persuasive and comfortable:

> Sarah Althea Sharon was in court, he admonished, as a matter of honor; she was not here because of perfidy and greed. No Sarah Althea is not a seductress, as her enemies would have one believe, quite the contrary, she is an uncontaminated, un-Sharonized maiden [who] by her silence in this marriage has made a sacrifice not unlike the sacrifice made by [every] married woman" (silence in the face of marital mistreatment). "Is there any doubt that the rapacious Senator Sharon wanted to coax her into his bed and when this failed he devised a bogus marriage plan."
>
> It was a plan to remove the plaintiff's scruples and to gratify his own passions. But to reach this end he introduced that [infamous] 'silent clause.' It was intended to vitiate the contract, [and] I do not believe that he ever expected to carry out his promise to her; no he intended to perpetrate a fraud upon her. But, like it or not, he married himself to her as firmly as the church could have ever done. A state of affairs that remained amicable, [until] the defendant having tired of her [attempted to take back] the contract, [only to be] put off by Mrs. Sharon when she told him that it had been lost, {whereupon] he abandoned all restraint and treated her outrageously.[16] Then Terry slowly raised his voice and enunciating each word carefully, declared. "[T]his trial will find for the plaintiff and the Senator will be dismayed to discover that he has blundered into marriage!"

Terry's case for the plaintiff had been made, but before sitting down he directed the courtroom's attention to a handful of lesser accusations, speculations that had occupied newspapers for weeks. The infamous suicide attempt Terry called "utterly false, she toppled from a chair, while reaching to remove a painting that hung on Lloyd's office wall—[whereafter in a dazed condition] she mistakenly overdosed on laudanum." On the charge that her family had abandoned her, he reversed the accusation, pointing out that the defense could have easily called the family to the witness stand if they truly believed that their testimony would have been damning to Hill. "But they didn't," he added using the lawyer's well-know injunction "because Barnes was afraid of what they might say." (Given the truth of Terry's assertion—that the defense was fearful of the family's answers—one can only wonder why he did not call them—perhaps for the same reason?)

Next he turned to the issue of Hill consorting with people below her own station (Negroes)—a question intended to stir the feelings of a courtroom full of class-conscious people. Terry's reply rarely exhibits the "purple patches [so] highly regarded by the legal lights of the time."[17] There is nothing unnatural [about] her relationship with a Negro, Mammy Pleasant:

> We who have gone to our colored nurses for relief from every childish affliction, we who have looked upon them as second parents, know that the friendship and respect for them continues until late in life. We know how staunch and true they are—faithful even to death. I am one who possesses this knowledge of the character of the colored "mammies" of my youth, and the plaintiff is another.[18]

Finally, in an effort to cast his client in the most sympathetic light possible, he concluded with the "exclusionary gambit," a gambit commonly employed by 19th century trial lawyers. "My client," he brashly declared, "is prepared to divorce Sharon without compensation [so as] to clear her name, [for either] she is a virtuous woman or the contract is a fraud, both cannot be true. She goes from this courtroom either vindicated as an honest and virtuous wife, or branded as an adventuress, a blackmailer, a perjurer, and a harlot." Perhaps Hill was sanguine with Terry's "all or nothing" proposal, but one can be certain that the other lawyers who represented her were not. Tyler had too much invested—rumors had it that the lawyers were to receive 50% of any award Hill might win. Possibly, though, Terry believed what he was saying. Everyone knew that with him there was never any middle ground. Either Allie was the innocent victim of Sharon's lascivious ways, as he had argued, or she did not deserve Terry's unsullied loyalty. And he reminded the court that those who charged him with dishonoring his calling by knowingly defending an extortionist failed to understand that "honor imbues my [every] cause. [I]f I am defending a strumpet I would be unworthy to practice law, but even my worst enemy has never attacked my integrity."

So it was that he concluded his defense of the plaintiff with an empathic defense of his own behavior—and a circular argumentation thrown in for good measure. Specifically, Sarah Althea Sharon was an innocent victim and the court can accept this to be true, for he, Judge Terry, declare it to be so, and what I say must be judged true because I am a man incapable of speaking before this court untruthfully. This all-or-nothing challenge ended Judge Terry's four-and-one-half-day summation. He rested the plaintiff's case. It was September 16, 1884.

Now the case was in the hands of the inscrutable Judge J.F. Sullivan. The trial had taken 83 court days and had produced a record of 1,142 pages. Legal historian Robert Kroninger tallies up the score:

> Some trial followers were partisans on one side or the other even before it had commenced. As it progressed there appeared to be more general sentiment for Sarah's side than for the Senator and, by the time the last witness had stepped down from the stand and the last exhibit had been marked in evidence, a referendum would have given Sarah an easy victory. The final arguments, while uniformly good, did nothing to change popular opinion.[19]

It remained to be seen, however, whether the presiding judge's view of the trial would conform to popular sentiment—some on the defense's side were fearful that Sullivan, as a former elected school board official, would allow the pressure of public sentiment to influence his decision.

Three months and ten days later, just in time to spoil Christmas for the losing litigant, Judge Sullivan summoned the parties back into court. It was Christmas Eve morning, a few minutes past 9 a.m. The litigants were in their places—Hill and her lawyers Tyler & Tyler, and the defendant's lawyers, Barnes, Evans, Flournoy and Levy were there. Only Senator Sharon and Judge Terry were missing. During the night, Sharon had become too overwrought to face the verdict, and Terry's absence was not a surprise to anyone, for he was grieving the death of his wife. Cornelia had died eight days earlier.

The San Francisco Chronicle described the 9 a.m. hour at City Hall as "a misty, moisty morning," and once again a *Chronicle* reporter offered his readers a word-rotogravure describing Sarah Hill's final appearance in Sullivan's courtroom:

> She was on time and affecting an air of confidence. She was dressed in a cloak of richly embossed velvet-trimmed otter, an otter boa thrown about her neck provided warmth against the cold. She wore black gloves and a bonnet crowned with blue beads. When she removed her leather coat in the courtroom, she revealed a black silk dress trimmed in blue velvet that matched the bonnet. Her entire attire was a dark hue except for a band of pink ruffles around the wrists.[20]

At ten minutes past nine, Sullivan entered the courtroom and seated himself at the elevated bench. He began to read, his voice a mere whisper in a hushed courtroom, spectators and lawyers straining for every word. "It had been a difficult decision to render," Sullivan began. "There has been much perjured testimony. It was hard to find the truth in the fable." "But worst of all," he said, glowering directly at Hill, "the plaintiff's testimony was filled [with] frightful perjury." He offered examples: He didn't believe that the senator had ever introduced Hill to friends as his wife, nor did he believe that Sharon at any time had referred to her in public as "his wife." Moreover, he continued, the special pleading by the witnesses on both sides made most of the testimony superfluous, "for this trial was not about unreliable witnesses—of which there were many too many; [no it was about] the validity of the marriage contract." Sullivan read on, "[two questions needed to be answered]; was the contract a forgery and, if not, was it legal?"

To the surprise of many, Sullivan then turned to the testimony of Max Gumbel, the defendant's conflicted handwriting expert. Until this point General Barnes had appeared tranquil, but with the judge's comments about Max Gumbel, his countenance began to darken. Max Gumbel was to become the lynchpin of the trial. It was his testimony, said the judge, that carried the greatest weight, for he was the one witness without partisan attachments. In other words, when Gumbel declared the signatures on the contract authentic, Sullivan had no choice but to take him at his word, he said, for he had no reason to lie. "The document is not a forgery so the quintessential issue becomes its legality."

With these words it was apparent to most in the courtroom that Terry's remarks had been, in degree, persuasive to the judge. He had agreed with Terry that the senator had signed the marriage contract, but more than that, he also agreed that Sharon "believed" he was signing a legally bogus document, one that would have no standing should matters force the issue into court. Then Sullivan avowed, that the senator sadly had been much too clever for his own good. Both parties, he explained, having freely signed, had met the Civil Code's requirements—the document met the legal test *bona fides exigit ut quod convenit fiat* (what is agreed upon shall be done). What is more, he added, the "Dear Wife" letters were not forgeries. They were an intentional part of Sharon's scheme to perpetuate his "vile deception." "[Sharon is an incorrigible reprobate] who signed and dated the contract because he could not do otherwise. [H]e was a man of unbounded wealth, [s]trong animal passions, [e]xcessive indulgence, [not] accustomed to restraint, [a man with] passions stronger than good judgment. He regarded [the] contract as a trifle, light as air, [a] miserable bit of paper behind which a weak woman could shelter her virginity (much too late for that) [while] she sought standing in the community."

Again Sullivan continued to see it Terry's way. He agreed that when the senator paid her expenses and appeared as her escort in public he had sealed his fate. He had validated the contract that he had unquestioningly believed was a legal fake! Sullivan summed up:

> William Sharon by virtue of the secret contract of marriage [has] become and now is the husband of Sarah Althea *Sharon.* [He is] guilty of willfully abandoning his wife. [Therefore] under the laws of the State of California [she] is entitled to a decree of the court devolving the bonds of marriage now existing between her and her husband, William Sharon, the defendant herein. The plaintiff is, in my judgment, entitled to a decree of divorce on the grounds of willful desertion, and a division of common property.[21]

Sullivan then closed the binder on his opinion and instructed the attorneys to consult a referee who would work out a just division of the "couple's property." In slightly more than two hours, Sullivan had lighted a litigious firestorm that would take a decade to extinguish. The sides had been drawn and the details of the trial became irrelevant; imposing a political victory became imperative for everyone connected with what was to follow. Tyler & Tyler's 50-percent contingency fee with Sarah Sharon had now come due. Terry's posturing aside (that the plaintiff wanted only to clear her name), lawyers were expecting to be paid. Two weeks later, the financial deposition was posted by the referee—Sharon must pay $2,500 alimony each month until final determination of property. The Tylers would receive $25,000 while the assistant counsels were to distribute another $25,000. But everyone knew that they were in for a bitter appellate fight before they would see a single penny of Sullivan's judgment.

As far as Sharon was concerned, he vowed to resist any payment "whatsoever" and in January 1885 he revived his appeal with the Ninth Circuit Court (the federal appeal had been in abeyance during the length of the state trial). "[I will] fight it to the bitter end. [F]ight] it in all the courts, and fight it on all sides. I will never give in to the last," Sharon said. Rumor was that the verdict had so angered Sharon that he deducted a percentage of Barnes' fees for "sheer incompetence." It was also whispered that he was paying $1,000 a day for his legal defense, and was altogether persuaded that he had not received anywhere near his money's worth.[22]

Sharon did not live to see the end of the litigation, for on November 13, 1885, he died, and the Federal Ninth Circuit did not release their opinion until December 26, 1885. Yet as almost everyone had suspected, once the case went before the federal court, the decision went the senator's way—this time it was the Sharon family's Christmas gift. Up until his last breath the senator had fought the state's judgment. A week before he died, he feebly instructed his aides:

> I am exceedingly weak in body and suffer great physical pain, but my mind is perfectly clear, [and I declare again] that I never signed [a marriage contract], I never addressed her as my wife in any communications [perhaps, only verbally, in social settings?]. [A]ll the "Dear Wife" letters [are] willful perjuries. [Therefore, I resist] her false claim to wifehood as I am duty bound to myself, my family and society, and [I divest my representatives] to contest her pretension in every legal and proper manner [as long as it takes to reverse the decision].[23]

Adolph Sutro, who was mayor of San Francisco at the time, did not mask his feeling when asked about Sharon's passing. He declared:

> That man is dead—I would not like to say much about him. I think that Sharon was a thoroughly bad man—a man entirely void of principles, honesty, and gentility—a selfish and grasping man capable of doing anything—committing any crime to accomplish his ends. Not a particle of generosity or character towards his fellow men—in his make-up. Utterly and entirely selfish—that's Sharon, and I think everybody will agree with me that knew him.[24]

Because one's station in life so often determines one's sympathies, it was not surprising that the popularity of Judge Sullivan's opinion fell consistently along class lines. Popular sentiment in most San Francisco neighborhoods sided with Terry's version of events, specifically, that the senator believed the document legally worthless and had used it to lure a hesitant Hill into an illicit affair. But the majority also believed that he had treated her as a companion, not as a harlot or a courtesan, since she had frequently appeared publicly within his inner circle of friends. Whether this meant that he had addressed or introduced her as his wife was never confirmed, but it was clearly a continuing topic of debate. Nonetheless, the public had no illusions about Hill's true nature and behavior—she was no innocent flower. She knew the contract was a contrivance and that her behavior was hardly exemplary. Still, most people thought that she honestly believed that the marriage contract had legal merit. Many people were inclined to believe the witness who had testified that Hill had talked to friends about filing a "breach of promise suit"—even while spying on the old roué. Hence, many agreed that more often than not she had acted more like a trollop than a wife.

More than a month after Hill's astounding victory in state court, Judge Terry had yet to make an appearance in San Francisco. People were not surprised, for his life had been in turmoil since the death of his wife, Cornelia.

During the summer her chronic illness of twenty years had worsened. For more than a dozen years, she had been seeking relief from her pain and vertigo in various California and Nevada health spas. Without the four boys to look after, she had recently been free to search for physical, and to a degree, emotional relief. Hence, she could be found soaking up minerals at hot and cold springs, choking down foul-smelling elixirs and enduring innumerable nauseating sulfurous poultices. But by the end of August 1884 she had become too frail to travel. She returned to Stockton, took to her bed, and was no longer strong enough to continue her search for medicinal deliverance. She contracted a persistent skin rash, her eyesight failed, she suffered from hypertension and nausea and she became dependent on large doses of opium to make each day bearable. Some speculated that she was suffering from "Bright's Disease" (disease of the kidneys). By mid-November, she was sleeping most of her days and nights away, so much so that her worried son, Sam, sent word to his missing and preoccupied father in San Francisco in a terse telegram: "Mother very much worse. Come home." Cornelia's death on December 16 had been expected by the family for several weeks. But when it finally came, Terry fell into a depression. A depression that was to deepen four months later when the rising star of the family, Sam, died of an infection following what everyone believed to be a minor surgical procedure. Sam had been the pride of the Terrys' older years. He had been the one son who had chosen to follow in his father's legal footsteps. In the Central Valley, Sam had become a successful lawyer and a politician, but unlike his father, neighbors and colleagues agreed, he was an engaging man, noted for his mother's calm level-headedness that was so conspicuously lacking in his father.

The sense of abandonment that possessed Terry after his wife's and son's deaths was reminiscent of the feelings he had had at the age of 12 when his mother had suddenly died. On both occasions it was for him a paralyzing experience. "Cornelia [u]nderstood his dispositions," wrote A. E. Wagstaff, "as no other person could, and she knew how to administer to his peculiar [habit of] overbearing bluntness."[25]

In the presence of women, Terry felt confident, and with their support his course of action seemed secure. His public and private words were forever laudatory and deferential whenever he spoke to women or of them. Women could restore order and they could be trusted, and his better and safer nature was manifested in the presence of loyal females. In contrast, men were different. Of them he was wary and mistrustful, and it seemed that when he was confronted by what he judged to be "disorderly and dishonorable" men, he could easily lose control. Short or long-term relationships with men were only rarely successful or satisfying. At age thirteen he had plunged into the aggressive military atmosphere of men in combat, and he carried the imprint of the aggressive male throughout life. When dealing with men, the boy-grown-into-manhood believed that he must be unflinching and fearless. Anything less would be personally destructive—for men meant to do him harm, unlike women, who had always protected him and provided him with a clear sense of direction.

When Terry finally did return to San Francisco at the end of January 1885 he threw himself into his largely neglected law practice. Facing him was a backlog of legal loose-ends, and to be expected, much of it pertained to *Sharon v. Sharon*. Tyler & Tyler had held onto their famous client for several weeks, but by March, Terry had become her sole legal counselor. This increased his legal burdens, but it also lifted his spirits and gave him a sense of purpose. It was a period of transition, and with past localities disappearing, his relationship with Sarah Althea Sharon also began to change. What at first had been simply a lawyer-client relationship became a relationship of confidant-friend, and eventually of lovers—with the constant encouragement (it was suspected) of a conniving Mammy Pleasant. "[Although] not a particularly rich man he was [surely] a famous one, she reasoned."[26]

News of this changing relationship was not a surprise to those who had been careful watchers of the two throughout the course of the trial. One reporter from *The San Francisco Chronicle* prattled, "The Judge and Sarah [were seen] sharing cherries and candy [during] a lull in the proceedings." "[The Judge and Sarah] engaged in light conversation [while the trial was continuing]." "While time hung heavy, Sarah demonstrated her penmanship to the Judge." "David Terry took up his old place in the courtroom beside Sarah Althea and looked pleased." *The Alta* added that "the two were seen at a social affair in the city," and the *Morning Call* revealed that while "Judge Terry was away on business, Mrs. Sharon stayed in his suite at the Palace." Perhaps this duality of empty lives and purposes made it inevitable that they would be drawn together. Terry was unable to live life without a sense of direction, and Mrs. Sharon had been directionless most of her life, and each seemed to fill a need in the uninhabited spots in the other's heart.

An announcement appeared in city newspapers a year after Cornelia's death that came as an unpleasant surprise to many of the judge's and Cornelia's old friends. Newspapers reported that on January 7, 1886, Sarah Althea Sharon (*nee* Hill) and David Smith Terry had been married. The marriage had been conducted by Father O'Connor at the Roman Catholic Parish House in Stockton—not at the Church high altar—"[for] the Judge is a Baptist deacon." The Southern Women's Guild of San Francisco—those devoted friends of Cornelia who had loyally stood by Terry through his ordeal with the Vigilance Committee, publicly protested his behavior in various city newspapers. Even ministers in Sunday pulpits could not remain silent.

Terry's oldest friends shrugged their shoulders and assumed he had gone mad—and said as much. Terry's long-time political ally, Stephen White, wrote to a friend, "Terry is just about old enough now to begin to get weak on the fair sex. These venerable mashes do funny things now and then."[27] Relatives on both sides of the families were displeased, but for the judge, incurring the resentment of his only living son, Clinton, was the most painful blow he suffered. Clinton Terry was so distraught by what he considered to be his father's dismal betrayal of his mother that he refused to attend the wedding. Later, in an attempt to make amends, the judge bought his son a large valley farm but his generosity did not seem to have any effect on his son's disappointed feelings.

Newspapers speculated excitedly about this odd relationship. The *Alta* wrote:

> [Sarah's] motives in contracting an alliance with so oppositely constituted a mate have been under discussion all day yesterday and today. [All] that is definitely settled is that Miss Hill has become Mrs. David Terry, and that she had clung to the name Sharon up to the moment of the transformation, as is shown by the name on the marriage license. [N]either party dressed for the occasion and immediately after the ceremony the Judge returned to his Fresno Law office where he spent the remainder of the day.[28]

It was also reported that the new "Mrs. Terry wanted no reporters in attendance nor would she be interviewed after the ceremony." A. E.Wagstaff's epigrammatic assessment of this unconventional union was as insightful as anyone's. It comes with the authority of interviews with the judge's nephew, John Warton Terry, some time after Terry's death:

> He had become attracted to [Sarah] for he firmly believed [that] she was villainously persecuted with gold. [He] recognized that she was a woman of talent and possessed a strong will and an unyielding determination. [These] qualities impressed him so deeply that he was blind to the subtle influences she employed in order to gain his confidence.
>
> [He] was disarmed by her audacity and her native brilliancy, and remarked to a friend [that] she was the smartest woman he ever met, for [l]ike some majestic Oak, whose huge trunk and rugged arms have defied the winds, the storms, and fury of the hurricane for centuries, the twining tendrils of the deadly ivy, with loving embrace, were quietly and insidiously undermining his strength and destroying his vital energies. Age had left no visible marks of its displeasure upon him, no warning of approaching decay, his majestic form still erect, [his] physical manhood, [his] intellectual power full-fledged; [but] the hour of greatest trial was approaching slowly but surely, and he was in the breach. Samson had his Delilah.[29]

Yet, it remained for one nectarial reporter to capture Hill's reasons for this Victorian mismatch. "After [months of] struggling unaided and alone, with the numerous minions of Mammon, [she] at last decided to let her head rest upon the bosom of her stalwart legal friend and defender and to be henceforth protected by him. Judge Terry has stood by her nobly [in her troubles] and the lady should be well satisfied with the kind fate that has landed her in such a safe harbor."[30]

The perfunctory tenor of their wedding day, however, gives no hint of the bitter disappointment and tragic outcome that the infatuation with this strong-willed, obsessed young woman would so shortly visit on this aging and sadly woebegone judge. He was a man who, perhaps in the inner reaches of his soul, knew that he had, in some uncontrollable way, sullied his deepest principles.

NOTES

1. A.E. Wagstaff, *The Life of the Ex. Chief Justice of the Supreme Court of California,* (San Francisco: Continental Publishing Co. 1892), 307.
2. A. Russell Buchanan, *David S. Terry: Dueling Judge,* San Marino CA. H. H. Huntington Library Press (1955) 198. See also *The Morning Call,* May 29, 1884.
3. Oscar Lewis and Carroll D. Hall, *Bonanza Inn* (New York: A. A. Knopf, 1939) 143.
4. Carl Brent Swisher, *Stephen J. Field: Craftsman of the Law* (Washington D.C.: The Brookings Institute, 1930), 322.
5. *The San Francisco Chronicle,* July 15, 1884.
6. David S. Terry. *The Political Record,* February 16, 1889 (San Francisco: California Poltical Record Publishing Co.) See also *The Political Record,* September 25, 1889.
7. Oscar Lewis, *Bonanza Inn,* 120.
8. —— *Bonanza Inn,* 148.
9. Robert H. Kroninger, *Sarah and the Senator* (Berkeley CA.: Howell-North, 1964), 105.
10. —— *Sarah,* 106.
11. Oscar Lewis, *Bonanza Inn,* 131.
12. Mammy Pleasant, who made it clear that she did not want to be called "mammy" was the object of much tabloid journalism during and after her life. Lynn M. Hudson makes the charge in her *The Making of Mammy Pleasant.* University of Illinois Press, (2003). Not only the tabloids but also later biographers were guilty of this practice. E.g, Helen Holdridge. *Mammy Pleasant.* (1953).
13. *Sharon v. Sharon*, 26 Fed. 337, October 3, 1883.
14. Oscar Lewis, *Bonanza,* 170.
15. —— *Bonanza,* 172.
16. —— *Bonanza,* 171.

17. —— *Bonanza,* 170.
18. —— *Bonanza,* 167.
19. Robert H. Kroninger, *Sarah,* 142.
20. December 24, 1884.
21. Oscar Lewis, *Bonanza,* 175–176.
22. Robert H. Kroninger, *Sarah,* 149.
23. Oscar Lewis, *Bonanza,* 181.
24. San Francisco Chronicle. April, 28, 1994.
25. A. E. Wagstaff, *Terry.* 61. The argument has been made that the excitement of Sharon-Hill trial, the long illnesses, and the times apart that Terry and Cornelia experienced weakened their bond in later years. It would be hard to confirm this argument one way or the other. But there is no doubt that Terry's love for his wife was deeply felt and enduring. In November of 1869, seventeen years into their marriage, Terry wrote from Nevada, during his mining adventures, to Cornelia in California the following: "You ask me if I [thought] of you on the 25th (their wedding anniversary)? No day passes [w]ithout thought of you. You [have been to me] my conscience, my priceless jewel, the 'fairest of ten thousand.' [I thank] the beneficent Ruler of the world for the blessing he has given me in you. This might seem strange language from a man of forty six to a women of forty to those who have not loved as we have, but you, my darling, will feel the truth." November 27th 1869. Terry Collection. Huntington Library, San Marino CA.
26. Holdrege, Helen. *Mammy Pleasant* (NY: G.P. Putnam's Sons 1953), 212; see also A. E. Wagstaff. *Terry*. 316–317.
27. Stephen Mallory White MSS, January 11, 1886. Cited in Swisher 330.
28. January 18, 1886.
29. A. E. Wagstaff, *Terry.*317–319.
30. *Daily Democrat*, January 7, 1886. Cited in Buchanan. 204.

Chapter Ten

Injury Unrequited

Nothing was settled and David Terry knew it. *Sharon v. Hill* was back on the federal docket, and local jurists were well aware that the "federals" rarely gave the state judiciary the attention it thought it deserved. Even more troubling for the newlyweds, the reviewing judges they were to face were two of Field's staunchest allies, Judge Matthew Deady and Judge Lorenzo Sawyer of the federal Circuit Court in San Francisco. The joyful victory celebration of the Christmas of '84 had become a faded memory for Sarah Althea Terry, even as the Christmas of '85 was certain to bring lamentable loss. And so it did—on December 26, just a year and a day after the Sullivan opinion, Judges Deady and Sawyer overturned Sullivan's decision. The federal judges did not mince words—they declared Sullivan's opinion "devoid of common sense."

Sullivan, the court declared, had made a false distinction between the legal validity of a secret marriage and the authenticity of a document. If the marriage document was a forgery—and the federal judges had no doubt that it was—then Sullivan's distinction was without merit. The authenticity of the document, not the propriety of marriages performed in secret, was the crux of the dispute. "In *Sharon vs. Hill*," said Deady, "the court need look no farther than the document itself for it is an inept fraud."[1] Even at the state trial, Deady insisted, all experts save Max Gumbel agreed that the document was fraudulent, and Gumbel was a "vile charlatan who had participated in forging it" (evidence for this charge was never presented).

Deady began his reversal with the statute of *domicilium*. The federal court should hear the case, he wrote, only if the domiciles of the litigants are in different states. In *Sharon v. Sharon,* Sarah Hill's lawyer, George Tyler, had gotten it wrong, said Deady—the litigants' domiciles were not in the same state. "Home is [not] where the heart is; it is where documents say it is." The fact that Senator Sharon had been living in a San Francisco hotel for more than a decade was irrelevant—it was not his legal residence.[2] Moreover, the federal case had been filed six months before the state suit had gone to trial, and even though the state opinion had been rendered, a final settlement was yet to be reached. Deady insisted that Senator Sharon "has a legal right to have his federal case go forward"—for a case not settled is a case not binding.

Then Deady turned to Terry's contention that Sharon had deceptively endorsed a document that he knew to be a forgery. Even were this true, he observed, and notwithstanding the ignoble behavior of both litigants, the document is no less fraudulent. A valid document of marriage requires the knowledgeable and willing consent of both participants by the right of the law *(de jure)*; moreover, a forged document cannot be made legal by a signee's state of mind.

Seemingly anxious to make Sharon's case for him, Deady next engaged in a series of arguments that can only be described as *petitio principii ad hominem*, i.e., question-begging personal attacks. Moreover, his arguments did not appear to give him the slightest pause. Deady began:

> Sarah is no ungathered rose. [She is] an hysterical dissembler. An obscure, unimportant person, without property or position in the world, [who] has deliberately [selected] as her friends doubtful persons from the lower walks of life. In contrast, Sharon is a person of standing [in] the community, [a man] of large fortune and manifold business and social relations, [one] bound to speak the truth [for] he is responsible for the correctness of his statements. Other things being equal, therefore, property and position are [a] guaranty of the truth of the possessor [for he who possesses them] has more to lose. [I]t is a fact founded on common experience, that [infidelity] in a man does not usually imply the moral degradation and insensibility that it does in a woman.[3]

When the judge put down his pen, his colleague, Lorenzo Sawyer, picked it up and composed arguments that were no less circular or charitable in the senator's defense. One would expect that if a man of Sharon's standing engaged in such a vile deed, there would be "producible evidence," he wrote, but there was none. Yet in contrast, Hill's confidants, all persons of lower position, confirm that she was lying, for if the document were authentic she would have confided, not in persons of poor reputation but in her brother who has been "her protector and guardian" for many years. Then Sawyer, after making it clear that poor people can frequently be social miscreants, followed it up by discussing his own version of 19th-century sexual politics: A woman accused of being unchaste cannot be believed when she denies the charge, nor can she be believed when she enters into a secret marriage, for only a woman of defiled character would make such an agreement. Said he:

> A woman who voluntarily submits to live with a millionaire for hire ought not, after she finds herself supplanted or discharged, be allowed to punish her paramour for the immorality of which she was the cause by compelling him to recognize her as his wife. If society thinks it expedient to punish men and women for the sin of fornication, let it do so directly. But until so authorized, the courts have no right to assume such function. [Therefore,] the estate is entitled to the relief prayed for, [hence] the Defendant Hill's contract shall be cancelled and surrendered.[4]

Robert Kroninger concisely lays out the judicial circularity that Deady and Sawyer employ:

> If she was not to be believed, then she did not enter into the extraordinary contract; if she did not enter into it then she should not be discredited as a person who would do so; if she was not discredited, then her testimony should be believed; [but] if her testimony was accepted then she did enter into the contract.[5]

The senator's victory in the federal court had come a year too late for him to embrace, so the legal repercussions, as inevitable as they were to be, would pass to his son. Fred Sharon, who from their first meetings had been fond of Hill, nonetheless, remained the loyal son faithful to his father's wishes. Fred Sharon was determined to pursue the matter until his father's name had been cleared.

This confirmed for David Terry what he had suspected from the outset. His wife would never get a fair trial in California's federal courts—Senator Sharon's connection with the federal judiciary was incorrigible. Federal judges in California, Terry fumed, were no less than the toadies of U.S. Supreme Court Justice Field. "Doubtless," he hinted, "when Field was serving as presiding Circuit Court justice of the federal court in San Francisco in the summer of 1885, he and his judicial comrades had laid the groundwork for winning in the federal what Sharon could not win in the state court."[6] As to be expected, the Sullivan reversal left the Terrys feeling cheated; but, in a certain inestimable way, the shabby personal treatment to which Mrs. Terry was being subjected in the public press was more disconcerting to her husband. The more the Terrys mulled over the federal opinions, the more determined Sarah Terry was to fight to restore her reputation—by "whatever means available," she often said.

In January of 1888, the Terrys enjoyed for fleeting moments a bit of good news. Judge Sullivan's opinion had been upheld in the state's highest court. The decision had come as something of a surprise to most San Franciscans who had long forgotten Sharon's appeal; it had been languishing in the high court for more than two years. Yet, for the Terrys, when Sullivan was finally upheld, it was a victory that had come at a high price, for later it was revealed that the court had been badly divided. The final opinion, to say the least, was tortured. The opinion was upheld by a single vote, and only after a majority (four judges) insisted on slashing the alimony and counsel fees to a minimum. The authenticity of the contract was debatable, they wrote, but the legality of its secrecy was moot, for the litigants' public cohabitation made it a free act by consent—thereby removing any issue of secrecy as an impediment. The upshot was that this politically important, but legally empty, opinion brought the Terrys only a moment of relief, for as quickly as the euphoria had come, it was gone again when Justice Field summoned the newlyweds before the Ninth Circuit Court of Appeal to face contempt charges for failing to surrender the marriage contract to the federal court as had been ordered.

Mrs. Terry curiously had been energized by the state's tepid Supreme Court opinion. Knowing that she again had been upheld made her more determined than ever to resist the federal order, "forever, if need be," she bawled at anybody who had the patience to listen. She would never turn over the marriage contract to anyone, for it was the only "document of evidence" that could prove her charges against Sharon—but, above all, she would certainly never turn it over to Field's corrupted federal court.

Her court date in front of Field would be early September of 1888. In the three years that had passed friends of the Terrys noticed that Mrs. Terry was becoming progressively more fragile of mind. She was more detached from the security of thinking things through rationally—her moods alternated between aspirations and agitations. So that by 1888 she was no longer willing to submit to any negative judgments that the courts might render, and this meant that she had become the driving force behind the couple's continuing litigation. Losing court cases was for her irrelevant, while having her position heard in public was everything. By contrast, her husband, fully aware of his wife's deteriorating mental state, found himself facing the upcoming district court appearance before Field fraught with danger. He may have been losing his zest for protracted legal fights, but he was also determined to confront their impending appearance before Field's federal court, as detached from Sarah's irrationalities as he could be.

In 1888, Justice Field was making his summer courthouse rounds in California, and Terry knew that the September hearing in front of Field would not be easy. Field would be eager to personalize the hearing by scolding and moralizing about Mrs. Terry's behavior—just the sort of thing that would cause his wife to explode emotionally. It would be more than a simple matter of listening to Field's judgments, for his colleagues who were to share the bench with him, Judges Sawyer and Sabine, had their own reasons for resenting

Sarah Terry. In particular, since the District Court ruling in 1885 against the Terrys, District Court Judge Sawyer had found the portentous Mrs. Terry to be a nuisance. In August of 1888, a month before the Terrys, appearance in Field's court, Sarah Terry had attempted to publicly humiliate Sawyer with a childish prank.

It happened when the Terrys found themselves traveling from Fresno to Stockton City on the same commuting train with Judge Sawyer. Mrs. Terry had, in the course of making her way down the train aisle, happened upon Sawyer, who was slouched in a lounge chair absorbed in a newspaper. Stopping behind him, she gave the hair curling out from beneath his hat a sharp upward tug, "a good wooling," she would later say—after which she gleefully scurried to her seat reporting her performance to a seemingly bemused husband. Onlookers said that they both enjoyed a hearty laugh. Later, by way of explanation, Terry said that he did not approve of his wife's behavior, but all the same could not help but laugh about it.

When the Terrys were next in San Francisco reporters asked her about the incident, but unfortunately, her response would not prove helpful. "I was paying 'Old Sawyer' back for his court decision (of 1885) and will do more to him when the time is right. Next time we will throw him in the bay."[7] The episode, trifling as it was, served again to energize San Franciscans' interest in the Terrys. Reporters, thereafter seizing on the opportunity to manufacture a narrative that would keep readers interested, would take every occasion to get Mrs. Terry's latest opinions on her impeding appearance before Judge Field. Well aware that her emotional stability was at best a thin reed, newspaper accounts whetted the public's appetite with her ill-advised and erratic outbursts. She made reporters' efforts worthwhile. Her defamatory insults and threats against Judges Field and Sawyer could be found in newspapers almost daily. Sadly, led along by his wife's impulsive behavior, Terry soon joined her with insults of his own. He, who had not forgotten the Harvey Lewis (clerk of the court) episode when he served on the California Supreme Court with Field, had always felt that Field, deep down, was pusillanimous. Intimidating Field, Terry concluded, would be easy and might very well lead the justice into altering his federal court opinions. These judges must understand, Terry reasoned, that it would not be the last time they would hear from them should the verdict go against Sarah.

Nonetheless, as David Terry's apprehension of the coming court date continued to grow, Sarah Terry's eagerness to face Field was without bounds. She thrived on newspaper coverage and was unrestrained in her comments: "I'll shoot the old man if he orders me to give up my marriage contract." David Terry's comments, on the other hand, were more circumspect. He sought to minimize outright threats, offering instead unproven albeit not unbelievable charges against the federal judges. "[W]e cannot expect justice, because the court already has been bribed by Sharon's millions," he said publicly.

On the day of the hearing, September 3, 1888, the courtroom was jammed with excited spectators, all waiting to hear the court's decision to be read. The daily reports of squabbling had increased interest so much that people filled every open space in the courthouse, every seat and aisle. The crowd anticipated a good show, and they were not to be disappointed. J.C. Franks, the U.S. Marshal in charge of order and security, unsure of what to expect, had circled the courtroom walls with peace officers. At precisely 10 o'clock three sober-faced judges entered the courtroom and seated themselves at the high bench. Their presence caused the cacophony of voices in the courthouse to fade away, and soon every eye was fixed upon the justices. The tensions in the room were palpable. Lewis and Hall describe the moment as "[a]rmies on the eve of battle."[8] The Terrys and Porter Ashe, son of Terry's old vigilante comrade P.B. Ashe, sat together at a table to the judges' right; while on the left were the Sharon family's three notable attorneys. The Sharons were represented by some of San Francisco's most experienced and high-priced lawyers—Richard Mesick, whose success rate and fees were higher than the region's Mount Tamalpias, and Sam Wilson and William Herrin, known to be two of San Francisco's best corporate lawyers, both of whom were accumulating fortunes as counselors for the Western railroad magnates. Wilson had been active in Field's aborted campaign for the presidency in 1884, and Herrin was soon to be the president of the Southern Pacific Railroad.

As presiding judge of the court, Justice Field sat between Circuit Court Judge Lorenzo Sawyer and District Court Judge George Sabine. Once all were seated, Field looked up from his papers and paused a moment waiting for the drone of muffled voices to fade away. The room becalmed and Justice Field drew his spectacles from a breast pocket, polished them, and nodded to the bailiff that the proceedings should begin. The bailiff announced the business of the court, and Field began reading what, if uninterrupted, would take about an hour to complete.

Judge Terry was hoping for the best but feared the worst. He looked over at his wife and saw that she was listening attentively. She was, he knew, searching for certain words and phrases—and how they were said meant almost as much to her as what was said. Terry was hoping that Field would stay on technical issues of law, for were he to stray off the matter of contractual fraud and onto the issue of his wife's moral deportment, he knew she would be hard pressed to control herself. Ten minutes into the recitation, however, and it was clear to the couple that their plan of preemptive verbal threats and intimidation had failed to alter Field's effort to besmirch Mrs. Terry's personal character. After an introduction of four or five pages summarizing the history of the litigation Field launched into a bitter attack on her character and behavior. Any objective person knew full well, he said, that the marriage document Mrs. Terry possessed could only be fraudulent for "she [has been throughout her entire life] an incorrigible cheat and liar—a woman without moral restraints." "Even Judge Sullivan," he added, "who found in her favor has said as much." As Field continued, Judge Terry struggled to keep his temper under control; for no matter how galling it was to listen to his old adversary describing his wife as a "woman without honor," he seemed determined to remain seated and silent. The same could not be said of Sarah Terry, however, who squirmed in her chair, fidgeted with her handbag clasp and finally, when Field declared "[that she] forthwith must hand over the contract," climbed onto her chair and screamed at Field, "How big was the sack that you have been paid by the Sharons for this verdict? I will never give up my contract."[9] Field doubtless was not surprised by her outburst for he did not flinch though he took a sip of water. Finally, he raised his eyes from the document and said in a subdued but steady tone, "Madam, sit down." She of course ignored him. He said it again, but she continued disgorging choice invectives that she had been saving for the occasion, whereupon Field turned to the Marshal of the court and said, "Mr. Marshal, remove the woman from the room." Marshal Franks quickly moved to remove her, but as he drew closer, Terry, no longer able to restrain himself, rose and placed himself between the Marshal and his distraught wife. He was determined, he said later, that no one should "manhandle her." "Sir," he growled at the marshal, "don't put a finger on my wife—get a written order." Ignoring Terry's warning, Franks reached around him in an effort to grasp Sarah Terry's arm. Terry, seeing that his warning had gone unheeded, instantly fell into to his celebrated state of impulsive anger and rage. With a massive right fist, the judge struck a blow full on the lawman's mouth. It was a blow so forcefully delivered that it dislodged one of Frank's teeth and sent it clattering across the hardwood floor. In an instant, four deputies were upon the judge. It took several minutes of furious tugging and hauling before they subdued the energized old man of sixty-four, but finally they wrestled him into a chair.

Sarah Terry, at the same time, was ushered from the courtroom. With her out of sight, Terry stopped resisting. On the surface he appeared calm, and when he muttered, "Let me go. I'll go quietly, I want to go to my wife," they released him. The crowd parted and the judge made his way to the foyer where he discovered Sarah again struggling with two guards in the marshal's anteroom. Terry's flashpoint returned, and again his reason became slave to his passions, and again several deputies blocked his way to his wife's side. This time, however, he drew an eight-inch knife from a shoulder sheath, and demanded that "[his] wife be unhanded."

The deputies returned Terry's fury in kind. Three of them locked his arms to his side while a fourth rested a pistol's steel barrel tip to his temple. For a fraction of a moment, Terry stiffened, but then he uncoiled and slowly relaxed. One deputy wrested the knife from his hand (Terry later contended that he had given it up freely) while others released their grip on him and allowed him to join his wife in the anteroom. By now she was sitting in a chair head down, attempting, not very successfully, to stifle sobs of rage and frustration.

The courtroom without the Terrys lost its appeal for most spectators—most vanished from the courthouse and were to be found in the streets spreading their own versions of what they had just witnessed. Meanwhile Justice Field continued reading the court's opinion to an almost vacant courtroom. He ended by declaring "petition denied." Terry and his wife, still under guard and with their patience wearing thin, demanded that the marshal release them for lunch: "Tell that bald-headed son-of-a-bitch, I want to go to lunch!" Terry shouted. In hindsight, it is clear from the Terrys demeanor that they had not expected to be detained, nor had they any notion of the severity of the treatment that was coming.[10]

After lunch, Field and his judicial colleagues engaged in a whispered debate for close to an hour on what should be done with the unruly pair. They emerged from consultations at mid-afternoon and announced to a crowd of puzzled reporters that the Terrys will pay for their transgression "[for] they have offended the majesty of the federal court and its offices. [Their] offenses [will] not go unpunished." Only later that evening did the Terrys and the reporters learn the full extent of the punishment. The charges and penalties were posted on the courthouse message board, and proved to be extremely harsh. Both Terrys were charged with "contempt of a federal court." Sarah Terry was sentenced to serve a month in jail for disturbing the peace and surreptitiously carrying a loaded pistol into the courtroom in her handbag. Judge Terry's punishment was even harsher. He was sentenced to serve six months in jail for disturbing the peace, drawing a weapon in the courtroom, and striking a U.S. Marshal who had been in the act of performing an assigned duty by a federal judge. Terry later said that he had expected to face contempt charges, but he was noticeably disturbed and insulted by the vindictiveness of the penalties leveled against his wife.

"How could a trifling outburst in court warrant a month in jail?" he asked. "She should serve no time in jail. What is more, she is gravid [pregnant], and has no business being in jail." Concerning his own sentence, Terry accused Field of lying about the incident—he had only defended himself, and he had not drawn a weapon in the courtroom. Not until he was outside in the courtroom's vestibule did he draw his knife, he said, noting that it was a "small knife." "What self-respecting man could do less in the defense of his wife?"

To these complaints Sarah Terry added a list of her own. She resented the "rough treatment" she had received at the hands of the deputies—it was especially rough treatment for a pregnant woman, and they had no right to search her handbag or to confiscate her pistol (she carried it, she said, because people on the street insisted on following her).[11]

Then, without pause, having finished her list of grievances, she slipped into a state of disconnected discourse that revealed more about her mania than it did about her circumstances. First in the order of her complaints, she lashed out at Justice Field's wife (Sue Virginia) for having had the temerity to attend the morning hearing. "What does she think I am, a prize elephant? I guess my husband has held as big positions as hers, and if she wants to see me she can call on me—she don't need to come to the courthouse to call."[12] Then she returned to her true nemesis; "I could have shot that old villain Field, but the time was not yet right." Many who heard her rambling that day were persuaded that her instability was becoming more and more unmanageable.

Twilight had settled over the mud-red flats of the bay shore line when the Terrys were finally escorted from the Lick House, (regarded by San Francisco the best hotel west of the Mississippi) through San Francisco's emptying streets to the wharf, where the ferry to Alameda-Oakland awaited. In an hour they would be in the Oakland jail (Marshal Franks felt that the situation would be more controllable if the Terrys were in jail on the other side of the bay). As the couple marched up the ferry gangway, Mrs. Terry bent over the hand railing and called down to a stevedore holding a mooring line. "Are you a member of the Laborers' Union?" she asked. He nodded that he was. "Well then," she said mournfully, "we need your support for we are the friends of labor." The seaman had just enough time to look puzzled before she was gone.[13] When the Terrys arrived at the Oakland jail their cells were resplendent with flowers and fruit from many sympathizers.

In the aftermath of this conflict, most legal observers believed that the penalties imposed on the Terrys were outrageously excessive and suggested that Field had once again turned vindictive. *The New York Herald Tribune* took the occasion to print the opinions of a dozen lawyers from New York and Washington, D.C., who declared that the Terrys' punishment far exceeded their crimes. Terry, of course, agreed and lost no time filing a petition to reverse the judgments, even though he warned his wife that she should not expect Field to lift a finger to remove the penalties unless public pressure forced him to do so. Terry's friends and colleagues agreed with this gloomy assessment and sought out former state Supreme Court Justice Solomon Heydenfeldt to intercede. Heydenfeldt had preceded Terry and Field on the California bench and was regarded as a friend of both men. He appeared willing to meet with Field, but only if Terry promised to abide by certain conditions. "My Dear Mr. Terry," he wrote, "[I shall] see Field tomorrow [and I hope you will allow me] to present a petition for your release. For it to be effective, [however, I must] be able to give assurance [that there] will be no violence or denunciation of Field after your release. Yours, as ever, S. Heydenfeldt, Sept. 10, 1888."

> Terry's reply came overnight: Dear Heydenfeldt, I reluctantly consent that an application be made. Field probably wishes to pay me for my refusal to aid his presidential aspirations four years ago. [Let me assure you] I will seek no personal satisfaction for what is past. You may say so as emphatically as you wish, that I will not commit a breach of the peace; [I will] avoid meeting any of the parties concerned; but I will not promise [to] refrain from denouncing the decisions of the authors. I believe [the decision] was purchased by the Sharon estate, and I would stay here ten years before I would say what I do not believe. If the judges wish to do what is right they would revoke the order imprisoning my wife. She was in [contempt] but she was [understandably] provoked by Field's besmirching her good name. When Field was a legislator, he thought that a court should be allowed to punish for contempt no more than five days. Yours Truly, D. S. Terry, September 10, 1888. (Terry was alluding to the contempt charges Field advocated in his 1850 encounter with Judge William Turner).[14]

The following afternoon, Heydenfeldt called on Field at his suite in the Palace Hotel. He presented Terry's petition. Field seemed to scan the request but then folded it several times over and tucked it into his vest pocket. He said nothing. Field's silence puzzled Heydenfeldt and made him uneasy, but not having the temerity to press the matter, he moved on to less sensitive topics. The justice would handle the matter in due course, Heydenfeldt thought to himself, and were he to push the matter further, he should do more harm than good. But despite Heydenfeldt's thoughts on the matter, it was soon evident that Field was in no mood to forgive and forget. Early the next morning he summoned Marshal Franks and three of the deputies who had been involved in the courtroom skirmish to his rooms. Together the men prepared affidavits refuting, point by point, Terry's account of the courtroom brawl, and whenever it appeared that the officers were stumped for a proper response, Field was more than willing to supply them with one. A week passed, and when Field appeared on the Circuit Bench in San Francisco, he announced in his familiar air of studied sobriety, "We have read [Judge Terry's] petition with great surprise at its omissions and misstatements. [He] has insulted the emblem of the Nation's majesty. Therefore I have denied his petition." The Terrys, he added gratuitously, would be expected to serve every minute of their sentences, and this court would make sure that they did.

With his "prayed-for relief" denied, Terry filed "petitions of revocation" with every state and federal court that he thought might conceivably have jurisdictional influence. His petition rested on the assumption that Field had filed false charges, specifically, that he had lied when he accused Terry of drawing a knife in the courtroom. He had not, and Terry insisted that he had newspaper accounts of the event that would prove the falsity of Field's claim; in fact Terry was hoping that Field would repeat his version of the September morning skirmish under oath. Field, however, was never going to fall into such an obvious trap. Rather, as the presiding judge of the court, he denied the petition and then, adjusting his initial charge—never admitting that he had misstated the situation—he inserted the conditional word *if* into the original charge:

> If the weapon had not been drawn in the courtroom it was only because a valorous deputy had prevented Terry from drawing it out from under his waistcoat, [for] any other [explanation] would be childish credulity. There is nothing [in the petition that warrants consideration for reversal that justifies] any remission of the imprisonment. [N]o one would be safer if the denial of a wrongful or criminal act would suffice to release the violator [from] the punishment due [his] offenses.[15]

In a fashion most galling to Terry, Field had settled the dispute, and as a consequence, Terry remained in jail without further review or relief. Several weeks later, the ruling was again challenged in the U.S. Supreme Court by friends of Terry on the grounds that Terry and his wife had been faced with sentencing by Field's court without legal representation. But Field turned the challenge away with the briefest response: "[Terry] needed no representation on the matter for his offense [was] committed in the presence of the Court." Field was letting the petitioners know, frequently to the astonishment of legal analysts, that as presiding judge he had witnessed Terry's behavior for himself, and no legal representative of Terry's need waste time arguing that the episode and Terry's performance were otherwise than he (Field) had declared them to be.

Terry's battle for a "reduced sentence," however, had not completely run its course. He would suffer one more indignity. In keeping with the Oakland jail's standard policy, the sheriff petitioned Judge Sawyer for Terry's release at the end of his fifth month in jail. The policy stipulated that for every month of good behavior, a prisoner earned five days of reduced time, and under these conditions, Terry had earned the right to be released from his sixth month of imprisonment at the end of the fifth month. Judge Sawyer, however, did not immediately pass judgment on the request, but instead wired Field—now safely sheltered on the East Coast—asking for guidance. The justice's wired response was immediate and unequivocal. Under no circumstances should Terry gain early release, for he had not yet demonstrated a proper "humility" before the court. Sawyer, Field insisted, must issue a public order denying the petitioner any time off. As a result, Sawyer's exegesis denying Terry's release was a paean of obfuscation. "Terry's contempt," he wrote, "was *sui generis*, the Judge did not qualify for early release for good behavior because unlike other prisoners [he] was not a criminal, but an offender of court protocol." The reduced sentence proviso applied only to criminals in state prison, Sawyer explained, not to officers of the court who by acts of misbehavior are being punished in a city jail for an offense against a federal officer.

A word should be added concerning Field's relationship with his judicial colleagues. He was never very close with any of them. His judicial gifts and his immense ego made it difficult for colleagues on the Supreme Court or the western district courts to form enduring positive relationships with him. Professionally, of course, they had great respect for him, but none was on intimate terms with him. Moreover, he was not reluctant to publicly describe some of his colleagues as fair-minded but "intellectually limited." Concerning his California associates he wrote, "It is not pleasant to find that the moment one leaves the State, all spirit and courage ooze out from the Federal Judges in San Francisco." Measuring Field's affiliation with the western federal judges, Judge Deady had the most positive relationship with him, judges Sawyer and Sabine seemed to be in a "sometime" brotherhood, and he and Judge Ogden Hoffman never cared for each other in the least. On the east coast, even his brethren on the U.S. Supreme Court referred to him as the "damned rascal" or the "wild bull".[16]

This jailing episode seemed to touch Terry in a profoundly life-changing fashion. To his mind, these public penalties of dishonor had been unfairly placed upon him, and as a result his feelings of resentment, frustration and powerlessness were exacerbated. And as jail-time dragged on his mood grew darker and his anger deepened—eventually turning his helplessness into irrational rage and spite. He vented this anger by publicly embracing rumors and accusations against Field's character—something he had always refused to do publicly while they were colleagues on the California Supreme Court.

Terry had heard of these rumors since Field's first days in Marysville and apparently had believed them but had refused to perpetuate them publicly lest he be judged spiteful, petty and, above all, dishonorable. But now this dishonored justice's confinement had made it impossible for him to repress these frustrations any longer. He repeated, in public correspondence and monthly editorials, every charge that people had, over the years, dredged up about Field. In a series of letters in the *San Francisco Political Record* Terry lashed out at Field accusing him of unbridled greed, cowardice and compromise. He borrowed passages from *The Gold Key Court* pamphlet of 1860—passages that had suggested that Field and Joseph Baldwin had taken bribes while on the state's highest court. He reminded readers that the pamphlet writer, James MacDougal, had claimed that "Terry had been the only honest judge on the California Supreme Court at the time." On the Judge Turner and Judge Barbour affairs of the 1850s, Terry put Field in the worst possible light. In those episodes, Field had cast himself as a courageous and principled man. Not so, Terry insisted. Field was a perfidious rogue, cowardly and unprincipled, and what was even worse, an obsequious sycophant who crafted legal opinions to fit the wishes and wants of powerful people.

Terry's sense of personal degradation now seemed to be complete. Reasonableness had vanished from his assessments, while passion provoked every response he had harbored for so many years toward his old enemy. Early on, his anger had been spontaneous—evoked when he perceived that his honor had been sullied. But now inner fatigue and the anguish of persistent defeat had become the pattern of life. Whenever Field or the federal courts were the objects of his musements, reason was subordinate to manic rage. From his cell he lamented:

> [K]nowing [Field's] past life and character and after watching his career for nearly forty years, [I am] strongly impressed with the belief that he is the same Field as ever, with all his vices intact, and age has only thrown the mantle of a more adroit hypocrisy over all. [S]uch judges, so appointed and inspired, are a scandal to the Republic, as well as a great peril [to the powerless].[17]

With his wife Sarah constantly by his side, the subject of the inequities they shared was seemingly the only important topic for discussion. When Cornelia was alive, she could restore Terry's sense of prudence and equilibrium, but with her gone, he was left with the succor of a woman who was herself in an endless state of self-pity and mental hand-wringing. She could not allay his discontent; she could only enervate his mistrust and foreboding. Even a presumed miscarriage suffered while Mrs. Terry was confined to the Oakland jail was to be blamed on Field. The unrequited jailhouse blues drove Terry to launch one legal appeal after another—appeals that in more reflectively cool and collected times he would have rejected as a waste of time, and in fact beneath his sense of propriety. As was inevitable, these legal fights also began to chew away at the Terrys' assets. Nevertheless, Terry fought on, goaded by a wife whose diminishing grasp on reality was making level-headedness, even in her best moments, ephemeral during his last two months of confinement.

Terry wrote furiously. He produced a protracted and somewhat tortured analysis of the legality of secret marriage contracts, he revived appeals before every state and federal court, he wrote personal letters to friends and colleagues, and he filed a *bill of revivor* (a request for the continuance of an abated suit) before the U.S. Supreme Court asking that the order requiring Mrs. Terry to yield up her contract to the federal court be rescinded. Finally, the U.S. Supreme Court ruled that the *bill of revivor* "idle." The claim, they wrote, had been directed against the wrong party. It should have been filed against Sharon's estate, not against the deceased Sharon. In point of fact, after Sharon's death, his attorney, William Barnes, had waited for a hushed two years' time to pass before filing a decree demanding that Sarah Terry hand over the contract as mandated by the 1885 federal court. Barnes' delayed filing of his decree provoked an additional confusion that was compounded at an 1888 hearing when Field calmly acknowledged that Terry had been caught on the horns of a dilemma. "[Judge Terry had attempted an appeal in due time]," Field wrote, "but as this was before the case had been revived, it was without efficacy—where a suit has abated by the death of a plaintiff after judgment, no appeal can be taken by the defendant until the case has been revived."[18]

From his cell Terry reacted: How could the U.S. Supreme Court declare the appeal frivolous? After all hadn't Field, one of the court's own, admitted that an appeal could not be filed until Sharon's lawyers brought charges on behalf of the estate? This additional confusion only corroborated Terry's conviction—the court was the puppet of the aging Field. At the end of each denial from the U.S. Supreme Court, Terry was forced to read the vexing disclaimer: "Justice Field [had, abstained] from taking part in the decision." Not likely, thought the impassioned Terry. "Sharon's wealth and Field's vindictiveness was manipulating every facet of this controversy." And Terry had no doubt that Field's hidden hand lay behind all of these legal setbacks. Setbacks that he accepted as just one more act of personal humiliation.

Every appeal brought only more bad news, and eventually even the California Supreme Court was to "betray" Terry. The state Supreme Court of 1888 had set aside the forgery question and supported the Terrys, but by July of 1889, with the makeup of the court having changed, the Terrys were left with but one court ally. The other six were loyal confederates of Justice Field. "Even," wrote the new court majority, "if the parties had believed themselves married, secret marriages in California are not legal, for such unions fail to have any acknowledged status before the world. It seems to us, [that] Sharon and Sarah lived not as man and wife but as man and mistress. [At no time did they cohabit; there was no common dwelling place—she visited his rooms and he visited hers]. Therefore, the Sullivan decision must be reversed. A new trial is ordered."

The most distressing aspect of this opinion, for Terry, was the court's willingness to allow Sullivan's position on the document's authenticity to remain unchallenged while a majority of the court argued for reversal on the strength of the litigants' moral behavior. Therefore, (Mrs. Terry), they declared, is a "dissembler," a "tainted woman." "Who could ever find her assertions believable? Even as [Sharon] was a man who had so long and so openly sinned, that he did not take care even to conceal his behavior from his family."

In contrast to her husband's attitude, Sarah Terry's view of the court's opinion was much less troubled but much more memorable. "Ask these Judges," she asserted, "what they would do if I were married by Father Burchard and the marriage was kept secret. My marriage with Mr. Sharon was just as binding as if I were married by a priest." She believed, as did many San Franciscans, that it was not the law's requirements that reversed the Supreme Court's own opinion but Sharon's money and Field's rank fear of "Terry on the loose." Field, Sarah Terry imagined, had refused to free her husband until he was safely ensconced 3,000 miles away on the eastern seaboard and Sharon's money had bought and paid for the court's new majority.

Terry, on the other hand, while apparently not discouraging his wife's delusional notions, believed that the roots for the harsh treatment he was receiving from Field ran much deeper; in part they arose from Terry's opposition to Field's appointment to the Supreme Court, and in part they were the result of his opposition to the justice's run for the presidency in 1876, 1880 and 1884. Terry and his friends judged Field to be vindictive and unforgiving, and clearly not a man to hold the most powerful office in the United States (the presidency). Terry's anti-monopolist colleague Stephen White reflected on Field's character: "[When Field] hates, he hates for keeps, and will do anything to win."[19] Terry was certain that these traits, plus Field's overweening opportunism, had been the real reason Terry had been forced to serve every minute of his sentence.

Some years after the story of Field's personal vendetta against Terry had become a popular explanation of their association, George C. Gorham, Field's law clerk and lifelong friend, made an effort to staunch this version of their relationship. Gorham wrote that Field had next to no connection with Terry at any time, and noted that the so-called witness to Terry's 1884 opposition to Field's presidential aspirations, Solomon Heydenfeldt, had roundly denied knowing that Terry had ever offered such an account. Heydenfeldt's letter of denial, printed in *The San Francisco Examiner,* was uncharacteristically harsh, Gorham pointed out, including such epithets against Judge Terry as "devoid of truth" and "a vile falsehood." But unfortunately, Heydenfeldt's disclaimer did not appear to fit the evidence available at the time.[20] Ten days after his note appeared in the *Examiner*, Heydenfeldt wrote Field reaffirming the accuracy of the newspaper article—apparently forgetting the letter that Terry had written to him promising not to harm Field if he were released (Terry's letter had contained the presidential story). A.E. Wagstaff, in his inimitable style, responds to Heydenfeldt's confusing charges against Terry: "Judge Heydenfeldt, willing to do homage to living power, or suffering by softening of the brain, denied [such a note from Terry, but] needless to say, there are but few men living who do not believe the statement made by Judge Terry [was true]."[21]

Nine months after Terry's release from jail, the Terrys, with a pressing need to improve their financial prospects, moved from Stockton City one hundred miles south to Fresno. By 1885, Fresno had become the hub of tree and vine agriculture in the southerly end of the Central Valley. In order to be closer to this shipping and financial center, in July of 1888, the law offices of *Terry & Bennett* moved to Fresno's Donahue block; but a month later this cluster of wood-laced buildings that comprised most of the block burned to the ground. *Terry & Bennett* lost not only their law offices, a large number of law books, legal drafts, and briefs, but seemingly also Mrs. Terry's cherished marriage contract. In reality, the contract may or may not have disappeared in the Fresno fire, but there was no question that the sense of injustice that David and Sarah felt they had suffered at Field's hands had not been quenched. They continued to ridicule and threaten the justice in the public press so severely, in fact, that Field's California colleagues and friends urged him not to return to California during the summer of 1889. These concerns, however, appeared to vanish when it was announced in Washington, D.C., that the justice and his wife were planning a long vacation in Europe during the summer (in fact, the justice was not scheduled to preside over the San Francisco federal court for another two years).

It was, therefore, a surprise to his friends when it was published that Field had cancelled the European trip and was planning to return to California for the summer—perhaps, as later events would seem to suggest, with a willingness to confront the Terrys and settle their differences once and for all. When asked by reporters several weeks before leaving Washington whether Terry's threats gave him pause, Field replied with his customary pious cant:

> I cannot and will not allow threats of personal violence to deter me from the regular performance of my judicial duties at the times and places fixed by law. As a judge of the highest court of the country, I should be ashamed to look any man in the face if I allowed a ruffian, by threats against my person, keep me from holding the regular courts in my circuit."[22]

But as fearless as this declaration sounded, it was also obvious that he had no intention to venture into the frequently "lawless" west defenseless. He and U, S. Attorney General William H. Miller hatched a plan. The two agreed that, while in California, federal and state deputies would track and report the Terrys' whereabouts around the clock, and that the San Francisco marshal's office would be given the responsibility of coordinating this surveillance through the state's newly expanded telegraph service. It was also understood that the U.S. Deputy Marshall David Neagle would remain by the justice's side as long as he was traveling on the west coast.

Deputy David Neagle, Field's bodyguard, was a familiar figure around San Francisco, for he had grown up at the base of Telegraph Hill in the city's Irish ghetto. He was no stranger to Terry's reputation, for as a schoolboy the judge had been a sometime hero in Neagle's neighborhood. (Neagle was a 10-year-old when Terry stabbed Sterling Hopkins and thirteen when the judge shot and killed Senator David Broderick.) When Neagle had become a man he was known to the newspaper-reading public as "the smallish deputy who had courageously wrested [the knife from Terry's hand]" during the nefarious courtroom fracas of 1888.

Neagle was in his mid-twenties when he left San Francisco seeking a fortune mining silver in the Dragoon Mountains of Arizona. But digging for silver ore in the Arizona Territory proved to be as fraught with failure as it was exhausting, and his dreams of overnight riches melted away in the relentless heat of the desert. By year's end, however, he had found work as a bartender-bouncer and peacekeeper in Arizona's famous saloon-town Tombstone. In short order he had become Tombstone's chief of police. Arizonans described him as "tough and fearless and cocksure," His physical size (5 foot 5, and 130 pounds) was not indicative of his physical skills. He was said to be, agile, dogged, and "as quick as a cat."

Years later he relished telling neighborhood listeners of his first encounter with one of Tombstone's famous Earp brothers. On a breezeless summer's afternoon while napping on the jailhouse porch, Neagle would begin, one of the Earps (which one was never made clear) approached and ventured, "So you're running this camp?" "Well yes I am," Neagle replied. "Wait a moment while I get my pistol." Then the deputy would pause before finishing his tale, offer a sly smile, and declare that when he returned to the porch, pistol securely strapped to his side, the Earp brother was nowhere in sight.

When Justice Field reached San Francisco in June of 1889, a telegram from Attorney General Miller awaited him. Miller cautioned him to keep their arrangement secret, "lest the Terrys find out."[23] It was a puzzling and somewhat foreboding warning that seemed out of place, since public knowledge of Field's arrangement with Miller might have provided just the deterrence they were looking for to keep the unrequited Terrys at bay.

Nevertheless, Field's California summer trip proceeded much as planned without any "unpleasantness from the Terrys" through June and July. During those months Field traveled up and down the state, while the Terrys seemed to be minding their own business at home in Fresno. Terry stayed close to home preparing for yet another of his wife's appellate court appearances in San Francisco—it was scheduled for the second week of August.

However, on the afternoon of August 13, uneventful days were about to become eventful. Field was in Los Angeles, and having finished his judicial hearings earlier than anticipated, he decided to board the Southern Pacific overnight train to San Francisco, rather than wait for the morning commute.

The hot afternoon light was fading into the cooler shades of evening when Justice Field boarded the night train for San Francisco. It was 5 p.m, and as usual, the ever-vigilant Neagle was close by his side. Minutes before the train pulled away from the station heading for San Francisco the deputy received word by telegram that the Terrys were planning to board the train in Fresno. (The Terrys' court date had arrived, and they were due in San Francisco's appellate court on the morning of August 14. Having known of Terrys' plans makes one think that San Francisco deputies had been staking out his home all summer.)

As was his habit, Field was already in his sleeping berth when Neagle brought him news that the Terrys would board the train at Fresno, and as was also his habit, whenever the subject of David and Sarah Terry came up, Field would feign no concern. Neagle and Field knew from earlier conversations that they'd be "ready for them whatever their intentions." The justice and his deputy had discussed what to do about the Terrys many times before, and both agreed that Judge Terry was a dangerous, mercurial-tempered man of immense size and strength, a person whose uncontrollable habits made him entirely unpredictable. Yet now, making matters worse, he was married to a licentious, unstable woman whom he seemed prepared to follow into all manner of madness. The two men calculated that the Terrys would be on board the train for the last three hours of the trip into Oakland, and that Neagle would keep an eye out for them. By the evening of the next day, at the end of what would prove to be a momentous, albeit tragic day, many people were lead to wonder if it had been a secret plan or mere coincidence that the bitter rivals were riding the same train on the same day. Later Mrs. Terry explained that it never had been their intention to be on board the train that Field was riding. In fact, she added, they had been keeping track of Field's whereabouts through daily newspaper reports, and the news accounts had indicated that Field would not be heading northbound until the evening of the 14th. Nevertheless, the rumor persisted; it was no coincidence that their paths crossed. And, were it not a coincidence, many maintained, it was not likely to have been in the Terrys' plans, because their court date on the 14th had been set for months prior to Justice Field's appearance in California.

The sun had disappeared below the rusty-colored waters of the Pacific Ocean when Field finally fell asleep in his private sleeping compartment. The Southern Pacific made numerous stops east of the mountains before turning northeast on its slow grind up and over the Tehachapi Mountains. At the summit, as commuters well knew, the train would finally pick up speed and rattle down the northern slope into the central valley where it would then begin its long crawl north from the little rail stop at Mojave (the length of the state made the journey through the Central Valley seem an arid, endless trek). Travelers agreed that the basin's interminable sameness and the train's innumerable stops throughout made it the most irksome part of the entire north or south trip.

Neagle sipped strong coffee to keep himself awake while he checked passengers boarding or disembarking at each dusty stop. As expected, slightly after 2:30 a.m. the train labored to a clangorous, metallically odorous stop in Fresno, and the ever-vigilant bodyguard, leaning well-out from the sleeping car platform, spied in the slate darkness the silhouette of a tall man and a petite woman. They carried a "grip pack" between them, suggesting that they did not plan to stay at their destination for long. Neagle was certain that the silhouetted couple boarding the train four cars forward were the Terrys—but they did not act as if they knew that their nemesis, Justice Field, was aboard.

At 8:30 that morning after numerous stops the train pulled into the depot at Lathrop for a 35-minute breakfast stop. Lathrop, located seven miles south of Stockton, still held pretensions of competing with Stockton for control of the San Joaquin Valley's shipping trade (after all, it was still the central valley storage center for the Central and Southern Pacific's rolling stock). Neagle advised the awakening Field that, as had been expected, the Terrys indeed had boarded at Fresno. Neagle added that it might be wise for Field to remain on the train and take his breakfast in the passenger's buffet. Field, however, waved him off. He would not change his plans for the Terrys. He had had decent meals in Lathrop's travel restaurant before, and he meant to have another. The bodyguard shrugged and assisted the hobbling old judge off the train and into the restaurant (Field's youthful knee collision with a New York City coal wagon had grown into a chronic pain of old age).

When the two men entered the restaurant they positioned themselves at a table in mid-room facing the double-door entrance so that they might see the Terrys if they entered the dining room. Scurrying patrons crowded the dining room—60 or 70 of them, about a third of whom were women. There was much confusion and clatter as passengers hurriedly ate breakfast—a thirty-minute train stop meant that there was no time to dawdle.

Field and Neagle had been seated for only a few minutes when the Terrys pushed their way through the doors into the dining hall. The restaurant's proprietor, James Stackpole, met them at the entrance and beckoned them to follow him to a table. Judge Terry fell in behind Stackpole, but Mrs. Terry, brought up short when she caught sight of Field watching them from his seat in the middle of the room, wheeled about and returned to the train without saying a word to her husband—Field and Neagle feigned indifference and continued eating. Stackpole, who was a friend of Terry's and had been warned by wire that the two judges were on the same train, wanted to avoid trouble. He led Terry to a far corner of the room away from Field. Once seated, Stackpole leaned toward Terry and whispered, "Is Mrs. Terry planning to make a disturbance?" Terry's first reaction was a quizzical gaze. "Why do you ask?" he replied. "Because Judge Field is sitting over there," Stackpole said, nodding in Field's direction. Terry first looked surprised and then agitated. "I don't know, there may be trouble. Go to the entrance and don't let Mrs. Terry back into the restaurant," he said.

What next transpired took but a few moments, even though it has been the subject of countless hours of heated debate and reams of legal depositions. When Terry was satisfied that Stackpole was in a position to intercept his wife's return to the restaurant, he rose and headed down an aisle that was directly at Field's back. Both Field and Neagle were aware that Terry was approaching, but neither man pretended to give the slightest notice. Many have wondered what was going through Terry's mind as he moved along the line of diners toward the justice's place at the table. Terry's long-time law partner, W. T. Baggett, later ventured at least one plausible answer:

> I have had frequent conversations with Terry about Field and he has often told me that Field used his court and his power as a judge to humiliate him, and that he intended to humiliate Field in return. "I will slap his face if I run across him, but I shall not put myself out to meet him. I do not intend to kill him; I shall insult him by slapping his face, knowing that he will not resent it as he is a coward".[24]

Assuming Baggett's assessment is correct, one might speculate that Terry was on his way out of the restaurant in an effort to head off his wife's return, but that on the way out, perhaps by impulse or plan, he maneuvered himself toward Field's table. "I'll slap the old man's face"—hadn't he so often told his wife he would do it? "When would there ever be a better chance?" "Sarah would laugh." "It would help salve her resentments." "Perhaps an insult would be enough, as it had been when 'Allie' had pulled Judge Sawyer's hair." In any event, he may have thought, Field would be humiliated and much too cowardly to respond—but best of all, "Allie" would laugh and be pleased.

When Terry reached Field's right side he bent forward and slapped the justice on the right cheek—it was a slap that was hard enough to cause diners to look up from their egg plates and oatmeal bowls. Neagle, sitting to Field's left, instantly rose halfway from his chair. Perhaps edgy from too much coffee and sleeplessness, Neagle drew his 44-caliber Colt pistol from his waistband. Holding it with both hands, he swung it into Terry's chest and fired point-blank. The bullet struck Terry's right lung and plunged downward severing his lower spine. The force of the shot at so close range instantly knocked the huge man backward onto the floor. As he fell, Neagle shouted, "Stop, I am a United States Deputy Marshal" and fired again. The second bullet creased Terry's ear but did no more real damage. Yet no more damage was needed. As Terry fell onto the sawdust floor his face was frozen in the sightless gaze of a dead man. The weapon's blast was deafening, and in an instant the room was filled with smoke and the acrid smell of spent gunpowder. People in panic rushed for the doorway. In the doorway Mrs. Terry broke free from Stackpole and hurried to her husband's fallen body—a bystander ripped her handbag from her arm. Later it was found to contain a Derringer. When she reached Terry, she fell across his chest, and in seconds her bodice was covered with blood. The shot to his lung had produced little external bleeding, but his punctured ear lobe was bleeding profusely, so much so that many later testified that the second bullet had found its mark in Terry's skull.

The sight of the stricken Sarah was piteous to behold," said one bystander. "Madness has overtaken her," said another. Her actions were alarming to all who witnessed them. At one moment she lay prostrate over her husband's bloody body in unbridled resignation or on her knees stroking his lifeless face. The next moment she was on her feet and clinging to the coats of burly men, demanding that they get a rope and "lynch the murderers, for they have slain an unarmed man, and have killed the only friend I had on earth." Sarah Terry repeated this behavior for several minutes—first hurling herself at her husband's lifeless form, and then darting about beseeching bewildered onlookers to help her mete out the justice her husband's murderers deserved.

All the while this was going on, Neagle was retreating to the rear wall of the dining room, fanning his pistol about in an effort to keep at bay anyone who might attempt to restrain him. "Stand back," he shouted, "I'm a U.S. Deputy Marshal and I'm protecting a Justice of the United States Supreme Court." Men prudently kept their distance, and moments later when the crowd seemed to be calming, Neagle cleared a path and returned to Field's side. Surprisingly, throughout the entire uproar, Field had stayed frozen to his table—"he remained fixed in his chair, motionless, and white as a marble," reported *The New York Herald*.[25] When Neagle reached Field's side, he firmly pulled the justice to his feet and pushed him before him out the door toward the train that was now pressurizing its boilers in preparation to leave the station. As they made their way through the crowd, Field paused long enough to offer a hasty explanation to a restless crowd. "My name is Judge Field. Judge Terry threatened my life and attacked me and my deputy marshal has shot him." Then, sensing that he was in the Central Valley where sympathy was decidedly in the stricken man's favor, he said no more but moved toward his sleeping car and quickly scrambled aboard. Neagle followed and slammed the stateroom door behind them. Then he bolted it.

By now Sarah Terry was pounding on the Pullman's side panels with a heavy ladle she had taken from the restaurant. It was noisy enough to cause Neagle to shout through a half-open window, "Keep that woman away from us or I'll shoot her." Mrs. Terry, inattentive to the threat, continued to plead with the crowd: "Why don't you hang [them]? They have shot an unarmed man. [Field] is too cowardly to be given a trial, [he] hired an assassin. They shot [my husband] down like a dog in the road. [My husband] was the soul of honor." Back inside the restaurant a group of men removed Terry's body to an adjacent barbershop where it was laid out on the floor with a barber's apron as a shroud. Later in the day, it was moved to the Stockton morgue where a coroner performed an autopsy and submitted a report, then the body was moved to a nearby funeral home where mourners and spectators gathered. Some were there to pay respect to a fallen hero, but others had gathered merely to observe the curious behavior of the widow. Throughout the night Sarah Terry's noisy mortuary lamentations could be heard by passers-by, unremitting, unrestrained and unconsoled. For two nights and a day she sat beside her husband's body, neither eating nor sleeping.

On August 16, two days after the shooting, the body was moved to Stockton's Episcopal Church. A thousand mourners crowded into the church's pews where they fanned and perspired their way through a two-hour service for the dead. Outside stood another thousand in the noonday sun, waiting for a procession to leave for the cemetery. When the retinue finally did leave for the Rural Cemetery, fifty carriages joined the cortege, and as had been the case at the mortuary, many who gathered at the grave side were authentic mourners, grieving the judge's death, but others were just onlookers curious to see if Sarah could control her "jim-jams." A curious reporter pointed out that, with the exception of an initial greeting, no words passed between Sarah Terry and her stepson, Clinton. As the judge's only living child, Clinton had insisted on making the burial arrangements—arrangements that only added to Sarah Terry's misery, for Clinton was unyielding on the matter of how his father was to be buried. He must be buried between the bodies of his mother Cornelia and his older brother Samuel. Clinton was determined to make sure that when stepmother Sarah died there be no burial space available by his father's side.

The day of the funeral had been blistering hot since sun up, and it stayed that way well after the sun had fallen out of sight. The Episcopal priest was ill, so the interment service was conducted by a church layman assigned to the duty. Newspapers reported that the pervading sounds at graveside were the stirring of a hot breeze rustling leaves of cottonwood trees and the spasmodic groaning of an increasingly erratic widow. After the last words were uttered and most of the crowd had moved away, and the harsh summer sun had begun to release its grip on the land, the curious who lingered watched as the disconsolate Sarah Terry was pried from her husband's casket top and carried to a waiting carriage by her brother and his friends.

As the bitter days of August faded into the month of September, the memory of the slain jurist grew in the esteem of neighbors up and down California's largest inland valley, but very few tears were shed for the widow. *The San Francisco Chronicle* framed the situation candidly. "The day Sarah married David S. Terry, was the day she signed his death warrant."[26] Nor was this irony lost on the editor of *The San Francisco Call* when he published a prescient poem Sarah Terry had written in the Oakland jail cell four months earlier. It was addressed to Judge Lorenzo Sawyer, but it was just as appropriate for her old judicial enemy Justice Field. It was a fitting *hic jacet*:

Hark! From the tombs
Warning sound Thine ears attend the cry,
Thou unjust Judge, come view the ground
Where you may shortly lie.

Oh, do not let the power of wealth
Blind your judicial eye;
Nor let [one] get by stealth,
What gold ought not to buy?

Oh, cursed gold that would corrupt
The judges of the land,
Give way to honesty and truth,
And let the mighty stand!

Broadway Jail
San Francisco
April 7, 1889.[27]

NOTES

1. *Sharon v. Hill.* 26 Fed. 337, October 1883.
2. Robert H. Kroninger. *Sarah and the Senator* (Berkeley CA.: Howell-North, 1964) 180.
3. *Sharon v. Hill,* 26 Fed. 361. October 1883.
4. Robert H. Kroninger. *Sarah,* 186.
5. —— *Sarah,* 187.

6. David Smith Terry, *Character and Career of Stephen J. Field,* (1889). 2.
7. George H. Gorham, *The Story of the Attempted Assassination of Justice Field* (New York Da Capo Press, 1968). 274. See also: *Some Opinions and Papers of Stephen J. Field.* v. 5 pamphlet 11, The Ninth Circuit Court, United States Supreme Court.
8. Oscar Lewis and Carrol D. Hall. *Bonanza Inn.* (New York: A.A. Knopf), 189.
9. *The San Francisco Chronicle,* September 4, 1888.
10. This account appears in O. Lewis *Bonanza Inn,* 191, but is disputed by many Terry supporters.
11. *The San Francisco Chronicle,* September 4, 1888.
12. *San Francisco Call,* September 4, 1888.
13. H.R. Harris transcript. 223. Printed in Swisher, *Craftsman of the Law.*336.
14. George C. Gorham. *The Story of the Attempted Assassination of Justice Field,* 1893, in Stephen Field's *Reminiscences,* 1893, 288–289.
15. *In re Terry,* 36 Fed. 419, September 1888. See also: *Some Opinions and Papers of Judge Stephen J. Field.* The Ninth Circuit Court of the United States Supreme Court. Vol. v, Pamphlet 11. September 3, 1888. *Bill of Revivor,* rendering Judge Sullivan's decision on William Sharon's opinion. See. *Some Opinions:* v. 5 pamphlets 5,7, Appendix 1, and pamphlet 6. (U.S. jurisdiction first attaches). Notice that Field overtly condemns Sarah Terry toward the end of judgment using Judge Sullivan's own words, but by the time he does she has already been ushered from the courtroom. What angers Sarah is the dictum that she must give up the marriage license that Field, once again, calls a forgery. Stephen J. Field to J. DeBarth Shorb. October 27, 1886, J. DeBarth Shorb Collection, The Huntington Library. (San Marino, A.).
16. *Memoirs.* Cornelius Cole, 15, (1908). Cited in Christian Fritz, *Federal Justice in. California*: 1851–1891, (1991). 40.
17. David S. Terry. *Political Record,* February 16, 1889. 59.
18. *Sharon v. Terry,* 36 Fed. 337. September 1888.
19. White to W.D. Grachy, August 21, 1889 White MSS. Carl Brent Swisher. *Stephen J, Field: Craftsman of the Law* (Washington D.C: The Brookings Institute, 1930). 356.
20. George C. Gorham, *Assassination,* 296–297.
21. A. E. Wagstaff. *The Life of the Ex. Chief Justice of the Supreme Court of California: David Terry* (San Francisco: Continental Publishing Co.:1892). 396.
22. George C. Gorham. *Assassination,* 299.
23. In a letter to Marshall Franks on April 27, 1889, Miller warns the marshall to keep the arrangements secret from the public (especially the Terrys). See Swisher, *Craftsman,* 344.
24. *The Daily Examiner.* August 16 1889. *The San Francisco Chronicle,* August 16, 1889.
25. *The New York Herald.* August 15, 1889.
26. *The San Francisco Chronicle,* August 16, 1889.
27. Robert H. Kroninger. *Sarah,* 168.

Chapter Eleven

Dishonor in Absentia

R.B. Purvis, sheriff of Stanislaus County, who was traveling on the same train as the two judges (apparently by chance) did what he could to bring order out of the confusion that had descended on Lathrop. After Field and Neagle had left the restaurant, Purvis ordered that Terry's body be removed from the restaurant to an adjacent barbershop. (A barber's apron was used as a shroud.) Then, he returned to the sleeping coach to confront Justice Field and his bodyguard Neagle. As the interrogation proceeded, the crowd milling about the train was becoming more and more restless, demanding that Field be brought before them. It was a situation that led Purvis and Field to agree that it would be prudent to move the train north to Stockton. The seven-mile trip to Stockton gave Field more than enough time to convince the sheriff that under no circumstances would he submit himself to an arrest without the proper warrant. Purvis, however, seemed equally determined not to allow a justice of the United States Supreme Court and his bodyguard to disappear from the scene without an official investigation. Purvis offered to let the justice continue on to San Francisco, but only on the condition that Neagle be held in Stockton until Field had returned to Stockton and Purvis had had time to finish his investigation. Under no circumstances, said the sheriff, would Neagle be released from custody without there being a proper hearing conducted.

By the time the train had reached French Camp just minutes from Stockton City, each man's bargaining position was firmly in place, and a deal was struck. It was agreed that Field would not be detained. He would continue on to San Francisco, but in exchange Neagle would submit to arrest with an assurance from the sheriff that he would be locked away in the Stockton jail, safe from the anger of any mob that might appear outside the jail. Field affirmed that after he had had a few days to put his affairs in order, he would return to Stockton for a formal hearing on the entire incident. Once the arrangement was settled Purvis and Neagle disembarked at French Camp and Field continued on to San Francisco. Purvis and his prisoner rode the rest of the way into Stockton by covered carriage, making sure to keep to the back roads. In Stockton, Neagle was locked in an inner cell in the city's jail as far away from the sight and sound of passers-by as it was possible for him to be. For a time, no one knew his whereabouts.

The astonishing news, however, had preceded Field into San Francisco by wire service and the recent installation of a telephone hook-up, so that when the justice stepped off the Oakland ferry, a crowd of reporters was waiting with anticipation. He had little to say to them, but one writer described Field as ashen faced but calm, "as if killing a man were [an] everyday occurrence." It soon became clear as events unfolded that at no time was it ever in Field's mind to return to Stockton City. Quite the contrary, he was making plans to deliver Neagle from the Stockton jailhouse from the moment he left Sheriff Purvis.

Even as Field was forging his plan to free Neagle, his antagonist, Sarah Terry, was busy pressing her charge that both men be brought to justice in a Stockton courtroom. On August 15, therefore, the morning after the shooting, Mrs. Terry appeared at the Stockton County Courthouse and filed complaints against both Neagle and Field, charging the deputy with cold-blooded murder and Field as accessory to the crime. The Stockton Justice of the Peace, H.V.J. Swain, did his best to discourage Sarah Terry from filing, arguing that it was a futile gesture, an utter waste of everybody's time. Yet, not surprisingly, and true to her nature, she remained unyielding. "I shall not change my mind; I want that old unjust judge tried along with his bodyguard." Eventually Swain relented after some local political and business leaders rallied to her support. Thereupon, the city council agreed that Stockton's Deputy Sheriff Thomas Cunningham go to San Francisco with a simple but impossible task—if the justice refuses to return to Stockton willingly, then he should be forcibly returned to Stockton City. Understandably, Cunningham faced his assignment with not a little trepidation.

While many San Joaquin County residents were caught up in the excitement of arresting a federal justice, most political and legal city leaders privately agreed that Cunningham was wasting everybody's time. Stockton's young prosecutor, District Attorney Avery White, however, was an exception. White thought Cunningham's effort was never vain posturing. White signed the document of complaint, stating publicly that he confidently awaited the prospects of confronting the powerful federal justice in a San Joaquin County courtroom. Nonetheless, not too many days had passed when White realized that the prospect of facing the old judicial lion inside or outside Stockton's city limits would prove to be a daunting affair—one that was well beyond his powers to advance. Interestingly, White talked about the episode with a *San Francisco Examiner* reporter some 30 years later—"[In the span of three days I learned] that the laws are what men want them to be; that men are bought and sold; [and] that judges are men. I should have known it in advance. But even today, as I look back, I cannot see that I acted wrongly for a boy."[1]

When it came to finding someone to blame for Terry's death, however, most Californians had no illusions. In reality, it was neither Field nor Neagle who was responsible for the judge's death. Terry's body lay in Stockton's Rural Cemetery of his own choosing. His death was the consequence of his deeply-rooted mania, for had he not been a slave to his own eccentric sense of honor—that is to say, had he not put his own head on the block—things would have turned out differently. Of course most citizens in the central valleys also believed that, given half a chance, Field would not have hesitated to punish the man he despised. They believed that Field, with the assistance of highly placed friends in Washington, had been planning a showdown with the Terrys for months—that Field intended to have Terry shot if the Terrys were to give Field the slightest provocation. There were hundreds of farmers and laborers up and down the inland valleys, moreover, who had no doubt that Field ambushed Terry. As the valley's conspiratorial slang put it, "Terry had been bushwhacked by Field's nervous deputy, a man who had [already earned a name for himself] as one who pulled a mighty quick trigger." Such sentiments were held as much by prominent state leaders as they were by workers. Los Angeles District Attorney Stephen White, for example, in a letter written to George R.B. Hays asserted, "To be candid, it makes me tired to listen to the flunkey talk that is going on at this time about a man [Field] who, in my judgment, is one of the most dishonest characters that has ever discharged the function of a judicial office."[2] A later letter from White to Terry's friend James McCreery, however, also makes it clear that Terry's sympathizers harbored no false hopes: "That Terry-Field episode was a most unfortunate affair. [But] I think it [would be] a grave mistake to assert federal control of the case."[3] By contrast, the business and legal establishments in San Francisco and Sacramento held no such disapproving feelings toward the justice and his bodyguard. In the eyes of the financial classes, Field was "a civilizing force out West." He represented a political change, a change from "frontier" or "miners' law" toward a judicial system that was ordered and hence predictable. If California were to have an orderly society the kind of society that protected "entrepreneurial endeavors and financial enterprise then the lawless [read: southerners and their henchmen] must be stopped."

Because conglomerates controlled the wire services and the news releases that reached the East Coast (telegraphic services in the west were usually owned and operated by the railroads or its subsidiaries), the events of that fateful day were cast in the most heroic and complimentary light possible for Field and Neagle, even as the Terrys suffered the most ignoble characterizations.

The news releases reaching the East Coast concerning Terry and his wife were more than exaggerated—they were intemperate to the point of fanaticism. The wire-service bulletins were filled with turgid accounts of the judge's "barbarism." He was described as a "lawless, bloodthirsty monster—a law unto himself, [a] vicious outlaw, with friends in high places." *The New York Tribune's* description of the shooting proved to be a verbatim account of the railroad-owned *San Francisco Daily Alta* account. It was repeated many times in Eastern newspapers. It was a frenzied account of Terry as a "fire-eating, blood-drinking renegade." His enemies agreed that Terry was a man whose violent end had been truly "earned."

On Thursday afternoon the 15th of August, a day after the shooting, Deputy Sheriff Tom Cunningham boarded the train for San Francisco. In his breast pocket was a warrant for the arrest of a United States Supreme Court justice. He had misgivings about the journey; he felt himself in water that was well beyond his depth. *The Daily Alta*'s account of Cunningham's first encounter with the justice captures a sense of the mismatch:

> In no way to embarrass the Sheriff, [Justice Field], with several personal friends, waited in his apartments at the hotel until a late hour. [T]he Sheriff did not reach town until 8:45 p.m., and after registering at the Russ House, went to the police station. [The clerk] told him that Chief Crowley wished to see him at the Palace Hotel. [When he arrived at the Palace he met] Marshal Franks in the corridor, [and together] the two [men] went to Justice Field's apartment. [The] hour was late and Justice Field exceedingly wearied, so the Sheriff very courteously withdrew after a few minutes' conversation in which they [arranged to meet the next afternoon] at the Appraiser's Building, where the Federal Courts were locate[d].[4]

The next afternoon at precisely one o'clock, Cunningham walked into the Appraiser's Building at Washington and Sansome Streets. It was the most imposing building on the bayside of town, towering like a citadel over the shipping and packing houses. Once inside, the deputy was ushered into an ancillary courtroom on the second floor, where he was confronted by an impressive array of federal officials—three federal judges, the federal district attorney, James Carey, and Federal Marshal, J.C. Franks. And sitting placidly in their midst was Justice Field. This phalanx of officials gave poor Tom Cunningham pause; he hesitated, and Field, sensing his indecision, seized the moment. "I am ready," he said expansively, "[for you to] proceed with your duty.

[An] officer should always do his duty. I recognize your authority, sir, and submit to the arrest; I am, sir, in your custody." But lest anyone forget the true origin of their troubles, he added: "Because I may be a judge, I am not excused from the proper processes of law. Judges should be all the more amenable to the laws which they are selected to maintain."[5] Cunningham, noticeably put off balance by Field's performance, was only able to mumble, "You are"—leaving bystanders to deduce for themselves whether he intended his remark to be a statement of fact or merely a question. If, however, Cunningham believed for a moment that this meant that he would be returning his charge to Stockton City, he was straightway disabused. Once Field was satisfied that Eastern papers would report that judicial decorum had been maintained, he would call a halt to "their performances."

Conducting the hearing was Federal Circuit Court Judge Sawyer, who then nodded in Marshal Franks' direction, and Franks beckoned for a clerk to come forward. The clerk presented the perplexed deputy with a federal writ of *habeas corpus* signed by Judge Sawyer. Then Sawyer ordered Field's immediate release from custody. Cunningham, writ in hand, was then led into an adjoining courtroom, where the ubiquitous Judge Sawyer took his place on the bench. At Cunningham's side was District Attorney Carey who handed the befuddled deputy a "return order" transferring the "prisoner Field" from the city of Stockton to the city of San Francisco. By now, the deputy sheriff was no longer hesitating. When asked to sign the release form, he did so straightaway, convinced as he was by then that he had done his duty. The people had been "served." By two o'clock that afternoon, Field was no farther from his Palace Hotel suite or closer to the Stockton jail than he had been when the deputy stepped off the ferry the night before. For all of five minutes Field had been Cunningham's prisoner! As Kroninger writes:

> To prove that Field was not the only person there with a sense of humor, Sawyer winked slyly at the appreciative reporters and asked. 'What shall be done with the prisoner?' After a few minutes of witty repartee, a five thousand dollars bond was agreed on and immediately posted, pending a hearing the following Thursday. This meant that the sheriff could not in the meantime hold Field nor take him to Stockton. The preliminary hearing on the murder charge was scheduled to take place in Stockton City on [the following] Wednesday.[6]

The *San Francisco Chronicle*, rarely given to irony on matters pertaining to Justice Field, concluded its own account of the afternoon's "frolic," to use Kroninger's word, by stating: "Field then retired with his friends, having given the best proof possible of the equality of all American citizens before the law."[7]

Doubtless Stockton's authorities had underestimated Field's ability to halt the state's judicial machinery in its tracks. Yet, the next day, when Cunningham stepped off the train in Stockton City accompanied by a federal lawyer named Charlie Ackerman, his encounter with District Attorney Avery White did not go well. Ackerman had with him a federal writ signed by Judge Sawyer directing White to release Neagle to the federal court authorities in San Francisco under Cunningham's custody.

When Stockton citizens who had gathered at the city hall learned of the Sawyer writ they began a slow march around the city jail, shouting as they went, that nothing could prevent them from breaking into "this paper-box" and "seizing the blackguard." Some suggested that it was now time "[to call] Judge Lynch to the bench." The next day confusion and anger heightened when San Francisco's newspapers appeared in Stockton heralding the arrival of Marshal Franks the next morning, Saturday August 17th. News reports declared that Franks intended to guarantee Neagle's safe return to San Francisco under "federal colors."

As midnight approached on Friday, August 16th, two days after the shooting, the lamps continued to burn at the Yosemite Hotel in Stockton City as council members gathered to argue how best to deal with the Marshal's arrival on Saturday. In reality they needn't have bothered. What the San Francisco papers failed to report was that, even as the councilmen bickered about the proper strategy for the morning showdown, a special train was making its way south from Oakland to Stockton.

At three a.m., the train inched into the Stockton station without its customary whistles and bells, and by 10 a.m. on the 17th (when the newspapers were reporting the arrival time for Franks in Stockton City,) the "rescue train" was well on its return trip to San Francisco with Ackerman, Cunningham and Neagle safely aboard. Federal Judge Sawyer had given Deputy Cunningham the authority (plus the honor) of releasing Neagle from the Stockton jail and escorting him to San Francisco's federal jail—and the elated bodyguard was well on his way north even before the drowsy city fathers of Stockton had adjourned to their beds. By Sunday the 18th, valley residents could only marvel at Field's formidable connections with the railroad barons when they learned that the rescue train—consisting of an engine pulling a single passenger car with its lights covered—had plowed its way through the warm night air, at full throttle, almost sixty miles per hour, on a track that had been cleared all the way into Oakland. By the end of the day, the Stockton Council would learn that Marshal Franks had never intended to make an appearance in Stockton. It was a ruse meant to catch the city of Stockton off guard, and it had. Marshal Franks had been Field's decoy, and his trip had been a planted story. It seems that only Sarah Terry had been suspicious for she warned the city council to suspect a trick—but who on the council was going to pay attention to the ramblings of an unstable, untrustworthy widow in the throes of grief and a growing state of madness?

Safely back in federal hands, Neagle cheerfully gave "a hundred newsmen" his version of the entire "ruckus." "The six days in the Central Valley had been more fun than a bear hunt," he said, "yet, I breathed easier as the train passed over the San Joaquin County line into Alameda County—it was good to be away from the heat and mosquitoes of the Central Valley." When news of Neagle's escape and rescue reached the Eastern newspapers, most editorial pages were effusive in their praise of the daring mission taken and its successful outcome. "Escape from Dogberry," exalted *The New York Herald Tribune*.[8] In San Francisco, of course, Field and friends applauded the results, while Terry's supporters became more irate and frustrated at their helplessness. A weak protest was mustered by a contingent of women from San Francisco's Southern States Social Register who paraded around the federal jail shouting insults through the barred windows of the cell in which it was supposed that Neagle was being housed.

Terry's political influence among valley residents, however, vanished as quickly as a Tule fog in August, and national support for the memory of the ill-fated Terry was insignificant, even in southern states. Only a handful of labor newspapers came to his defense. One such paper, *The New York Sunday Mercury*, went so far as to call for the dismissal of all federal officials connected with the affair, including the United States Attorney General, W.H. Miller, who the Mercury insisted, should be indicted as an accessory "to murder."[9] Labor papers in California lamented the fact that a "single" federal agency could turn the authority of the "entire" state into "mere whimsy," while also chiding Field's perfidy—expressly, his posturing as a defender of California's states' rights, while he was "single-handedly" overturning the wishes of state officials who were demanding that Neagle be prosecuted as a man charged with violating the state's homicide law.

The Field hearing was to begin in Judge Sawyer's federal courtroom on Thursday morning, August 22, but there was a fruitless, five-day delay while Stockton lawyers struggled to reverse the Neagle writ. By the 28th it became clear to everyone that they would be unable to reverse, so the hearing was set to begin the next day on Thursday the 29th. In the morning, Justice Field limped into the courtroom on the arm of his old comrade, Judge Sawyer. Court watchers jammed the courtroom hoping for a reprise of the theatrical events in the *Sharon v. Sharon* trial. But sadly, the spectators' enthusiasm diminished when word came that Sarah Terry had no plans to attend. The extra week's delay, moreover, had given Field all the time he needed to assemble a powerful cast of political and legal characters from both state and federal governments to plead his case. The governor of the state, P.R.W. Waterman, declared in a letter made public in the San Francisco newspapers that "senior state officials disavowed any action taken by the Stockton District Attorney against Justice Field." The justice should be released immediately, Waterman declared, "lest it be a burning disgrace to the [entire] State." How, he went on, borrowing directly from Field's own terminology, "[can we accept] the charges of a woman of abandoned character and utterly unworthy of belief respecting any matter whatever?" Nor were spectators astonished when Judge Sawyer, in a short 20-minute decision, agreed that "it had been a shameless, reckless, unfounded charge."

> [We] are extremely gratified to find that [we shall] be spared the necessity of further inquiring as to the extent of the remedy afforded the distinguished petitioner, by the Constitution and laws of the United States, or of enforcing such remedies as exist, and that the stigma cast upon the State of California by this hasty and, to call it in no harsher terms, ill-advised arrest, will not be intensified by further prosecution. [Any] further review of the matter will be dismissed.[10]

As it turned out, the Stockton District Attorney had anticipated what was coming and had not sent a single representative to court to raise objections on the widow Terry's behalf.

The following day, Neagle's lawyers (eight in number), sensing that the court was ready to logroll the entire procedure, offered to waive objection to whatever irregularities might be facing their client and go directly to trial. This time the Stockton lawyers were in the courtroom prepared to offer a compromise. Having decided that it would be sheer folly to attempt to try Field on the charge that he was aiding and abetting a murder, they offered to drop all charges against the justice in exchange for a favorable jurisdictional ruling on Neagle's case. This had been suggested earlier by the Los Angeles District Attorney Stephen Mallory White. White had no illusions about the direction the investigation was heading. In a letter to Terry's friend, James McCreedy, White had recommended dismissing the state's case against Field in order to fight a "possibly" winnable case against Neagle. "I think it is a mistake to assert federal control of the case. The United States Judges are hostile to the Terry side and I believe they will take jurisdiction and discharge Neagle without a trial. The case is practically being tried by Field, though he is behind the scenes."[11]

White's assessment proved to be correct. Not only did Judge Sawyer ignore the Stockton proposal without comment, he also announced that the order of the hearing's proceedings would be reversed. Instead of first ruling on the question of jurisdiction, he would begin by hearing the evidence in the case. Not unexpectedly, Terry's representatives howled in protest. How, they pleaded, can the Court ask for the presentation of evidence in a case over which it may not have jurisdiction? The facts could be set forth in sufficient detail, they argued, so as to enable the judge to rule on jurisdiction without revealing the plaintiff's entire presentation. To do otherwise would allow Neagle and his lawyers to hear the case against him without the safeguards of a formal trial; hence, Sawyer's order would prejudice the plaintiff's case before it had begun. Facts relating to jurisdiction, the Stockton lawyers insisted, should be set forth by Neagle as petitioner *in traverse* (plea of denial), showing why he should not be returned to the Stockton jail. If the plea failed, they concluded, the matter would then be ended and federal jurisdiction would not be a relevant consideration. "The State owes the petitioner no apology—after all, one Californian has shot another Californian."

Judge Sawyer listened but remained unmoved, and when the presentation ended, he chose to say little more than to declare that the attorneys for the contending parties should be prepared to present their evidence in court on Monday morning, September 2. Robert Kroninger writes:

> When Neagle's *habeas corpus* hearing finally began several days later no state attorneys were present to protest the granting of the writ. The hearing lasted two full weeks, even in the absence of any opposition, but proceeded amicably. Justice Field, the case against him dismissed, sat in the empty jury box making of it a sort of reserved spectators' gallery. He sauntered in and out of the court and into chambers with Judge Sawyer at every recess. He was to be a major witness, of course, but perhaps he wished to assist Sawyer by interpreting and explaining the evidence as it was presented.[12]

Without adversarial objections, things went smoothly, though not as rapidly as might have been expected under such circumstances. On Monday, a boisterous albeit attentive crowd heard the magniloquent Field give his version of the incident for the first time under oath. As had happened before when Field discussed the Terrys, he insisted on beginning at the beginning. This meant reviewing the entire saga: the first trial, Sarah Terry's incorrigibility, the pertinacious David Terry, the fraudulent marriage contract, the courtroom brawl, the contempt citation of 1888, and the numerous subsequent state and federal appeals. Finally, but only after more than an hour of historical review, were the listeners to hear the actual details of the shooting—but not before Judge Sawyer had joined in Field's prologue with his own description of the insolent "wooling" he had suffered at Sarah Terry's hands.

When Field reached the substantive matters, he began on a fulsome note. He told the listeners that he was unable to understand Judge Terry's resentments, for until the 1888 contempt citation, they had had the most amicable long term professional relationship. They had always been congenial colleagues. Whatever bitterness and resentment may have arisen in the last few years, Field hinted, came not from their personal relationship but from the destructive influence of Terry's mercurial second wife. In effect, Field said, Terry's suspicions and resentments began only after this second marriage, a union that had plunged him into a dishonorable defense of an ignoble woman, a loss of prestige and withering financial reversals.

Field then turned to the fateful day in question and with Sawyer's assistance offered a cryptic explanation for Terry's "strange" performance at Lathrop—he was there that day, said the justice, to "murder me." On this point there was total agreement among the defendants. (During the entire week of testimony, neither Field, Neagle nor Sawyer would ever acknowledge any other motive than murderous intent for Terry's "strange" behavior in the Lathrop restaurant. Moreover, no subsequent judicial review of the Lathrop events was ever to attribute to Terry any motive but murderous intent.) Field insisted from start to finish that, had not Neagle taken the decisive action that he did, there would have been—to use Sawyer's phrase—"a vacancy on the bench of one of the most august judicial tribunals in the world." Field cast Neagle as no less than a heroic functionary warding off the slathering rage of "a monster out of control." Only by resolute courage was Neagle able to save the moment and bring the demented giant to his knees (once and for all). Moreover, Sawyer added gratuitously, the state of California could not be trusted to treat the "great Justice and his noble armor-bearer [fairly]." Field's biographer George Gorham summed up the sentiments of the Field contingent with a joke that was, he said, making the rounds: "Newsboy: 'A man tried to kill [Justice Field] in California!' Customer: 'What was done about it?' Newsboy: 'Oh! They arrested the Justice.'"[13]

As the hearing proceeded, there was conflicting testimony offered; but without opposing council present to raise questions about these discrepancies, nothing was ever challenged, and spectators were left to draw whatever conclusions they might. Field testified, for example, that Terry had struck him two blows and was about to deliver a third, but Neagle testified in direct contradiction that Terry struck the justice one violent blow and then reached for a Bowie knife that was concealed in his coat—Field had nothing to say about a knife. Field insisted that Neagle fired his weapon twice as he arose from the table, but Neagle testified that he placed himself between Field and Terry just as Terry was about to brandish a knife, before he fired the first shot. Field declared that the first shot did not stop Terry's onslaught, so Neagle was obliged to shoot a second time, even though the bodyguard described Terry as sinking to the floor after the first shot. Both men agreed that Terry was armed. A bystander from Los Angeles, George L. Lidgerwood, when called to the stand, testified that he had seen Sarah Terry surreptitiously extract a knife and scabbard from beneath her husband's coat while she lay across his bloody body. At the hearing no one rebutted Lidgerwood's story, but the next day newspapers pointed out that since Terry always carried his knife in a scabbard looped over his shoulder there was no possible way for his wife to remove these without first removing his coat. Bystanders in the restaurant, who were not called to testify, had declared that Terry had "slapped," "tapped" or "brushed" Field's face, but Neagle and Field insisted that Terry had struck the justice a "fierce and heavy blow."

Sheriff Purvis, who was not present at the hearing, had testified that immediately after the shooting, he had "examined [the justice's] face carefully and there was not as much as a red mark on it."[14] Field testified that Neagle had shouted, "Stop! I am an officer, stop!" before he fired the fatal shot, but other customers told reporters that Neagle shouted "stop" only after he had fired two shots. There was incredulity on the faces of courtroom spectators when Field testified that he did not understand why Neagle had asked him to take breakfast on the train that tragic morning; perhaps, Field offered, Terry may have been trying to provoke a duel. "No one knew better than Judge Terry that [I] would resent any personal indignity." This comment would appear to be at odds with Field's earlier remark that Terry's stealthy approach from the rear demonstrated an intention to kill him. However, conflicting testimony was never of much significance at the hearing, for there were no witnesses present with opposing versions of the Lathrop confrontation. When Judge Sawyer summed up, moreover, he never wavered from his friend Field's thesis:

> It is necessary to repeat the facts in full, "for when the deceased left his seat, some 30 feet distant, walked stealthily down the passage in the rear of Justice Field, and dealt the unsuspecting jurist two preliminary blows, doubtless, by way of reminding him that the time of vengeance had at last come, Justice Field was, already, at the traditional *wall* of the law. He was sitting quietly at a table, back to the assailant, eating his breakfast, the side opposite being occupied by other passengers, some of whom were women, similarly engaged. When, in a dazed condition, he awoke to the reality of the situation, and saw the stalwart form of the deceased with arm drawn back for a final mortal blow, there was no time to get under, or over, the table, had the law, under any circumstances, required such an act for his justification. Neagle could not seek a 'wall' to justify his acts, without abandoning his charge to certain death. When, therefore, he sprang to his feet and cried, Stop! Stop! I am an officer, and saw the powerful arm of the deceased drawn back for the final deadly stroke instantly, change its direction to his left breast, apparently, seeking his favorite weapon, the knife:

> and at the same time heard the half-suppressed, disappointed growl of recognition of the man, who, with the aid of half dozen others, had finally succeeded in disarming him of his knife, at the court-room, a year before, the supreme moment had come: or, at least, with abundant reason, Neagle thought so, and fired the fatal shot. The testimony all concurs in showing this to be the state of facts, and the almost universal *consensus* of public opinion of the United States seems to justify the act. On that occasion, a second, or two seconds, signified, at least, two valuable lives, and a reasonable degree of prudence would justify a shot one or two seconds too soon, rather than a fraction of a second too late. Upon our minds the evidence leaves no doubt, whatever, that the homicide was fully justified by the circumstances.[15]

Sawyer's rendition reveals that he was fully aware of the criticisms that had been coming from Eastern legal reports when he added:

> We have seen in an Eastern law journal [s]ome adverse criticism upon the act of the petitioner. [B]ut it is not for scholarly gentlemen of humane and peaceful instincts [s]itting securely in their libraries, 3,000 miles away, looking backward over the scene, to determine the exact point of time when a man in Neagle's situation should fire at his assailant, in order to be justified by the law. It is not for them to say that the proper time had not yet come. To such, the proper time would never come.[16]

Midway through the second week of the hearing, Sawyer halted testimony and announced that he and his associate, Judge George Sabine, had heard enough and were prepared to rule on the matter of jurisdiction. This announcement brought George A. Johnson, California's Attorney General, and the ever-zealous Stockton District Attorney Avery White into court on the next working day. Both men, of course, pressed the case for state jurisdiction, but they may as well have stayed at home and saved traveling expenses. Sawyer and Sabine were not prepared to accept any version of the shooting and the events that followed but that of Associate Justice Field. Neagle's constitutional right wrote Sawyer, "entitles him to be discharged on a federal writ of *habeas corpus* because [he] is under color of federal authority. [W]hen Federal and State laws conflict the state law is subordinate [for] two valid laws cannot conflict." The federal government has a right to protect its federal judges, Sawyer continued, in point of fact, Neagle was protecting a federal judge. Moreover, the president of the United States has a duty to appoint police officers who are responsible for the welfare of federal judges. "If they have duties to protect the United States mail, surely then they have a duty to protect U.S. judges as well." It was agreed. There is no constitutional statute requiring federal deputies to protect federal judges—but who can doubt that it is "a principle of Common Law, and where the code is silent the common law governs." Kroninger, at this point, argues that Sawyer had returned to "the rule of the Roman arena—[n]ewspaper editorials supplanting thumbs—in aid of his decision."[17]

Sawyer, not forgetting devout observers who might be listening, goes so far as to draw an analogy from religion to underscore his argument. "Even as the *Holy Host* sanctifies the humblest abode as the Church, so does the judge transform his surroundings into a court." When acting in his official role the judge and the court are one and the same—where the judge goes, so goes the court. Governor P.R.W. Waterman, one might say, had become Field's bailiff *in transitus*. The U.S. attorney general, through the office of the U.S. Marshall, was required to assign a federal constable to protect Field, and since the evidence had shown that the Terrys were murderous conspirators, it was not unreasonable for the justice's bodyguard to believe that a mortal assault was underway in the restaurant that August morning. On numerous occasions, the Terrys had made it clear "that they intended to horsewhip the old man and throw his body in the bay."[18]

Therefore, the deputy was acting "under the color of law" when he shot Terry, Sawyer announced, and under such mitigating conditions, "the laws of California do not pertain. It is a matter of federal jurisdiction and the federal writ of *habeas corpus* stands—David Neagle is released from the custody of the San Joaquin County Sheriff."

It would not have been unreasonable to believe that the issue of jurisdiction had been ordained well before the hearing was ever gaveled to order, but what followed the adjournment of proceedings was sure to remove any lingering doubt about it. Standing in the midst of a throng of well wishers, Neagle was approached by Field who, after quieting the crowd, made a little speech in which he solemnly announced, "I would not be in the land of the living [were it not for my bodyguard], and were I a rich man I would present him with more than this gold watch." Whereupon he handed Neagle an embellished watch on which was inscribed, "Stephen J. Field to David Neagle, as a token of appreciation of his courage and fidelity to duty under circumstances of great peril at Lathrop, Cal., on the fourteenth day of August, 1889."[19] After the celebrants wandered away, Neagle was led before Judge Sawyer, where his friends and supporters posted a $5,000 bond.

And so it was that the shooting of the unarmed David S. Terry, chief justice of the California Supreme Court, had cost Neagle no more nor no less than thirty-two days of jail time.

In April of 1890 the U.S. Supreme Court settled the remaining questions pertaining to federal or state jurisdictions, and this jurisdictional decision lives on with numerous citations since its inception.[20] Before the U.S. Supreme Court, the appellant, Attorney General of California George Johnson, argued that Sawyer had erred when he asserted that the state had no jurisdictional claims over the so-called "official" actions of federal employees. "Common law is [always] the province of the states, for the statutes of the Constitution nowhere speak of a 'national common law.' Federal employees, therefore, are subject to the jurisdiction of the state in which they act."

In short order, however, the nation's highest court disallowed Johnson's appeal. Yet, no one was astonished (least of all Johnson and his staff), for Californians had no doubt that Field was behind the scene "pulling the strings," even though, on innumerable occasions, he had made public profession denying any undue influence.

Most noteworthy to some observers was the fact that the court's opinion was not unanimous, the divided opinion reflecting the age-old division of civil strife that had torn the country apart 30 years earlier. The dissent of two justices was unequivocal—Chief Justice Melville Fuller and Associate Justice Lucius Lamar, both faithful sons of the south, reminded the court majority that an *ex parte* proceeding taken on Terry's behalf by the state against Neagle "as a prisoner in custody of a state court of a competent jurisdiction [could not] be taken from that jurisdiction and discharged on *habeas corpus* issued by a court of the United States, simply because one is not guilty of the offense for which one is held."[21] Neagle was not under "U.S. color of authority," for at no time was he held in U.S. custody before a U.S. court, or restrained by a U.S. decree. He, no less than any other citizen, had the burden of demonstrating his guilt or innocence before the authorities who hold him. "We can [a]sk the Congress to make new law that exempts federal employees from the legal provisions of state government," they continued, "but at this moment Congress has offered no such provision. [Presently], the President is powerless to authorize protection for federal employees' *contra jus commune* (against common law). The powers of the general government are made up of concessions from the several States; [and] whatever is not expressly given to the former the latter expressly reserves." Congress has not made a law protecting the life of justices nor does 'common law' supply one. On the contrary, the government is composed of twenty-four sovereign and independent states, each of which has its own local usages and customs—its "own common law." The United States government, therefore, has no common law assented to by the sovereign states—save for those crimes committed on the high seas, or on overseas territories.

> The gravamen (burden) of this case, concluded Justices Fuller and Lamar, is in the assertion that Neagle slew Terry in pursuance *of a law* of the United States. He who claims to have committed a homicide by authority must show the authority. If he claims the authority of law, then *what law*? And if a law, how came it to be a law? Somehow and somewhere it must have had an origin.[22]

Sawyer's claim that the United States court is wherever Field is in his official capacity, and that Neagle is his traveling bailiff, say the justices, is utterly preposterous! A judge is not *the* court. Terry's crime in striking Field (if it was a crime) was certainly not contempt of court. If, Fuller summarized, Terry had murdered Field, he would have been charged with committing a state crime and would have been tried by a state court; and had Neagle been tried in a state court as properly he should have been, Fuller concluded confidently, he would have been, no doubt, acquitted.[23]

Neagle's and Field's exoneration in the nation's highest court finally brought the Field-Terry conflict to its long overdue ending—it had been 33 years since they had first eyed each other suspiciously at the opening of the California court in October of 1857.

Postmortem of the astonishing ordeal has never been kind to the memory of Terry. Newspapers that had vilified him in life continued to vilify him in death. In New York, the reaction of Field's brothers David Dudley and Cyrus were published in major newspapers and were typical representations of how the business community viewed the conflict. Dudley Field framed the episode as one more example of the country's growing disrespect for the "rule of law." Justice Field had been singled out to be a victim of lawlessness, while Terry, he argued, had been one of those restless southern adventurers who had refused to accept the consequences of the war that they had lost. Terry was an abuser of a citizens' right to expect legal order, he concluded.

Brother Cyrus' interpretation of events, on the other hand, was somewhat more explicit. He insisted that Terry's attack on Field had not been a coincidence; it had been from the beginning personal and conspiratorial. When the justice entered California in June, wrote Cyrus Field, the Terrys stalked him. The attack at Lathrop was the result of a year's planning engaged in by the Terrys and their clandestine (but unnamed) anti-monopolist henchmen. They were fully expecting to kill Justice Field and were frustrated to the point of rage when the plan failed. It was no happenstance, Cyrus Field conjectured, that they boarded the train on that fateful morning, for they had been following Justice Field's whereabouts in the daily newspapers since the day he arrived in California in June. In fact, it was determined that the railroad restaurant at Lathrop was the ideal place to perform "their cowardly deed," because the Terrys would be surrounded by friends in the Central Valley who were certain to protect them. What is more, witnesses would be inclined to support whatever version of the incident the Terrys would lay out. Lieutenant General William Tecumseh Sherman, now free to declare his true allegiances, reflecting back on those years when he had faced Terry and the Vigilance Committee, wrote expansively of Terry's manly heroism and irreconcilable resentments.

Most newspapers' editorial pages throughout the country were in agreement with these anti-Terry sentiments. Most papers were eager to defame his memory. The judge's death, they wrote, was a "useful lesson for the southern scofflaws," or "Californians have finally avenged the death of Senator Broderick." (Years later, even Neagle came to believe that reprisal for Broderick's death was the proper explanation for the restaurant shooting. In an interview in 1939, Neagle told a reporter that "[when] I felled Terry on that restaurant floor in Lathrop I shouted that this one is for Broderick)."[24] During the trial, of course, he had not mentioned such heroics, nor had there been testimony from bystanders to this effect. Other newspapers, particularly those in the east that had shared the railroad-controlled Western wire services, described Terry as "a fire-eating, blood-drinking desperado." "All honest men," said *The Argonaut*, "who respect the law will breathe more freely, [for had Neagle not acted as he did], Field would have been left in the claws of a [vicious] tiger."[25] Other newspapers engaged in the social piety of attributing the tragedy to his "second marriage," pointing out that at the end even "Terry's own clergyman had refused to bury him" (this was, however, not true, the family minister was ill, and the other Episcopalian priest in Stockton was vacationing out of town.) The *Nation*, again evoking the memory of the Broderick incident, wrote, "[s]omebody ought to have killed [this man] a quarter of a century earlier for this antebellum [renegade] is as out of place in these post-Civil-War times as a tiger is in a barnyard."[26] But by far the most acrimonious attack came from Field's hometown newspaper, *The Placerville Observer*:

> The timely official shot which killed David S. Terry [it declared] arrested and avenged a brutal assault, characteristic of the assailant, [it] closed a criminal career, distinguished by shameless infamies. The cold-blooded blackguard belonged to a class of treacherous and brutal ruffians, whom unwept and unregretted, are passing rapidly away. [A]n inglorious death [c]aused by a drastic dose of his own medicine. The doom he invited and deserved was only too long deferred. Dust to dust, earth to earth, and peace to his ashes.[27]

This nation-wide rebuke continued unabated for several weeks, but then loyal Terryites could remain silent no longer. Typical of their responses was a sardonic rebuttal from the *Stockton Mail*:

> Terry had a Bowie knife all the way from a foot to eighteen inches long, with the blood of his last victim still upon the blade. He stood picking his teeth with it when the Rev. Mr. Neagle, a distinguished prelate from Arizona entered the room upon the arm of Stephen J. Field, a sacred personage descended from Heaven to execute the will of God upon earth. (It is unusual for a person to pick his teeth before eating, but any person hesitating upon this point will be in contempt of the Federal Circuit Court and may be shot at any time convenient to the Shooter).[28]

Terry's name suffered the greatest public humiliation, however, not from the nation's newspapers but from the legal community in his adopted state. The day after the shooting (August 15th 1889), his law partners, William T. Baggett and James L. Crittenden, traveled north to Sacramento to present a petition before the Supreme Court requesting recognition of the passing of a former chief justice of California's highest court. Baggett and Crittenden arrived in the afternoon while the court was in session, but it was not until the end of the session that Chief Justice William Beatty acknowledged their presence. After Beatty asked the two men to state their business, Baggett began, "I am here, your honor, to ask the Court to remember the passing of Chief Justice David Terry who . . ." Beatty cut him off in mid-sentence. "We shall discuss this matter amongst ourselves," he said. Baggett took his seat and waited while the justices held a somewhat desultory discussion among themselves. Finally the chief justice turned and addressed Terry's two friends, announcing that the court thought it wise to postpone any decision on the matter until the next morning. In the morning, before a handful of reporters and Terry's two visibly annoyed partners, Beatty declared that, "upon full consultation we thought it better that [a formal statement not be presented by the court]. [Given that] the circumstances of Judge Terry's death are notorious, and under these circumstances this court has determined to pass on this matter in silence, and not to take any action upon it."[29] Beatty's tenure on the bench lasted twenty-five years, and throughout these years, Chief Justice Terry was without honor *in absentia.*

Stephen Field would serve eight more years on the bench. He was 81 years old when he retired from the U.S. Supreme Court, and after his retirement he lived another sedentary year and a half, housebound but not forgotten or ignored. He died in Washington, D.C., on April 9, 1899. The Sunday evening he died was damp and chilly. His wife, her sister Sarah, and Associate Justice David Brewer were by his side, and the Reverend Edward Mott, son of Gordon Mott of Marysville who had been Field's dueling second in the William Barbour controversy, conducted prayers at Evensong.

Field had made it plain to colleagues several years before he left the bench that he was determined to stay on the court until he had surpassed Chief Justice John Marshall's record for longevity. He reached his declared goal but there was a cost. During his last three years it was noticeable to court lawyers, clerks and court aids that his mental and physical powers were waning and that he was unable to sustain the mental rigor demanded of an officer of the country's highest court.

Finally it was agreed that one of the justices should confront Field on the matter of his continued service and insist that it was now time for him to step down. Members of the court agreed that Justice John Harlan, Field's long-time friend, should approach the old man and candidly declare that it was his duty to go. After several days of ambivalence, Harlan summoned the courage to approach Field on the matter. Harlan couched his request in the most innocuous fashion possible. He asked Field if he remembered when the two of them had been forced to go to the declining Justice Robert Grier and request that he retire from the court. Harlan paused, waiting for Field's reflective response. Slowly as the old man grasped the implication of Harlan's question he became, Carl Swisher writes, "alert and [with his] eyes blazing with the old fire of his youth, burst out: 'Yes! And a dirtier day's work I never did in my life!' [That] was the end of the [Brethrens'] effort to induce Justice Field's retirement."[30] Thereafter they waited with forbearance until he surpassed Marshall's lengthy tenure. By then they all knew that Field's resignation would be on a day of his own choosing.

Field resigned on December 1, 1897, and by his own count he had written 620 opinions while on the federal Supreme Court, 57 on the Tenth Circuit Court and 365 as a justice of the California Supreme Court. It was a remarkable total of 1,042 opinions during his lifetime. The sense of calling, as he understood his entire legal tenure to be, was revealed in a letter to a colleague. The letter read in part:

> "When my resignation takes effect my period of service on this bench will have exceeded that of any of my predecessors, while my entire judicial life will have embraced more than forty years. I may be pardoned for saying that during all this period, long in comparison with the brevity of human life, though in retrospect it has gone with the swiftness of a tale that is told, I have not shunned to declare in every case coming before me for decision the conclusions, which my deliberate convictions compelled me to arrive at, by the conscientious exercise of such abilities and acquirements as I possessed."[31]

Sarah Althea Terry was thirty-eight years old when Judge Terry died, but her efforts to secure justice were not curtailed either by his passing or by her failures. Her painful losses only jolted her into greater activity in order to right the wrongs, and to find the public vindication that she felt had been taken from her. From a neutral perspective, a better course of action might have been to return to her Fresno home and accept the wise and frugal counsel of her husband's financial administrator, C.G. Sayles, to attend to the responsibility of running her home. But true to her nature, she would not hear of it. Her claim to property and insurance became equivocal, and eventually her title to her husband's property was challenged, as was her right as benefactor to any of his death benefits. Through it all, however, she remained undeterred. She continued to press her claim for a share of the Sharon estate.

With each legal and financial loss she became more and more unstable, more erratic in behavior and more incoherent in mind. Initially her friends noted that she was able to carry on so long as she limited her conversation to everyday discourse, and that she strayed into madness only when the topic turned to her legal battles with Sharon and Field. But eventually, as her comments grew more and more the result of hallucination and, hence incomprehensible, she became unable to deal with the reality of her situation. This was especially evident when news reporters took the time to follow her around town. Even her loyal friend Mrs. Pleasant, who seemed genuinely interested in her welfare, finally acknowledged that Sarah Hill-Sharon-Terry had reached a stage of moodiness, suspicion and despondence that brought her ever closer to a self-destructive state—often she was unable to recognize the difference between her friends and her enemies. Seemingly, without rhyme or reason, she frequently planned revenge on many individuals, while increasingly falling under the sway of fortune-tellers, seers and spiritualists.

Two years after the death of her husband, Mrs. Terry was completely at the forbearance of friends, and when finally even their patience had run thin, she was left tragically trapped in circumstances of her own making. She took to wandering the streets of San Francisco, and was seen wading in gutters and begging and borrowing for room and board. Mrs. Pleasant, who initially had protected her whenever she needed help, eventually was forced to have her restrained and locked up while a series of sanity hearings pended. Her compulsive paranoia had made her a threat to herself, if not to others. At her hearing, two physicians agreed that she was indeed insane, and on March 10, 1892, Judge Levy pronounced her so and committed her to the state asylum in Stockton City. (Ironically, Judge Terry had been one of the founding governors of the Stockton asylum.) No longer the striking beauty of the Sharon trial, she had become a pitiable creature, one described by the *Chronicle*, a week before she was confined to the hospital at Stockton, as a "[rain drenched figure] dripping wet and soggy [wearing] a hat, from which ribbons hung limp as rags, fastened far back on her head, exposing a broad forehead framed in damp clusters of light hair, [she] was covered with mud and presented a sorry appearance. Few who saw her recognized her as the celebrated Mrs. Sarah Althea Terry."[32]

By the end of March 1892, she had become a permanent patient in the Stockton State Hospital, and as her ability to recall the past declined, so also seemingly, did her ability to recall her life's most dramatic moments. Toward the end of life, all she could remember from her days of legal travail was that William Sharon was a very rich man, that she had been married to more than one man, that Judge Terry was a man as large as a doorway, and that George Tyler had been her attorney and General Barnes had been an adversarial attorney in a famous trial. When asked about the infamous marriage contract and its authenticity, however, she claimed no recollection. Speculating rhetorically, Oscar Lewis and Carroll Hall wrote, "[h]ad she really forgotten [about the marriage trial] or was she refusing to say, cannily 'protecting her interests'?"[33]

Sarah lived forty-five more years at the state hospital and died on Saint Valentine's Day, 1937. Cornelia Terry McClure, the daughter of Clinton Terry, having decided that the passing of almost a half-century was enough time to respect both the memory of her father and her grandfather, buried Sarah Terry in the family plot at Stockton's Rural Cemetery. No more poignant assessment of this harsh episode, and this troubled woman can be found than the one that is portrayed in Ambrose Bierce's column in the Sunday edition of *The San Francisco Examiner* that appears in Lewis' and Hall's, *Bonanza Inn*: "The male Californian—idolater of sex and proud of abasement at the feet of his own female—had now a fine example of the results entailed by his unnatural worship. Mrs. Terry, traipsing the streets, uncommonly civic, problematically harmless but indubitably daft—is all his own work, and he ought to be proud of her."[34]

But as it was to Hamlet's Horatio, the last word on the saga should be left, so to speak, to the last man standing—Stephen Johnson Field. In an 1889 article in the *Overland Monthly* the California politician and journalist E.G. Waite wrote a brief account of the life and character of David Terry in which he attempted to offer one of the few dispassionate appraisal of Terry. A closing passage refers to Terry as a man possessed of "sterling integrity of purpose."[35]

Some time later, Waite was nominated by President Benjamin Harrison to be registrar of the land office in San Francisco, but when Field heard of the nomination, he raised such strong objections to it that Harrison thought it wise to withdraw Waite's name. Field's explanation for his vigorous objection to the nomination appeared in *Themis* for May of 1890:

> When Waite's nomination for registrar was made I handed to a senator an article written by Waite in the *Overland Monthly* of October (1889), eulogistic of the late David S. Terry. Much surprise was expressed by the senator at the tone of the article, the senator stating that it was a reflection upon the administration in designating the marshal to protect Judge Sawyer and myself from murderous assault by Terry, for if he was, as represented by Waite, a 'man of sterling integrity of purpose,' it was meant, if it meant anything, that Terry was a man of high principles and pure character, having honorable principles of action. It was quite evident from what the senator to whom I gave the article and other senators said that it would be impossible for the nomination of Waite to be confirmed. Quite certain I am that neither Governor Stanford, who was his

> friend, nor the whole delegation from California, could have secured his confirmation.[36]

Carl Brent Swisher concludes: "This act of Justice Field's had an appearance of vindictiveness and cheapness of purpose which cast an unpleasant reflection upon him [that brought] disillusioned sneers at the reputed dignity of the judges and the courts. The enmities that were made and the hatreds that were stirred were destined to live until all the principal characters themselves were gone. Seen from any angle whatever, it was a sorry affair. Justice Field failed to forget things that he might well have allowed to pass from his mind."[37] In point of fact, given the vindictiveness that developed between these two judges, as their paths crossed numerous times in the latter half of the nineteenth century, it is not overstated to say that their relationship was marked not only by the appearance of vindictiveness, but by an unrepudiated malice in the mind of each toward the other until the end.

NOTES

1. *The San Francisco Examiner,* May 21, 1921.
2. Stephen Mallory White, MSS, Stanford University. (Palo Alto, California). See also Carl Brent Swisher, *Stephen J. Field: Craftsman of the Law,* (Washington D.C. The Brookings Institution, September 11, 1889). 356.
3. C J. Swisher. *Craftsman,* 350–51.
4. August 16, 1889.
5. Gorham, George C. *The Story of the Attempted Assassination of Justice Field by a Former Associate on the Supreme Bench of California* (New York: De Capo Press. 1968). 325.
6. Robert H. Kroninger. *Sarah and the Senator.* (Berkeley CA.: Howell-North, 1964). 221.
7. *San Francisco Chronicle.* August 19, 1889. Cited in Kroninger, *Sarah and the Senator* (Berkeley CA.: Howell-North, 1964). 221.
8. August 8, 1889.
9. Richard H. Kroninger. *Sarah,* 223.
10. George C. Gorham, *Assassination,* 338.
11. Carl Brent Swisher. *Craftsman,* 356.
12. Richard H. Kroninger. *Sarah,* 224.
13. George H. Gorham. *Assassination,* 339.
14. *The Daily Examiner,* August 15, 1889; see also Buchanan. *Dueling Judge,* 224.
15. *United States v. Terry,* 39 Fed. 864.
16. *United States v. Terry,* 39 Fed. 864.
17. Richard H. Kroninger. *Sarah,* 228.

18. Gorham, G.H. *The Story of the Attempted Assassination of Justice Field.* (NY. Da Capo Press 1968) 274.
19. *San Francisco Chronicle,* September 17, 1889.
20. *In re Neagle,* April 1890, 135 U.S. 1.
21. *In re Neagle,* 135 U.S. 40. 1890.
22. *In re Neagle*, 135 U.S. 76. 1890.
23. *In re Neagle,* 135 U.S. 99. 1890.
24. Harry M. Gorham, *My Memories of the* Comstock. (1939).
25. August 26, 1889.
26. Harry M. Gorham, *Memoirs of the Comstock.* (San Francisco: 1939). 171.
27. Placerville Observer; see also, A.E. Wagstaff, *The Life of the Ex-Chief Justice of the Supreme Court of California: David S. Terry,* (San Francisco: Continental Publ. Co. 1892. 515–516.
28. August 20, 1889. Citing Buchanan. 226.
29. Carl Brent Swisher, *Craftsman*, 354. Also, A. Russell Buchanan. *Dueling Judge.*
30. —— *Craftsman,* 444; see also, Charles Evans Hughes, *The Supreme Court of the United States.*
31. —— *Craftsman,* 445.
32. *The San Francisco Chronicle* Cited in Lewis, *Bonanza Inn,* 1939, 206.
33. Oscar Lewis. *Bonanza Inn*, 213.
34. *San Francisco Examiner,* in Oscar Lewis and Carroll Hall. *Bonanza Inn,* 208.
35. E. G. Waite. "An Estimate of the Life and Character of David S. Terry," *Overland Monthly,* Oct. 1889.
36. Carl Brent Swisher, *Craftsman,* 360.
37. —— *Craftsman,* 361.

Selected Bibliography

JOURNAL ARTICLES

Ayres, W.O., Personal Recollections of the Vigilante Committee, *The Argonaut,* v. 25 no.7, (August 19, 1889).

——, "Public Opinion of the Death of Judge Terry," *The Overland Monthly,* (14, Sept. 1889).

Bakken, Gordon Morris, "California Constitutionalism: Politics, the Press and the Death of Fundamental Law." *Pacific Historian,* (30, 1986).

Boden, *Charles R.,* "David Terry's Justification." *Wasp Newsletter,* (p.55, 1933).

Botts, Charles T., *Hastings Constitutional Law Quarterly,* Fall 1989.

Coleman, W. T., *Century Magazine*, (November 1891).

Ellison, Joseph. "California and the Law 1846–1869: Federal Relations of a Frontier Community." *Southwestern Historical Quarterly, (October* 1922).

——, "California and the Nation." *Southwestern Historical Quarterly,* (v. 30, no. 2. 1926).

Florcken, H. G., "Law and Order View of the San Francisco Vigilance Committee of 1856." Taken from the Correspondence of Governor J. Neely.

Field, Stephen J., "Attack on E. G. Waite," *Overland Monthly,* v. 15, 16, 17.

Hittel, John S., "The Character of David C. Broderick." *Overland Monthly,* v. 13, (January 1889).

Holland, James K., "Diary of a Texan Volunteer in the Mexican War," *The Southwestern Historical Quarterly,* 30 (1926).

Hurt, Peyton, "The Rise and Fall of the 'Know Nothings' in California," *California Historical Society Quarterly,* (v. 9, March 1930. 16).

J. Neely Johnson, *California Historical Society Quarterly,* (v 14, p. December 1935).

——, California *Historical Society Quarterly*, (15, Pt. 2, 1936) 350.

McMurray, Orrin Kip, "An Historical Sketch of the Supreme Court of California." *Bench and Bar in California.* (1926).

——. "Seventy-five Years of California Jurisprudence," *California Law Review,* (v.13, no.6 1925).
Merkel, Philip L. "Railroad Consolidation and Late Nineteenth Century Federalism: Legal Strategy in the Organization of the Southern Pacific System," *Western Legal History,* (11, 1998).
Mooney, Ralph J. "Justice Stephen Field." *Western Legal History,* (*v*. 11, 1998).
Oaks, Henry L. "Dr. Royce's California." *The Overland Monthly*, (Sept. 1886).
Olmstead, Roger. The American West, (v. 7, 1970).
Pomery, Earl, "California 1846–1860, The Politics of a Representative Frontier State." *California Historical Society Quarterly,* (*v*. 32, 1953).
Potts, Charles, S. "The Romantic Story of a Great Texan." *Southwest Review,* (v. 19, 1934).
——. "Mexican Land Grants," *Southwestern Historical Quarterly,* (v. 30, 1926).
——. *Southwestern Historical Quarterly,* (p. 296, 1944).
Royce, Josiah. "Royce's California." Editor, American Commonwealth, *The Overland Monthly,* (Sept. 1886).
——. "The Squatters Riots of the 50*'s* in Sacramento." *The Overland Monthly*, Sept. 1885.
Scheiber, Harry N. "Race, Radicalism and Reform: Historical Perspective on the 1879 California Constitution." *Hastings' Constitutional Law Quarterly.* (Fall 1989).
Sherman, William Tecumseh, "Sherman's Letters to Thomas Ewing, June 16, 1856." *The Century Illustrated Monthly Magazine,* (43, 1891).
Terry, David S., *The Political Record.* (San Francisco, 1889).
Themis, Aug. 17, 18, (1889). May 24, 1890. Waite, E.G. "An Estimate of the Life and Character of David S. Terry." *The Overland Monthly,* (Oct. 1889).
——. "Communications in Answer to Criticism." *The Overland Monthly,* (Nov. 1889).
Henry, William, "The Movement for State Division in California 1849–1860." *Southwestern Historical Quarterly,* v. 18, October. 1913.
Willey, S.H. "Personal Recollections of the Vigilance Committee." *The Overland Monthly,* (Vol. 8, August 1886).

BOOKS

Adams, Henry. *History of the United States,* (N.Y.: Viking Press. 1986). v 9.
Bancroft, Hubert Howe, *History of California,* 1848–1859, 1860–1890. (San Francisco: A. L. Bancroft 1898). v. 6&7.
——. *Political Tribunals.* (San Francisco: The History Co. 1887).
Bean, Walton, *California: An Interpretive History.* (N.Y.: McGraw-Hill & Company. 1968).
Black, Chauncey, F., and Samuel Smith. *Some Account of the Work of Stephen J. Field as Legislator, State Judge and Judge of the Supreme Court of the United States.* (N.Y.) (s.n.) 1881.

Bodenhamer, David J., *Fair Trial: Rights of the Accused in American History.* 1992.
——, and James W. Ely Jr., *Ambivalent Legacy: A legal History of the South* (Jackson: University of Mississippi. 1984).
Bryce, James, *The American Commonwealth.* v. II 1891 (London: Macmillan 1889).
Burnett, Peter H., *Recollections and opinions of an Old Pioneer* (N.Y.: D. Appleton and Co. 1880).
Buchanan, A. Russell. *David S. Terry of California: Dueling Judge*. (San Marino California: The Huntington Library Press. 1956).
Bynon, A.A., *The Constitutional Convention 1878: State of California* (San Francisco: J.T. White 1878).
Byxbee, Robert G., *Letters to his Sister*. Ed. Doyce Nunis. (Calhoun & Benhem: Thomas Hays. 2000).
Carroll, John A., *Richard A. Brown: Pivot of American Vigilantism* (Tucson: University of Arizona. 1969).
Caughy, *Their Majestics, The Mob.* San Francisco, (1960).
Clark, Malcolm, *Pharisee Among the Philistines: Diary of Matthew Deady 1871–1892.* (Portland: Oregon Historical Society, 1935).
Cleland, Robert Glass. *History of California: The American Period.* (New York: The Macmillan Co. 1922).
Coblentz, Stanton A. *Villains and Vigilantes.* (New York: Wilson-Erickson Co. 1939).
Colton, Walter, *Three Years in California* (N.Y.: A.S. Barnes 1851).
Coronel, Don Antonio Franco, *Tales of Mexican California 1817–1894.* Ed.
Doyce Nunis (Santa Barbara CA.: Bellerophon books, 1994).
Crosby, Elisha Oscar, *Reminiscences of California and Guatemala: 1849 to 1864*, Edited by Charles A. Barker, (San Marino California: The Huntington Library Press. 1945).
Cross, Ira B., *Labor Movement in California* (Berkeley CA.: University of California. 1935).
Currey, John, *The Terry-Broderick Duel* (Washington D.C.: Gibson Bros. 1896).
Davis, Winfield J., *History of Political Conventions in California 1849–1892,* (Sacramento, CA.: 1893).
——. *Themis: Seventy-Five Years in California Law* (Sac. CA.: A.J. Johnston & Co. 1889).
Delma, D. M., *Speeches and Addresses* (San Francisco: A. M. Robertson, 1901).
Dobie, Edith, *The Political Career of Stephen M. White.* (Palo Alto: Stanford University Press, 1927).
Dressler, Albert, ed., *Letters to a Pioneer Senator.* (San Francisco: H.S. Crocker Co. 1925).
Ellison, William H., *A Self Governing Dominion 1849–1860.* (Berkeley California, Univ. of California, 1950).
Fargo, F., *A True and Minute History of the Assignation of James King of William at San Francisco, California*. (San Francisco: Witton, Towne, & Co. 1856).

Farragut, Loyall, *The Life of David Glasgow Farragut.* (New York: D. Appleton and Co., 1872).
Field, David D., *The History of Berkshire*, Speeches at the Chicago Democratic Convention: the electoral votes of 1876 (N.Y.: D. Appleton & Co. 1877).
Field, Henry, *The Record of the Family of the late Reverend David Dudly Field.* (New York, printed by family, 1899).
Field. Stephen J., *Personal Reminiscences of the Early Days in California.* (New York, D: De Capo, Press 1968).
——. *Biographical Notes.* (private printing, 1892).
Fritz, Christian, *Judge Ogden: Federal Justice in California* (Lincoln: Univ. of Nebraska 1991).
Goodwin, Cardinal, *The Establishment of State Government in California 1848–1850.* (New York: The Macmillan and Co., 1914).
Gordon, John D., *Authorized by No Law.* (Pasadena, CA.: Ninth Judicial Circuit Court of the United States, Historical Society 1987).
Gorham, George, *Biographical Notice of Stephen J. Field.* (N.Y.: De Capo Press. 1968).
Gorham, Harry M., *My Memories of the Comstock.* (Los Angeles: Suttonhouse Publishers, 1939).
Gray, Henry M., *Judges and Criminals: Shadows of the Past.* (San Francisco, 1858).
Gray, Paul Bryan, *Forster vs. Pico: The Struggle for the Rancho Santa Margarita.* (Spokane WA. The Arthur H. Clark Company, 1998).
Griswold del Castillo, Richard. *The Treaty of Guadalupe Hidalgo.* (Norman OK.: University of Oklahoma, 1990).
Hall, Carrol Douglas, *The Terry-Broderick Duel.* (San Francisco: Colt Press 1939).
Hall, Kermit, *The Oxford Companion to the SUPREME COURT* of the United States (Oakland: Biobooks 1992).
Hansen, Woodrow James, *The Search for Authority in California.* (Oakland California: Biobooks, 1960).
Hirshson, Stanley P. *The White Tecumseh.* (New York, John Wiley & Sons, Inc., 1997).
Hittell, John, *History of California.* (San Francisco, Stone & Co.1898).
——. James W. Marshall, Edwin G. Waite, *The Discovery of Gold in California* (Palo Alto: Lewis Osborne, California, 1968).
Holdredge, Helen, *Mammy Pleasant.* (New York: Putnam. 1953).
Hopkins, Archibald, *Stephen J. Field,* (Green Bag, 1899).
Howard, John Raymond, *Remberances of Things Past.* (1895).
Hudson, Lynn M., *The Making of Mammy Pleasant* (Urbana: University of Illinois, 2003).
Hunt, Rockwell D., *California Firsts.* (San Francisco: Fearon Publishers. 1957).
Johnson, J. Edward, *History of the Supreme Court Justices of California, 1850–1900.* (San Francisco: Binder-Moss, 1963).
Kens, Paul, *Justice Stephen J. Field.* (Lawrence Kansas: University of Kansas. 1997).
Kroninger, Robert H., *Sarah and the Senator.* (Berkeley California: North Point Press, 1964).

Lamar, Mirabeau, Bonaparte. *Papers of M.B. Lamar*, (Austin: A.C. Baldwin, 1921).

Lawson, John D., *American State Trials.* #15 (St. Louis: Scholarly Resources, Inc.1972).

Lewis, Oscar. *This Was San Francisco.* (D. Mc Kay Co. 1962).

Lewis, Oscar and Carroll D. Hall, *Bonaza Inn.* (New York: A.A. Knopf. 1939).

Lipsky, Eleazar, *The Devil's Daughter*, (New York, Meredith Press. 1969).

Lotchin, Roger W., *San Francisco 1846–1856: From Hamlet to City.* (N.Y.: Oxford University, 1974).

Lungum, David J., Law and Community of the Mexican California Frontier 1821–1846. (Norman OK: The University of Oklahoma Press 1987).

Lynch, Jeremiah, *A Senator for the Fifties: David C. Broderick of California.* (S.F.: A. M. Robertson 1911).

McClosky, Robert, *The American Supreme Court.* (Chicago: University of Chicago Press. 1960).

McCurdy, Charles, *The Fields and the Law.* (1986).

McCowan *California Vigilantes 1857.* (San Francisco: Biobooks, 1946).

McGown, Edward, *Vigilance Committee 1856: Adventures and Perils.*

Mills, Frank R., *Rail and Water:* (The Owl Limited 1898).

Myers, Gustauos, *History of the Supreme Court.* (Chicago: C.H. Kerr and Co. 1925).

Myers, John M., San Francisco Reign of Terror, (San Francisco: Doubleday 1966).

O'Meara, James, *Broderick and Gwin.* (San Francisco: Bacon & Co. 1881).

Owens, Kenneth N., *Gold Rush Saints,* (Spokane WA: The Arthur H. Clark Company, 2004).

Nunis, Doyce, *The San Francisco Vigilance Committee of 1856.* (Los Angeles: Westerners 1971).

Pomeroy, John Norton, Introduction to *Some Account of the Work of Stephen J. Field.* (N.Y.: Chauncey Black 1881).

Pound, Roscoe, *Spirit of the Common Law.* (Boston: Marshal James. 1963).

Powell Richard R., *Compromise of Conflicting Claims: A Century of California Law, 1776–1860.* (Dobbs Ferry N.Y.: Oceana Publishers, 1977).

Royce, Josiah, *California from Conquest in 1846 to the End of the Second Vigilance Committee in San Francisco:* A Study of American Character. (Boston: Houghton and Mifflin. 1897).

——. *Fugitive Essays* (Cambridge: Harvard University Press 1920).

Scherer, James, *Lion of the Vigilantes* (New York: Bobbs-Merrill Co, 1939).

Senkewicz, Robert M., *Vigilantes in the Gold Rush.* (San Francisco: Stanford University Press 1985).

Shatlock, D. O., *David S. Terry.* (San Francisco 1856).

Sherman, William Tecumseh, *Memoirs.* (Bloomington IN.: Indiana University Press 1957).

Shinn, Charles, H. *Mining Camps: A Study in American Frontier Government* (N.Y.: Scribners 1885).

Shirley, Dame, The Shirley Letters. (Santa Barbara CA.: Peregrina-Smith, 1920).

Shuck, Oscar T., *Bench and Bar in California.* (San Francisco: Occidental printing house 1888).

Soule, Frank, John H. Gihon M.D. and James Nesbit, *The Annals of San Francisco,* (San Francisco: D. Appleton & Co. 1858).
Starr, Kevin, *America and the California Dream.* (New York: Oxford University Press, 1973).
Swisher, Carl Brent, *Stephen J. Field: Craftsman of the Law.* (Washington D.C. The Brookings Institute. 1930).
——. *Motivation and Political Technique in the California Constitutional Convention*, 1878–1879. (Claremont, CA.: Pomona College. 1930).
Taylor, Bayard, *Eldorado: Adventures in the Path of Empire.* (Lincoln NE: University of Nebraska Press. 1949).
Terry, David S., *The Character and Career of Stephen J. Field.* (San Francisco: SI, 1889).
——. *Arrested for Conspiracy and Murder of the Hon, D.S. Terry.* (1889).
——. *The Trial of David S. Terry* (San Francisco: R. C. Moore and Co. 1856).
Thomas, Lateley, *Between Two Empires: The Life of William Gwin.* (Boston: Houghton-Mifflin 1969).
Tinkham, George H., *Men and Events 1769–1890.* (Stockton Ca.: Record Publishing Co. 1915).
——. *History of San Joaquin County.* (Los Angeles: Historical Record Co. 1923).
——. *History of the State of California and the Historical and the Biographical Record of the San Joaquin County.* (Los Angeles, Historical Record Co. 1909).
——. *History of Stockton.* (San Francisco: W. M. Hinton and Co.1880).
Truman, Ben C., *The Field of Honor.* (NY: Fords Howard & Halbert. 1884).-
Tuthill, Franklin, *History of California.* (San Francisco: H.H. Bancroft & Co.1866).
Wagstaff, A. E., *The Life of the Ex. Chief Justice of the Supreme Court of California: David S. Terry*. (San Francisco: Continental Pub. Co. 1892).
Waldon, D.C. and T. J. Vivian, *Biographical Sketches of the Delegates to the Convention,* (San Francisco: 1878).
Williams, David D., *David C. Broderick.: a political portrait* (San Marino CA.: Huntington Library Press, 1969).
Williams, Mary Floyd, *History of the San Francisco Committee of Vigilance of 1856.* (Berkeley, The Univ. Of California Press, 1921).
Williams, R. Hal, *The Democratic Party and California Politics 1880–1899.* (Palo Alto CA.: Stanford University Press.1973).
Wistar, Issac Jones, *Autobiography*. 1827–1905. (Philadelphia: Wistar Institute, 1914).
Woolley, L. H., *California 1849–1913.* (Oakland CA. De Witt & Snelling,1913).
Wright, William, *Dan DeQuille of the Big Bonanza*. (San Francisco: Book Club of California. 1980).

MANUSCRIPTS AND DOCUMENTS

Browne, J. Ross. *Report of the Debates in the Convention of California on the Formation of the State Constitution*, Huntington Library, San Marino, California. 1849.

——. *Debates and Proceedings of Constitutional Convention of the State of California, Sept. 28, 1878.* Huntington Library, San Marino, California, (1879).

Character and Career of Stephen J. Field as it is Know in California: Field's Infamy is Judge David S. Terry's Vindication. 1889. Huntington Library, San Marino, California

Documents in Relation to the Charges Preferred by Stephen J. Field and others before the House Assembly of the State of California against William R. Turner, district judge of the Eight Judicial District of California June 15, 1851. Huntington Library, San Marino, California.

Gold Key Court or the Corruption of a Majority of It. Huntington Library n.n., n.d., n.p., San Marino California.

Gorham, George C. *The Story of the Attempted Assassination of Justice Field by a Former Associate on the Supreme Court of California.* n.p. opinions and papers, Huntington Library, San Marino, California, (1893).

Field, Stephen J. Arrested for Conspiracy and Murder of the Hon. David S. Terry, 1889 Fresno. California.

Field, Stephen, J. "A Possible Solution of the Chinese Problem." *The Argonaut,* August 9, 1879. Huntington Library, San Marino, California.

——. "The Taxation of Property of Railroad Companies in California," San Francisco, 1883. Huntington Library, San Marino California.

Mason, Richard Barnes, *Laws for the Better Government of California.* (Glendale California: Pacific Historical Review, 1933).

Journal of the Senate of the State of California, Session #1 San Jose, (1850).

Latham, Milton S. *Stephen J. Field, Facsimile of letter to A. Lincoln concerning appointment S.J. Field as judge of U.S. Courts for California.* (S.F.: Grabhorn Press 1945)

O'Meara, James. *Vigilance Committee, 1856.* The Henry Wagner Collection, Huntington Library, San Marino California, (1887).

Piper, Richard Upton, *An Examination of the 'marriage contract,' and other documents,* San Francisco, 1885. Huntington Library Collection, San Marino, California.

Shattach, D.O., "Terry's Resistance of Vigilance Committee Not Criminal." San Francisco, 1856. The James DeBarth Shorb Collection. Huntington Library, San Marino California.

Terry, David Smith, *Arguments of David S. Terry,* Stockton California, 1887, Huntington Library, San Marino California.

The David Smith Terry Collection, *Letters and Documents.* Huntington Library, San Marino, California.

NEWSPAPERS & MAGAZINES

The Argonaut, San Francisco, Oct. 5, 1878; July 26, Aug. 9 1879; June 25, Aug. 25, 1880; June 28, 1884; Jan 31, 1885, July 11,18,30, 1885; Aug. 23,25, 1880; Aug. 19,26 1889.

The Daily Alta California, San Francisco, Feb. 7,10,19, 1852; July 14, 1857; June 22, 1880, June 12, 18, 26. Sept. 11, Nov. 17,18, Dec 27, 1884, May 10, 1885, Jan. 18, 1886.

The Daily Examiner, San Francisco, Oct, 2, 22, 1879, Aug. 15, 1889, May 12, 1921.

Fresno Weekly Expositor, June 24, Aug. 7, 1855, July 14, 1857; May 22, 1878. May 19,26, 1880.

The Los Angeles Times, Sept 4, 1888. The Daily Tribune, New York, June 18,22,23,24, 25, 1880.

The New York Herald, Aug. 23, 1880; June 22, 1888; Aug 15,16,18, 1889. *The New York Herald Tribune,* June 24,25,26 1880; Aug 17,18,21,28, 1889.

The New York Times, June 2,17,18,21,22,23,24,25,28, 1880.

The Political Record, San Francisco, 1884

The Sacramento Daily Evening Bee, Apr. 4, 1859.

The San Joaquin Republican, Aug. 27, Sept. 4, 1882; Aug. 11, Aug. 16, 1855. *The San Jose Tribune*, Aug. 15, 1855.

The San Francisco Chronicle, May 24,26, 1876; Sept. 20,30, 1878; May, 1,14,19,22,23, June 22,24,25, 1880; March 11; April 1,6,9,10,17,23, July, 15,25, Aug. 12, Dec. 25, 1884; Apr. 18, Sept. 1,30, Nov. 17, Dec. 26, 1885; Jan. 8, 1886; Sept 3,4, 1888; August 15, Sept. 17, 1889; March 2, 1949.

The San Francisco Herald, Dec. 3, 1850.

The Stockton Daily Evening Mail, Aug. 19,20, 1889.

LEGAL CASES

California Reports:

The People, ex rel Mulford et al. v Turner. 1 Cal., 143, (June 1850).

People ex re Field v Turner. 1 Cal., 152, (1850).

Ex parte Field, 1 Cal., 187, (Dec. 1850).

The People ex re. Field v Turner. 1 Cal., 189, (Dec 1850).

Hicks et al. v Bell. 3 Cal., 219, (July 1853).

Johnson v Gordon. 4 Cal., 368 (Oct. 1854).

Stokes v Barrett & Co. 5 Cal., 36, (Jan. 1855).

Castro v Gill. 5 Cal., 40, (Jan. 1855).

Lin Sing v. Washburn. 20 Cal., 142, 534, (1862).

In re Archy on *Habeas Corpus.* 9 Cal., 147, (Jan. 1858).

Ex Parte Newman. 9 Cal., 502, (Apr. 1858).

Ferris v Coover. 10 Cal., 589, (Oct. 1858).

Ferris v Coover. 11 Cal., 176, (Oct. 1858).

Hyman v. Read. 13 Cal, 445, (Apr. 1859).

Biddle Boggs v Merced Mining Co., 14 Cal 279, (Oct. 1859).

McCracken v the City of San Francisco. 16 Cal., 591, (Oct. 1860).

Moore v Smaw. 17 Cal., 199, (Jan. 1861).

Grogan et al. v The City of San Francisco. 18 Cal., 590, (July 1861).

Lin Sing v Washburn. 20 Cal., 534, (July 1882).
The Stockton and Visalia Railroad Company v The City of Stockton. 51 Cal 328, (July 1876).
The Central Pacific Railroad Co. v The State Board of Equalization. 60 Cal 35, (Jan. 1882).
Sharon v Sharon. 67 Cal., 185, (June 1885).
Sharon v Sharon. 68 Cal., 29, (Nov. 1885).
Sharon v Sharon. 75 Cal., 1, (Jan. 1888).
Sharon v Sharon. 79 Cal., 633, (July 1889).
Sharon v Frederick Sharon, 84 Cal., 424, (June 1890).

Federal Reports
US, Federal Circuit Court, Ninth District.
2 Sawyer 667; cited in Swisher, p. 211.
3 Sawyer 144; cited in Swisher, p. 212.
Ah Fong Fed. Cases, #102, (1874).
Ho Ah Kow *v* Nunan, Fed. Cases, #6546 (July 1879).
In re Qoung Woo 13 Fed. 229, (Aug. 1882).
In re Ah Sing, 13 Fed 286, (Aug. 1882).
In re Ah Tie, 13 Fed 291, (Aug. 1882).
San Mateo *v* Southern Pacific R.R. 13 Fed 145 (1882).
San Mateo *v* Southern Pacific R.R. 13 Fed 722 (Sept. 1882).
In re Neagle, 39 Fed. 833 (1889).
Santa Clara *v* Southern Pacific R.R. 18 Fed 385, (Sept. 1883).
In re Low Yam Chow. 13 Fed. 605, (Sept. 1882).
In re Ah Lung. 18 Fed 28, (Sept. 1884).
Sharon *v* Hill. 20 Fed. 1, (Mar. 1884).
In re Ah Moy. 21 Fed. 785, (Sept 1884).
In re Cheen Heong. 21 Fed. 791, (Sept. 1884).
Sharon *v* Hill. 22 Fed. 28, (Oct. 1884).
Sharon *v* Hill. 23 Fed. 353, (Mar. 1885).
Sharon *v* Hill. 24 Fed. 726, (Aug. 1885).
Sharon v Hill. 26 Fed. 337, (Dec. 1885).
Sharon *v* Hill. 26 Fed. 722, (Apr. 1886).
Sharon *v* Terry. 36 Fed. 337, (Sept. 1888).
In re Terry *et al.* 36 Fed. 419, (Sept. 1888).
In re Terry. 37 Fed. 649, (Feb. 1889).
US *v* Terry *et al*. 39, Fed. 355, (May 1889).
In re Neagle. 39 Fed. 833, (Sept. 1889).
In re Terry *et al.* 41 Fed. 771, (Mar. 1890).

United States Supreme Court Reports
Cummings v The State of Missouri. 71 US 277, (Dec. 1866).
Ex Parte Garland. 71 US 333, (Dec. 1866).
Ex Parte McCardle. 73 US 318, (Dec. 1867).

Slaughter-House Cases. 83 US 36, (Dec 1872).
Bradwell v Illinois. 83 US 130, (Dec. 1872).
Bartsmeyer v Iowa. 85 US 129, (Oct 1873).
Chy Lung v Freeman et al. 92 US 275, (Oct. 1875).
Munn v Illinios. 94 US 113, (Oct 1876).
Sinking-Fund Cases. 99 US 700 (Oct. 1873).
Butchers' Union Slaughter-House and Live-Stock Landing Co. v Cresent City Live-Stock Landing and Slaughter-House Co. 111 US 746 (Oct. 1884).
Barbier v. Connolly, 113 US 27, (Oct. 1884).
Soon Hing v. Crowley, 113 US 703, (Oct. 1884).
San Mateo County v Southern Pacific R.R., 116 US 138, (Oct. 1885).
Santa Clara County v Southern Pacific R.R., 118 US 394 (Oct. 1885).
In re Terry. 128 US 289, (Oct. 1888).
Chae Chan Ping, v US. 130 US 581, The Chinese Exclusion Case, (Oct. 1888).
Terry v Sharon 131 US 40, (Oct. 1889).
In re Neagle, 135 US 1, (Oct. 1889).
Central Pacific Railroad Company v California. 162 US 91, 1895, (Oct. 1895).

Index

Ah Fong v. California: Field legal opinion on, 168

Ah Tie v. California, 163–164

Alaska Commercial Company: and "Chinese" problem, 178

Alta California, vi

"American Party" (also "Native American Party"), 21–22,130

Appomattox, 147

"Archy" (*In re "Archy"*): legal opinion on, 58; issue of slavery in early California, 58

Argonaut, The: support of railroad interests, 56,182

Arizona Territory: silver mining in, 246

Arthur, Chester A. (U.S. President) 189

Ashe, Porter: Law and Order Society, 87, 235

Atlanta Constitution, The Field's *Personal Reminiscences,* 106

Baker, E.D., 85; and Cora trial , 85

Baldwin, Joseph G,: California Supreme Court Justice, 125,128

Ballowe Sam (Captain): Battle at Monterey, 5

Bancroft, Herbert H.: *History of California* ,86,104, 193

Bank of California, 199

Barbour, William T. (Judge): Eight District Court of California, 110,112

Barnes, William: defense counsel to Sharon, 204,216

Belmont Hotel (San Francisco) 147, 200

Benicia, CA: early history of California, 85; education of Terry son, 145

Bennett, Nathaniel: Assoc. Justice, first California Supreme Court, 108

Biddle Boggs v. Merced Mining Co., 120

"Big Four" of railroads, 174

Bigler, John, 20; "free soil" governor of California , 110

Blackburn, Andrew (Judge): early California judicial decisions on capital punishment, 58

Blue Wing Saloon, the, 26

Board of Equalization: corporate attacks on, 159–160

"*Bonanza Inn*", *The,* 198

Botts, C.T.: and property rights of women, 42

Boutwell, E.B., (U.S. Navy Captain) 92, 102

Bradley, Joseph. *See* Bradwell, M ,155.

Bradwell, Myra, 155; right to pursue legal career ,155

Bragg, Braxton (General) 146; Terry at Battle of Chicamauga, 147
Broderick, David C.: and patronage, 132: Broderick-Moore exchange,112–113, 131; death of, 139; duel against Terry,137,140; U.S. Senator from California, 131
Browne, J. Ross: *Debates* (California Constitutional Convention of 1855), 38, 49–50
Buchanan, Russell A., 105; Terry biographer, 148, 193
Bulletin, The ("Workingman's' Newspaper) 77, 126; on bribery of Field , 123, 193, 241
Burlingame Treaty: and immigration policy, 163, 178
Burnett, Peter: Assoc. Justice, Supreme Court of California, 25, 115; Chief Justice, Supreme Court of California, 25; first elected governor or California, 58

California Board of Equalization, 159–160
California Civil Code on Marriage, 208
California Constitutional Convention , (1849) 34, (1878) 175–177
California Democratic Party: (1853) nomination of Bigler, 110
California Democratic Convention: (1884) 190, 199
California State Assembly: on "Chinese" question, 162
California Republican Party, 175
Californios (see Vallejo, Carrillo) 31, 33
Carey, James, Federal Judge: and Terry assassination, 257
Carpenter, Matthew Hale. *See* Bradwell, 115
Carrillo, Jose Antonio, 33
Cavillaud, Charles, 9
Central Pacific Railroad, 156, 170, 174
Central Valley, 174; Stockton as shipping center, 174; populist politics of
"Chinese" problem, "the Mongols," 162–163, 174
"Chivs", the, 140–141
Chy Lung v. Freeman, 163
Circuit Court of Appeals (San Francisco), 157; Field term on, 157
Civil War, the, 146
Clark, Malcolm: populist criticism of Field, 157
Cleveland, Grover (U.S. President): National Democratic Convention (1884) 191
Coleman, William Tell: and Vigilance Committee, 101; action in Cora case, 74, 80, 101
Colton, David, (see Broderick): President of Santa Fe Railroad, 156; second to Terry in duel, 138
Colton Hall (Monterey, CA): site of first California, Constitutional Convention, 34
"Commissioners of the Funded Debt" (San Francisco Board of Supervisors) 124
Cope, Warner Walter (Judge) 125–126
Cora, Charles, 125–126; murder of William Richardson,76, 80
"Cotton Whigs," 20
County of Santa Clara v. Southern Pacific Railroad Co. See Fields, railroad interests, 158
Crescent City Livestock Landing and Slaughter Co., 153; Louisiana statute on public health, 53
Crocker, Charles. *See* "Big Four" of railroads, 174
Cummings, John, Rev.: and post-Civil War loyalty issues, 152
Cummings v. Missouri 151
Cunningham, Thomas (Deputy Sheriff. Stockton) 257; and Terry assassination, 248
Cushing, Caleb, U.S. Atty. General. *See* Franklin Pierce, (U.S. President), 92

Daily Alta, The: railroad controlled newspaper, 257; and Terry trial , 204, 215
Daily Call, The: comment on *Sharon v. Hill,* 211
Daily News, The: on death of Broderick, 139
Democratic National Convention (Cincinnati, 1880) 184; Field presidential nomination
Democratic State Convention of California (1854), 21
Dempster, C.J. threat against Terry's life, 92
DeToqueville, A., 160
Dixie Democrats, post war, 190
Donner Party Expedition (1846), 10
Douglas, David: Secretary of State of California, 83
Douglas, Frederick, 133
Douglas, Stephen A., 133; criticism of U.S. President James Buchanan, 133
Dows, John: Vigilance Committee, 91
DuPont, James (Captain, *USS Cyrano*), 33
Durkee, John: and vigilante action, 87

Earp Brothers (Tombstone, AZ): and Neagle, 246
equal protection (14th Amendment), 152
Evans. Oliver J.: repudiation of Hill against Sharon, 217–218
Evening Bulletin, The: on Hopkins killing, 89
Ex parte Garland, 151–152

Fairfax, Charles S. (last Lord Fairfax) 127
Farragut, David (U.S. Naval commander) 84, 101. *See also* Boutwell, E.B.
Ferris v. Coover, 118
Fiat Justitia Ruat Coelum, 74
Field, David Dudley, 2, 8, 10, 13, 149, 152, 187
Field, Stephen Johnson: alcalde of Marysville, 11, 12, 106; children of, 2; connection to Lincoln, 66, 143, 149; defense of railroads, 155; early theological education, 7; family of origin, 2; in Panama, 8; marriage of, 123; presidential campaign (1876) 184; Supreme Court of California (10th Dist.), 157; U.S. Supreme Court (Assoc. Justice), 149
Los Filibusteros ("freebooters"), 72
First Congregational Church of Sacramento, 173; pre-convention meeting (1855) 23. *See also* "Preserving the Union" speech, 23
"Fort Gunnybags," 79, 102
Fort Vigilance (see Farragut, D) 98, 101
Fourteenth Amendment (to U.S. Constitution) 154
Fox & Connor Liquor Emporium: site of Richardson murder , 76
Franks, J.C. (Federal Marshall): and Terry assassination, 235, 239, 257
freedom of religion debate, 114–116
Fremont, John C.: first U.S. Senator from California, 46
Fremont v. United States, 121
Fresno: agricultural center , 245

Garfield, James A., (U.S. President), 189
Garland, A.H.: Congressman of the Confederacy, 151–152; post-Civil War loyalty issues, 150
Garland v. Cummings, 151
The Gold Key Court: Or The: *Corruption of the Majority of It*, 123
Goodwin, Jesse, 107; legal associate of Field, 107
Gorham, George C.: law clerk to Field, 224, 263; and 1884 presidential election, 234
"Grangers" 62, 173
California Constitutional Convention (1878) 173

Grand Hotel (San Francisco). *See* Sarah Hill , 201
Gum Saan (Gold Mountain) 178
Gumbel, Max 222
Gwin, William M., (U.S. Senator from California) 46, 49, 133; defense of Terry against railroads, 99; elected to U.S. Senate, 46; on Field presidential candidacy, 131

Hall, Carroll D., 198. See also "*Bonanza Inn*"
Hammond, Dr., 139. *See also* Broderick
Hancock, Winfield Scott (General): presidential nominee (1880), 189
Haskell, Leonidas, 139; death of Broderick
Hastings, L.W., 41; *see* Treaty of Guadalupe Hidalgo; slavery debate in early California, 41
Hastings, Serranus Clinton: First Chief Justice of California Supreme Court, 65; established first California law school , 73. *See also* Bennett, N; Lyons, H.
Hayes, Rutherford B. (U.S. President)
Herrin, William: attorney to Sharon, 235; corporate lawyer, 235; defense of railroads, 235
Heydenfeldt, Solomon (Justice, California Supreme Court), 117–118; 1884 presidential election , 239
Hicks v. Bell, 117
Hickox, George: handwriting analyst, Hill trial, 219
Hill, Sarah Althea ("Allie"), 196, 230
History of the Supreme Court Justice of California, 26–27
Ho Ah Kow v. Nunan (1877) 164
Holmes, Oliver Wendell, Jr., 53
Hopkins, Mark (see "Big Four"), 174
Hopkins, Sterling A.: Vigilance Committee, 88–89; murder of, 93
"Hounds," the (& Sydney "Ducks") 174
Houston, Sam, 93; and Texas Rangers
Howard, Volney, 85–86. *See also* Cora, Charles
Huntington, C.P. (President, Central Pacific Railroad): Colton-Huntington correspondence, 156; of California (1878) 176

Irwin, Wlliam , Governor of California (1887), 130

Jackson, Andrew (U.S. President) 20
Jackson Street Armory, 88
Jalisco, Mexico (1865): Terry residence in, 147
Johnson, Hiram: opposition to railroad interests, 182
Johnson, J. Neely, 79, 83; Governor of California , 79, 83; confrontation with vigilantes, 8 80
Johnson v. Gordon, 119
jura regalia vs. *jura signa,* 117

Kearney, Dennis: Workingman's Party (1878), 173–174
Kearneyites, 173
"Know-Nothing" Party, 21, 24

Lagoarde, Bernard, 140
Langum, David, legal historian: *Law and Community on the Mexican Frontier*, 68–69
Lathrop, CA: site of Terry assassination, 263
Law and Order Society, 79; and Law Officers Society of 1849, 79
"Lecompton" Democrats, 130
("Lecomptonites"), 130
Lee, Robert E. (General): surrender at Appomattox, 147
Lewis, Harvey, 127–128; Terry on California Supreme Court, 127
Lin Sing v. Washburn. See Burlingame Treaty, 163

Lippitt, F.J.: on property rights for women, 42
Lloyd, Rueben. *See* Sarah Hill , 197, 213, 216–217
Lone Mountain Cemetery (San Francisco): death of Broderick, 81
Lyons, Henry Augustus, Assoc. Justice, California Supreme Court, 65. *See also* Bennett, N., Clinton, S.

MacDougal, James A. (Atty. General of California, 1859), 123
Magna Carta (1215), 61
Maloney, James Rueben ("Rube"): Law and Order Society, 87
Manrow, J.P. (elected "judge advocate"), 93–94. See also *People v. David S. Terry*, 93; Truitt, Miers, 93
Marion Rifles Brigade, 88
Las Mariposas, 120
Marysville Appeal, The hometown newspaper of Field, 149
McCarty, John: presidential candidate, opponent of Field, 13
McCreery, James: legal consequences of Terry assassination, 256
McCurdy, Charles: *Fields and the Law* (1986) x, 166
McDougal, John, (Lt. Governor of California), 46, 49. *See also* Burnett, P.
McElrath, J.E.: Field presidential nomination, 188
McKibben, J.C. (Colonel), 136, 138. *See also* Broderick
McNabb, James: Vigilance Committee, 87
Merced Lake: site of Broderick-Terry duel , 137
Merced Mining Co., 120–121
Mesick, Richard: attorney to Sharon, 235
Mexican War, 28; Treaty of Guadalupe Hidalgo, 29
Miller, John F.: on "Chinese" problem, 165
Miller, Samuel (Assoc. Justice, U.S. Supreme Court), 154. *See also* Fourteenth Amendment
Miner's Distribution Center, 19
Moore, B.F.: defense of Judge William Turner against Field 112. *See also* California State Assembly
Morning Call, The: on Broderick case, 138
Mott, Gordon, N. (Judge, 8th Dist. Court of California) 110–111. *See also* Bigler, John
Mulford, Samuel: legal associate of Field, 107–109
Mulligan, Billy: arrest by Vigilance Committee, 83. See also *San Francisco Chronicle*
Murray, Hugh (Chief Justice, 25 California Supreme Court): and Terry , 65; and "landed-interests." *See also* Burnett, Peter, 65

Native American Party, 21–22, 130
Neagle, David (U.S. Deputy Marshall): bodyguard to Field, 260, 246
Nevada's Comstock Lode: silver mining, 198
New York Evening Post, The: and anti-slavery oratory, 106
New York Times, The: on Field, 187–188
New York Herald Tribune, The: allegations of bribery against Field, 193; Field on loss of presidential nomination (1880), 190
New York Tribune, The: on Terry assassination, 257
New York State Codes of Legal: Procedure, 10
Norton, Edward: colleague of Field, 162; on "Chinese" problem, 162–163

Non-Partisan Alliance: California Constitutional Convention (1878), 175, 177

Oakland Jail: and Terry prosecution, 238–240
"oaths of loyalty" (post-Civil War), 151
O'Meara, James, 17, 76, 140; on Field's run for U.S. Senate and Blue Wing Saloon., 17, 76, 140
Osborn, William, 57; *The Wild Frontie,* 57

Pacific Express, 77
Pacific Railroad Act, 181
Palace Hotel, 198
Palmer-Cook Bank Building: Headquarters of Law and Order Society, 88
Pennsylvania Engine House, 89
People v. David Smith Terry, 83
Perley, Duncan: supporter of Terry in Broderick case, 102, 134
Philips, John G.,87
Pierce, Franklin (U.S. President), 92
Placer Times, The, Field disbarment, 108
Pleasant, Mary Ellen ("Mammy") 197, 213, 220, 228. *See also* Sarah Hill
Pound, Roscoe, 64–65; embrace of common law on Western frontier
"Preserving the Union" speech (Terry, 1855), 23
"Protocol of Queretaro": land rights in early California. 32. *See also* Treaty of Guadalupe Hidalgo
Purdy, Sam opponent of Terry, 20
Purvis, R.B. (Sheriff, Stanislaus County) 254; and Terry assassination, 254

Reminiscences (Field) 185
Republic of the Pacific", 91; Terry position on, 22
Richardson, William H. (General, U.S. Marshall), 76; killed by Cora, 76
Riley, Bennett (military governor of California) 33
Royce, Josiah, 30; early years in California, 75; Harvard professor , 75
Runnels, Hiram, Mississippi Congressman, 6. *See also* Terry, D..S.., marriage of, 6
Ryan, Arabell, 76. *See also* Cora, Charles

Sabine, (Judge): Terry jailed by, 235, 265
Sacramento Bee,The: and Terry-Field controversy, 127, 129
San Francisco Chronicle, The: on Terry's marriage to Sarah Hill, 251
San Francisco Daily Alta, The: on Terry assassination, 257
San Francisco Examiner, The: on Terry family life, 161
San Francisco Political Record, The: on Terry-Field controversy, 272
San Francisco Post, The: pro-business reportage, 192
San Joaquin Republican, The: Miners' Distribution Center, 19; reputation of Terry in Stockton, 19
San Mateo v. Southern Pacific Railroad, 157
San Jose Tribune, The: and Know-Nothing Party, 157
"sand-lotters," 174
Sawyer, Lorenzo (Judge, Federal Circuit Court) 231; hearing on Terry assassination, 258
Scannell, David (Sheriff): Law and Order Society, 83
Semple, Robert: on issue of slavery in early California, 39
Sherman, William Tecumseh ("Cump"), 82, 85–86, 103, 268
Sicard. *See* Cavillaud, Charles, 9
Sing-Sing Prison. 77
Sinking Fund Cases, the, 160
Sharon, Frederick, 199

Sharon, William (U.S. Senator from Nevada) 198; arrest warrant filed by Hill (1884), 198; children of, 198
Sharon v. Hill, 230
Sharon v. Sharon, 203
solvent debt taxing ("double taxation"), 159
Southern Pacific Railroad, 156
sovereign domain proviso, 63. *See also* Treaty of Guadalupe Hidalgo
St. Ignatius College, 203
Stackpole, James: and site of Terry assassination, 248–250
Stanford, Leland (Governor of California), 181
"States rights" Democrats (1855), 260
statute of *domicilium,* 230
Stockton Daily Independent, 172; Terry judgments against railroads, 172
Stockton City, CA: site of Terry law firm, 169; dealings with Central Pacific Railroad, 170; dealings with Western Pacific Railroad, 170; reaction to Terry assassination, 257
Stockton/Visalia Railroad (V.R.R.): and Stockton City, 171
Sullivan, Jeremiah (Judge, California Superior Court) 203, 221. See also *Sharon v. Sharon*
Sutter, John A. (Captain) 106
Sutter County gold strike in, 106
Sutro, Adolph, Mayor of San Francisco, 224
Swain, H.V.J., (Justice of the Peace, Stockton) 255; Terry assassination, 254–55
Swisher, Carl Brent, 11, 274; Field family biographer, 11; hostility to new constitution, 193; on California Constitutional Convention, 172
Sydney" Ducks," 74. *See also* "Hounds" 74

Tammany Hall, 131; West coast version of, 131
"Tammany Hall criminals," 138
Taylor, Bayard, ix; journalist and traveler in early California, 30
Taylor, Zachary (U.S. President) 38
Terry, David Smith: assassination of , 250; appointment to Supreme Court of California, 24; children of, 3, 144; family of origin, 3; legal and public service career, 71–172; marriage to Cornelia Runnels, 229; marriage to Sarah Hill, 226, 271; military recruitment in Texas for Confederacy, 148; Terry-Field controversy, 130f; opposition to corporate interests, 180
Texas Legislature, 93
Texas War for Independence, 4
Treaty of Guadalupe Hidalgo (1848), 2, 53
Truitt Buildings, 78
Truitt, Miers: defense counsel to Terry, 94
Turner, William, (Judge, 8th Dist Court of California) 106, 109; controversy with Field, 106–107
Tuthill, Franklin: overlander historian, 57
Turnverein Hall, 80
Tyler, George Washington, 216; counsel to Sarah Hill, 209. See also *Sharon v. Hill*

Union Railroad, 158
U.S. Army of the Pacific, 32, 82
U.S. Department of War, 33
U.S. Constitution: discussion of Amendments, 13–15
USS John Adams, 102. *See also* Farragut, D.
U.S. Supreme Court: ruling on *San Mateo v. Southern Pacific Railroad*, 157

Vallejo, Mariano Guadalupe (General): land donation. See also *Californios*, 31, 33
Vigilance Committee: army of, 80

Vigilance Society, 78
Visalia, CA: and railroads, 170–171

Wagstaff, A.E., 104; Terry biographer, xi, 227
"War of Secession," 143
Washoe Mountains ("Washoes"): gold and silver mining, 144
Wellock, William, 173. *See also* Kearneyites, 173
Western Pacific Railroad: and Stockton City, 169–170; purchase of interests by Central Pacific Railroad, 170
White, Stephen Mallory (Dist. Attorney of Los Angeles), 187; and Terry assassination, 261; anti-monopolist, 192
Workingman's Party: California Constitutional Convention (1878), 173; merger with California Democratic Party, 176–177
The Wild Frontier, 57
Wilmot Proviso (1846), 33
Williams College, 7; Fields, higher education, 7
Wool, John E. (General) 82–84; at Benicia, 82–84; in Mexican War, 82

Yuba county miners' political support of Fields, 106, 109

www.ingramcontent.com/pod-product-compliance
Ingram Content Group UK Ltd.
Pitfield, Milton Keynes, MK11 3LW, UK
UKHW041142300926
15471UKWH00011B/104

9 780761 848912